Teach
Yourself
ODBC

in 21 Days

Teach Yourself
ODBC
in 21 Days

Bill Whiting
Bryan Morgan
Jeff Perkins

SAMS
PUBLISHING

A Division of Macmillan Computer Publishing
201 West 103rd Street, Indianapolis, Indiana 46290

I would like to dedicate this book to my wife, Becky, for her love and support. Once again, you're the best.—BM

To my three girls, Leslie, Laura, and Kelly, and to my parents, Ruth and Perk, without whose love and support this would not be possible.—JP

Copyright © 1996 by Sams Publishing

International Standard Book Number: 0-672-30609-3

Library of Congress Catalog Card Number: 94-67514

99 98 97 96   4 3 2 1

Interpretation of the printing code: the rightmost double-digit number is the year of the book's printing; the rightmost single-digit, the number of the book's printing. For example, a printing code of 96-1 shows that the first printing of the book occurred in 1996.

Composed in AGaramond, Bodoni, and MCPdigital by Macmillan Computer Publishing

Printed in the United States of America

Publisher *Richard K. Swadley*
Acquisitions Manager *Greg Wiegand*
Development Manager *Dean Miller*
Managing Editor *Cindy Morrow*
Marketing Manager *Gregg Bushyeager*

Acquisitions Editor
Christopher Denny

Development Editor
Tony Amico

Production Editors
Tonya R. Simpson
Katherine Stuart Ewing

Copy Editors
Margaret Berson, Joe Williams

Technical Reviewers
Bryan Morgan
Jeff Perkins

Editorial Coordinator
Bill Whitmer

Technical Edit Coordinator
Lynette Quinn

Formatter
Bill Whitmer

Editorial Assistants
Sharon Cox
Andi Richter
Rhonda Tinch-Mize

Cover Designer
Tim Amrhein

Book Designer
Alyssa Yesh

Production Team Supervisor
Brad Chinn

Production
Mona Brown
Michael Brumitt
Charlotte Clapp
Christopher Cleveland
Jason Hand
Ayanna Lacey
Kevin Laseau
Casey Price
Brian-Kent Proffit
Bobbi Satterfield
SA Springer
Susan Van Ness
Colleen Williams

Overview

Contents

Acknowledgments

Bill Whiting

Chris Denny, acquisitions editor, for keeping the faith with this project despite the many pitfalls. My co-authors, for picking up the slack when I fell behind and was ill. The entire Sams editorial team for not letting this book gather dust, but rather making it a better product in my absence. My family, for tolerating my efforts with this book. I was away from them a lot while I was working on this book, and they encouraged me anyway, which meant a lot to me.

Bryan Morgan

Special thanks to the following people:

My wife, Becky Morgan, for her patience and understanding, Chris Denny and Tony Amico at Sams Publishing for their guidance, and Bill Whiting and Jeff Perkins for their hard work and assistance in completing this book.

About the Authors

Bill Whiting has been involved in computer development since 1967. He has also pursued careers as a printer and a paramedic. Bill currently is working as a data access and systems integration consultant. He has presented classes and spoken around the world on the subject of client/server technology. Bill lives in Rochester, Minnesota with his wife Judy and grown daughter Lindsay, and his grown son Will recently moved to Texas. The family enjoys boating, but often had to share the boat with a laptop while book development was in progress! Bill can be reached on CompuServe at 70631,315 or the Internet at `billw@usa.net`.

Bryan Morgan is a member of the technical staff at The Analytical Sciences Corporation (TASC) in Fort Walton Beach, Florida. He holds a Bachelor of Science degree in Electrical Engineering from Clemson University and is currently pursuing a Master's degree in Electrical Engineering from the University of Florida. Bryan has application development experience on a variety of platforms using Oracle, Sybase, Informix, Access, and InterBase. In addition to this, he co-authored *Teach Yourself SQL in 14 Days* and was the technical editor for *Developing Client/Server Applications with Visual Basic*. Bryan lives in Navarre, Florida with his wife, Becky.

Jeff Perkins is a Senior Software Engineer with TYBRIN corporation in Shalimar, Florida. He is a graduate of the United States Air Force Academy and has over 2,500 hours of flying time as a navigator and bombardier in the B-52. Jeff is a co-author of *Teach Yourself SQL in 14 Days*.

Introduction

This book is all about learning how to use ODBC when you are programming with Microsoft's Visual C++ using the Microsoft Foundation Class Libraries (MFC) or Visual Basic. You will need the following tools for this endeavor: a Visual C++ compiler or Visual Basic (the Professional Edition is recommended), the Microsoft ODBC Software Development Kit (SDK), which is only available as a component within the Microsoft Developer's Network Level II subscription, and a computer powerful enough to run these compilers. If you intend to use the alternate C++ class libraries such as odbc/ClassLib mentioned in this book, you will also have to purchase that from Intersolv.

The skill you should have to get the greatest gain from this book is a good understanding of C++ or Visual Basic, depending on which development environment you are planning to use. You do not have to be an expert with either, and if you are only interested in using one of these two environments, you can ignore the other.

This book is intended for those who can create their own programs in Visual Basic or Visual C++ without help. There are many techniques that are omitted or simplified for the sake of clarity, expecially in the C++ sections. Visual Basic provides a set of data access objects (DAOs) that are designed to use ODBC as a middle layer when accessing data sources. These DAOs are not discussed at all in this book because they are viewed as another, opposite approach to data access from that taken here. The approach presented in this book with Visual Basic will generally take more programming effort that using the DAO controls and objects, but will invariably produce better performance. The use of Visual C++ with MFC is a middle ground between making direct calls to the ODBC API and using data access objects as available in Visual Basic. In most cases, the ODBC API function calls in C are shown for those who want to build their own class libraries.

Special Features of This Book

This book contains some special elements that help you understand ODBC features and concepts as they are introduced.

- ☐ Syntax boxes
- ☐ Notes
- ☐ Cautions

Syntax boxes explain some of the more complicated features of ODBC. Syntax boxes consist of a formal definition of the feature followed by an explanation of the elements of the feature. Here is a sample syntax box:

VB**4** Syntax

The *SQLConnect* Function

The general syntax for the SQLConnect function in Visual Basic is

```
RETCODE SQLConnect(hDBC, szDSN, cbDSN, szUID, cbUID, szAuthStr, cbAuthStr)
```

The function will attempt to load and connect to the data source specified by DSN. If that data-source name is not valid, the Driver Manager will follow the guidelines listed in Table 8.1 while attempting to establish a connection. The parameter hDBC specifies the connection handle for this connection. The parameter szDSN specifies the data-source name. The parameter cbDSN is the length of parameter szDSN. The parameter szUID is the user identifier to be used to access the data source. The parameter cbUID is the length of parameter szUID. The parameter szAuthStr specifies the password or other authentication string for this user. The parameter cbAuthStr is the length of parameter szAuthStr.

Notes are explanations of interesting properties of a particular program feature. Here is an example of a note:

> **Note:** Each keyword returned in the browse-result string is followed by a colon and a word or short phrase before the equal sign. These words are the user-friendly description of the attribute, which can be used for prompting with a dialog box.

Cautions warn you of programming pitfalls to avoid. Here is a typical caution:

> **Caution:** If changes are made to the Setup1A.MAK project and then the SETUP1.EXE application is rebuilt, the SETUP1.EXE file must be compressed using the COMPRESS -d option. If this is not done, your install application will fail without any appropriate error messaging. Also, the SETUP.LST file must not be compressed using the COMPRESS tool.

Programming Examples

Each chapter of this book contains many useful programming examples complete with explanations; these examples show you how you can use ODBC features in your own programs. The examples contain a listing of the program, as well as an analysis of how the program works. Special icons are used to point out the parts of the example: Type and Analysis.

The type icon appears next to some listings and indicates when you should type in a program.

The analysis icon appears next to the text after a listing. You should read the text after an analysis icon to learn the purpose of the listing and the important parts of the code.

➡ The code continuation character tells you that the single line of code continues on the following line.

End-of-Day Q&A and Workshop

Each day ends with a question-and-answer section containing answers to common questions relating to that day's material. There is also a Workshop at the end of each day that consists of quiz questions and programming exercises. The answers to these quiz questions, as well as sample solutions for the exercises, are presented in Appendix A, "Answers."

Conventions Used in This Book

This book uses different typefaces to help you differentiate between ODBC code and regular English, and also to help you identify important concepts.

☐ Actual code is typeset in a special monospace font. You'll see this font used in listings, as well as in code snippets. In the explanations of code features, commands, statements, variables, and any text you see on the screen also is typeset in this font.

☐ Placeholders in syntax descriptions appear in an *italic monospace* font. Replace the placeholders with the actual filename, parameter, or whatever element it represents.

☐ *Italics* highlight technical terms when they first appear in the text and are sometimes used to emphasize important points.

This week provides the foundation for your knowledge of ODBC. By the end of the week you will have enough knowledge to set up ODBC on your computer and will be on the verge of writing your first program.

Day 1, "Getting Started," is about how to best use this book. Day 2, "Overview of ODBC Concepts and Theory," presents a broad perspective of what ODBC is meant to do, its background, theory, and basic implementation. This prepares you for the program design using ODBC discussed on Day 3, "Application Design Considerations."

In preparation for the programs you will learn in week two, Day 4, "Installing Drivers and Configuring Data Sources," walks you through ODBC driver installation and data source configuration. With your environment set up, the next logical step is to go over the tools you will use to exploit the power of ODBC. On Day 5, "The Microsoft ODBC Software Development Kit (SDK)," you learn the most important of these tools, the Microsoft ODBC Software Development Kit. Day 6, "Development Tools," focuses on Microsoft's Visual C++

and Visual Basic as ODBC tool builders. And to end the week, Day 7, "Data Types," prepares you for the programs to come with a discussion of data types.

Let's get started!

Getting Started

Welcome to the world of programming with ODBC! Your adventure in exploring and using this new world of database connectivity begins today. Most of the information in today's lesson gives you the tools you need to program the ODBC Application Programming Interface (API). You'll learn about the following topics:

- [ ] What is ODBC?
- [ ] Programming with Visual Basic versus programming with C++
- [ ] Tools needed for development
- [ ] Sample applications and sample data
- [ ] ODBC driver to use for exercises

What Is ODBC?

Most people who first try to use the acronym to refer to Open DataBase Connectivity (ODBC) seem to scramble the letters. Although it might come out OCDB, OBDC, or OBCD, those using the term usually know it has something to do with a database. The question is: What does it have to do with a database?

What ODBC Is Not

Perhaps it would be easier to say first what ODBC does not do:

- [ ] ODBC does not limit an application to using one database type.
- [ ] ODBC does not limit an application to using one database server.
- [ ] ODBC does not restrict what communications to a data source can be used.
- [ ] ODBC does not automatically make data access slower.
- [ ] ODBC does not force you to select from a small list of applications already written.
- [ ] ODBC does not require using the "lowest common denominator" in functionality to be portable.
- [ ] ODBC does not require that Microsoft programs be used on Intel-powered PCs for database access.
- [ ] ODBC does not require years of programming experience to use.

Defined by the Name ODBC

Now that you know what ODBC does *not* do, are you closer to knowing what it *does* do? The answer to what ODBC is and what it's used for is in the name: *Open DataBase Connectivity.*

ODBC defines a method of connecting to data sources that is open to as many applications and data sources as possible. To accomplish this openness, the application and the database must agree on a common method of accessing the database. This agreement is implemented as a published standard defining a complete set of API function calls and a similarly complete SQL syntax set.

To use ODBC, an application program must use the ODBC API calls as defined in the standard. In addition, the SQL statements used must comply with the ODBC SQL syntax.

The database side of this open connectivity is provided by drivers, which are contained in Dynamically Linked Libraries (DLLs). These drivers will transform the ODBC API functions into function calls supported by the particular data source being used. Similarly, the drivers transform the ODBC SQL syntax into syntax accepted by the data source. Different data sources can be accessed by just loading a different DLL. These drivers were originally produced by the manufacturers of the databases, but now there are many third-party vendors as well.

One of the interesting side benefits of the ODBC concept is that many file formats can now be accessed by applications as if they were a database when they might be just a text file. ODBC drivers can connect to true database servers such as DB/2 on IBM mainframes, AS/400, and DEC RdB systems, and SQL Server, Oracle, and Informix servers, to name a few. In these cases, the ODBC driver transforms the ODBC function calls to native database server calls and passes the calls to the server. In the case of local file-based data sources such as text files, dBASE, Excel XLS, Access MDB, and other file types, the ODBC driver does not use the native application that created the file. Instead, the ODBC driver acts as the server, performing file input/output itself.

Components of ODBC

The ODBC architecture consists of four major components, which are described as follows. Figure 1.1 presents a flowchart illustrating the relationship among these components.

Data Source	This component consists of several parts as defined in a single data-source entry in the ODBC.INI file or registry. These parts could include the data itself, the associated DataBase Management System (DBMS), the platform on which the DBMS is running, and the network used to access that platform. Many data sources do not include a network or even a DBMS.
Driver	The driver is a DLL, which functionally sits between the Driver Manager and the data source and processes ODBC function calls. The driver connects to a data source on command from the application, receives SQL statements from the application, and passes them to the data source after possible translation. It also receives result-set information from the data source and passes it back to the application.

Note: The ODBC interface provides for access to data that is not contained in a conventional SQL DBMS, such as Xbase or text files. When the DBMS does not provide SQL support, the ODBC driver must process the SQL statements and return results as though the DBMS had done so. Similarly, an ODBC driver can supplement functionality provided by a rudimentary SQL DBMS. In this way, applications are able to call a common set of functions, secure in knowing that the driver will figure out how to provide the requested functionality.

Driver Manager	This DLL, generally provided by Microsoft as a part of the ODBC Software Development Kit, provides access to the individual ODBC drivers. The Driver Manager loads driver DLLs and directs function calls to them. The Driver Manager does limited error processing and handles some ODBC function calls.
Application	A program that processes data. This program can be written in one of many programming languages, generally running on the Microsoft Windows operating system. The application calls ODBC functions to interact with data sources.

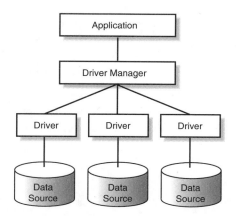

Figure 1.1. *Four components of ODBC architecture.*

In contrast to what ODBC does not do, here are a few of the things that ODBC does do:

☐ ODBC enables an application to use heterogeneous data sources.

☐ ODBC enables simultaneous connections to multiple database servers.

☐ ODBC drivers support multiple communications protocols to data sources, enabling programs to ignore the communications protocols in use.

☐ ODBC enables a non-SQL DBMS to be a data source.

☐ ODBC enables programs to be fully interoperable between databases.

Industry Commitment to ODBC

By now, you should have a basic understanding of what ODBC can do when programmed properly. On Day 4, "Installing Drivers and Configuring Data Sources," you'll have an opportunity to compare the ODBC API with others and discover many reasons why programming using ODBC is a better choice than using other interfaces.

Some programmers—even when convinced that ODBC is the best overall database programming interface—have been afraid to commit to using ODBC because they fear it's just a fad and won't last once a new method comes along. They should set their fears aside because ODBC is here to stay.

On Day 2, "Overview of ODBC Concepts and Theory," you will learn how ODBC developed and about the worldwide acceptance it has received. Microsoft and many

other major application vendors and database vendors have made a commitment to supporting and using ODBC. Currently, there are 16- and 32-bit ODBC drivers on the market for most data sources, and most of the major client/server application development tools provide an ODBC connectivity option.

History has shown that once the industry adopts a paradigm, support for that way of doing things will be carried forward at great expense. ODBC has achieved critical mass such that it would be difficult for a vendor to discontinue support for ODBC functionality. Therefore, you should feel comfortable choosing ODBC as a data-access standard, knowing that the standard will remain as stable as anything in the industry.

Programming with Visual Basic Versus C++

Some of the great debates of all time are centered on "which is better" choices:

☐ Ford versus Chevy

☐ Corn versus green beans

☐ Visual Basic versus C++

How many times have you heard people argue strongly that their way is better than all others? They'll debate at great length how green beans are better for you than corn, or Fords drive better than Chevys. When listening carefully to such discussions, you have to admit that usually both sides have valid reasons to support their arguments, and the deciding factor is little more than personal preference. Such arguments illustrate the futility of trying to subjectively determine "better" or "best" between objects that are either not comparable or are functionally identical.

To evaluate whether Visual Basic or C++ is better for programming using ODBC is probably more like comparing doctors to lawyers than comparing Fords to Chevys. That is, although both Visual Basic and C++ are programming languages, they are perceived as meeting needs at opposite ends of the fast development/fast performance spectrums.

You can count on a significant learning curve as you begin programming with the ODBC interface regardless of the language used. On Day 4 you'll learn about the specific advantages of using the ODBC API versus other APIs. In addition, you'll see a high-level logic flow, which can be used in calling the ODBC API.

The high-level program logic flow is the same for C++ and Visual Basic. The difference between the two languages is in the handling of the data within the application program itself. Most programmers agree that C++ is much faster than Visual Basic when it comes to executing input and display operations as well as performing computations. Early versions of BASIC were all interpreted, and its reputation for slowness was well deserved. All references in this book are to Visual Basic version 4.0, which is thought by many to execute very quickly.

Assuming that C++ does execute faster than Visual Basic, the question might be: Why use Visual Basic? The answer is easy: Visual Basic shortens development time. For a simple program with basic dialog controls, it will take equally proficient programmers less time to develop with Visual Basic than with C++. As program speed becomes more important and the user interface becomes more complex, C++ gains the advantage.

Using Visual Basic Data Controls

One of the real advantages of Visual Basic is the ability to use it to prototype an application module or working dialog quickly. Using the Microsoft Visual C++ App Studio tool, you can also prototype the dialogs quickly, but populating the prototype with data is more of a problem.

By using the data controls included in the Visual Basic version 4 Professional Edition, you can connect to ODBC data sources and do simple data access easily. Unfortunately, ODBC has gotten a bad reputation among some who have tried this technique as their only development effort. Although the development cycle is short and the learning curve is low, the performance with such applications tends to be disappointing.

The performance penalties paid when using the data controls vary depending on the data source involved and the type of access being used. It is not unheard of to achieve an increase in performance of 20 times or more when moving from data controls to accessing the ODBC API directly. If the application is going to be used only sparingly, such performance could be acceptable in light of the development time required to program to the API. On the other hand, if an application is to be used regularly, the payback of extra development time can be realized quickly.

The Jet Engine

Many first-time programmers will build an application in Visual Basic with data controls or in Microsoft's Access and be very disappointed with the application's performance. Typically, because they are also using ODBC for the first time in this same project,

ODBC will be blamed for the slow data-access speed. Because the majority of these programmers don't know how to write to the ODBC API, they can't see for themselves how wrong their assumption is about ODBC's speed.

It appears that the Jet Engine was written to provide a DBMS supporting PC-based tools such as Access. In this scenario, the Jet Engine is efficient at handling data in a local file-based database. When the Jet Engine has to access remote data sources using ODBC, it has more difficulty because the local file system can perform some operations much faster than a remote DBMS can. The Jet Engine tries to perform its usual functions by mapping them to ODBC functions. What you end up with is one DBMS (the Access Jet Engine) trying to provide an "outer wrapper" for another DBMS (the ODBC data source, such as SQL Server).

Version 2.0 of Microsoft Access solved many of these performance problems by making better use of the ODBC API, but Visual Basic version 4.0 does not share the same Jet Engine, and so the problems persist with Visual Basic. Both products (and many others) provide a SQL Passthru technique to overcome these problems and enable use of DBMS-specific features by forcing the application to pass an SQL command directly to the DBMS without changing or parsing the command.

Even when you turn off application functionality with the SQL Passthru option, performance won't compare with that achievable by a well-written application making its own calls to the ODBC API. It's your job to write that application well. In the next 21 days, you'll learn just how to accomplish that goal.

To return to the issue of which language to use, Visual Basic or C++, the best answer might be: Use both depending on the particular need. For a prototype or *ad hoc* application, use Visual Basic. For a production application, use C++.

Tools Needed for Development

Before you begin to develop an application using ODBC, you must have a minimum set of tools to work with. This book was written with the following *minimum* set of tools in mind:

☐ Microsoft Visual C++ Professional Development Environment, version 1.5 or higher

   or

   Microsoft Visual Basic Professional version 3.0 or higher

☐ ODBC Software Development Kit (SDK) (contained in Microsoft Developer Network Level II Kit)

☐ Microsoft *ODBC 2.0 Programmer's Reference and SDK Guide*

> **Note:** If you plan to use the Microsoft Visual C++ Development Environment, make sure that your version is compatible with the target platform you want your application to run on. If your application is to run on Windows 95 systems, it must be built with Visual C++ version 2.0 or higher. Note also that Visual C++ version 2.0 will run only on Windows NT or Windows 95.

Sample Applications, Sample Data, Sample Disk

Most of the sample programs throughout this book are built against the same target application. This application is a database of music CDs, which was chosen because just about everyone, regardless of his or her business background, is familiar with a music album on CD or vinyl. The final sample application can display data only from this database, insert new CDs, and manipulate the data in the manner expected from a typical business application.

The sample data consists of a small set of entries that might be found in a fictitious music database if one were to be created. The point is not taste in music or accuracy of the data content (in the samples, that is), but rather how to use ODBC to achieve the desired results.

Sample ODBC Driver for Exercises

You need to do all the exercises in this book and all testing and practicing against actual ODBC drivers. It's assumed that if you will be developing for a particular ODBC driver or data source, you already have that driver.

Because each driver has its own capabilities and peculiarities, it's strongly recommended that you develop and test against the drivers your application is most likely to run against. If you are going to develop an application for the general market that is designed to run against any ODBC driver, you should obtain as many different drivers as possible.

As stated earlier, having the Microsoft Software Development Kit for ODBC is a minimum requirement for developing an ODBC application. This SDK includes some sample drivers that you can use for testing purposes but cannot redistribute with your application. These drivers might be sufficient for testing purposes, but they're limited in conformance, functionality, and features. You'll need to look elsewhere to find 32-bit drivers for testing against the 32-bit Driver Manager, Administrator, and your application if it too is written using a 32-bit compiler.

Summary

This chapter introduced you to ODBC as you prepare to program using ODBC throughout the rest of this book. The chapter covered the following topics:

- ☐ ODBC is a method of connecting to data sources in a common way no matter how different the source or location of the data itself.

- ☐ Programming to the ODBC API can be done with many languages; Visual C++ and Visual Basic are two of the most popular. The pros and cons of using each depend on application usage.

- ☐ To develop an ODBC application, you'll need more than just a development language compiler. You'll also need the SDK, which provides header files, samples, and the definition of the ODBC API itself.

- ☐ Testing an application requires the use of a working ODBC driver. Although several are included with the ODBC SDK, you should have one for testing your application's final target.

Q&A

Q If my application will use more than one data source, do I have to code different SQL syntax for each?

A No. One of the major advantages of using ODBC is that the application passes standard ODBC SQL syntax to the driver, and the driver converts that to syntax appropriate for the DBMS being used.

Q Won't using ODBC slow down my application?

A Generally not. As is the case with any application development, final speed is determined by the quality of the code written. If the ODBC calls are made wisely, performance can be excellent. Likewise, sloppy coding can cause terrible performance.

Q Can my application connect to more than one data source at a time? Can I mix data from these data sources?

A You can have many connections open to many data sources at the same time from within the same application. Because you are in complete control of the data returned, you can mix and match data as much as needed to accomplish your needs.

Overview of
ODBC Concepts
and Theory

This chapter begins by presenting the history of ODBC and then focuses on the theory of ODBC and how it is implemented. Today, you'll learn about the following:

☐ The history of ODBC

☐ Driver and SQL conformance levels

☐ Driver Manager functionality

☐ One, two, and three-tier driver differences

☐ Calling ODBC APIs

The History of ODBC

To understand why ODBC was developed, one needs to look back at the evolution of data processing during the past decade.

When personal computers (PCs) were first introduced by IBM in 1982, the market was small and undeveloped. There had been a few machines on the market prior to that time, but they were considered toys that were purchased by hobbyists to experiment with rather than tools for serious computing. At that time, all business computing was done on mainframe systems. Most of these systems were made by IBM, with others from Univac, Sperry, Control Data, and a few other manufacturers. During this period, IBM was the runaway market leader, with a high percentage of computer terminals attached to IBM mainframes.

These terminals, typically of the 3270 type, were strictly display devices connected to the mainframe through a controller, with coaxial cable providing the connecting medium. These terminals had no built-in intelligence or functionality. They provided no graphics-display or color-display capability; the only display color was green.

Note: The term *3270* has become a generic reference to a character-mode "dumb" terminal attached to an IBM mainframe computer. Although there have been many models of terminals, almost all have included the capability of emulating a model-3270 terminal.

The programs running on the mainframe systems to drive the 3270 terminals were often monstrous in size and complexity. As a result, any changes or additions to these programs could be made only by experienced programmers who were familiar with the programs already. Because these programmers were often in short supply and very busy, the lead times required to make programming changes were long.

Eventually, frustration at such long lead times made users receptive to new and innovative systems coming on the market. These new systems were different in that they did not run on mainframe computers, but rather on minicomputers. These systems were small enough to be physically located in the departments where they were being used. They were inexpensive enough to be purchased outright, at a fraction of the cost of a mainframe system. Finally, and perhaps most importantly, these new systems were completely self-contained. The department that purchased the system had complete control over that system without having to wait for or work with a corporate Information Services (IS) department that had been traditionally slow in meeting user needs.

At the same time that these new minicomputer systems were showing up in some corporate offices, desktop PCs were starting to be seen. Typically they were not easy to use, and there were not many software packages to purchase at first, but the word-processing and spreadsheet packages being used were very popular. In addition, PC users began to notice that they did not have the same delays in response from their PCs that they had on their 3270 terminals attached to the mainframe.

These three developments—lengthy programming lead times on mainframe programs, the introduction of cost-effective minicomputer systems, and the acceptance of PCs for desktop applications—all played a part in the evolution of client/server programming.

Currently, there seem to be as many definitions of what client/server computing means as there are consultants in the industry. Most agree that it involves splitting the processing needed for an application between two or more computers, allowing each to perform the tasks for which it is best suited. When Microsoft Windows version 3.0 was released, the graphical user interface (GUI) became very popular among users, who found it easy to use and understand. Some analysts claim that client/server applications have caught on because users demanded GUI front ends to their programs that were "fun to use" rather than necessarily providing any extra functionality or performance.

Some of the first examples of client/server computing merely put a graphical front end on an existing program running on a mainframe or minicomputer. But as soon as efforts were made to do more processing on the PC, problems arose. These first programs were coded to use the proprietary programming interface and query language provided by the back-end system. This would make the application work fine with the original system, but it completely blocked movement to another system or the integration of more than one system.

A need developed to access not only those applications and data residing on the mainframes, but also those running on the newly acquired departmental minicomputer. When mergers took place, there was a need to access data on the other company's systems, but if they weren't the same type, that was not possible.

The only solution was either to have a different program or terminal on each desktop to access each different system, or to develop a standard that would allow programs to access many different data sources transparently.

ANSI and SAG CLI Specification

To overcome the problem of a lack of standards, the SQL Access Group (SAG) developed a call-level interface (CLI) specification. The SQL Access Group is a consortium of leading software and hardware database vendors. From this SAG SQL CAE specification and the X/Open specification, the ODBC interface was developed. The ODBC API enables developers to write applications that use one common set of code for accessing databases. The API is then converted by ODBC drivers into a format that can be used by the back-end database management systems (DBMSs) that are being accessed.

One of the early results of attempted database standardization was the adoption in 1986 of a standard for SQL. At that time, the American National Standards Institute (ANSI) defined SQL as a language that was to be separate from any other programming language. Since that initial effort, there have been several major additions to the standard.

In 1989, the standard created three different methods of interfacing with SQL programmatically, as follows:

Direct Invocation	Programmatic access using direct invocation is implementation-defined.
Module Language	Specifies the creation of SQL procedures from within compiled program modules. These procedures are then called from a conventional program in the same manner as a subroutine. The module language uses parameter passing to return values to the calling program just as a conventional subroutine does.
Embedded SQL	Enables SQL statements to be embedded directly within the code of a program. This 1989 specification defined embedded statements for COBOL, FORTRAN, PL/1, and Pascal.

In 1992, ANSI released its latest SQL specification, known as SQL-92. This specification has become an international standard. SQL-92 included several new features which had a direct impact on ODBC, whose creation followed the release of the SQL-92 standard very closely.

The two new features of SQL-92 that had the greatest impact on the ODBC standard were the definition of three levels of functionality and the addition of connections to database environments (which addressed the needs of client/server architectures). Additionally, the 1992 standard added additional data types, including date and time, support for dynamic SQL, scrollable cursors, and full outer-join support.

Concurrent with the ANSI standards introduction was the development of the SQL Access Group's call-level interface, which was based upon and fully supported the ANSI standard. This particular CLI for SQL consists of a group of function calls that support SQL statements. The CLI that was defined by SAG and X/Open in 1992 is similar to the dynamic embedded version of SQL described in the SQL Access Group and X/Open SQL CAE specification (1992). The ODBC interface is modeled directly from this CLI.

Dynamic Versus Embedded SQL

Initial programmatic access to SQL databases was done using embedded SQL from within COBOL or other language programs. The processing of SQL statements using this method involved the following three steps:

1. **Precompilation.** The program source code, including the embedded SQL statements, are processed by a language-specific precompiler. This precompiler would remove the SQL statements from the remainder of the source code, check the syntax of the SQL statements, and insert calls to private DBMS routines in place of the SQL statements.

2. **Bind.** In this step, a special DBMS-specific program analyzes and optimizes the SQL and creates an application plan or access path for each SQL statement. This plan is actually stored in the DBMS for later execution.

3. **Execution.** The application program is executed. When the database access is encountered, the execution plan that was created in the Bind step is executed. Data is returned from the query to the application program using host variables.

This technique of SQL execution is very effective for many applications, and it provides very fast database access when the pattern of database access can be determined at development time by the programmer and the SQL can be hard-coded into the program. The method of using embedded SQL from within a program is known as *static SQL*.

The two distinguishing features of static SQL are hard-coded SQL statements and binding to one DBMS. These features make static SQL fast to execute but very inflexible. Consider the usability of an ad-hoc query tool or even a spreadsheet such as Microsoft Excel if, each time it needed to get data from a DBMS, the request had to be recompiled.

To meet this need, the SQL-92 standard defined dynamic SQL. Dynamic SQL enables an application to generate and execute SQL statements at program runtime.

Dynamic SQL statements can be executed in two ways, either prepared or immediate. With a *prepared statement*, the DBMS prepares an access plan for the particular SQL statement. The actual statement can then be executed many times without the expense of generating the access plan each execution. The other way to run an SQL statement is with the *EXECUTE IMMEDIATE* statement. This method sends the SQL statement directly to the DBMS and tells it to prepare and execute the statement on the fly.

Dynamic SQL does not provide the same amount of speed or efficiency as static SQL. If, however, a programmer needs the flexibility to be able to defer until runtime the construction of the actual SQL statement or the association with a particular data source, then dynamic SQL is the only choice available. Figure 2.1 illustrates when the various steps in SQL execution take place.

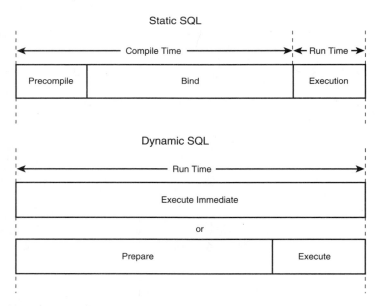

Figure 2.1. *SQL statement processing.*

Driver and SQL Conformance Levels

In creating the SQL-92 standard, the ANSI group understood clearly that each DBMS supports a different set of SQL functionality and syntax. For this reason, the SQL-92 standard first set out the three levels of SQL functionality: entry, intermediate, and full.

The ODBC standard goes a step further in defining conformance levels for drivers in two areas: ODBC SQL grammar (including ODBC SQL data types), and the ODBC API. These conformance levels make an application programmer's job easier by defining a standard set of functionality that both the driver developer and application developer can rely on and easily determine.

By definition, if a driver claims conformance to a certain API or SQL conformance level, it must support *all* of the functionality in that conformance level. If there is a single piece of the conformance level that is not provided by the DBMS, the driver developer must either provide the missing functionality from within the driver or claim a lower level of conformance. However, the converse is not true. If a driver supports all pieces of one level and a few of the next level, it works to everyone's advantage. The application can determine the functionality provided by a driver by making runtime calls to SQLGetInfo, SQLGetTypeInfo, and SQLGetFunctions. (The use of these functions will be detailed on Day 9, "Determining Driver and DBMS Capabilities.")

Because the ODBC API defines many functions beyond the CLI specification from X/Open and the SQL Access Group, the ODBC API functionality is split into three levels. The core API includes all functions in the SAG CLI, whereas Level 1 and Level 2 functions go beyond that minimum.

Core API Functionality

- [ ] Allocate and free memory and handles for environment, connection, and statements.
- [ ] Connect to multiple data sources. Allow multiple statements per connection.
- [ ] Execute SQL statements immediately. Prepare and execute SQL statements.
- [ ] Assign application storage space for parameters in an SQL statement and its result columns.
- [ ] Retrieve data from a result set and information about the result set.
- [ ] Roll back or commit transactions.
- [ ] Get error information.

Level 1 API Functionality

- [ ] Include core API functionality.
- [ ] Connect to data sources with dialog boxes to collect driver-specific attributes.
- [ ] Set and inquire about values of connection and statement options.
- [ ] Send all or part of a parameter value when data length is large.
- [ ] Retrieve part of all of result column values when data length is large.
- [ ] Retrieve catalog information about tables and columns, including information about them.
- [ ] Retrieve capability information about the driver and data source.

Level 2 API Functionality

- [ ] Include core and Level 1 API functionality.
- [ ] List available data sources and browse-connection information.
- [ ] Send and receive arrays of parameter and result-column values.
- [ ] Retrieve the number and description of parameters.
- [ ] Use a scrollable cursor.
- [ ] Retrieve the SQL statement in the form native to the DBMS.
- [ ] Retrieve catalog information about procedures, privileges, and keys.
- [ ] Call a translation DLL.

> **Note:** Common practice among commercial application developers is to assume that all Level 1 API functions are supported. Driver developers are being strongly urged to support this level of conformance. It can therefore be considered safe to assume in your application development that only Level 2 functions are optional.

ODBC defines its own set of SQL-grammar conformance levels. The three levels of ODBC SQL are minimum, core, and extended. The core level roughly matches that level of SQL grammar specified in the X/Open and SQL Access Group SQL CAE specifications of 1992. The minimum grammar is for a very limited level of ODBC conformance, and the extended grammar is designed to allow for extensions to the grammar to utilize features specific to a particular DBMS.

The standards break the grammar into two language subsets: Data Definition Language (DDL), used to define the data schema, and Data Manipulation Language (DML), used to access and change the data. Each level of grammar support is broken down by support for the DDL, DML, the expressions allowed, and the data types supported.

Minimum SQL Grammar Support

☐ DDL: CREATE TABLE and DROP TABLE

☐ DML: Simple SELECT, UPDATE SEARCHED, INSERT, and DELETE SEARCHED

☐ Expressions: simple

☐ Data types: CHAR and VARCHAR

Core SQL Grammar Support

☐ Include minimum SQL grammar

☐ DDL: GRANT, REVOKE, CREATE VIEW, DROP VIEW, CREATE INDEX, DROP INDEX, and ALTER TABLE

☐ DML: full SELECT

☐ Expressions: set functions (MIN, MAX, SUM, and so on), and subqueries

☐ Data types: NUMERIC, DECIMAL, SMALLINT, INTEGER, REAL, FLOAT, and DOUBLE

Extended SQL Grammar Support

☐ Include minimum and core SQL grammar

☐ DML: positioned UPDATE and DELETE, SELECT FOR UPDATE, unions, and outer joins

☐ Expressions: date, time, and timestamp literals, and scalar functions such as ROUND and SUBSTRING

☐ Data types: BIT, TINYINT, BIGINT, BINARY, VARBINARY, LONG VARBINARY, DATE, TIME, and TIMESTAMP

☐ Procedure calls

☐ Batch SQL execution

> **Warning:** A change in the ODBC specification between ODBC 1.0 and ODBC 2.0 has redefined which level of conformance contains positioned update, positioned delete, SELECT FOR UPDATE, and the UNION clause. These have all been moved from core SQL grammar to extended grammar in version 2.0. If your application will use SQL conformance levels to determine whether any of these statements are supported, you will also need to check the version number of the driver.

Driver Manager Functionality

All of this discussion about conformance levels has been referring to the features of drivers, but earlier you learned of the existence of a driver manager. Because not all drivers support all functions, it seems dangerous to link an application to the driver when you do not know what API calls are supported.

This is why any application program only needs to link to the Driver Manager. The Driver Manager, which is furnished by Microsoft along with an import library, exports all ODBC API functions. The individual drivers actually export functions to the ODBC Service Provider Interface (SPI). The ODBC API and SPI are syntactically very similar. Applications write to the API to receive the benefits provided by the driver manager. Although the primary purpose of the driver manager is to load driver DLLs, it also performs the following tasks:

- [ ] Maps data-source names to specific driver DLLs by looking in the ODBC.INI file or the registry
- [ ] Provides entry points to ODBC function calls for each driver
- [ ] Performs some ODBC initialization calls
- [ ] Provides sequence and parameter validation for ODBC calls

One-, Two-, and Three-Tier Driver Differences

A final point of clarification about types of drivers. At times, the conformance level of a driver's API levels and SQL conformance can be confused with whether a driver is single-tier or multiple-tier. The easiest way to determine whether a driver is single- or multiple-tier is to determine where the SQL statements are being processed.

If the ODBC driver is processing the SQL statements internally and returning the data to the application, the driver would be considered single-tier. This type of driver, which does all of the database file processing internally, is typically employed to access files from dBASE, Excel, or Access. These files are Indexed Sequential Access Method (ISAM) files created by their native applications to hold the data. When accessing this type of file, the ODBC driver is performing all DBMS processing internally to the driver, and the application that created the file is not involved.

If the ODBC driver passes the SQL statement to another process to retrieve the data, it is called a two-tier or multiple-tier driver. Examples of this type of driver would be ones that process requests for Oracle, SQL Server, or AS/400 databases. Some drivers also employ an intermediate processor to perform some conversion or communications functions before passing the SQL request to the database. These intermediate systems are commonly called *gateways*. Three-tiered drivers utilizing a gateway are available for mainframe systems to access DB/2 databases, mid-range systems for AS/400 databases, and systems to access RdB databases on Digital Equipment Corporation (DEC) systems.

Calling ODBC APIs

Now that you have learned ODBC in broad strokes, it is time to get a little more specific. ODBC's Application Programming Interface is the key to the extraordinary things ODBC makes available to you. In the next sections you see how you access these API functions.

Parameter-Passing Differences Between Visual Basic and C++

The passing of parameters to ODBC API functions is the same whether the function is called from C++ or Visual Basic. The prototypes and sample code shown later in this book illustrate that point. When developing against the ODBC APIs, you must take note of whether you are passing by value or by reference. Normally, this is very straightforward and is determined logically by whether the parameter is input or output and whether the function is returning a numeric value or a string.

All of the prototypes shown in this book use the Hungarian notation naming convention, so that the parameter name starts with a "p" if it is a pointer. All pointers are FAR pointers.

Note that in Visual Basic there is no concept of a pointer. Therefore, prior to making a function call that requires a pointer, a Windows API call such as LSTRCPY will have to be performed to obtain a pointer to the data.

Application Input and Output Buffers

It is the responsibility of the application to create both input and output buffers for use in passing data to the ODBC driver. The input and output refer to data direction relative to the driver. That is, the input buffer is used to pass data to the driver, and results are passed from the driver to the application in the output buffer. The memory needed for these buffers must be allocated and maintained by the application. Care should be taken to ensure that the buffer is large enough to accommodate the null termination byte passed at the end of string data.

In addition, the application programmer must ensure that the memory remains intact between functions if two different functions refer to the same buffer by using pointers. Some functions, such as SQLBindCol, will pass in to the driver the pointer to a particular buffer area. Subsequent function calls, in this case SQLFetch, will use that pointer for returning data to the buffer. If, between the time of the two calls, the location of the buffer has changed or become invalid, unpredictable results will occur.

This can be a common problem when programming in Visual Basic using variable-length string variables. Visual Basic allows the declaration of a string variable with no length specified. At runtime when the program fills that variable, memory is allocated to match the size of the data filling the field. This action will cause data storage for variables to move around in memory to accommodate the new allocations. If a pointer refers to an address before the new allocation, when the SQLFetch is performed it could return data to unknown areas of data or program code.

Care should also be taken to avoid allocating buffer space that crosses segment boundaries in Windows 3.1 programs. If a buffer is larger than a 64KB segment, the application owning that buffer should request the data in pieces, broken on segment boundaries. This is not a problem when writing to a system using a flat memory model such as Windows 95 or Windows NT.

When passing data in an input buffer to a driver, the application actually passes the address and length of the buffer. The length field can contain a numeric value of 0 or greater, which is the actual length of the data in the buffer. If the length value is 0, the buffer contains a zero-length or empty string. A NULL value has a completely different meaning in SQL and is never equal to an empty string. If a length value is specified, the character data in the buffer does not need to be null-terminated. The buffer-length field can also contain the values SQL_NTS or SQL_NULL_DATA. If the value equals SQL_NTS, this specifies that the character data in the buffer is a null-terminated string. When performing an SQLExecute function against a previously prepared SQL statement, the input buffer contains the actual values to be substituted into the parameter markers. When the length field contains SQL_NULL_DATA, the driver is to ignore the data in the buffer and use a NULL data value.

When an application calls a function that will return data in the output buffer, it must pass three values about the buffer to the driver. These values are the address of the buffer, the allocated length of the buffer, and the address of a variable in which the driver will return the length of the data actually returned. If the application passes in a null pointer as the address of the buffer, the driver will not return any data and will return SQL_SUCCESS if no other errors occur. All data conversion happens before data is placed into the output buffer. Any character data receives a null-termination byte. The variable receiving the length of the data will receive the number of bytes of actual data, not including this null-termination byte. The length is the length of the data following conversion. If the buffer is not large enough to hold all of the data, the driver will attempt to truncate the data without losing precision. If it is able to do so, the driver will return SQL_SUCCESS_WITH_INFO; otherwise it will return SQL_ERROR. If the value of the data to be returned is NULL, the driver will return SQL_NULL_DATA.

Summary

This chapter looked at the history and background of ODBC to understand how the interface was developed and what need it filled. The theory of ODBC and how it works was also explored. In this chapter, you learned the following:

☐ The origins of ODBC came as demand for client/server development expanded and the need was seen for an open interface to multiple databases.

☐ Because there are many database products on the market with diverse capabilities, the ODBC standard had to allow for varying levels of functionality using defined API and SQL conformance levels.

☐ The driver manager provides a common calling interface for all drivers, but little other actual functionality.

☐ There can be drivers that process SQL requests internally, called single-tier drivers, and others that pass the SQL to a separate database engine, called multiple-tier drivers.

☐ Calling ODBC APIs involves passing data values into and out of the driver using buffers.

Q&A

Q Why wasn't the ODBC interface introduced earlier?

A Until dynamic SQL was included in the SQL Access Group's standards in 1992, the ODBC interface was not practical. Use of embedded SQL would have required recompilation for every data source.

Q How can I program to the ODBC API using Visual Basic when the ODBC standard is all written for C?

A Although the ODBC APIs are written for use by C-language programs, Visual Basic provides for calling C-language DLLs. It is very common to call Windows APIs from Visual Basic, and the techniques are identical for calling ODBC APIs.

Q Won't I have to change my application source code depending on whether the driver I use is single- or multiple-tier?

A No, this won't make any difference to the application. The whole concept behind ODBC is that the application calls the standard APIs, and the driver hides how and where the function is processed.

Q There are three API conformance levels and three SQL levels. Are these levels always the same within any one driver?

A No. A driver can support extended SQL grammar and only be fully compliant with the Level 1 APIs.

Workshop

The Workshop provides quiz questions to help you solidify your understanding of the material covered and to give you experience in using what you've learned. Try to understand the quiz and exercise answers before continuing on to the next day's lesson. Answers are provided in Appendix A, "Answers."

Quiz

1. What memory constraints should the programmer be aware of when using the ODBC API?

2. What will be the return value of your ODBC function if it is successful? If it is not?

Application Design Considerations

Now that you're acquainted with the foundations of ODBC, today you examine actual program design using ODBC. This chapter presents a high-level view of program logic in database access using ODBC and explores the trade-offs you'll face when you use ODBC drivers to create an interoperable application. You'll learn about the following topics:

- ☐ Comparing ODBC to other CLIs
- ☐ Determining the proper level of interoperability
- ☐ Handling missing functionality
- ☐ High-level logic flow with ODBC

Comparing ODBC to Other CLIs: The Interoperability Factor

As an application developer, one of the first decisions you must make when designing an application that needs database connectivity is: What interface is most appropriate for use in this situation?

If your design specifications call for an application that must interoperate over more than one database environment, you'll have chosen ODBC as the CLI of choice to provide the interoperability. Many times, that decision is easy to make because there are few practical alternatives.

The more difficult decision is to determine how much interoperability to build into the application. This is hard to specify because the options are less clear-cut. You must have a clear set of interoperability goals laid out before starting application development, or the project will either come in over budget or not work for all the intended data sources.

Developing for Known Data Sources

The task is easiest if you are using ODBC to provide interoperability between two or three different data sources and you are certain that they are the only data sources to ever be used by your application. In this case, the specific differences in API function and SQL grammar support between the data sources can be mapped and analyzed. Sometimes, depending on the complexity of the application, it can help to have an idea of what ODBC functions will be needed in the application before you start mapping database differences. In this manner, you can avoid studying functions you will not be using.

Note: It might not be possible to determine all of the functions supported by a particular ODBC driver by reading the documentation. In such cases, using the ODBC Test tool is invaluable. This tool is shipped as a component of the Microsoft ODBC Software Development Kit. Its usage is detailed on Day 21, "Using ODBC Test and Trace Tools." Using this tool, you can execute the `SQLGetInfo` calls and the other functions that are explained on Day 9, "Determining Driver and DBMS Capabilities," and Day 10, "SQL Syntax for ODBC."

After determining the differences in functionality and SQL grammar between the specific ODBC drivers to be used for a particular application, the designer is left with one final choice: whether to allow for these differences in the design and coding stage of the application, or to test and respond to them at runtime. The trade-offs here are somewhat obvious. That is, if you design the program code to call certain ODBC API functions and use certain SQL syntax based on known driver behavior, the application will fail if that behavior changes. On the other hand, if you test the environment at runtime and your program responds appropriately based on the output from those tests, your application will continue to work as long as the drivers that are used do not employ functionality not originally planned for. The trade-offs are in ease of development versus greater flexibility.

Many or Unknown Data Sources

When the application design is conducted before the ODBC drivers are known, interoperability becomes a much larger issue for the application developer. In this situation, very few assumptions can be made about the functionality or SQL grammar supported by the drivers. As a result, if the application is to be truly interoperable, you must choose an approach that will work best for the application. It has often been said that to use ODBC you must use the lowest common denominator approach, but this is not the only choice to make. Broadly stated, there are three approaches that can be used, as described in the following sections.

No Common Denominator

In this method of using ODBC, the application makes no assumptions at all about the functionality or features provided by a DBMS. Each time a function is used, it must be surrounded by conditional code that checks conformance levels and capabilities with the driver. Developing with this method would provide the broadest possible interoperability

and would take advantage of all optional features provided by the DBMS. It is seldom used, however, because any effort to develop an application in this manner would be a huge undertaking, and the application would be nearly impossible to maintain once it was developed. This method of ODBC implementation is utopian in philosophy, but nearly impossible to implement in the real world.

Lowest Common Denominator

This method uses only those functions that are certain to be available in every data source the application might want to use. By picking a low level of functionality such as this, the developer avoids having to write any conditional code in the application. However, it makes it impossible to take advantage of any special features provided by the back ends, and it makes every DBMS look the same.

This *lowest common denominator* approach was used by many of the earliest front-end applications and tools that were released shortly after the introduction of ODBC. These tools would only work with drivers that provided a minimum set of conformance, usually Level 1, but they were limited by this design. Microsoft Access was an example of this. In version 1.1 of Access, it was very difficult to utilize any DBMS-specific functionality. An add-on Dynamic Link Library (DLL) was available to enable DBMS-specific SQL to be passed through, but this was not officially supported. When Access version 2.0 was released, it contained a much higher degree of ODBC flexibility. SQL passthrough support was built into the product. As other products mature, they will also enable and provide greater flexibility and functionality from the DBMS through the ODBC driver.

Lowest common denominator has been used as a derogatory reference to ODBC itself, but it is easy to see how this is really a reference to how the ODBC CLI is implemented by a front-end application.

The Mixed Approach

This method of application design is a middle ground between the lowest common denominator and no common denominator approaches. In this method, the application assumes a certain minimum level of functionality provided by all the drivers to be used. Then the application queries for additional features above that minimum level. A good example comes when examining outer-join functionality. Because only some DBMSs support outer joins, the lowest common denominator approach would assume that no ODBC drivers can perform outer joins, and the application would provide this functionality itself. This is what Access version 1.1 appears to do. The smarter, mixed approach asks the driver if it can perform outer joins. If it can, the application sends SQL asking the DBMS to perform the outer join, but if the DBMS does not support this, the application does it internally. Microsoft Access version 2.0 works in this fashion.

Handling Missing Functionality

As you design your application, you might discover that your application requires functionality that is not provided by the DBMS you plan to use. If this is functionality that is essential to the purpose of the application, you must select another DBMS or provide the missing functionality within your application. The preceding example of outer joins is a case in which if the DBMS cannot process an SQL join statement, your application can submit separate SELECT statements against each table and then join them internally.

Some functionality cannot be provided with the application, however. If a particular set of data is not updatable on the DBMS, there is nothing the application can do to emulate or provide this capability of changing the data in the database. In this case, your options are limited to proceeding with the application in read-only mode, giving the user the option of proceeding, selecting another data source, or quitting—or the application can just post an error message and abort.

When evaluating how such problems can affect your application, keep in mind that problems such as the inability to update data can come from three or more places, depending on the data source. Your application must be prepared for these circumstances. If you choose to implement a key-based system in your application, such as that used in Microsoft Access and Visual Basic Data Controls, the lack of a unique index on the table being used will prevent updatability because of the logical inability to uniquely identify the row to be updated within the application. The functions SQLSpecialColumns and SQLStatistics can be called to obtain information about indexes on specific tables. These functions will be introduced on Day 9. Keep in mind that this type of limitation is imposed by the application design, and therefore it can be removed by changing the design of the front-end application.

There are some ODBC drivers that provide read-only access to the DBMS as a security measure. These are typically seen in situations in which the DBMS provides read/write access, but for security or data-integrity reasons, some users are only to be given read access for performing queries. The function SQLGetInfo, when called with the fInfoType of SQL_DATA_SOURCE_READ_ONLY, will indicate whether the data source itself is set to READ ONLY. The functions SQLGetConnectOption and SQLSetConnectOption can be called with the option SQL_ACCESS_MODE to determine and set how the driver supports SQL statements that cause updates to the data. (These functions are also explained on Day 9.)

The final possibility in the example of data updates is that the DBMS attempts an update and fails. This could occur because of insufficient privileges on the data source, log-file problems, or many other difficulties depending on the environment. The application designer must be prepared for such errors to occur and handle them gracefully. On Day

13, "Determining the Return Status of a Call," you learn about how to handle such errors and present the error information to the user. The important design decision in this case is whether to present the error and abort, retry the update, or continue without the update.

High-Level Logic Flow with ODBC

The single question heard most often from beginning ODBC developers is "Where do I start?" It is useless to have a high level of knowledge and experience using C++ or Visual Basic without knowing at a high level what sequence in which to use the ODBC functions. Even (or perhaps most particularly) experienced SQL users can be quickly frustrated when they first begin experimenting with ODBC and they receive a series of "function sequence error" messages. Although there is plenty of flexibility in the use of ODBC functions, there are some basic sequences that must be followed.

You might find it helpful as you first explore the ODBC environment to use the ODBC Test tool to execute functions without having to write any code. In this way, you can see the result of changing the sequence of execution as well as the impact of changing parameters and options. At the highest level, the ODBC functions can be broken into two categories: environment functions and data functions. The *environment functions* establish and maintain the environment ODBC uses, whereas the *data functions* request queries or changes to the data source and handle the results.

ODBC Environment Functions

The ODBC environment functions are those that establish or clean up parts of the ODBC environment, query or change the behavior of that environment, or connect and disconnect with a data source. As shown in Figure 3.1, no SQL statement processing can occur until at least the first four basic environment functions are performed. The first three of these functions—SQLAllocEnv, SQLAllocConnect, and SQLConnect—are explained in detail on Day 8, "Connecting to the Data Source," and SQLAllocStmt is detailed on Day 11, "Running SQL SELECT Statements." The clean-up functions performed after all SQL processing is completed are covered on Day 19, "Ending Transactions and Connections."

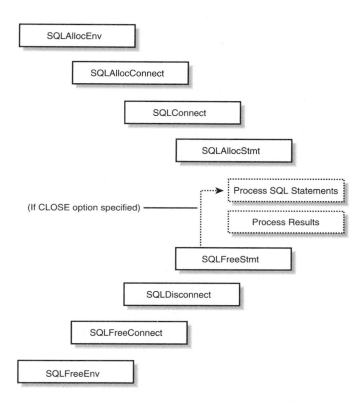

Figure 3.1. *Diagram showing the highest-level ODBC function calls necessary to process SQL requests.*

In Figure 3.1, the functions are paired and indented to indicate which functions logically work together. Generally speaking, the functionality can be repeated many times at each level. That is, if you want to connect to more than one data source simultaneously in an application, call SQLAllocConnect and then SQLConnect together to create one connection, then call SQLAllocConnect and then SQLConnect again for the second connection. It is then necessary to call SQLAllocStmt one or more times for each connection that has been established.

Because not all data sources support more than one concurrently active statement, you must be careful before you allocate multiple statements. For example, SQL Server supports only one statement per active connection, whereas Oracle supports many. To check this behavior, call SQLGetInfo with an fInfoType value of SQL_ACTIVE_STATEMENTS. This is another of the many options to be covered on Day 9. If the application finds that

the data source supports only one active statement at a time, the SQLFreeStmt function must be executed to free or release the previous statement handle (and all of its pending results, if any) before allocating a new statement.

As indicated by the dotted line in Figure 3.1, many functions have behavior that varies depending on the parameters specified with the function call. In the case of SQLFreeStmt, you can specify a CLOSE option or a DROP option. If the DROP option is used, the application would need to allocate a new statement handle before attempting any additional SQL processing. On the other hand, if a statement is to be reused, the statement can be freed with the CLOSE option, in which case the same statement handle can be reused without allocating a new handle.

It is important to keep in mind that if the application will be developed using C++ with classes written elsewhere, the developer must have a good knowledge of which of these environment functions are already included in the initialization code of the classes and therefore do not need to be explicitly written by the application developer. If you use Microsoft's Visual C++ version 1.5 with the Microsoft Foundation Classes (MFC) version 2.5, it is possible to create a very simple application that will use ODBC to query data from a data source and display it without explicitly coding any ODBC function calls. This same simple use of ODBC is also available in MSVC 2.*x*, Microsoft's 32-bit compiler, through the 3.*x* MFC it ships with.

The use of classes such as the Microsoft Foundation Classes represents a compromise between speed of development and flexibility in the application. If all of the function calls are made for you, the flexibility to tailor the application to the data source is lost. This is why it is important to be intimately familiar with the classes you are using, so that you can modify and add to the code being used to create an application that maximizes functionality for you. As you evaluate what the classes are doing, remember that they will also be following the outline diagrammed in Figure 3.1. Any additions you make to this code must still fit into this basic framework of ODBC function sequencing.

ODBC Data Functions

After the ODBC environment is initialized as diagrammed in Figure 3.1, it is time to interact with the actual data residing on the DBMS that is selected as the data source(s). In this loose context, *interaction* could mean querying the data, changing the data, or learning about the attributes of the data. Although the functions for learning about the data are ODBC-defined API functions, the specific steps addressed in the diagram in Figure 3.2 use SQL statements to query or change the data.

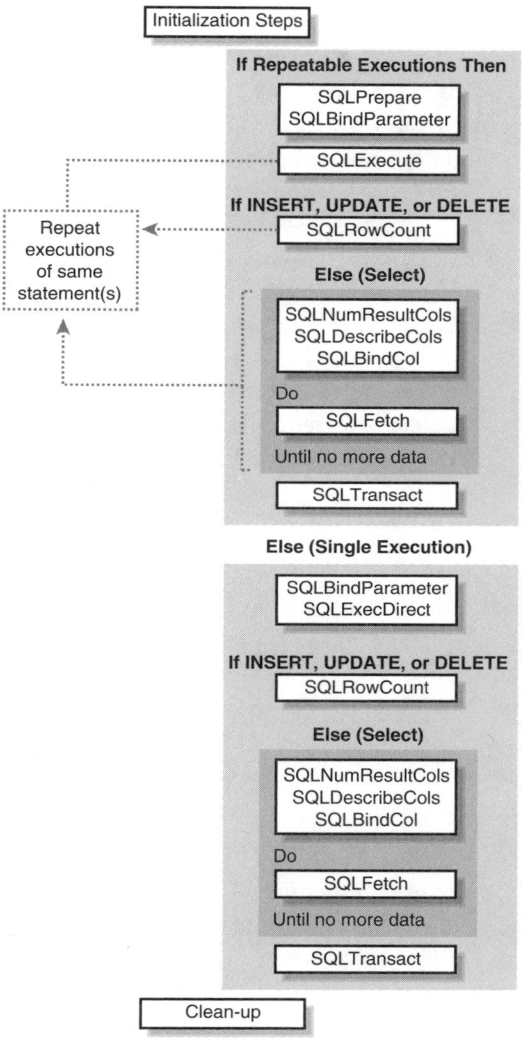

Figure 3.2. *A diagram showing the ODBC function calls used to execute SQL statements.*

The first feature to note in Figure 3.2 is that between the initialization at the top and the cleanup at the bottom, there are two large blocks of code. These blocks both perform the same functionality; the only difference is that the top block takes advantage of preparing the SQL statement to give better performance during multiple executions. The bottom block assumes a single execution and leaves out the preparation step.

The core ODBC functionality provides two different methods for SQL execution, depending on need. These are prepared execution using SQLPrepare followed by SQLExecute, and direct execution using SQLExecDirect. If the same SQL statement is going to be executed many times, even if the data values change, prepared execution will provide performance benefits. In addition, if the application needs information about the attributes of the result set before data is returned, preparing the statement will enable you to obtain information about the result set. This is because when a data source receives an SQLPrepare statement, it will compile the statement and produce an access plan for that statement which is available to the driver. When a statement is to be executed many times, the performance benefit is achieved because the compilation and access plan have to be accomplished only once. However, if a statement is to be executed only once, it should be executed directly to avoid the extra overhead involved with preparing the statement. (Further details on running prepared statements versus direct execution are presented on Days 11 and 14.)

In Figure 3.2, the function SQLBindParameter is shown being executed just before the execution of the SQL statement, whether prepared or direct. This function, which is explained on Day 14, "Using Prepared Statements and Parameter Markers," binds a buffer to a parameter marker within the SQL statement. A parameter marker is the question-mark character (?) placed in an SQL statement in place of a value. When used in this manner, when the SQL statement is executed, the value is either placed into the buffer from the data source or sent to the data source from the buffer, depending on the SQL statement. The obvious power of this functionality is that the actual value does not have to be known at compile time but is inserted at runtime. In addition, the same SQL statement when prepared can be executed multiple times without change just by changing the values in the bound buffers.

Following SQL statement execution, Figure 3.2 diagrammatically breaks the handling of results into two classes: results from SELECT statements, and results from all other types of SQL statements. Speaking again at a high level, with the details to come in later chapters, the only result available from SQL statements that change the data is the number of rows affected by the statement. This value is obtained by calling SQLRowCount (which is detailed on Day 15, "Running INSERT, UPDATE, or DELETE Statements").

> **Note:** Many new ODBC developers complain that SQLRowCount does not work correctly in returning the count of rows returned by an SQL SELECT statement. In the ODBC specifications, SQLRowCount is only defined to return the number of rows affected by an UPDATE, INSERT, or DELETE statement or their equivalent operations in SQLSetPos, a cursor-based

operation. Contrary to what might be implied from the function name, this function is not designed to return the number of rows in a query-result set. Some drivers might make this value available in such a manner, but this behavior cannot be relied upon. Most applications that need this information are forced to scan the result set, performing a count once the data has been fully returned to the application.

In the case of a SELECT statement, Figure 3.2 diagrams a set of data-preparation steps followed by a loop to fetch the data until all data is returned. This is an example of one form of high-level data retrieval. In actual practice, there could be more or fewer steps involved, depending on the type of data, whether the application developer knows the data schema ahead of time, and whether this will be a single row or a large amount of data.

The first function called, SQLNumResultCols, is used if the number of columns being returned is unknown. This would be the case typically when the returned result set is to be displayed in a grid or other general type of display format. If the SQL statement SELECT * FROM ALBUM is executed, the number and order of columns returned would be unknown. By calling SQLNumResultCols (which is explained on Day 12, "Returning Data to the Program"), the application can learn at runtime how many columns are in the result set. This can be useful to set up for and receive the data when looping within the application. Obviously, if the developer is requesting specific, known columns of data explicitly in the SQL statement, this function is not needed.

The next function commonly called when returning data is SQLDescribeCols. This function, also described on Day 12, is used to get a full description of a particular column in the result set. This information includes the data type, size, and column name. If the data is to be used in a form or other data-specific display organization, this function is probably not needed, but if a general display is being set up at runtime, the information returned by SQLDescribeCol is essential.

When the ODBC driver returns the data values composing a result set, these values must then be moved into data-storage areas defined by and accessible to the application. This binding can be done either before the result row is returned to the driver, or after. These options, also discussed on Day 12, involve either the use of SQLBindCol to bind a column to a specific data storage area before fetching the data, or SQLGetData to move the data into storage after the entire row has been fetched.

Because SQLBindCol has to be performed only once per column, regardless of the number of rows returned, it offers obvious performance benefits on multirow result sets over SQLGetData, which must be performed for each column in each row. When using bound columns, the data movement between the driver's buffer and the application data storage area is automatic, and occurs when the SQLFetch is performed. On the other hand, if not bound, the data for each column must be moved using SQLGetData programmatically for each value.

Although it might seem foolish to use anything other than bound columns, consider the case in which not all of the data is needed. In this situation, you could bind only the columns containing data that is always needed or which defines criteria for the other columns. Then, if the data from the remaining columns is needed, as might be the case if a user selected the row, the remaining data for unbound columns in that row can be returned to the application only using SQLGetData calls.

The SQLTransact function call is shown on Figure 3.2 to depict where it would appear in the sequence of calls if transaction control is being used. This call would be made to commit or roll back the current transaction. (This functionality is explained on Day 18, "Using Transactions and Commitment Control.")

Summary

Today's lesson presented a high-level overview of the logic flow needed in an ODBC application. You learned about the following topics:

☐ The ODBC CLI has advantages and disadvantages over other CLIs. If interoperability is not needed between different DBMSs, a DBMS-specific CLI will suffice. However, if interoperability is needed, ODBC is the best (and many times the only) choice.

☐ Interoperability is not a black-or-white concept, but one of variable shades of gray. The application designer must decide before writing code how much interoperability his application will provide.

☐ When using a variety of database drivers supporting many systems, there will be different levels of support. Not all features are supported by all drivers. Design decisions must be made as to how to handle missing functionality.

☐ The logic flow used in calling ODBC functions must follow a specific pattern in order to be successful. This logic flow can be broken into the environment functions and the data functions.

Q&A

Q **If a certain ODBC driver does not provide the functionality my application needs, can't I just select and use a different driver?**

A Sometimes, but usually not. At the time of this writing, there was only one ODBC driver available for Oracle databases. If that driver did not provide the needed function, it would need to be provided in the application. On the other hand, there are many different versions of drivers for ISAM file types and even SQL server systems. If a particular driver does not meet all needs, you should certainly check with other vendors.

Q **The Microsoft Foundation Classes, version 2.5, limit me to one data source per record set. Can't I overcome this limit?**

A Because this is a limitation in the MFC version 2.5 classes, and not in ODBC, the limit can be overcome. You can write application code to access multiple sources; other commercial classes, such as the odbc/ClassLib from SWDI, do not have this restriction.

Q **Must I choose and stick with using bound columns for an entire connection, or can I change?**

A You can bind only those columns desired, and they can be unbound at any time.

Workshop

The Workshop provides quiz questions to help you solidify your understanding of the material covered and to give you experience in using what you've learned. Try to understand the quiz answers before continuing on to the next day's lesson. Answers are provided in Appendix A, "Answers."

Quiz

1. Does SQLRowCount return the number of rows in a result set?
2. What functions does the ODBC core provide for SQL execution?

Installing Drivers and Configuring Data Sources

Now that the lessons so far have covered the background of ODBC and looked at high-level program design, it's time to get to work. Before programming or even testing with ODBC, you need to install and configure ODBC drivers. This chapter shows you how to install typical ODBC drivers and how to configure data sources. You will learn about the following:

- [ ] Installing drivers using Setup
- [ ] ODBC configuration files and registry entries
- [ ] Differences between 16- and 32-bit tools
- [ ] Configuring data sources using ODBC Administrator
- [ ] Configuring data sources programmatically

You learned in the past three days that the ODBC interface consists of the ODBC Driver Manager from Microsoft and DBMS-specific drivers from many different driver vendors. In addition to these dynamic link libraries (DLLs), each workstation also needs configuration information that these DLLs use to determine where the data is located and how to access that data.

Each driver vendor will ship along with their driver the ODBC Driver Manager and the ODBC Administrator, a program to perform the configuration. In addition to these pieces, which many users and developers might know about, there are lesser-known components, which you will use today. These include the Installer DLL, cursor-library DLL, 3D-controls DLL, driver-setup components, and help files. On Windows 95 and Windows NT systems, a variety of 16- to 32-bit and 32- to 16-bit thunking DLLs are also installed.

Unlike many networked applications that can be configured and run as shared network applications, ODBC must be run using at least a local configuration. This does not mean that the files previously mentioned cannot reside on a network server, but they must be in the local systems path.

Installing Drivers Using Setup

Virtually all ODBC drivers written for Windows systems can be installed with a standard setup program from Microsoft. This setup program is part of the Driver Setup Toolkit, which is included with the ODBC Software Development Toolkit (SDK). (This is explored on Day 5, "The Microsoft ODBC Software Development Kit (SDK).") The components distributed and installed by Setup are also included in the ODBC SDK.

When you install new drivers, you run the program SETUP.EXE, usually from floppy disk. After some preliminary screens specifying the installation directory and other features, you are usually presented with a choice of which drivers to install. Figure 4.1 shows such a selection for the Microsoft SQL Server driver, which is the only driver shipped on that disk. In contrast, Figure 4.2 shows the selection dialog box presented by the Q+E ODBC Pack. This dialog box features a long list of drivers that can be installed.

Figure 4.1. *Driver selection during installation of Microsoft SQL Server driver.*

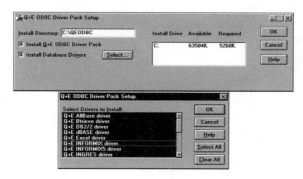

Figure 4.2. *The selection dialog box from Q+E Driver Pack showing many drivers installable from one setup.*

Although the driver vendor has a great deal of flexibility in configuring how the setup operation works, the installation process will generally avoid installing older files over newer versions of the same file. Figure 4.3 shows a typical error dialog box that appears in such a situation. In this case, the user installing the driver is given the option of installing the older file or continuing the setup without installing that particular file. Figure 4.1 shows the Advanced option button, which presents a dialog box providing control of these events during the installation. These options enable the user to select always installing the driver or administrator regardless of date and other variations of these options.

Figure 4.3. *The warning dialog box that appears when the installation is about to copy a file over a file of the same name with a newer date.*

Caution: Although setup programs usually check file dates to determine the newest version, these can be incorrect. Because the file date can be manipulated during the setup process, this date cannot always be relied upon to reflect which file is a newer version. The actual version number should be coded within the DLL or EXE file. You can view this by selecting the file within File Manager and pressing Alt+Enter. You should always use the files with the newest (highest) version number. In addition, it is always a good idea to only have one copy of a particular file such as ODBC.DLL on the entire system.

Once the setup program has completed copying all the needed files to the system, the configuration process is started. This configuration is identical to that presented by the ODBC Administrator, a Windows Control Panel application. You can either configure a data source now during the setup operation or perform it later using the Administrator. If setup was run to update a driver that has previously been installed and configured, re-creating the data source is not always necessary.

Note: You do not have to re-create or reconfigure a data source when you are upgrading the corresponding driver, but it might be a good idea. Careful reading of the installation documentation and readme files that shipped with the new driver should indicate whether this reconfiguration is necessary. Such configuration or re-creation is at times needed in order to include new parameters or attributes in the data-source definition.

The first dialog box of the configuration process, whether during setup or from the ODBC Administrator, is shown in Figure 4.4. If this is the first driver to be installed, the Data Sources (Driver) list will be empty, and the Setup and Delete buttons will be grayed out.

Figure 4.4. *The Data Sources dialog box from configuration or ODBC Administrator.*

Notice that the two bottom buttons on this dialog box are active. The Options button is used to turn on or off trace logging and to specify a log file. This logging is for all drivers, but it is not as useful as some of the other trace tools available. (These tools are presented on Day 21, "Using ODBC Test and Trace Tools.") The Drivers button, when pressed, will bring up a list of installed drivers. By selecting a driver in this list and pressing the About button, you can also see the version number and other details of a particular driver. To begin the creation of a new data source, press the Add button. This will bring up a similar list of installed drivers, as shown in Figure 4.5.

Figure 4.5. *The Add Data Source dialog box where the driver to be used for the new data source is selected.*

Once the driver to be used for this new data source is selected, a driver-dependent dialog box will be presented. Figure 4.6 shows the dialog box used for the Microsoft SQL Server driver.

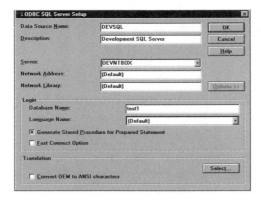

Figure 4.6. *The driver-specific configuration dialog box for the SQL Server.*

In this example with SQL Server, the user must enter a data-source name and a server name. All of the other information is optional, with defaults being provided by the driver. Some of the optional information, such as the network address and library, must be changed using the ODBC Administrator, and the database name can either be changed with the Administrator or by an attribute in the connection string during the SQLDriverConnect function.

ODBC Configuration Files and Registry Entries

Once the configuration dialog box has been completed, the administration routine will complete the creation of the data source by writing the configuration entries either to the ODBC.INI file or to the registry. The ODBC.INI file is used in Windows 3.1 and Windows for Workgroups systems, whereas Windows 4.0 and Windows NT have replaced the INI files with the registry. When a 16-bit driver is installed on Windows NT in the Windows on Windows (WOW) subsystem, an ODBC.INI file entry is generated.

The ODBC.INI file and the registry contain the same information; only the location and access method are different. This information includes the data-source name and description, the driver DLL being used, and any driver or data-source specific attributes as defined by the driver. The ODBC.INI file appears as shown in Listing 4.1 when the SQL Server installation and configuration are completed.

 Listing 4.1. ODBC.INI file with SQL Server entry.

```
;--------------------------------------------------------------------
; WARNING:  Do not make changes to this file without using the ODBC Control
;           panel device or other utilites provided for maintaining data
;           sources.
;
;           Incorrect changes to this file could prevent ODBC from
;           operating or operating correctly.
;--------------------------------------------------------------------

[ODBC Data Sources]
DEVSQL=SQL Server

[ODBC]
TraceAutoStop=0
Trace=1
TraceFile=\SQL.LOG

[DEVSQL]
Driver=C:\WINDOWS\SYSTEM\sqlsrvr.dll
Description=Development SQL Server
Server=DEVNTBOX
FastConnectOption=No
UseProcForPrepare=Yes
Database=test1
OEMTOANSI=No
LastUser=
```

The ODBC.INI file consists of four main groups. The first group, which is really only one section, generally found at the top of the file for ease of reading, is the ODBC Data Sources section. This contains the name of each data source currently configured and its corresponding driver name. The second options group consists of those sections that apply to all ODBC data sources. These sections would be used for tracing and other debug functions. In Listing 4.1, there is only one such section, headed ODBC. This section controls the trace log generated by the Driver Manager. The Default data-source section contains a single section with a data-source name of "Default." This section is not listed in the ODBC Data Sources section and is a duplicate of one of the configured data sources. The final group consists of one section for each configured data source. Each section has a section header containing the data-source name, and all attributes follow, one per line.

In Windows 95 and Windows NT, the data-source configuration information is stored in the registry. Figure 4.7 shows the registry entry for the SQL Server data source using a 32-bit SQL Server driver. As you can see from this figure, the ODBC.INI entry is a subkey of ODBC under the CURRENT_USER hive. Each section in the ODBC.INI file will

have a corresponding subkey in the registry, and each keyword-value pair has a matching entry in the registry. All of these entries can be viewed using the registry-editor application. In Windows 95, this application is REGEDIT.EXE, whereas in Windows NT it is REGEDT32.EXE. The view shown in Figure 4.7 is from REGEDIT.EXE.

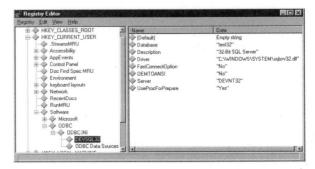

Figure 4.7. *Registry Editor showing hierarchy of entries for ODBC.INI.*

A second initialization file is also created and maintained when you modify data sources using the ODBC Administrator. This file, named ODBCINST.INI, contains the name and description of each available driver, as well as a section containing the driver DLL, the setup DLL, and any driver-attribute keywords. Translation DLLs are also enumerated in the ODBCINST.INI file. Listing 4.2 shows the ODBCINST.INI file following installation of the 16- and 32-bit SQL Server drivers and configuration of their corresponding data sources.

Listing 4.2. ODBCINST.INI file with SQL Server driver installed.

```
;------------------------------------------------------------------------
; WARNING:  Do not make changes to this file without using the ODBC Control
;           panel device or other utilites provided for maintaining data
;           sources.
;
;           Incorrect changes to this file could prevent ODBC from
;           operating or operating correctly.
;------------------------------------------------------------------------

[ODBC Drivers]
SQL Server=Installed

[ODBC Translators]
MS Code Page Translator=Installed

[SQL Server (32 bit)]
Driver=C:\WINDOWS\SYSTEM\sqlsrv32.dll
```

```
Setup=C:\WINDOWS\SYSTEM\sqlsrv32.dll
32Bit=1

[ODBC 32 bit Drivers]
SQL Server (32 bit)=Installed

[SQL Server]
Driver=C:\WINDOWS\SYSTEM\sqlsrvr.dll
Setup=C:\WINDOWS\SYSTEM\sqlsrvr.dll
APILevel=1
ConnectFunctions=YYY
DriverODBCVer=02.01
FileUsage=0
SQLLevel=1

[MS Code Page Translator]
Translator=C:\WINDOWS\SYSTEM\mscpxlt.dll
Setup=C:\WINDOWS\SYSTEM\mscpxlt.dll
```

Note that this file, from a Windows 95 system, shows two drivers installed, but the ODBC.INI file shows only one data source. This is because the 32-bit driver and data sources are configured using the registry rather than the ODBC.INI file. When you compare the preceding listing to the registry entry shown in Figure 4.8, it is easy to see the similarities between the two. In fact, it would be easy to confuse the 16- and 32-bit drivers in this case because they are nearly identical. The name of the data source, driver, and DLLs are the only clues to which version is being used. If the version information for the driver DLL that is listed were to be checked, it would show whether a 16- or 32-bit driver was being referenced.

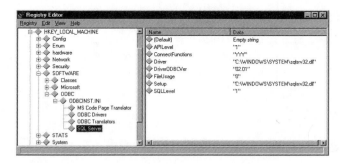

Figure 4.8. *The Registry Editor showing ODBCINST.INI values.*

Note that both of the initialization files for 16-bit drivers are kept in the WINDOWS directory, but the registry equivalents are kept in different hives. The hierarchy for ODBC.INI entries is as follows:

```
HKEY_CURRENT_USER
    Software
        ODBC
            ODBC.INI
```

Instead of being kept in a user context, the driver-information hierarchy in the registry for ODBCINST.INI is as follows:

```
HKEY_LOCAL_MACHINE
    Software
        ODBC
            ODBCINST.INI
```

The obvious implications of the data-sources information being kept in the CURRENT_USER hive is that if more than one person logs onto a system using the registry (Windows 95 or Windows NT), the ODBC configurations will be different. If two different users plan on using the same data sources, they will have to create those data sources two times using the ODBC Administrator, or else their application will have to create the data source for them.

Caution: Although the initialization files are simple ASCII text files that can be modified with any text editor, they should only be changed using the tools provided specifically for ODBC administration. The same is true of the registry entries. Text editors or the registry editor can be used to view the contents of ODBC configurations, but attempts to modify the information using these editors can be disastrous. Often the user is unaware of interactions between different areas of the configuration, and manual editing provides no error checking. An example of this is with the SQL Server driver. If a network address and library are entered in the configuration dialog box, they are not only saved as part of the ODBC.INI information, but they are also written to the SQLSERVER section of the WIN.INI file. Future revisions of the driver could change the options and keyword-value pairs without notice. All of these reasons justify the need to *not* edit the ODBC configurations by hand.

Differences Between 16- and 32-Bit Tools

ODBC has been developed so that 16-bit applications can use both 16- and 32-bit drivers on the appropriate platforms, and similarly, 32-bit applications can use both types of drivers in some scenarios. In tomorrow's lesson, you will see what components are needed to perform these transformations and how they are used. For today, just keep track of the data sources and the tools used to maintain them.

For most ODBC data-source administration, the ODBC Administrator is used. This is an application that ships with the ODBC SDK, and it can be run as either a control panel applet or a regular application. Because Windows 3.1 is strictly a 16-bit operating system, only the 16-bit version of the Administrator is loaded whenever a driver is installed. However, with Windows 95 or Windows NT, there could be 16- or 32-bit drivers, or both. To avoid confusion, you need to be careful in matching administrator with driver. Figure 4.9 shows the Control Panel with both flavors of ODBC Administrator shown.

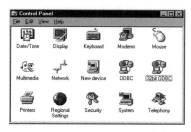

Figure 4.9. *Control Panel on Windows 95 system showing icons for both 16- and 32-bit ODBC Administrators.*

This potential for confusion becomes even greater when the administrator applications are opened, as shown in Figure 4.10. In this figure, the 32-bit administrator is shown on the left. They are both open at the same time on the same workstation, and they do not show the same data sources. If you were to select the Drivers display on both, you would see that they also show different drivers installed. If the data source DEVSQL32 did not have the "32" in its name, you would not be able to determine which version of the administrator, drivers, and data sources you were working with unless you used the About button to look at driver details. Then you would see that one driver filename is SQLSRV32.DLL, and the other is SQLSRVR.DLL.

Figure 4.10. *Opened administrator applications.*

Configuring Data Sources Using the ODBC Administrators

Data sources can either be configured using the ODBC Administrator or by calling the installer DLL from within a program. Creating or changing a data-source configuration using the Administrator offers flexibility; the user can enter a wide variety of values into the configuration dialog box. The data-source name, for instance, can be nearly any character string of up to 30 characters, as long as it does not contain some special characters.

In addition, the user needs to know very little about the actual DBMS or the configuration parameters in order to create a data source using the administrator. A good example of this is the SQL Server configuration shown in Figure 4.6. Here, the user is prompted for a data-source name, which the user can create, and a description, which can be anything, because it is merely descriptive text. The Server name must be entered, but the driver provides a drop-down list box here to enumerate the known servers for user selection.

Although not all drivers are equally easy to configure, use of the dialogs provided in the administrator tool make this job very simple. It is this simplicity and flexibility that can also create problems for the application developer. If the developer does not want the user to be prompted to select a data source, but rather wants this to be coded within the application, there must be a way to ensure that the data-source name is always the same. It would be very difficult to ensure that two users entered the same name, and ridiculous to assume this could be done across an entire department or enterprise. (Users just don't type that well.)

Configuring Data Sources Programmatically

The solution to this problem is to not depend on the user configuring the data source. Instead, the application program can create the needed data source if it does not already exist. Just as driver developers often have their setup programs configure a data source for their driver at the time it is installed, the application program can check for the existence of a data source and create it if it's missing.

The negative side of configuring data sources programmatically is that if the driver is upgraded and requires new or different attributes, the application program must be changed. In addition, the moment DBMS-specific code is placed in an application, portability is lost for that application. Although this is a factor for generic, general-use applications and tools, when an application is written for a specific purpose, it might be the only way to meet a practical need.

VB

The *SQLConfigDataSource* Function

The general syntax for the SQLConfigDataSource function in Visual Basic is as follows:

```
BOOL SQLConfigDataSource(hwnd, fRequest, Driver, Attrib)
```

This function is part of the installer DLL API. This DLL, ODBCINST.DLL, ships with the ODBC SDK, and it must be in the system's path when calling this function. The parameter hwnd is the handle of the parent window; it is used if dialog boxes need to be displayed to prompt the user for additional information. If this parameter is NULL, no displays will be generated. The parameter fRequest can have values of ODBC_ADD_DSN to add a new data source, ODBC_CONFIG_DSN if the request is to modify an existing configuration (data source), or ODBC_REMOVE_DSN if the request is to remove an existing data source. The parameter Driver is the name of the driver, exactly as defined in ODBCINST.INI. The parameter Attrib contains a list of attributes as keyword-value pairs. These keyword-value pairs are DBMS-specific. Many times the easiest way to determine what is required here is to use the ODBC Administrator to configure a data source for the desired driver, and then use the keyword-value pairs placed in the ODBC.INI file for the new data source.

An example of using SQLConfigDataSource from Visual Basic is shown in the following section.

C++

Syntax

The *SQLConfigDataSource* Function

The prototype for the SQLConfigDataSource function is as follows:

```
BOOL INSTAPI SQLConfigDataSource    (HWND      hwndParent,
                                     WORD      fRequest,
                                     LPCSTR    lpszDriver,
                                     LPCSTR    lpszAttributes);
```

This function is used to create, modify, or remove a data source. The parameters are the same as the previous Visual Basic example.

It might be premature to go into much detail about how to use this function before detailing the prerequisites. However, in Listing 4.3, you'll see a small Visual Basic sample program that you can enter and run in order to see how this function works. Don't worry about functions such as SQLAllocEnv; this is covered on Day 8, "Connecting to the Data Source."

At this point, just enter the code as shown in Listing 4.3 and experiment, noting the results in your ODBC.INI file or ODBC.INI section of the registry. These files, with the file extension of .BI, are part of the ODBC SDK and cannot be distributed. However, because you need the SDK to develop ODBC code, you should have it already. These files are located in the vbdemo subdirectory under the samples subdirectory.

Type

Listing 4.3. Source code for the Form_Load subroutine in the VBADDDSN.EXE program.

```
Sub Form_Load ()
  Dim DSN As String * 32
  Dim Desc As String * 255
  Dim DSNLen As Integer
  Dim DescLen As Integer

    'Allocate and initialize ODBC environment upon program startup
  rc% = SQLAllocEnv(henv)          'Allocate environment
  If rc% <> SQL_SUCCESS Then
    MsgBox ("Unable to allocate environment")
    End
  End If
  AddBtn.Enabled = True
  rc% = SQLDataSources(henv, SQL_FETCH_FIRST, DSN, 31, DSNLen,
➥Desc, 255, DescLen)

  Do While rc% = SQL_SUCCESS
    If Mid$(DSN, 1, DSNLen) = "Chap04" Then
      OutBox.Caption = "Chap04 Data Source Already Exists"
      Label1.Enabled = False
      AddBtn.Enabled = False
      ExitBtn.Default = True
      Exit Do
```

```
     End If
     rc% = SQLDataSources(henv, SQL_FETCH_NEXT, DSN, 31, DSNLen,
     ➥Desc, 255, DescLen)
   Loop

End Sub
```

Note: This program should be compiled with the 16-bit version of Visual Basic 4.0. Otherwise, the ODBINST.DLL, which you need for the `SQLConfigDataSource`, and the other DLLs it needs to run cannot be referenced without moving them into the SYSTEM32 subdirectory.

Note: See Day 5 to learn about Visual Basic setup procedures.

The code in Listing 4.3 initializes the ODBC environment by calling `SQLAllocEnv`, and then checks for the existence of the data source by repetitively calling `SQLDataSources` to obtain the names of the currently configured data sources. In this example, if the data-source name is found, a message is posted and the Add button is disabled. In normal practice, if the data-source name was found, the remainder of the code would be skipped and normal processing would begin.

If the data source is not found, the Add button is active. By pressing this button, the code shown in Listing 4.4 is executed, causing the new data source to be configured. Again, in the real world, this would take place without user intervention. Figure 4.11 shows the dialog box for the sample program VBADDDSN.EXE.

Figure 4.11. *The dialog box for the sample program VBADDDSN.EXE.*

Listing 4.4. Source code from VBADDDSN.EXE for the AddBtn subroutine.

```
Sub AddBtn_Click ()
  Dim Driver As String * 30
  Dim Attrib As String * 255
  Dim ZSTR As String * 1
  Dim hwnd As Long

  hwnd = 0
  ZSTR = Chr(0)
  Driver = "WATCOM SQL" & ZSTR
  Attrib = "DSN=Chap04;Description=Sample data source for Chapter4;
➥Database=D:\ODBCPP20\samples\watcom\sampledb.db;Start=rtstartw %d;
➥PreventNotCapable=1" & ZSTR & ZSTR

  rc% = SQLConfigDataSource(hwnd, 1, Driver, Attrib)
  OutBox.ForeColor = &H80000008
  OutBox.Caption = "Data Source Created"
End Sub
```

Once the Add button has been pressed and the SQLConfigDataSource function executed, the only thing left to do in this sample is to exit from the program. This sample has no error-checking or success-signaling built-in.

The only way to check the true success of this program is to examine the ODBC.INI file to see if the added data source has appeared and if the attributes are correct. It is a good idea to test this newly created data source using a test tool before attempting to use it from a newly created application. In this way, you can isolate problems, to see whether they are in the data-source definition or the application program, using the data source.

The ODBC.INI file with the new data source, Chap04, is shown in Listing 4.5. Note that the data-source name is added to the ODBC Data Sources section at the top, and a section titled Chap04 is added at the end of the file.

Listing 4.5. ODBC.INI file after running VBADDDSN.EXE, showing new data source Chap04.

```
;----------------------------------------------------------------------
; WARNING:  Do not make changes to this file without using the ODBC Control
;           panel device or other utilites provided for maintaining data
;           sources.
;
;           Incorrect changes to this file could prevent ODBC from
;           operating or operating correctly.
;----------------------------------------------------------------------
```

```
[ODBC Data Sources]
DEVSQL=SQL Server
Chap04=WATCOM SQL

[ODBCSPY]
TargetDSN=
TargetDriver=

[ODBC]
TraceAutoStop=0
Trace=1
TraceFile=\SQL.LOG

[DEVSQL]
Driver=C:\WINDOWS\SYSTEM\sqlsrvr.dll
Description=Development SQL Server
Server=DEVNTBOX
FastConnectOption=No
UseProcForPrepare=Yes
Database=test1
OEMTOANSI=No
LastUser=

[Chap04]
Driver=C:\WSQL\wsqlodbc.dll
Description=Sample data source for Chapter 4
Database=D:\ODBCPP20\samples\watcom\sampledb.db
Start=rtstartw %d
PreventNotCapable=1
```

4

Summary

Today's lesson presented the configuration of data sources and the tools to perform such configurations. You learned about the following topics:

- [ ] How the setup program installs the files needed for an ODBC driver and also enters the configuration program for configuring a data source using the new driver.

- [ ] What the ODBC configuration files are and what information they contain; how the registry entries are similar to the initialization files, and where each is used.

- [ ] That there is a difference in administration tools for 16- and 32-bit drivers and how to spot the difference.

☐ How using the ODBC Administrator to configure a data source provides great flexibility for the user but offers no way to enforce naming rules when needed.

☐ Data sources can be easily configured from within an application program. This provides the uniformity of naming required for some applications, depending on the existence of a specific data-source name.

Q&A

Q **Can I install my ODBC driver DLLs to whatever directory I want?**

A No. Accessory files and tools can be installed into a private directory, but the driver and setup DLL files must be installed into the Windows\System directory, if there is one. The driver manager, administrator, and installer DLL files must also be installed into the same system directory. The initialization files must also be in the Windows directory or the configuration information must be kept in the registry.

Q **When installing a new driver, I get a message saying my driver manager is newer, but I know it's actually outdated. Is this possible?**

A Yes, because the file data does not determine which file contains the latest code. Each ODBC DLL file has a version stamp within the file. By examining the file properties in File Manager, you can see the version number of the code itself. Always use the highest version number.

Q **If I create a data source from within my program, can I only modify it from a program?**

A No. Once a data source is created, it is the same as all others. It can be modified or removed either from a program or from the administrator.

Workshop

The Workshop provides quiz questions to help you solidify your understanding of the material covered and exercises to give you experience in using what you've learned. Try to understand the quiz and exercise answers before continuing on to the next day's lesson. Answers are provided in Appendix A, "Answers."

Quiz

1. Can more than one data source be created using the same driver? Specify why or why not.
2. Can the return from SQLConfigDataSource be checked against SQL_SUCCESS, and can the standard ODBC error routines be used if it fails?
3. If the SQLConfigDataSource function needs to be used to provide a common data-source name, but the other attributes can be user configurable, how is this done?
4. On a Windows NT system that uses a 32-bit SQL Server driver, can the ODBC.INI file be distributed on the network to other workstations to copy the data source configuration rather than running the administrator or configuring programmatically at each workstation?

Exercise

1. Modify Listing 4.4 to use the Access (32-bit) driver, create a connection named MUSIC, and connect to a database named music.mdb in the \samples subdirectory.

The Microsoft
ODBC Software
Development Kit
(SDK)

This chapter presents the details of the Microsoft ODBC Software Development Kit. This kit is a necessary tool to have on hand before you develop an ODBC application. Today, you learn what benefits are derived from this kit; you also learn about the following topics:

- [ ] An introduction to the ODBC SDK
- [ ] Compiler files in the SDK
- [ ] Sample applications and code
- [ ] Test tools
- [ ] Documentation
- [ ] 16- and 32-bit application components

When considering development of an application using ODBC, the average programmer will usually try to find out what resources and tools are needed for such development. Unfortunately, in the past it was difficult to determine what resources were really needed, and even more difficult to obtain these resources. Now that you already have the most important tool for ODBC development—namely, this book—you can start looking for the other tools.

Obviously, if you are going to be writing code, you need a compiler. This book discusses only the use of Microsoft's Visual Basic and Visual C++. On Day 6, "Development Tools," you will explore why these two compilers work so well for ODBC development. In addition, tomorrow's lesson covers add-on tools to enhance or add to the capabilities of these compilers. Today, however, we will restrict our discussion to the ODBC Software Development Kit.

An Introduction to the ODBC SDK

When the SDK is mentioned to first-time ODBC programmers, they might know something about software development kits from their experience with Windows programming, but not know of the existence of the ODBC SDK. And someone without any Windows or similar programming background might be completely unaware of this method of packaging the essential tools needed for developing to a particular platform or standard.

The ODBC SDK goes far beyond its predecessors in terms of content, sophistication, and value. For all practical purposes, it is impossible to develop any code to the ODBC

standard without using the SDK. Unfortunately, some programmers become upset when they first learn that they cannot purchase the SDK as a stand-alone product. It must be purchased as part of the Microsoft Developer Network (MSDN) Development Platform Kit. This collection of operating systems, SDKs, and device driver kits (DDKs) is sold as a yearly subscription service, which includes four quarterly shipments on CD-ROM. Although the price of $498 U.S. might not seem like much when you consider all that is included, if you only need the ODBC components, the price can be a hindrance.

When you install the ODBC SDK, it is not necessary to install any other components than the ODBC kit itself. Figure 5.1 shows the initial setup dialog box from the MSDN installation. This dialog box shows the various tool categories available for installation from the various MSDN Level 2 CD-ROMs. The ODBC SDK is installed as a piece of the Windows 3.1 category.

Figure 5.1. *Tool-category selection dialog box from the SDK Setup.*

5

The next dialog box presented in the SDK installation gives a good view of all of the tools available through this medium. Figure 5.2 shows part of a list of the tools that can be installed as part of the Windows 3.1 category. Although the Windows 3.1 Chinese DDKE might not have a lot of appeal to the average programmer, some of the other goodies might. This friendly dialog box enables you to select one or more tools to be installed before you proceed any further.

The dialog box shown in Figure 5.3 shows the start of the actual ODBC SDK installation. In this dialog box, it is easy to see the component parts in the ODBC SDK as well as their sizes when installed. You can use this dialog box to avoid installing some components in order to save disk space, but this will probably lead to nothing but trouble. If you are so short on disk space now that you can't install everything, you will almost certainly run out of space right in the middle of that important compile. Don't fight it—fix it! Get that bigger disk drive *now.*

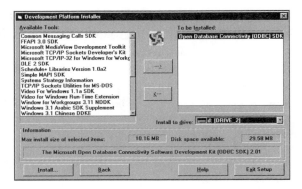

Figure 5.2. *Available tools selection dialog box from the SDK Setup.*

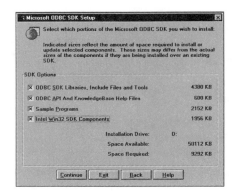

Figure 5.3. *The ODBC Setup dialog box with selectable options.*

If you select the Win32 SDK components for installation, they will present a warning message if they are being installed on a Windows 3.1 or Windows 95 system. This is because Win32 components cannot be run on a 16-bit Windows 3.1 system, and Windows 95 was not released before the version-2 ODBC SDK, so it doesn't know about Windows 95. You can and should override this warning message and install these components if you will be targeting a Win32 system with your Visual C++ compiler. Later today, we will evaluate the various components necessary to build against 16-bit and 32-bit platforms.

When all of the other SDK components can be installed, the Setup routine will present a list of available ODBC drivers and prompt you for a selection, as shown in Figure 5.4. These drivers, with the exception of the Template Sample Driver, are from the Microsoft Desktop Driver set. These drivers are included in the SDK for use in developing an

ODBC application, but you cannot distribute them with the application. There are a number of redistributable components included in the SDK, but these are generally shipped with drivers rather than the application. Complete documentation on what files may be redistributed is included with the SDK.

Figure 5.4. *Dialog box prompting for selection of ODBC drivers to be installed from the SDK.*

While installing the selected drivers, the SDK Setup will also create data sources for each driver. These data sources include appropriate matching data sample files, which are loaded on your workstation at the same time the drivers and data sources are copied. For the sake of clarity, each of these data sources has _sdk20 appended to its name, as shown in Figure 5.5. These data sources and data files are included for more than testing purposes. If you are developing using Visual C++ with the Microsoft Foundation Classes (MFC), version 2.5 or higher, the AppWizard will prompt for you to select the data source when creating the application. If your target is to use one of these desktop drivers, you will need a configured data source before proceeding, so this step makes it easier.

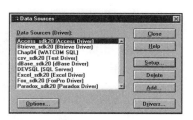

Figure 5.5. *The list of created data-source names following SDK installation.*

Compiler Files in the SDK

The SDK installs files into three directories that are absolutely essential for program development using ODBC with Visual C++ or Visual Basic. These files are the compiler INCLUDE files and the library definition files.

C and C++ *INCLUDE* Files

The INCLUDE files are placed in the INCLUDE subdirectory. These files are for use with C or C++ compilers. This directory should be placed in the front of the compiler INCLUDE path. Generally, the INCLUDE files shipped in the SDK will be the newest unless an incremental fix is posted on CompuServe by Microsoft. If this happens, the old SDK files should be renamed and the new files placed in the SDK INCLUDE subdirectory. It is not uncommon to have more than one copy of these same files loaded on your system, so make sure that the INCLUDE path is set up correctly. As an example, on a system with Microsoft Visual C++ version 2.0, Microsoft ODBC SDK, and South Wind Design, Inc.'s odbc/ClassLib loaded, there were three copies of the SQL.H file, among others. Although the version shipped with MSVC had the newest date, the copy that shipped with the ODBC SDK was slightly larger but had an older date. The SDK file was in fact the newest; the size change was caused by additions put in for version 2.01. The other two copies had shipped with version 2.0. Table 5.1 lists the files included in the INCLUDE directory with a description of the contents of the file.

Table 5.1. INCLUDE filenames and their contents for use with C and C++.

Filename	Contents
CTL3D.H	Defines and prototypes for use with CTL3D.DLL to provide three-dimensional controls.
ODBCINST.H	Defines and prototypes for use when calling functions from the ODBC installer. Includes functions such as SQLConfigDataSource used to set up drivers and data sources.
ODBCVER.H	Defines the ODBC version, as well as company and platform definitions.
SQL.H	Defines, prototypes, and typedefs for the SQL core functionality. This is the main INCLUDE for ODBC. Provides definition of return codes and parameters such as

Filename	Contents
	SQL_SUCCESS. This file only covers the core functions and their corresponding data types.
SQLEXT.H	Defines, prototypes, and typedefs for the extended functions at both Level 1 and Level 2. Because most drivers and their corresponding applications provide and use at least Level 1 functionality, this file will almost always be needed.
W16MACRO.H	A set of "window cracker" defines. Used as a minimum set of Windows message macros for message handling in some of the sample programs.

The ODBC .LIB or library definition files are installed into two subdirectories if the WIN32 support is selected. The 16-bit libraries are defined by .LIB files in the LIB subdirectory, and the 32-bit .LIB files are in the LIB32 subdirectory. These files correspond with DLLs found in the BIN and BIN32 subdirectories. Table 5.2 lists the .LIB files and their descriptions.

Table 5.2. Library definition files and their descriptions.

Dir	Filename	Description
LIB	CTL3DS.LIB	Import library for use with CTL3D.DLL. For creating 3-D controls in dialog boxes.
LIB	CTL3DV2.LIB	Version 2 of 3-D controls. For use with CTL3DV2.DLL.
LIB	GATORTST.LIB	Import library for use with ODBC Test functions.
LIB	ODBC.LIB	Import library for use with all ODBC functions as exported from the driver manager.
LIB	ODBCINST.LIB	Import library for use with ODBCINST.DLL, the installer library.
LIB32	CTL3D32.LIB	Import library for 32-bit edition CTL3D32.DLL.
LIB32	CTL3D32S.LIB	Import library for static linking of CTL3D32.

continues

5

Table 5.2. continued

Dir	Filename	Description
LIB32	GTRTST32.LIB	Import library for use with test functions in 32-bit version of ODBC Test application.
LIB32	ODBC32.LIB	Import library for use with all 32-bit ODBC functions as exported from the 32-bit driver manager.
LIB32	ODBCCP32.LIB	Import library for use with 32-bit ODBC installer functions as exported from the ODBCCP32.DLL installer.

Note: Don't forget to add the appropriate INCLUDE and library directory paths to your INCLUDE and LIB environment variables preceding those entries for the compiler and other tools. In Windows 3.1, add these paths in the AUTOEXEC.BAT file. In Windows 95 and Windows NT, add the directory to the registry HKEY_CURRENT_USER hive under the Environment key.

Visual Basic *INCLUDE* Files

Unlike the INCLUDE files provided in the SDK for use with C and C++ compilers, the Visual Basic INCLUDE files are a little more hidden. The INCLUDE files must be used to write a C++ program that calls the ODBC API, whereas Visual Basic provides bound data controls that will access ODBC data sources without the user writing any direct ODBC calls. If there are no direct ODBC calls, the function prototypes are not needed. It seems that Microsoft has assumed that most users will use the bound controls rather than programming directly to the API, so it originally did not produce any INCLUDE files with the prototypes. Because the benefits of programming directly to the API became more obvious, Microsoft has quietly released some basic INCLUDE files.

The Visual Basic INCLUDE files are located in the ODBC SDK when installed under the samples subdirectory. These files, as listed in Table 5.3, are part of the files in the VBDEMO sample subdirectory. To use them in a Visual Basic project, you must go to the Visual Basic File menu and select Add File. Note that these files have a nonstandard file extension, so they will not show up in the File Open dialog box until you select All

Files (*.*) as the file type.

Table 5.3. ODBC INCLUDE files from sample VBDEMO.

Filename	Contents
ODBCOR_M.BI	Module definitions for core ODBC functions.
ODBCOR_G.BI	Global definitions for core ODBC functions. Includes constants, named return codes, and data types.
ODBEXT_M.BI	Module definitions for extended ODBC functions. These include both Level 1 and Level 2 prototypes.
ODBEXT_G.BI	Global definitions for extended ODBC functions. Includes constants, named return codes, and data types specific to Level 1 and Level 2 functions.

The four basic INCLUDE files listed here are updated to include ODBC version 2 features, but care must be taken to ensure that they remain current as new versions of the SDK are released. In addition, these files do not include prototypes for the ODBC installer functions, such as SQLConfigDataSource, which was used yesterday in the VBADDDSN sample. In that case, we had to manually add a prototype for this function in the GLOBAL.BAS file within the project.

Sample Applications and Code

To assist with the development of ODBC applications and drivers, the ODBC SDK includes several sample programs. Table 5.4 lists the directories and programs included with the SDK.

Table 5.4. Sample programs included with ODBC SDK.

Directory	Sample Description
ADMNDEMO	C-language program that will perform a connect, execute manually entered SQL statements, run scripts, and perform other special ODBC tasks.
CPPDEMO	Very simple C++ demo program showing basic use of C++ classes within an ODBC application.
CRSRDEMO	C program showing how to use the ODBC cursor library.

continues

Table 5.4. continued

Directory	Sample Description
	Includes using the cursor for scrolling and positioned updates and deletes.
QURYDEMO	Query demo showing the use of multiple simultaneous connections performing concurrent queries. User is able to type in SQL query and view results.
VBDEMO	Visual Basic demo showing calls to the ODBC API rather than using the bound data controls.

Although these samples are worthwhile to study, they are not an exhaustive compilation of every ODBC usage. It is a good idea to examine the samples that are shipped with the Visual C++ or Visual Basic compilers and with SWDI's odbc/ClassLib if you have it, as well as looking in the CompuServe libraries in the WINEXT and MSMFC forums.

Test Tools

Included with the ODBC SDK are two of the most powerful tools you will have at your disposal to learn about the ODBC API in general and specific drivers in detail, as well as to debug problems.

The ODBC Test tool, which is described in detail on Day 21, "Using ODBC Test and Trace Tools," enables you to perform ODBC API calls interactively, setting the parameters and examining the results between each call. With this tool, you can alter the order of function execution to see the impact on results. If you are uncertain what value a particular driver will return to a query function, you can find out by executing that query.

The ODBC Test tool, previously known as GATOR.EXE, provides an unequaled opportunity to test functionality without writing a single line of code. Test scripts can be stored and rerun on demand. There are two versions of ODBC Test—a 16-bit and a 32-bit version—found in their respective BIN directories.

Two trace tools are included with the ODBC Driver Manager and the SDK. These are the trace function built into the driver manager and ODBC SPY, which is shipped with the ODBC SDK. (These utilities are also covered in detail on Day 21.)

In addition to these tools shipped with the Microsoft products, there are third-party tools

that can make ODBC application development and debugging much easier. The tool line from Dr. DeeBee Tools includes such tools as an application semantics checker, an ODBC call recorder, a call counter and timer, and others. These tools and a few others are described in detail on Day 21.

Documentation

There are multiple opportunities to obtain the ODBC SDK documentation, but the recommended method is to purchase the printed copy of Microsoft's *ODBC 2.0 Programmer's Reference and SDK Guide*. This book, available from Microsoft Press, is a complete reference guide to the ODBC API.

For immediate assistance while in the middle of application development, an Online Help API Reference is included in the ODBC SDK. This help file presents the reference information for each of the ODBC API functions as well as a code example and a related functions list. This hypertext help file is very useful for a quick lookup. A similar online document covering the entire ODBC API is available with the odbc/ClassLib C++ Class Libraries.

Although all of these API references show the ODBC API functions as C functions, it is easy to convert that information to the appropriate call from Visual Basic.

16- and 32-Bit Application Components

When you install the ODBC SDK, the components will be installed to correspond to the version of Windows onto which you are installing. For Windows 3.1 or Windows for Workgroups 3.1 and 3.11, only the 16-bit driver will install. For Windows 95 and Windows NT, both the 16-bit and 32-bit components can be installed, depending on the compiler being used. The components involved include a 16- or 32-bit driver manager and administrator, and "thunking" DLLs that convert 16-bit addresses to 32-bit and vice versa.

16-Bit Application and 16-Bit Driver

The pure 16-bit environment was all that was available when ODBC was first introduced until ODBC version 2 was released in April 1993. Until more 32-bit drivers become available, this combination will remain the most used.

This combination of all 16-bit components can be used on Windows 3.1, Windows for Workgroups, Windows 95, and Windows NT systems. In the case of Windows NT, rather than thunking up to the operating system's 32-bit mode, this combination of components will run in the Windows On Windows (WOW) subsystem.

16-Bit Application and 32-Bit Driver

This combination can be seen on Windows 95 or Windows NT systems, typically where a new 32-bit version of a driver has been substituted into an existing application.

When thunking from 16-bit to 32-bit is indicated, the application is still calling the ODBC functions from the 16-bit Driver Manager, ODBC.DLL. This DLL in turn calls the ODBC16HT.DLL generic thunking DLL, and that DLL calls the 32-bit ODBC32GT.DLL generic thunking DLL. This final thunking DLL makes the actual calls to the 32-bit driver rather than the calls coming from a 32-bit Driver Manager.

32-Bit Application and 16-Bit Driver

If a new application is written that is available only in a 32-bit version, but the driver is available only as a 16-bit driver ("The new driver will be released next month"—famous last words!), the platform options are limited. Windows NT and Windows 95 do not support calling 16-bit drivers from 32-bit applications.

If you do encounter this configuration running on a Win32s system, it is easy to see that the 32-bit Driver Manager is not a real driver manager, but rather a very thin thunking layer that calls the 16-bit universal thunking DLL. This universal thunking DLL in turn calls the real 16-bit Driver Manager, which then calls the 16-bit drivers.

If the real 32-bit Driver Manager is substituted in this scenario, the SQLAllocEnv function will return SQL_ERROR. Because this error occurs so early in the ODBC initialization process, it is possible that the user would only see an error dialog box with the return code -1 error message. You can easily simulate this behavior by substituting the wrong DLL for the correct one. They are named the same and are differentiated only by their size.

32-Bit Application and 32-Bit Driver

This combination of components is simple like the all 16-bit solution, but it provides better speed. If only 32-bit components are involved, you can certainly expect significantly improved performance over an otherwise identical 16-bit configuration.

Summary

Today's lesson taught you about the Microsoft ODBC Software Development Kit. You learned about the following topics:

- [ ] The Software Development Kit is a component that is absolutely essential to obtain before you attempt to develop an ODBC application. The SDK consists of many components that are used for either driver or application development, or both.

- [ ] The components included with the SDK include a variety of compiler files. These are both the INCLUDE header files and the import libraries for linking. Function prototypes and constant declarations are also included for use with Visual Basic development.

- [ ] A number of sample applications, including source code, are shipped with the SDK, for use by the application developer. These samples demonstrate development with C, C++, and Visual Basic, and they provide examples of how to use many of the more common ODBC functionalities.

- [ ] A set of test and trace tools are shipped with the ODBC SDK for both 16- and 32-bit usage. These tools are helpful both for debugging applications and for understanding driver behavior while writing applications.

- [ ] Documentation of the ODBC interface is available in both paper and online formats from Microsoft and other vendors. These are primarily reference works documenting the specifics of each ODBC API call rather than explaining in detail how and when to use these functions.

- [ ] ODBC provides support for 16- and 32-bit applications and drivers. The application developer needs to be aware of the DLLs involved in providing this thunking support and on which platforms it is supported.

Q&A

Q Can I distribute the ODBC Test tool with my application to help users debug their problems?

A No. Only those files installed into the REDIST16 and REDIST32 subdirectories of the SDK may legally be redistributed. All other components are licensed under a single-user license.

Q **Can I develop 16-bit applications using Visual C++ version 2.0 to run on Windows 3.1?**

A If you are using a 16-bit ODBC driver, you can build your application to the Win32s standard and use the thunking DLLs to access the driver.

Q **Can I use Visual Basic to create an application that will use a 32-bit driver?**

A Yes. Using Visual Basic version 3.0, the executable file is 16-bit. Calling 32-bit drivers from 16-bit applications is not a problem.

Q **If I have this book, do I really need the paper reference sold by Microsoft?**

A No. By using this book and the online API help reference included with the SDK, you should not need the paper reference manual. Many users find it helpful, however.

Development
Tools

This chapter discusses some of the tools you can use to develop your ODBC applications. This will include compilers for C++ and Visual Basic, as well as add-in or complementary tools for use with these compilers. For the C++ environment, you learn available class libraries, whereas for Visual Basic there will be mention only of third-party controls. Today you will learn about the following topics:

- ☐ Microsoft Visual C++
- ☐ C++ database classes
- ☐ Microsoft Visual Basic
- ☐ Other development tools

To put this chapter in perspective, a reminder is necessary that this book is only about using Visual C++ and Visual Basic as development tools for ODBC applications. The selection of tools or techniques could have been expanded considerably. The scope of this work was intentionally kept focused for two reasons:

1. Knowledge about the use of the two selected tools can be easily applied to the use of other tools.

2. Limiting the scope to the most widely used tools enables complete coverage of the material in a reasonable amount of time.

Expanding the scope of this book could have taken it in either of two directions. A vertical expansion would have included more tools working at the same level. These additional tools are mentioned later in this chapter. A horizontal expansion would include such tools as Microsoft Access and the Visual Basic bound data controls for developing to a different application programming interface (API).

Using Access and Visual Basic's built-in functionality does not preclude the use of ODBC data sources. In fact, the Jet Engine built into these products is ODBC-aware, and it produces the same ODBC function calls that you will be making from your program. The difference is primarily in how the ODBC functions are called and the differing impact on performance.

As you'll see in the section "C++ Classes," the Microsoft MFC classes use the same basic model as Access and Visual Basic, and they are therefore burdened with the same performance and flexibility problems. Because of the higher development overhead of creating an application directly to the ODBC API, it is unlikely anyone would use this technique unless it offered distinct advantages. The most obvious advantages are in performance and flexibility. You will explore how C++ can be used to combine the classes with direct ODBC API calls in order to provide the best mix between ease of code construction and performance.

Microsoft Visual C++

It is expected that before you use Microsoft's Visual C++ compiler to develop ODBC applications, you will have already learned about both the C++ language and the Visual C++ product with its environment and tool set. (There are several excellent books available from Sams Publishing to help you with this learning.)

If you do not yet have the Visual C++ product and will purchase it specifically for this project, be aware that several versions have been released. Which version of the Visual C++ compiler you need will depend on the target platform on which you expect your application to run.

Another factor to consider when you are choosing the version of the compiler you need is which version of the MFC database classes you need, if you will be using them. The next section covers the C++ classes in more detail, but keep in mind that each version of Visual C++ also shipped with a different version of MFC.

The original Microsoft Visual C++ product was released some time ago as an upgrade to the Microsoft C product. This first release was version 1.0. A second version 1.0 came out, but it was not the same. This "new" version 1.0 was actually called Visual C++ for Windows NT.

The first version of Visual C++ to enjoy any usage with ODBC application development was called version 1.5. This is because the MFC classes did not include database classes for database support until the release of MFC version 2.5, which was included with version 1.5 of the Visual C++ compiler.

Both version 1.0 and 1.5 of the standard Visual C++ products generated 16-bit output, either executable files (EXE) or dynamic link libraries (DLL). Version 1.0 of Visual C++ for NT was the first version that generated 32-bit outputs.

Visual C++ version 2.0, which was released in September 1994, was the first incarnation of the product that included both 16- and 32-bit versions. These are two separate compilers, instead of one that can be built for both 16- and 32-bit targets. Although Visual C++ version 2.0 can develop both 16- and 32-bit executables, if you are using the MFC database classes, you can only connect to the same-sized ODBC driver and not thunk as discussed yesterday.

This thunking limitation with MFC means that a 32-bit application might be able to thunk to a 16-bit ODBC driver in some cases, but it cannot do so when you build the 32-bit application using Visual C++ version 2.0. Because the code is very portable, it is recommended that you build two versions of the executable if it will be running on both 16- and 32-bit platforms. This should involve merely a rebuild of the same source code

6

with the different versions of the compiler. (Obviously, both 16- and 32-bit ODBC drivers of the same type would be needed in this situation.)

Microsoft's Visual C++ was chosen for this book not only because it provides broad platform support and is thought to generate very good code, but also because of the breadth and depth of documentation included with the product. The online documentation that ships with Visual C++ is very comprehensive, almost to the point of making it difficult to find the proper subject. However, the search tools and hyperlinks can overcome this, and no developer should be afraid or ashamed to use this valuable time-saving tool whenever a question or uncertainty arises.

C++ Classes

Although programs containing exclusively C code can be compiled by the Visual C++ compiler, they would lack the object orientation that is making C++ so much more popular. By combining objects of the same attributes and functionality into a class, and providing the capability to inherit from that class, C++ enables developers to share important constructs. This also enables classes and collections of classes to be useful to others and therefore sold or distributed to other developers if they provide a needed functionality.

Microsoft Foundation Classes

The Microsoft Foundation Classes (MFC) are an example of classes that are useful to every developer writing for a Windows platform. When Windows first gained widespread popularity with the release of version 3.0, developers groaned at the idea of developing with the Windows Software Development Kit (SDK), mostly because of the detail and sheer volume of function calls needed to manipulate the Windows interface.

The version 2.0 MFC libraries that shipped with Visual C++ version 1.0 provided a great deal of functionality for building and maintaining the standard Windows graphical user interface (GUI), but they did not have any classes that supported database functions. These GUI classes were very important in enabling developers to easily generate standard graphical objects without writing a lot of code. This in turn made the developers' time available for other aspects of their applications.

The release of MFC 2.5, and most recently MFC 3.0, added additional functionality and features to the basic GUI building classes that were already built-in. The most notable of these additions were classes to provide support for ODBC databases and Object Linking and Embedding (OLE).

The strength of the classes provided in MFC is in many ways also its weakness. If you want to provide a standard toolbar in your application that looks and acts like the toolbar in most other Microsoft applications, the MFC classes make that very easy. If you want to access ODBC data sources in much the same way you do with Microsoft Access or Visual Basic's bound data controls, the MFC database classes make it easy. However, if you want your toolbar to be different from the Microsoft norm, or if you want to access your ODBC data source without using a keyset-driven model like Access and Visual Basic, it becomes more difficult.

When designing and developing an application, the developer must be careful to avoid making broad generalizations about the tools available and how they can be used. Just because the MFC database classes seem to limit you to one table per connection does not mean you must also limit your application. It just means that you must explore how to modify or enhance the functionality provided by the MFC classes and use other classes or directly code the functionality not present. The MFC classes that come "out of the box" might suffice for simple applications; if so, use them and enjoy the ease of development. However, if your application needs more flexibility or the capability to do things differently, don't abandon MFC completely to go in another direction. Remember that MFC probably provides the easiest and most standardized GUI tools.

odbc/ClassLib

Another set of database classes is available from South Wind Design, Inc. (SWDI). At the time of this writing, the odbc/ClassLib classes were the only database classes marketed besides MFC. These odbc/ClassLib classes provide two differences from Microsoft's MFC database classes. First, the MFC and odbc/ClassLib paradigms are significantly different. This does not mean they each must be used in vastly different ways, but they are designed to be used differently. Second, the odbc/ClassLib product is designed to be used with Borland's C++ compiler as well as the Microsoft Visual C++ application framework. As might be expected, the Microsoft Visual C++ product and the MFC classes are bundled as one product and are designed to work with each other.

The paradigm difference between MFC and odbc/ClassLib is far more significant and can have a large impact on how an application is designed and built. The MFC class library is designed to provide a uniform appearance and functionality to all applications that are built using MFC. This paradigm features the document and the view. The *document* represents the whole of the data, whether it is a spreadsheet, a word processing document, or a database. The *view* represents that portion of the document that is visible on the screen at any given time.

Microsoft has implemented this document/view paradigm in the database classes of MFC by having both the CDatabase class and CRecordSet class inherited from the CObject class. The CRecordView class is inherited from the CView class. The CDatabase objects represent a single connection to a single data source, encapsulating both the ODBC environment handle and the connection handle. The results set from an SQL SELECT statement form the basis for a CRecordSet object. Again, Microsoft's stated intention was to make the MFC database classes act like—and be familiar to those who were already working with—Access and Visual Basic.

SWDI, on the other hand, has tried to model its odbc/ClassLib classes more directly to the ODBC model itself rather than to the Access or Visual Basic keyset-driven model. ODBC, as shown earlier, has a hierarchy within a connection. The application owns the ODBC environment (as represented by the handle), the environment owns the connection, and the connection owns the statement. The odbc/ClassLib classes have the odbcENV class at the highest level. The odbcENV class owns the odbcCONNECT class, which in turn owns the odbcSTMT class. The odbcCURSOR class and some special iterator classes are inherited from the odbcSTMT class.

The odbc/ClassLibs should be more familiar to a developer with ODBC experience, whereas the MFC classes will seem like home for developers with backgrounds building Windows applications that use the document/view paradigm. For anyone with no experience in either area, the odbc/ClassLib offering probably offers more flexibility, with the paradigm better following the existing documentation of the ODBC interface.

Microsoft Visual Basic

If your development is to be done with Microsoft's Visual Basic, the options are fewer and much less critical to the success of the project. With Visual Basic, there are no class libraries to consider and nothing particularly special about the versions.

Visual Basic version 4, like Visual C++ 2.0, uses two versions, both called VB 4.0, to generate both 16- and 32-bit code. The 16-bit version generates code for use with 16-bit drivers. And of course, the 32-bit version generates 32-bit applications for use with 32-bit drivers. Pick one.

The issue of whether to use the Standard Edition or the Professional Edition is not overly important either because the Professional Edition includes the bound data controls that you will not be using. However, there are a number of extra goodies in the Pro Edition that might make it worth having, such as the extra file you need to produce Visual Basic controls.

One area in which Visual Basic is drastically different from Visual C++ is in the capability to switch paradigms back and forth—using MFC where it's nice, and going to direct ODBC API calls when needed. Visual Basic does not allow this to happen because Visual Basic does not expose the environment handle for its bound controls, and so the developer cannot step into the middle of that connection and manipulate the data or the connection. For any given application or section of functionality within an application, you must decide at design time whether the ODBC interface will be managed by the Jet Engine built into Visual Basic or by you, the developer.

Other Development Tools

As mentioned previously, there are other tools and environments that can be used to develop ODBC applications. These tools will not be discussed any further beyond this chapter.

Borland C++ 4.5 Compiler

Borland has always been a major player in the PC-based development environment. Its Turbo line of compilers has always provided some of the best compiling speed and execution speed, and the integrated development environment was an industry leader for some time.

The Borland C++ 4.5 compiler was considered a step up in compiler technology for Borland. Although the Turbo products were widely sold, they were considered toys by many, suitable for learning but not for developing industrial-strength applications. Borland tried to change that perception of its compilers with the C++ offering, and it appears to have been largely successful.

If there were any criticism of the Borland C++ 4.5 compiler, it would be aimed at the class libraries rather than the compiler itself. The Borland OWL libraries do not provide the same GUI look and feel that developers get when using the MFC libraries. For some developers, this is a benefit; for most, it is a drawback.

In the context of this book, the greatest shortfall of the Borland OWL libraries is their lack of ODBC class support. The SWDI odbc/ClassLib will work with Borland's compiler, and SWDI includes samples for two versions of Borland's compiler. For many developers, however, close only counts in horseshoes and atomic bombs. The Borland compiler was not included in discussions in this book because it brings nothing new to the table, and it leaves out much of what MFC does offer.

CA Realizer

This BASIC application-development system from Computer Associates provides much of the same functionality as Visual Basic. Because the use of ODBC APIs from BASIC is the same whether from CA Realizer or from Visual Basic, either tool can be used to develop code programming to ODBC.

The lack of compatible third-party add-ins for CA Realizer could be a deciding factor whether or not to use this development environment instead of Visual Basic.

Integra and Other Add-Ins

Coromandel (with its Integra add-in tools) and several other add-in tool vendors have become very active in the marketplace, offering database development tools. None of these tools are evaluated in this book.

This is not to suggest that these tools are unworthy of evaluation. However, at the time of this writing, the only add-ins that had captured significant market interest using ODBC were those from Integra. Performance is a big issue in the success of any such products, and it seems to be lacking in many.

Each developer should look at these products in the context of his or her own development projects. Everything shown in this book can be done easily without any products other than those that are specified. If you think something else can enhance your productivity or your finished product, by all means give it a try. Innovation and enhancement are what makes our industry grow.

Summary

Today's lesson centered on the tools that are needed for development of an ODBC application. You learned about the following:

☐ Microsoft's Visual C++ integrated development environment is very well-suited for ODBC application development. The latest version, 3.0, offers both 16- and 32-bit application-development compilers, editors, and debugging tools.

☐ There are two major suppliers of database classes for ODBC development using C++. Microsoft includes its MFC libraries with Visual C++. South Wind Design, Inc., sells odbc/ClassLib, the other choice for ODBC development.

☐ Microsoft is the vendor of Visual Basic for low-end development needs. Visual Basic lacks the frills and flexibility available from C++, but it enables easy development of ODBC applications calling the API directly.

☐ Other development add-in tools are available, but they are not featured in this book. Borland makes a C++ compiler (as do other vendors), and there are many Visual Basic add-in products. However, none of these offerings provides more than the Microsoft tools featured here.

Q&A

Q **Can I write part of my application using Visual Basic and part using Visual C++, and then combine them?**

A No. There is no facility for linking the output from Visual Basic with the same from Visual C++. Visual C++ version 1.5 can use Visual Basic controls (VBX), but this compatibility has been discontinued with version 2.0 because VBXs are only 16-bit.

Q **Why can't I use the best part of the MFC classes together in the same code with the best part of the odbc/ClassLib classes?**

A You can. This is the beauty of both. You can use as little or as much of each as you like, and make the rest of the ODBC calls yourself.

Q **Can I use Visual C++ version 2.0 now to develop a 32-bit application against the 16-bit driver that I have, and then plug in the 32-bit driver when it is released?**

A You probably shouldn't do this. You can always develop a 16-bit application using Visual C++ version 1.5, and then rebuild using version 2.0 when the new driver is released.

Data Types

Before writing code, the developer must understand what data types are used in the ODBC SQL definition, and how these SQL data types map to C data types used in applications. This lesson looks at the range of values that can be stored in the various data types, and how transformations occur. Today you learn the following topics:

- [ ] SQL data types used in ODBC
- [ ] C data types as defined by ODBC
- [ ] Converting data types between the DBMS and the application
- [ ] Using data types for CREATE TABLE and ALTER TABLE statements
- [ ] Differences in Visual Basic data types

SQL Data Types Used in ODBC

Keeping track of the data types that are in use and the mapping between the various data types can be one of the most confusing aspects of ODBC development for the beginner. This seems to be because there are several different data type definitions, and they don't all map to each other on a one-to-one basis.

The two main categories of data types used in ODBC applications are the SQL data type and the C data type. The SQL data type is one of a set of specific data types defined in the X/Open and SQL Access Group SQL CAE specifications of 1992. The constants naming these SQL data types are found in the ODBC Software Development Kit (SDK) INCLUDE files SQL.H and SQLEXT.H.

You can see why this standard data type definition is needed if you look at the various implementations of character data. The minimum SQL grammar support in ODBC must include at least one character data type. This data type is defined in ODBC SQL as SQL_CHARACTER, and is ODBC data type number 1. This data type can be used as input to the ODBC function SQLGetTypeInfo, as shown following, to query the driver as to what that data type is called on the specific data source.

VB4

Syntax

The *SQLGetTypeInfo* Function

The general syntax for the SQLGetTypeInfo function in Visual Basic is

```
RETCODE SQLGetTypeInfo(hstmt,fSqlType)
```

If the function returns an error and the subsequent SQLError call shows that the error is Driver not capable, the particular data type passed in fSqlType is not supported by this driver. (SQLError is fully explained on Day 13, "Determining the Return Status of a

Call.") If the function call returns successfully, the result set is standard, as shown in Table 7.1, and is ordered by DATA_TYPE and TYPE_NAME.

Table 7.1. Standard result set columns from SQLGetTypeInfo.

Column Name	Data Type	Description
TYPE_NAME	varchar (128) not NULL	Name of the data type as used on the data source.
DATA_TYPE	smallint not NULL	SQL data type from SQL.H and SQLEXT.H or driver-specific data type from driver documentation.
PRECISION	integer	Maximum precision for this data type on the data source. NULL when precision is not applicable.
LITERAL_PREFIX	varchar (128)	Character(s) used to prefix a literal. Could be a single quote (') for character data or 0x for binary data. NULL when prefix character is not needed or appropriate.
LITERAL_SUFFIX	varchar (128)	Character(s) used to terminate a literal. NULL where literal suffix is not needed or appropriate.
CREATE_PARAMS	varchar (128)	Parameters needed when defining this data type. An example would be MAX_LENGTH for a variable-length character field.
NULLABLE	smallint not NULL	Specifies whether the data source accepts a value of NULL for this data type.
CASE_SENSITIVE	smallint not NULL	Specifies whether a character data type is case-sensitive for the purposes of comparison. Returns TRUE only if data is of type character and case makes a difference in comparisons.

continues

Table 7.1. continued

Column Name	Data Type	Description
SEARCHABLE	smallint	Specifies how the data type can be used in WHERE clauses. Returns SQL_UNSEARCHABLE if the data type cannot appear in a WHERE clause. Returns SQL_LIKE_ONLY if the data type can be used only in a WHERE clause preceded by a LIKE predicate. Returns SQL_ALL_EXCEPT_LIKE if data type can be used everywhere except with a LIKE predicate. Returns SQL_SEARCHABLE if data type can be used with all WHERE clauses.
UNSIGNED_ATTRIBUTE	smallint	TRUE if data type is unsigned, FALSE if data type is signed, NULL if data type is not numeric.
MONEY	smallint	TRUE if data type is a money data type, FALSE if the data type is not a money data type.
AUTO_INCREMENT	smallint	TRUE if the data type autoincrements, FALSE if the data type is not autoincrementing. NULL if the data type is not numeric.
LOCAL_TYPE_NAME	varchar (128)	Localized data-source name for use in user-interface dialog boxes. For display use only.
MINIMUM_SCALE	smallint	The minimum scale or number of digits to the right of the decimal on this data source. If the data source has a fixed scale (for example, a field representing money would have a fixed scale of 2, $20.50) then this value will be the same as MAXIMUM_SCALE.

Column Name	Data Type	Description
MAXIMUM_SCALE	smallint	The maximum scale for this data type on this data source. NULL if not applicable.

The value passed in fSqlType must be one of those listed in Table 7.3 or SQL_ALL_TYPES. If the value SQL_ALL_TYPES is used, the data source will return a row in the result set for all the supported data types that the data source reports. SQLGetTypeInfo might not return rows for all data types. For instance, it might not return information about user-defined data types. SQL Server is one of many DBMSs that enable you to create new data types dynamically, and these new data types usually will not be reported by the SQLGetTypeInfo function.

The *SQLGetTypeInfo* Function

The prototype for the SQLGetTypeInfo function is

```
RETCODE SQL_API SQLGetTypeInfo(
    HSTMT       hstmt,
    SWORD       fSqlType);
```

If you review the data types used in the result set from this function, you can see why using generic data types is confusing. In particular, notice the return data type SMALLINT. As shown in Table 7.3, this is an SQL data type that has different characteristics in Visual C++ version 2 and Visual Basic version 4.

To illustrate how SQLGetTypeInfo is used and to examine how data sources can differ, use the ODBC Test tool to perform the SQLGetTypeInfo function against different data sources. The ODBC Test tool is explained in detail on Day 21, "Using ODBC Test and Trace Tools," so don't get hung up on the tool—just concentrate on the results.

For the purposes of this small illustration, you'll perform connections using the ODBC drivers furnished with the ODBC SDK and with the SWDI odbc/ClassLib. The connections will be to an Access version 1.1 data source, a Btrieve data source, and a Watcom data source. The fSqlType parameter used is SQL_CHAR, as shown in Figure 7.1 from the ODBC Test tool. The results are shown in Table 7.2.

7

Note: Before you run this experiment, make sure your data sources are hooked up in the ODBC Administrator. See Day 3, "Application Design Considerations," or ODBC Administrator Help for details. If you don't want to use these specific data sources, use any data source available on your machine and note the differences.

Figure 7.1. *The input prompt for an SQL data type from the ODBC Test tool.*

Table 7.2. Output from `SQLGetTypeInfo` showing the results from three different data sources.

Data Source	Output
Access	`"TEXT", 1, 255, "'", "'", "length", 1, 0, 3, <Null>, 0, <Null>, "TEXT"`
Btrieve	`"STRING", 1, 255, "'", "'", "length", 1, 1, 3, <Null>, 0, <Null>, "STRING"`
Watcom	`"char", 12, 32767, "'", "'", "max length", 1, 0, 3, <Null>, 0, 0, "char"`

From this small example, you should be able to get a better appreciation for the way ODBC helps the application developer. In the case of a character data type, three different data sources call the character type by three different names, and allow two different sizes of data. By using the ODBC SQL data type of `SQL_CHAR`, the developer does not have to worry about the conversion other than to know that the driver will take care of this chore.

The current ODBC definitions, as derived from the X/Open SAG definitions of 1992, break the SQL data types into three conformance levels, just as the functions and SQL syntax are divided into groups. In Table 7.3, the data types are defined as one group rather than showing the three levels. The application developer seldom has to worry about what conformance level a data type is in; instead, he worries about whether the driver supports the data type. This information about the data type can be found from the `SQLGetTypeInfo` function call without regard to the conformance level of the driver (as long as the driver supports `SQLGetTypeInfo`).

Table 7.3. ODBC SQL data types.

fSqlType	SQL Data Type	Range of Values	Description
SQL_CHAR	CHAR(n)	$1 <$ length < 254	Character string of fixed string length
SQL_NUMERIC	NUMERIC(p,s)	Up to 15 digits	Signed, exact value depends on definition of precision (p 15) and scale (s precision)
SQL_DECIMAL	DECIMAL(p,s)	Up to 15 digits	Same as NUMERIC
SQL_INTEGER	INTEGER	-2,147,483,648 to 2,147,483,647	Exact numeric value with precision 10 and scale 0
SQL_SMALLINT	SMALLINT	-32,768 to 32,767	Exact numeric value with precision 5 and scale 0
SQL_FLOAT	FLOAT	10^{-308} to 10^{308}	Signed approximate numeric value with mantissa precision 15
SQL_REAL	REAL	10^{-38} to 10^{38}	Signed approximate numeric value with mantissa precision 7

continues

Table 7.3. continued

fSqlType	SQL Data Type	Range of Values	Description
SQL_DOUBLE	DOUBLE	10^{-308} to 10^{308}	Same as SQL_FLOAT
SQL_DATE	DATE	N/A	Date data
SQL_TIME	TIME	N/A	Time data
SQL_TIMESTAMP	TIMESTAMP	N/A	Date/time data
SQL_VARCHAR	VARCHAR(n)	1 length 254	Variable length character string
SQL_LONGVARCHAR	LONG VARCHAR	Data source	Variable length dependent character data
SQL_BINARY	BINARY(n)	1 n 255	Binary data of fixed length
SQL_VARBINARY	VARBINARY(n)	1 length(n) 255	Variable length binary data
SQL_LONG	LONG VARBINARY	Data source	Variable length VARBINARY dependent binary data
SQL_BIGINT	BIGINT	-2^{63} n $2^{63}-1$	Exact numeric value with precision 19 (if signed) or 20 (if unsigned) and scale 0
SQL_TINYINT	TINYINT	-128 n 128	Exact numeric value with precision 3 and scale 0
SQL_BIT	BIT	0 or 1	Single-bit binary data

In most of the numeric data types shown in Table 7.3, the range of values is shown for signed fields. An application must use the ODBC functions SQLGetTypeInfo or SQLColAttributes to determine whether a particular data type or a particular column of a result set is signed or unsigned.

> **Caution:** You can have problems when you use Table 7.3 to determine the data type based on precision. In particular, note that the SQL data type SMALLINT has a precision of 5 but an unsigned maximum value of 65,535. Because precision is defined as the maximum number of digits used by the data type, confusion could reign over values between 65,536 and 99,999. These are clearly precision 5, but will not fit in a SMALLINT data type. Where this possibility exists, it is always safest to err on the side of a larger data type to avoid overflow or truncation.

C Data Types as Defined by ODBC

Although data is stored on the data source in an SQL data type, it is stored in the application in ODBC C data types. Because the movement of data from the ODBC output buffer into the application program is performed by the ODBC driver rather than the application program, the calling application program must tell the driver what data type the data is being moved into. This is where the ODBC C data types are used.

The C data types are also defined in the SQL.H and SQLEXT.H include files from the ODBC SDK. Table 7.4 lists the ODBC C data types along with their corresponding C typedef and C types.

Table 7.4. ODBC C data types.

fCType	ODBC C Typedef	C Type
SQL_C_CHAR	UCHAR FAR *	unsigned char FAR *
SQL_C_SSHORT	SWORD	short int

continues

Table 7.4. continued

fCType	ODBC C Typedef	C Type
SQL_C_USHORT	UWORD	unsigned short int
SQL_C_SHORTa	SWORD	short int
SQL_C_ULONG	UDWORD	unsigned long int
SQL_C_SLONG	SDWORD	long int
SQL_C_LONGa	SDWORD	long int
SQL_C_FLOAT	SFLOAT	float
SQL_C_DOUBLE	SDOUBLE	double
SQL_C_BIT	UCHAR	unsigned char
SQL_C_STINYINT	SCHAR	signed char
SQL_C_UTINYINT	UCHAR	unsigned char
SQL_C_TINYINT[†]	SCHAR	signed char
SQL_C_BINARY	UCHAR FAR *	unsigned char FAR *
SQL_C_BOOKMARK	BOOKMARK	unsigned long int

SQL_C_DATE	DATE_STRUCT	struct tagDATE_STRUCT {
		   SWORD year;
		   UWORD month;
		   UWORD day;
		}

SQL_C_TIME	TIME_STRUCT	struct tagTIME_STRUCT {
		   UWORD hour;
		   UWORD minute;
		   UWORD second;
		}

SQL_C_TIMESTAMP	TIMESTAMP_STRUCT	struct tagTIMESTAMP_STRUCT {
		   SWORD year;
		   UWORD month;
		   UWORD day;
		   UWORD hour;
		   UWORD minute;

SAMS
Sams
Learning
Center
SAMS
PUBLISHING

fCType	ODBC C Typedef	C Type
		UWORD second;
		UDWORD fraction;
		}

† These values of fCType were valid in ODBC 1.0. ODBC 2.0 applications must not pass these values to ODBC 2.0 drivers, but they must be passed to ODBC 1.0 drivers.

Converting Data Types Between the DBMS and the Applications

The specification of ODBC SQL data types and ODBC C data types is done so the 1.0 driver will know how to convert data as it moves between the data source and the application. If all data was just one data type—for example, character data—the only data specification needed would be length. Obviously, you don't store everything in a database in character format, so specifying data types is necessary.

When the SQLExecute or SQLExecDirect functions are called, the driver checks to see if any parameters have been bound to the SQL statement using SQLBindParameter or if there are any data-at-execution parameters that should receive their data from an SQLPutData function. If so, the driver must convert the application data from its C data type to the data source's corresponding SQL data types. As explained in the last paragraph, you have already set (for ODBC 1.0) the data types of the sending and receiving fields, telling the driver what conversion to make while transferring the data.

In a similar fashion, when you move data in the other direction, the SQLGetData function, for unbound columns, and SQLFetch or SQLExtendedFetch, for bound columns, need to know the sending and receiving data types for data conversion during data retrieval.

An application can specify that the default ODBC C data type be used by passing SQL_C_DEFAULT for the fCType argument in the functions that bind or retrieve data. However, this is not recommended practice because some drivers promote SQL data types, and in so doing lose their capability to determine the default data type. If a driver cannot determine the data type of a result set column, no data will be transferred.

7

Table 7.5 shows the supported data type conversions from ODBC SQL data types to ODBC C data types and back. The first two columns show the default data type conversion. The third column shows allowed or unsupported alternative data type conversions. To convert from SQL data types to C data types, find your SQL data type in the first column down, then look in the second column to see the default conversion data type. Similarly, to convert from C to SQL data types, find your C data type in the second column, and then look in the first column to find the default SQL data type.

Table 7.5. Default and allowable conversions between ODBC SQL data types and ODBC C data types.

ODBC SQL Data Type	C Data Type	Additional Conversions
SQL_CHAR	SQL_C_CHAR	Any other data type
SQL_VARCHAR	SQL_C_CHAR	Any other data type
SQL_LONGVARCHAR	SQL_C_CHAR	Any other data type
SQL_DECIMAL	SQL_C_CHAR	All but SQL_C_DATE, SQL_C_TIME, SQL_C_TIMESTAMP allowed
SQL_NUMERIC	SQL_C_CHAR	All but SQL_C_DATE, SQL_C_TIME, SQL_C_TIMESTAMP allowed
SQL_BIT	SQL_C_BIT	All but SQL_C_DATE, SQL_C_TIME, SQL_C_TIMESTAMP allowed
SQL_TINYINT (signed)	SQL_C_STINYINT	All but SQL_C_DATE, SQL_C_TIME, SQL_C_TIMESTAMP allowed
SQL_TINYINT (unsigned)	SQL_C_UTINYINT	All but SQL_C_DATE, SQL_C_TIME, SQL_C_TIMESTAMP allowed
SQL_SMALLINT (signed)	SQL_C_SSHORT	All but SQL_C_DATE, SQL_C_TIME, SQL_C_TIMESTAMP allowed
SQL_SMALLINT (unsigned)	SQL_C_USHORT	All but SQL_C_DATE, SQL_C_TIME, SQL_C_TIMESTAMP allowed

ODBC SQL Data Type	C Data Type	Additional Conversions
SQL_INTEGER (signed)	SQL_C_SLONG	All but SQL_C_DATE, SQL_C_TIME, SQL_C_TIMESTAMP allowed
SQL_INTEGER (unsigned)	SQL_C_ULONG	All but SQL_C_DATE, SQL_C_TIME, SQL_C_TIMESTAMP allowed
SQL_BIGINT	SQL_C_CHAR	All but SQL_C_DATE, SQL_C_TIME, SQL_C_TIMESTAMP allowed
SQL_REAL	SQL_C_FLOAT	All but SQL_C_DATE, SQL_C_TIME, SQL_C_TIMESTAMP allowed
SQL_FLOAT	SQL_C_DOUBLE	All but SQL_C_DATE, SQL_C_TIME, SQL_C_TIMESTAMP allowed
SQL_DOUBLE	SQL_C_DOUBLE	All but SQL_C_DATE, SQL_C_TIME, SQL_C_TIMESTAMP allowed
SQL_BINARY	SQL_C_BINARY	Only SQL_C_CHAR allowed
SQL_VARBINARY	SQL_C_BINARY	Only SQL_C_CHAR allowed
SQL_LONGVARBINARY	SQL_C_BINARY	Only SQL_C_CHAR allowed
SQL_DATE	SQL_C_DATE	Only SQL_C_CHAR, SQL_C_BINARY, SQL_C_TIMESTAMP allowed
SQL_TIME	SQL_C_TIME	Only SQL_C_CHAR, SQL_C_BINARY, SQL_C_TIMESTAMP allowed
SQL_TIMESTAMP	SQL_C_TIMESTAMP	Only SQL_C_CHAR, SQL_C_BINARY, SQL_C_DATE, SQL_C_TIME allowed

7

Using Data Types for *CREATE TABLE* and *ALTER TABLE* Statements

One of the limitations of the standard ODBC SQL grammar and syntax as currently defined is that the standard ODBC SQL data types cannot be used in CREATE TABLE and ALTER TABLE statements. Although this might seem like a significant limitation, ODBC does provide a method to perform these statements using the data source-specific data types.

In the earlier example for the function SQLGetTypeInfo, you saw that the first column of the result set was named TYPE_NAME. For an SQL_CHAR ODBC SQL data type, this TYPE_NAME was "TEXT", "STRING", and "char" in the three examples. For most ODBC function calls requiring a data type, you would use the SQL_CHAR data type. However, for a CREATE TABLE statement where you are forming the SQL statement within your application, you would use syntax like the following:

```
CREATE TABLE newtable
  (colname TEXT(20))
```

Passing a CREATE TABLE SQL string with a column data type named something other than the types enumerated in SQLGetTypeInfo will fail. To avoid some of the problems with this naming restriction, the odbc/ClassLibs will provide this functionality for you built into one of their classes.

Differences in Visual Basic Data Types

You must exercise some care when comparing Visual Basic applications written for ODBC to those written in Visual C++ because of the differences in data types. The biggest difference is in the integer SQL data type expressed as SQL_INTEGER.

As you saw earlier, the default data type conversion is from SQL_INTEGER to SQL_C_ULONG for unsigned or SQL_C_SLONG for a signed integer. The problem is that the definition calls for this data type to be a numeric value with a precision of 10. The SQL_INTEGER data type is referring to a 4-byte storage length (32-bit value). Under Visual Basic and the 16-bit version of Visual C++, an integer is a 16-bit value, or precision of 5. A C short int will produce the same data type as a Visual Basic INTEGER; the Visual Basic LONG is the same size as a C long int.

There are similar differences in the handling of character fields. More specifically, the naming of character fields requires some attention on the part of the programmer. In Visual Basic, STRING data types can be either fixed or variable length, up to 255 characters, without a NULL terminator. The Visual Basic TEXT data type more closely corresponds with the SQL_LONGVARCHAR ODBC data type.

Summary

Today's lesson presented the concepts of ODBC SQL data types and ODBC C data types and how they correspond. You learned the following topics:

☐ SQL data types represent the data types used on the data source. Although these are a common set of data type definitions, not all SQL data sources are supported on all data sources. The SQLGetTypeInfo function enables the application to determine SQL data type information.

☐ The ODBC C data types are definitions of data types used in the application program to store data that moves between the data source and the application program storage areas.

☐ It is the responsibility of the driver to convert the data from the type used on the data source to the data type used in the application program. If specific data types are not given to the driver, it will try to use defaults.

☐ The names of the ODBC SQL data types cannot be used embedded inside a CREATE TABLE or ALTER TABLE SQL statement. Instead, the data type name must be queried from the ODBC driver and used.

☐ Visual Basic has data types similar to the ODBC C data types, but differences do exist. These differences relate as much to platform storage word size as they do to development tool differences.

Q&A

Q Can I have the driver convert my data source columns to any data type I specify within my application?

A Almost. The conversions listed in Table 7.5 show the conversions that are allowed and not allowed. For instance, an SQL_DATE field on the data source cannot be converted to an SQL_C_SHORT field in your application.

7

Q **Is any data validity testing performed during data conversion?**

A Yes. The tables in Appendix D of the Microsoft Press book *ODBC 2.0 Programmer's Reference and SDK Guide* list what tests are performed and what SQL states are returned when a problem is detected.

Q **Is there an easy way to maintain my data values inside my Visual Basic program and let the driver handle all conversions?**

A Yes. Again, as shown in Table 7.5, data of the C data type SQL_C_CHAR can be converted to any SQL data type. These conversions are legal as long as the data within the fields converts to valid values appropriate for the receiving data type.

Q **I'm getting compiler warnings from Microsoft's Visual C++ about my ODBC arguments not matching. What am I doing wrong?**

A The most likely problem is that all objects of the CString class in Visual C++ are signed, and string arguments in ODBC functions are unsigned. Cast your arguments as signed to avoid these errors.

Workshop

The Workshop provides quiz questions to help you solidify your understanding of the material covered and to give you experience in using what you've learned. Try to understand the quiz and exercise answers before continuing on to the next day's lesson. Answers are provided in Appendix A, "Answers."

Quiz

1. What are the two main categories of data types used in ODBC applications?
2. What ODBC functions must an application use to determine whether a particular data type or a particular column of a result set is signed or unsigned?

Exercise

1. Using the ODBC Test tool, connect to a database, use the SQLGetTypeInfo function, and then the Get Data All function to return the type information.

OK, the table is set. From what you have seen and done during this first week, you should

☐ Know the layout and purpose of this book (Day 1)

☐ Have some practical knowledge of the history and structure of ODBC (Day 2)

☐ Be ready to insert ODBC into an application (Day 3)

☐ Have set up the ODBC administrator on your computer and know how to configure a data source (Day 4)

☐ Obtained and set up the Microsoft ODBC Software Development Kit (Day 5)

☐ Be prepared to use Visual C++, Visual Basic, or both to write applications using ODBC (Day 6)

☐ Understand the basic data types used in ODBC (Day 7)

This first week is a big step. The rest of your ODBC skills will be built on the knowledge you gained in the first seven days of this book.

In the second week you will learn how to exploit the power of your database using ODBC. Starting on Day 8, "Connecting to the Data Source," you will learn how to open a session with your database. After you have a connection, Day 9, "Determining Driver and DBMS Capabilities," shows you how to use ODBC functions to find out what your database driver will and won't do.

Armed with this knowledge, Day 10, "SQL Syntax for ODBC," is a brief primer on Structured Query Language (SQL) and how SQL is supported by ODBC. Day 11, "Running SQL SELECT Statements," shows you how to execute SQL statements with ODBC. Once you start sending queries to your database, the next step, covered on Day 12, "Returning Data to the Program," is to retrieve the requested data.

Because life and programming are not perfect, Day 13, "Determining the Return Status of a Call," covers how to detect and recover from errors. And finally, on Day 14, "Using Prepared Statements and Parameter Markers," you will learn how to make SQL queries using parameters.

It's going to be a busy week, so let's get started.

Connecting to the
Data Source

This chapter presents the first steps in actually programming with ODBC. You learn the concept of an ODBC environment handle, the database connection handle, and the actual connection. Unless you create these elements in the proper order, you cannot access data in your database. This chapter teaches you the relationship between these elements and how they are created using the different C++ class libraries as well as with Visual Basic. Today you learn the following topics:

☐ Initializing the ODBC environment

☐ Requesting a connection

☐ Connection alternatives

Initializing the ODBC Environment

In order for any application to access data in a database, it must establish a connection to that database through its corresponding ODBC driver. To establish such a connection, the application must request a connection from the Driver Manager, specifying the data source desired.

In order for the Driver Manager to be able to accept such a connection request, it must have been initialized. This initialization, performed when an `SQLAllocEnv` call is made, both allocates memory for an environment handle and initializes the ODBC call-level interface (CLI) to be used by the calling application. This must be the first call made before any other ODBC functions are called. If other functions are called before `SQLAllocEnv` succeeds, the other functions will return -2 (`SQL_INVALID_HANDLE`).

Once the environment handle has been obtained, and before the driver connection can be requested, you must allocate the connection handle. You do this with a call to the `SQLAllocConnect` function, which will allocate memory for a connection handle and return the new connection handle.

It is important to note the relationship between the ODBC environment (of which there can be only one), the ODBC connection (of which there can be many), and active statements for each connection. This relationship is illustrated in Figure 8.1. Allocation of statement handles and the number of statements each connection can have open are presented on Day 9, "Determining Driver and DBMS Capabilities."

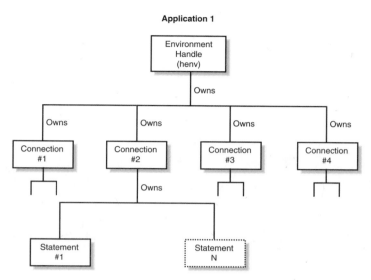

Application 1

Environment
Handle
(henv)

Owns

Owns — Connection #1

Owns — Connection #2

Owns — Connection #3

Owns — Connection #4

Owns

Statement #1

Statement N

Figure 8.1. *Each application can have one environment handle but many connection handles.*

Notice that there is and can be only one ODBC environment per application, and conversely, one application per ODBC environment. This means that the same environment handle cannot be shared among multiple applications. If you have two Visual Basic executables that need to access the same data, they must either do that sharing using DDE or OLE 2 links, or they must have their own separate connections to the data source. They cannot share the environment handle or the connection and its connection handle. If you need to perform such sharing, you should create a DLL that owns the environment and the connections that are needed. Then all applications that need to use this connection can do so by calling the DLL functions. The environment and connection handles remain under the ownership of one "application," in this case the DLL.

The *SQLAllocEnv* Function

The general syntax for the SQLAllocEnv function in Visual Basic is

```
RETCODE SQLAllocEnv(hEnv)
```

The function allocates memory for global information such as valid connection handles and active connection handles. It also initializes the ODBC interface to be used by the application. The function returns an environment handle and a success or fail return

code. The following code fragment declares the handle and return value as global and then tries to open the connection.

```
Global hEnv As Long
Global rc% As Integer

rc% = SQLAllocEnv(henv)
```

The variable henv now contains the address of (pointer to) the environment handle.

> **Note:** Although all the Visual Basic examples will refer to handles, Visual Basic does not support either the handle data type or the idea of a far pointer. The value of the handle is manipulated in an INTEGER data type variable, and the address contained in a pointer can be manipulated by the application programmer in a LONG Visual Basic data type.

C++ **Syntax**

The *SQLAllocEnv* Function

The prototype for the SQLAllocEnv function is

```
RETCODE SQL_API SQLAllocEnv(HENV    FAR *phenv);
```

The function initializes the ODBC interface for the application and allocates memory for the environment handle. It returns the pointer to the henv handle. For example:

```
HENV   henv;

RC = SQLAllocEnv(&henv);
```

The return code will be either SQL_SUCCESS or SQL_ERROR. If the function succeeds, it returns a pointer to storage for the environment handle. If it fails, it will set the henv referenced by phenv to SQL_NULL_HENV. This happens because a memory allocation error prevented the allocation of the needed memory.

The SQLAllocEnv function works in two places at two distinct times. When the function is called from the application, it executes the function within the Driver Manager only. The second half of the function, which is in the driver, is not performed until the application attempts a connection by calling SQLBrowseConnect, SQLDriverConnect, or SQLConnect. If the driver portion of SQLAllocEnv fails during a connect function, it is possible to call SQLError to determine the cause of the error. The full usage of SQLError is covered on Day 13, "Determining the Return Status of a Call."

The same henv must be used by all threads in a multithreaded application. It is your responsibility as the application programmer to ensure safe multithreading by controlling access to this variable. In some cases, such as when you use Microsoft Foundation Class (MFC) database code in a DLL or in two concurrent applications, you could be using different environment handles or losing your handle without being aware that this is happening. Because the MFC classes do not give you the ability to control such access easily, the potential for conflict to cause application crashes is high.

This problem happens because MFC code uses a global static variable to store the henv. The henv variable is assigned—and its memory allocated—when the first Cdatabase object is created. If this creation is done in a DLL, the environment handle is used for all Cdatabase objects created by all applications sharing that DLL. When the program that first caused the handle creation and memory allocation goes away, so does the memory allocated for the henv variable. All the other applications that still have Cdatabases open will now most likely crash. This scenario will happen when two applications are using the AFXDLL version of the MFC database code.

There are three approaches that can be used to avoid this problem, as follows:

1. Let only one application use the DLL at a time or let only one application at a time call into the DLL and create a Cdatabase object. In the latter case, the application that calls into the DLL to create a Cdatabase must delete it before letting any other application call into the DLL to create a Cdatabase.

2. Modify the MFC code in DBCORE.CPP so that it creates and uses a separate henv for each application. The Windows API function GetCurrentTask is available to associate specific task handles with their environment handle. The code can be modified so that it checks to determine if an henv has been allocated and associated with the current task. It will have to allocate and associate a new environment handle when a new task is seen. In addition, code would be needed to replace all references to henvAllConnections with a function call to retrieve the correct henv for the current task.

3. A final technique is to have one database application that acts as a DDE or OLE server. This application keeps all the database code in a central application. This central application queries the database and returns results to the individual applications.

The *SQLAllocConnect* Function

The general syntax for the SQLAllocConnect function in Visual Basic is

```
RETCODE SQLAllocConnect(hEnv, hDBC)
```

The SQLAllocConnect function allocates memory for the connection information. It accepts the environment handle henv as input and returns a pointer in the form of an Integer to the new connection handle just created.

Example:

```
Global hEnv As Long          'Pointer to handle for environment handle
Global hDbc As Long          'Pointer to handle for connection
Global rc% As Integer        'Return code

rc% = SQLAllocConnect(hEnv, hDBC)
```

The variable hDBC now contains the address pointing to the handle for the new connection. Errors from this function, which can be obtained by calling SQLError, are usually caused by not having a valid environment handle in henv or by the Driver Manager or the driver not being able to allocate memory for the connection.

The *SQLAllocConnect* Function

The prototype for the SQLAllocConnect function is

```
RETCODE SQL_API SQLAllocConnect(HENV henv, HDBC FAR *phdbc);
```

The function allocates memory for the connection handle and the connection information. It returns the pointer to the handle hDbc. For example:

```
HENV   henv;
HDBC   hdbc;

RC = SQLAllocConnect(henv, &hdbc);
```

Although both functions shown in the preceding examples are essential to using the ODBC interface, whether you will have to code these calls in your programs depends on what language and class libraries you are using. Visual Basic has no support for object-oriented concepts like classes, so Visual Basic programmers must explicitly call all functions in the correct sequence from their code.

C++ programming, on the other hand, does give you more decisions to make regarding the amount of code you want to write. The Microsoft Foundation Class libraries, versions 2.5 and higher, provide the programmer considerable isolation from the details of creating the environment and making a connection. As you learned on Day 6, "Development Tools," this isolation reduces the amount of code you have to write and greatly reduces the amount of flexibility you have when accessing an ODBC data source.

As you progress through this book, you will see C++ examples using MFC classes, the odbc/ClassLib classes from South Wind Design, and private classes created for these examples. Each has its advantages and disadvantages, and these will be pointed out where possible. Because you might want to build your own classes sometime, the base API call syntax that is used will always be illustrated in order to enable you to use the APIs within whatever class you choose.

Requesting a Connection

The wording of this section might sound strange, but don't forget that the Driver Manager is sitting between your application and the ODBC data sources. You must therefore "ask" the Driver Manager to make the connection for you. There are two functions used to connect to a data source, SQLConnect and SQLDriverConnect. The first is a simpler connection that has three fixed parameters and will not prompt the user for any missing parameters. The other connection function is used for data sources that require more parameters than the three used for SQLConnect or when the user is to be prompted for some or all the connection information. With both functions, the Driver Manager will look in the ODBC.INI file for data-source specifications to use in making the connection.

The *SQLConnect* Function

The general syntax for the SQLConnect function in Visual Basic is

```
RETCODE SQLConnect(hDBC, szDSN, cbDSN, szUID, cbUID, szAuthStr, cbAuthStr)
```

The function will attempt to load and connect to the data source specified by DSN. If that data-source name is not valid, the Driver Manager will follow the guidelines listed in Table 8.1 while attempting to establish a connection. The parameter hDBC specifies the connection handle for this connection. The parameter szDSN specifies the data-source name. The parameter cbDSN is the length of parameter szDSN. The parameter szUID is the user identifier to be used to access the data source. The parameter cbUID is the length of parameter szUID. The parameter szAuthStr specifies the password or other authentication string for this user. The parameter cbAuthStr is the length of parameter szAuthStr.

Table 8.1. Connection guidelines for the Driver Manager.

Order	Action
1	If the data-source name parameter contains a valid data source, the Driver Manager will use that name to locate the data-source specifications in the ODBC.INI file or the registry. Those specifications include the name and location of the driver DLL, which the Driver Manager

continues

Table 8.1. continued

Order	Action
	will load if it is not already loaded. The Driver Manager then calls SQLAllocEnv and SQLAllocConnect in the driver. Then the manager will call the connection function in the driver, passing all the SQLConnect arguments to the driver.
2	If the specified driver is already loaded on the specified connection handle, the Driver Manager will call only the specified connection function in the driver.
3	If a different driver DLL is currently loaded, the Driver Manager must call SQLFreeConnect and SQLFreeEnv in the driver that is loaded, and then unload that driver. The manager then performs the operations listed in step 1.
4	If the specified data-source name cannot be found or a null pointer is passed for the data-source name, the Driver Manager will locate the driver specified as the default data source and load that driver. The manager will pass each SQLConnect argument to the driver after it is loaded.
5	If the data-source name cannot be found or a null pointer is passed for the data-source name, and no driver is specified as the default data source, the Driver Manager will return SQL_ERROR and a SQLSTATE of IM002 (the data-source name is not found and no default driver is specified).

The function will return SQL_SUCCESS, SQL_ERROR, or SQL_SUCCESS_WITH_INFO. If the return is not SQL_SUCCESS, the SQLSTATE can be obtained by calling SQLError. The common SQLSTATE values from this function are listed in Table 8.2.

Example:

```
Global hDBC As Long          'Pointer to handle for connection
Global rc% As Integer        'Function return code

Dim DSource As String * 40   'Data source name
Dim User As String * 10      'User ID
Dim Pwd As String * 10       'Password
```

```
DSource = "LocalServer"
User = "WWW"
Pwd = "mypass"

rc% = SQLConnect(hDBC, DSource, Len(DSource), User, Len(User), Pwd, Len(Pwd))
```

The function returns `SQL_SUCCESS` if the connection is successful.

Table 8.2. Common errors from `SQLConnect`.

Error	Problem	SQLSTATE
Communication link failure	The communication link between the data source and the driver failed before the connection completed processing.	08S01
Connection in use	The specified connection handle had already been used to establish a connection and the previous connection was still open.	08002
Data source not found and no default specified	The data-source name specified in szDSN could not be found in ODBC.INI or the registry, nor was there a default data source specified. _or_ The ODBC.INI file could not be found.	IM002
Data source rejected connection	The data source rejected the establishment of the connection for implementation-defined reasons.	08004

continues

Table 8.2. continued

Error	Problem	SQLSTATE
Driver does not support this function	The driver specified by the data-source name does not support the function. (Use SQLDriverConnect.)	IM001
Unable to connect to data source	The driver was unable to establish a connection with the data source.	08001
Invalid authorization specification	The value specified for user ID or authorization information (password) was rejected by the data source. Check spelling and case of user ID and password.	28000
General Error	No SQLSTATE exists for this error. The error message returned by SQLError should explain the cause of this failure.	S1000
Specified driver could not be loaded	The driver listed in the data-source specification in the ODBC.INI file or registry was not found or could not be loaded.	IM003
Memory allocation error	Either the Driver Manager or the driver was not able to allocate the memory required for this function.	S1001
Invalid string or buffer length	The length specified for the data-source name was greater than 32.	S1090

Error	Problem	SQLSTATE
	or	
	The length specified for one or more of the string-length parameters was less than 0, but not equal to SQL_NTS (-3 from SQL.H).	
Timeout expired	The time-out period expired before the connection was completed. Increase the time-out value by calling SQLSetConnectOption with the option SQL_LOGIN_TIMEOUT.	S1T00

C++

Syntax

The *SQLConnect* Function

The prototype for the SQLConnect function is

```
RETCODE SQL_API SQLConnect(
    HDBC          hdbc,
    UCHAR   FAR *szDSN,
    SWORD       cbDSN,
    UCHAR   FAR *szUID,
    SWORD       cbUID,
    UCHAR   FAR *szAuthStr,
    SWORD       cbAuthStr);
```

The function loads the specified driver and establishes a connection to the data source using the user ID and password specified in the function call.

Example:

```
char  szDSN[SQL_MAX_DSN_LENGTH]
char  szUID[32]
char  szPWD[32]
//load the parameters
lstrcpy(szDSN, "LocalServer");
lstrcpy(szUID, "WWW");
lstrcpy(szPWD, "mypass");
//connect
  SQLConnect(
      hdbc,
      szDSN,
      SQL_NTS,
```

```
      szUID,
      SQL_NTS,
      szPWD,
      SQL_NTS
      );
```

The parameters used here are the same as those used for the preceding Visual Basic example.

> **Note:** In the last example, instead of passing the length of the parameters as the following parameter, the constant SQL_NTS is used. This signifies that the parameter is a null-terminated string.

VB4

Syntax

The *SQLDriverConnect* Function

The general syntax for the SQLDriverConnect function in Visual Basic is

```
RETCODE SQLDriverConnect(hDBC, hWnd, szConnStrIn, cbConnStrIn, szConnStrOut,
➥cbConnStrOutMax, pcbConnStrOut, fDriverCompletion)
```

This function is an alternative to SQLConnect. It supports data sources that require more information to make a connection than the data-source name, user ID, and password provided in SQLConnect. If more connection information is needed than is provided in the connection string, dialog boxes will prompt for the needed information.

SQLDriverConnect provides the following options when called:

☐ Establish a connection using the connection string passed as szConnStrIn. In this instance, the connection string would contain the data-source name, one or more user IDs, one or more passwords, and other information required by the data source being used.

☐ Establish a connection using a connection string that contains only some of the needed information. In this case, both the Driver Manager and the driver can prompt for needed information. (The example that follows includes such prompting.)

☐ Establish a connection to a data source that is not defined in the ODBC.INI file or registry. If your application passes a partial connection string in the function call, the driver can prompt the user for connection information.

The parameter hDBC specifies the connection handle for this connection. The parameter hWnd is the parent window handle, to be used if dialog boxes will be presented. The parameter szConnStrIn is the connection string. The syntax of this string is presented in the next section. The parameter cbConnStrIn is the length of parameter szConnStrIn. The parameter szConnStrOut is a pointer to the buffer where the completed connection

string is to be placed. Your application should allocate at least 255 bytes for this buffer. The parameter cbConnStrOutMax is the actual length of the szConnStrOut buffer. The parameter pcbConnStrOut is a pointer to the size, in bytes, of the actual connection string that was returned when the connection completed. If the buffer is smaller than the actual string, it will be truncated. The parameter fDriverCompletion is a flag that indicates whether the driver and Driver Manager should prompt for needed information to complete the connection. The values for this flag and their meanings are shown in Table 8.3.

Table 8.3. Driver completion flag guidelines.

Flag	Driver Manager Action	Driver Action
SQL_DRIVER_PROMPT	The Driver Manager displays the SQL Data Sources dialog box as shown in Figure 8.2. It builds a connection string based on the data-source name returned from the dialog box and the remainder of the original connection string. If the dialog returns no data-source name, it will return DSN=Default.	The driver displays a dialog box prompting for user ID, password, and other needed connection information as shown in Figure 8.3. The driver will use values from ODBC.INI or registry as initial values. When the user exits from the dialog box, the driver will connect and return the connection string with the values entered placed into the string.
SQL_DRIVER_COMPLETE or SQL_DRIVER_COMPLETE_REQUIRED	If there is a valid data source specified with a DSN parameter in the connection string, the Driver Manager will pass the entire connection string to the driver.	If the connection string is complete and accurate, the driver will copy it to szConnStrOut and complete the connection. If any information is

continues

119

Table 8.3. continued

Flag	Driver Manager Action	Driver Action
	If not, it will perform the same actions as with SQL_DRIVER_PROMPT.	missing or incorrect, the driver will prompt for it as shown previously. If the flag is SQL_DRIVER_COMPLETE_REQUIRED the driver disables the controls for any information not required to connect.
SQL_DRIVER_NOPROMPT	The Driver Manager copies the connection string as-is to the driver.	If the connection string contains enough information to complete the connection, the driver will connect and copy szConnStrIn to szConnStrOut. Otherwise, the driver will return SQL_ERROR.

Figure 8.2. *The SQL Data Sources dialog box.*

Figure 8.3. *The dialog box for additional information during connect.*

> **Note:** Normally, the SQLDriverConnect function deals with the data-source name (DSN) as a parameter. Beginning with ODBC 2.0 drivers, the DRIVER keyword can be used instead of the data-source name to refer to the driver name rather than the data-source name. In this case, no additional information is read from the ODBC.INI file or the registry, so enough keywords must be defined in the connection string to enable a connection.
>
> The use of the DRIVER keyword can be helpful in situations in which there are many client workstations connecting to the same server, such as an SQL server. Although each user could define the data source with a different name, or even variations in spelling and capitalization, the DRIVER name will always be the same.

Example:

```
Global hDBC As Long            'Pointer to handle for connection
Global rc% As Integer          'Function return code
Global ConnOut As String * 255 'Global connection string

Dim ConnIn As String * 255     'Temporary for first connection
Dim cbOut As Integer           'Receives length of actual connection string

ConnIn = "DSN=;DATABASE=rscdb;"
ConnOut = Space$(255)
rc% = SQLDriverConnect(hdbc, GetParent(GetFocus()), ConnIn, 255, ConnOut, 255,
➥cbOut%, 1)
```

The function returns SQL_SUCCESS if the connection was successful.

C++ **Syntax**

The *SQLDriverConnect* Function

The prototype for the SQLDriverConnect function is

```
RETCODE SQL_API SQLDriverConnect(
    HDBC        hdbc,
    HWND        hwnd,
    UCHAR  FAR *szConnStrIn,
    SWORD       cbConnStrIn,
    UCHAR  FAR *szConnStrOut,
    SWORD       cbConnStrOutMax,
    SWORD  FAR *pcbConnStrOut,
    UWORD       fDriverCompletion);
```

The function is an alternative to using SQLConnect when more information must be passed to the driver or the user is to be prompted for connection information at runtime. The following example shows how SQLDriverConnect is used.

Example:

```
void CCpconn01Doc::OnNewConnect()
{
    UCHAR szConnStrIn[256];
    UCHAR szConnStrOut[256];
    SWORD pcbConnStrOut;

    strcpy((char*) szConnStrIn, m_connect);
    VERIFY(SQLAllocConnect((((CCpconn01App*) AfxGetApp())->m_henv, &m_hdbc)
            == SQL_SUCCESS);

    if (SQLDriverConnect(
            m_hdbc,
            AfxGetApp()->m_pMainWnd->GetSafeHwnd(),
            (UCHAR FAR*) szConnStrIn,
            SQL_NTS,
            (UCHAR FAR*) szConnStrOut,
            255,
            &pcbConnStrOut,
            SQL_DRIVER_PROMPT) != SQL_SUCCESS) {
        AfxMessageBox("SQL connection error");
        return;
    }
    m_bConnected = TRUE;
    m_connect = (const char*) szConnStrOut;
}
```

The parameters used here have the same content and order as those used for the Visual Basic example of SQLDriverConnect.

The SQLDriverConnect function will return the same return codes as SQLConnect and will also return SQL_NO_DATA_FOUND if the Driver Manager or the driver prompts for additional information and the user cancels the dialog box. If the function returns

SQL_ERROR or SQL_SUCCESS_WITH_INFO, SQLError can be called to determine the nature of the problem. The SQLSTATE statements that are returned are covered in Table 8.2. Table 8.4 covers only those SQLSTATE statements that are unique to SQLDriverConnect because those shown in Table 8.2 are common to both connection functions.

Table 8.4. Common errors from SQLDriverConnect.

Error	Problem	SQLSTATE
Invalid connection string attribute	An invalid attribute keyword was specified in the connection string but the driver was able to connect anyway. (Function returns SQL_SUCCESS_WITH_INFO.)	01S00
No data source or driver specified; dialog prohibited	The connection string did not contain a data-source name or driver, and fDriverCompletion is SQL_DRIVER_NOPROMPT.	IM007
Dialog failed	The Driver Manager or driver tried to display a dialog box and failed.	IM008
Data truncated	The entire connection string would not fit in szConnStrOut, so it was truncated. The untruncated length is in pcbConnStrOut. (Function returns SQL_SUCCESS_WITH_INFO.)	01004
Invalid driver completion	The value for the argument fDriverCompletion was not valid.	S1110

Now look at sample programs in C++ and Visual Basic to see the connections take place. These programs do nothing more than make a connection and display the connection string. (Later chapters will add some real meat to these bare bones.) In the first program, Microsoft's Visual C++ was used. To create the example yourself, use the AppWizard to create the basic program. Use App Studio to add a menu selection to add a connection. Because this example is so simple, the message-handling function for that menu entry can go right in the main module, MAINFRM.CPP. Listing 8.1 shows the source code for program MAINFRM.CPP in the CPCONN01 project.

Listing 8.1. The source code for the program MAINFRM.CPP.

```cpp
// c++ program illustrating an ODBC connection
#include "stdafx.h"
#include "cpconn01.h"

#include "mainfrm.h"

IMPLEMENT_DYNCREATE(CMainFrame, CFrameWnd)

BEGIN_MESSAGE_MAP(CMainFrame, CFrameWnd)
    //{{AFX_MSG_MAP(CMainFrame)
    ON_COMMAND(ID_CONNECTIONS_ADDNEWCONNECTION, OnConnectionsAddnewconnection)
    //}}AFX_MSG_MAP
END_MESSAGE_MAP()

CMainFrame::CMainFrame()
{
    // TODO: add member initialization code here
}

CMainFrame::~CMainFrame()
{
}

/////////////////////////////////////////////////////////////////////////////
// CMainFrame message handlers

void CMainFrame::OnConnectionsAddnewconnection()
{
  UCHAR szConnStrIn[256];
  UCHAR szConnStrOut[256];
  SWORD pcbConnStrOut;

  strcpy((char*) szConnStrIn, m_connect);
  VERIFY(SQLAllocConnect(((CCpconn01App*) AfxGetApp())->m_henv, &m_hdbc)
          == SQL_SUCCESS);

  if (SQLDriverConnect(
          m_hdbc,
          AfxGetApp()->m_pMainWnd->GetSafeHwnd(),
          (UCHAR FAR*) szConnStrIn,
          SQL_NTS,
          (UCHAR FAR*) szConnStrOut,
          255,
          &pcbConnStrOut,
          SQL_DRIVER_PROMPT) != SQL_SUCCESS)
    {
      AfxMessageBox("SQL connection error");
      return;
    }
```

```
  else
    {
      m_bConnected = TRUE;
      m_connect = (const char*) szConnStrOut;
      AfxMessageBox(m_connect);
    }
}
```

Listing 8.2 shows the source code that must be added to MAINFRM.H after AppWizard has created the file. This code defines the parameters used in the connection function and defines the environment handle.

 Listing 8.2. Source code to be added to MAINFRM.H.

```
public:
  HDBC m_hdbc;  // ODBC connection handle
  BOOL m_bConnected;
  CString m_connect; // ODBC connect string
```

 The preceding listings show the major code entered to perform the connection. As mentioned at the beginning of this chapter, before a connection can be made, the application must create an environment handle that initializes the ODBC interface. In this example program, we added that function in the module CPCONN01.CPP. To create this handle add the following line just before the return statement in InitInstance:

```
SQLAllocEnv(&m_henv)
```

Create the project and build the executable. The main frame can look something like the example shown in Figure 8.4. The only active menu selections are Add New Connection and File/Exit. When you select Add New Connection, you should be prompted to select a data source. When a successful connection is made, you will see a message box displaying the completed szConnStrOut returned from the driver, as shown in Figure 8.5.

Figure 8.4. *The main window for the CPCONN01 example.*

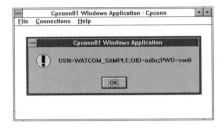

Figure 8.5. *The results from a successful connection in CPCONN01.*

Now try your hand at a Visual Basic sample program that does something similar to the program you just finished. In program VBCONN01, the environment and connection handles are displayed rather than the connection string. Listing 8.3 shows the code written for the Visual Basic form. The function declaration for the Windows API function GetFocus was added to the GLOBAL.BAS file. In addition, the ODBC API declarations were included in the Visual Basic project from the ODBC SDK VBDEMO sample.

 Listing 8.3. The VBCONN01 connection example.

```
Sub Form_Load ()
    'Allocating and initializing ODBC environment upon program startup
  Show
  rc% = SQLAllocEnv(henv)
  If rc% <> SQL_SUCCESS Then
    MsgBox ("Unable to allocation environment")
    End
  End If
  ShowEnv.Caption = "hEnv: " + Str$(henv)     'Display the henv
End Sub
Sub MenuAddConn_Click ()
  Dim ConnIn As String * 255       'Temporary for first connection
  Dim cbOut As Integer             'Receives length of actual connection string

    'Connection requested from menu - allocate conn handle
  rc% = SQLAllocConnect(henv, hdbc)
  If rc% <> SQL_SUCCESS Then
    MsgBox ("Unable to allocate connection")
    rc% = SQLFreeEnv(henv)
    End
  End If
  ShowDBC.Caption = "hDBC: " + Str$(hdbc)

  ConnIn = "DSN=;"
  ConnOut = Space$(255)
  rc% = SQLDriverConnect(hdbc, GetFocus(), ConnIn, 255, ConnOut, 255, cbOut%, 1)
  If rc% = SQL_SUCCESS Or rc% = SQL_SUCCESS_WITH_INFO Then
    MsgBox "Connect Successful!"
```

```
      Else
         MsgBox "Connect Failed"
      End If

   End Sub
```

Figure 8.6 shows the output from the VBCONN01 program, including the main form and the message box indicating successful connection. The environment and connection-handle values can be seen on the left side of the main form.

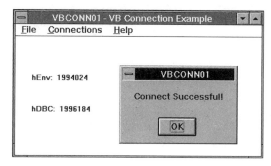

Figure 8.6. *The success message for VBCONN01.*

Tip: If an application needs to make more than one connection to the same data source, use the connection string output from the first connection as input to all of the other SQLDriverConnect calls. If any specifications such as user ID and password were prompted for during the first connect, the responses to those prompts will be in the output connection string. By using this string as input to the subsequent calls and having the driver completion flag set to SQL_DRIVER_COMPLETE, the user will not be prompted for the same input more than once.

Connection Alternatives

So far, you have seen the two most common methods of connecting to a data source: using SQLDriverConnect for the most flexibility, or using SQLConnect for simpler connections where the connection information is usually fixed and can be hard-coded

into the application or easily prompted for, such as a user ID and password. Critics might look at this and say that ODBC is not very flexible in allowing connections to complex or unknown data sources. Some of this criticism is warranted if you only look at using the ODBC interface from an environment such as that built using the MFC 2.5 database classes.

If you want your application to be more powerful or easier to use, the ODBC API has provided for your needs. While making a connection to an unknown (or forgotten) system, the SQLBrowseConnect function will enable the calling application to iteratively determine what connection attributes a data source needs. By prompting the user for choices from the lists returned, a successful connection can be made using SQLBrowseConnect without the application having to know what is needed ahead of time.

Similarly, the SQLDrivers and SQLDataSources functions enable an application to obtain a list of data sources or drivers before attempting a connection. The application can then build its own prompting dialog boxes to determine the connection specifications. Although the topic is not covered here, the ODBC API even enables your application to create its own data source before attempting a connection. This functionality is usually seen when installing a new driver, but nothing prevents it from being used in your application.

The *SQLBrowseConnect* Function

The general syntax for the SQLBrowseConnect function in Visual Basic is

```
RETCODE SQLBrowseConnect(hdbc, szConnStrIn, cbConnStrIn,
➥szConnStrOut, cbConnStrOutMax, pcbConnStrOut)
```

This function provides an iterative method of discovering and selecting the attributes needed in a connection string to connect to a particular data source. Each successive call to SQLBrowseConnect returns another level of attributes and their possible values. The calling application must specify which of the presented attributes and values are to be used for this connection. Once this process has covered all of the attributes for the data source, the function will return SQL_SUCCESS or SQL_SUCCESS_WITH_INFO, indicating a connection has been made.

When a connection is successfully made, the SQLBrowseConnect function will return the full connection string, which can then be used as input to an SQLDriverConnect call. The parameters used in the SQLBrowseConnect call match and are a subset of the parameters used in SQLDriverConnect. They have the same data types and meanings in both functions. The SQLBrowseConnect function does not use the fDriverCompletion or hWnd parameters because SQLBrowseConnect will never prompt for user input. The application program calling this function must format and display any user dialog boxes used.

8

Syntax

C++

The *SQLBrowseConnect* Function

The prototype for the function `SQLBrowseConnect` is

```
RETCODE SQL_API SQLBrowseConnect(
    HDBC          hdbc,
    UCHAR  FAR *szConnStrIn,
    SWORD         cbConnStrIn,
    UCHAR  FAR *szConnStrOut,
    SWORD         cbConnStrOutMax,
    SWORD  FAR *pcbConnStrOut);
```

This function supports an iterative method of finding and listing the attributes and attribute values needed to make a connection to a data source. The example that follows demonstrates the code flow that could occur when you use this function.

The following example shows how `SQLBrowseConnect` might be used to browse a fictitious connection on a networked server. The attributes that are shown apply only to this example, but they are intended to give a general example of the flow when using this function.

Before browsing the connection, the application must request a connection handle, as follows:

```
SQLAllocConnect(henv, hdbc);
```

Next, the application makes the first call to `SQLBrowseConnect` specifying just the data-source name, as follows:

```
SQLBrowseConnect(hdbc, "DSN=SuperDB", SQL_NTS, szBrowseBack, 300, &cb);
```

The driver will determine that this is the first time the driver has been called on this connection. In response to this first call, it will return the next level of connection attributes: `SERVER`, user ID, password, application name, and workstation ID. For some attributes, such as `SERVER` in this case, it might return a list of valid values. Lists of values are enclosed in braces {}. The return code from `SQLBrowseConnect` is `SQL_NEED_DATA`. The string returned back is as follows:

```
"SERVER:Server={acctg,mfg,sales,shipping};UID:Login ID=?;
➡PWD:Password=?;*APP:AppName=?;*WSID:WorkStation ID=?"
```

> **Note:** Each keyword returned in the browse-result string is followed by a colon and a word or short phrase before the equal sign. These words are the user-friendly description of the attribute, which can be used for prompting with a dialog box.

For the next iterative call to SQLBrowseConnect, the application must supply values for each attribute. In this example, this would be SERVER, UID, and PWD. The asterisk before APP and WSID indicates that these attributes are optional. The value returned for an attribute with a value list, such as SERVER, can be one of the list items or a value supplied by the user.

The application calls SQLBrowseConnect again with the chosen values in the connection string. The user-friendly words, asterisks, and unused optional attributes are removed, as follows:

```
SQLBrowseConnect(hdbc, "SERVER=sales;UID=Whiting;PWD=mypass",
➥SQL_NTS, szBrowseBack, 300, &cb);
```

The driver will attempt to connect to the sales server using the attributes given. If more attributes are needed to finish the connection, it will return SQL_NEED_DATA with a browse-result string, as follows:

```
"*DATABASE:Database={north,south,east,west};*TRANSLATE:Translate=?"
```

Because both attributes in this return string are optional, the application can omit them if appropriate. The application must call SQLBrowseConnect again anyway to indicate the omission of these last attributes. In this example, the application will select the north database with no translation needed. It will call SQLBrowseConnect one last time, omitting the asterisk before DATABASE, and leaving out the TRANSLATE completely, as follows:

```
SQLBrowseConnect(hdbc, "DATABASE=north", SQL_NTS, szBrowseBack, 300, &cb);
```

Now that the application has passed back the last attribute, DATABASE, browsing is complete and the application is connected to the data source. SQLBrowseConnect will return SQL_SUCCESS and fill the browse-result string with a full connection string, as follows:

```
"DSN=SuperDB;SERVER=sales;UID=Whiting;PWD=mypass;DATABASE=north"
```

This final connection string does not include the user-friendly words, asterisks, or unused attributes. The application can use this return string with SQLDriverConnect to reconnect to the data source on the current hdbc (after disconnecting) or to connect to the data source on a different hdbc.

Additional Listing Functions

The ODBC Driver Manager provides two additional functions that are very similar and can be helpful in applications that select a data source at runtime. The `SQLDataSources` function returns a list of data sources as configured in the ODBC.INI file or the registry. The `SQLDrivers` function similarly returns a list of drivers and driver attributes from the ODBCINST.INI file or the registry.

The generic prototype for `SQLDataSources` is as follows:

```
RETCODE SQLDataSources(henv, fDirecttion, szDSN, cbDSNMax, pcbDSN,
➥szDescription, cbDescriptionMax, pcbDescription)
```

The generic prototype for `SQLDrivers` is

```
RETCODE SQLDrivers(henv, fDirection, szDriverDesc, cbDriverDescMax,
➥pcbDriverDesc, szDriverAttributes, cbDrvrAttrMax, pcbDrvrAttr)
```

In both functions, the parameters passed include a buffer for the information returned and a pointer to the number of bytes returned into the buffer, while passing in the length of the buffer. The `fDirection` parameter can contain `SQL_FETCH_FIRST` or `SQL_FETCH_NEXT`. The name of the buffer describes the data passed.

Summary

Today's lesson presented the mechanism for connecting to data sources. You learned about the following topics:

- [ ] The ODBC environment and call-level interface (CLI) must be initialized before use. The `SQLAllocEnv` function initializes the environment, allocates necessary memory, and returns a handle to this environment.

- [ ] There are two primary calls that are used to connect to an ODBC data source. The `SQLConnect` function is used to make a simple connection to a data source. The application must have the data-source name, user ID, and password information coded in the program or must handle getting this information from the user. The `SQLDriverConnect` function provides more flexibility to connect when the data source requires more than the basic attributes to connect. This function will also prompt the user for needed connection information if needed.

☐ If a connection is desired to a data source whose attributes are not known or are dynamic, `SQLBrowseConnect` can be called to browse through the required and optional attributes needed for connection. `SQLDrivers` and `SQLDataSources` can be called to get a list of available drivers and configured data sources on a particular client workstation.

Q&A

Q When a connection fails, I call `SQLError` but it always returns `SQL_NO_DATA_FOUND`. How can I tell why my connection is failing?

A Check the actual return code from your connection function. `SQL_INVALID_HANDLE` indicates that allocating your environment or connection handle failed.

Q I need two connections in my application, but whenever I try to connect the second time, I get the message `Connection in use`.

A You must allocate a second connection handle and use that for the second connection request.

Q How is a default data source set up?

A In the ODBC.INI file, copy an existing data source section, changing the data-source name to `[Default]`. Do not include this default data source in the `[ODBC Data Sources]` section.

Workshop

The Workshop provides quiz questions to help you solidify your understanding of the material covered and exercises to give you experience in using what you've learned. Try to understand the quiz and exercise answers before continuing on to the next day's lesson. Answers are provided in Appendix A, "Answers."

Quiz

1. Will the following connection string return any syntax errors from `SQLConnect`:

   ```
   "DSN=mydriver;UID=Whiting;PWD=mypass;"
   ```

2. What is the problem with the following `SQLDriverConnect` connection string?

   ```
   "DSN=SQL Server;UID=Bill;DSN=SQL Server #2"
   ```

Exercises

1. Modify the SQLDriverConnect example to connect to each of the data sources on your desktop system. Code all of the connection attributes into your application and set fDriverCompletion to SQL_DRIVER_NOPROMPT.

2. Use the SQLDataSources to create your own dialog box prompts for the SQLDriverConnect function.

Determining Driver and DBMS Capabilities

Now that you know how to connect to an ODBC data source, you need to find out details about that data source. This chapter presents some of the functions that can be used to query the data source about its capabilities and about details of the data itself. You'll learn when it is important to know about specific capabilities and how they impact your development. Today you learn about the following topics:

☐ ODBC conformance levels

☐ Querying for a specific driver or server function

☐ Querying for index information

Before studying the functions that query driver- and DBMS-specific capabilities and settings, it is important to step back and analyze when and why this information about the data source is needed.

If you will be developing an application that will use only one or two specific data sources, you should know before writing any code how those data sources behave. If not, you can and should find out using tools such as ODBC Test. If you do know how the driver will act and what its limitations are, you should not have to write any conditional code enabling your application to act differently depending on how the data source acts.

On the other hand, if you don't know at the time of development what data sources your application will be using, the application must be able to determine its environment and respond appropriately. For example, the SQLGetInfo parameter SQL_ACTIVE_STATEMENTS is used to learn if a driver or data source will support more than one active statement at a time through one connection. If your application selects several rows of data at once, and the user wants to perform an update to the second row, if the data source supports multiple active statements, the select result set can be retained while the update is performed on another statement. If the active statement count is one, the application will have to discard the pending results from the select, perform the update, and then reselect the data and reposition to the current row.

Don't be discouraged by the number of parameters available for a call like SQLGetInfo. Rather than being a sign of complexity for ODBC programming, think of it more as an indication of how flexible and rich the ODBC interface really is, enabling you to maximize the utilization of DBMS power and features. It is not uncommon to develop an ODBC application that does not query data source capabilities if you already know what they are. In this case, knowing what you can find out using this function and others will make the ODBC Test tool that much more powerful.

On the other hand, the expert use of such functions by an application developer will result in an application that is truly portable and interoperable with any ODBC drivers

available. As you learned earlier, reality probably will dictate that an application not be interoperable with all ODBC drivers but will with those that meet a minimum ODBC conformance level.

ODBC Conformance Levels

On Day 2, "Overview of ODBC Concepts and Theory," you learned the conformance of an ODBC driver to the three levels of API calls and three levels of SQL grammar. The SQLGetInfo call can determine which of these levels a driver achieves by querying against info types SQL_ODBC_API_CONFORMANCE and SQL_ODBC_SQL_CONFORMANCE, but determining the driver level of conformance is not the primary goal of this chapter. Today you are more interested in subtle and not-so-subtle features and capabilities supported by the individual drivers within those conformance levels.

As the application developer, you really need to be aware of both the conformance levels and their restrictions and the distinguishable capabilities within individual functions. This will come mostly through experience in using the ODBC interface, as well as judicious use of the API references either through the Microsoft reference manual or the online help format API references.

Another consideration for the software developer is the version of ODBC being used. In the course of evolution of the ODBC standard, it is inevitable that some features of ODBC change or go away as they are replaced by newer and better features. The most evident change between ODBC version 1 and version 2 was the addition of many function calls and the addition of many info types to the SQLGetInfo call. This chapter minimizes these differences, assuming that most vendors will adopt the version 2 standards as soon as possible. When ODBC version 3 is published, the changes there will probably also need to be reviewed for future development work.

Querying for Specific Driver or Server Function

There are seven functions dedicated to either setting or retrieving information about a driver, a data source, or the current state of a connection to a data source. You learned the first of these, SQLGetTypeInfo, on Day 7, "Data Types."

There are two other sets of functions that are more difficult to classify. These consist of two retrieval functions, SQLGetConnectOption and SQLGetStmtOption, and their companion functions that change settings, SQLSetConnectOption and SQLSetStmtOption.

These are covered on Day 17, "Using ODBC Cursors," and Day 18, "Using Transactions and Commitment Control." These functions are difficult to classify because the `SQLSetStmtOption` function enables you to set a number of cursor control parameters, but also enables you to set the query time-out value, the maximum length of data returned in a column, and control asynchronous processing. All of the parameters queried and set by these four functions are covered in their respective chapters.

One of the remaining two functions is `SQLGetInfo`. This is probably the most powerful ODBC function in terms of determining the capabilities of any particular ODBC driver and data source. With the release of version 2.01 of the ODBC Software Development Kit (SDK), the `SQLGetInfo` call supports 115 different information types.

VB4

Syntax

The *SQLGetInfo* Function

The general syntax for the `SQLGetInfo` function in Visual Basic is

```
RETCODE SQLGetInfo(hDbc, fInfoType, rgbInfoValue, cbInfoValueMax, pcbInfoValue)
```

The function will return information specified by the `fInfoType` parameter about the driver and data source. The parameter `hDbc` is the handle for the connection being queried. The parameter `fInfoType` is the type of information being requested. These constant values are defined in the file ODBEXT_G.BI in the VBDEMO sample in the ODBC SDK. The parameter `rgbInfoValue` is a pointer cast as an integer which references the storage area receiving the output information. The information returning from the function will be either a 16-bit integer value, a 32-bit binary value, or a null-terminated character string, depending on the type of information requested. The parameter `cbInfoValueMax` is the maximum length of the `rgbInfoValue` buffer. The parameter `pcbInfoValue` is the number of bytes the function wants to return in `rgbInfoValue`. If this value is greater than the size of the buffer, the value returned is truncated.

The available values of `fInfoType` and their meaning is detailed in the following paragraphs. These are the same arguments for both Visual Basic and Visual C++, but not the same arguments for version 1 drivers and version 2 drivers, as noted. As new values are added for this function, they will be added to the ODBC SDK and documented by Microsoft on the ODBC forum on CompuServe—WINEXT, Section 10.

Example:

```
Dim cbOut As Integer          'Lengh of output data
   Dim rgbInfoValue As String    'Temporary for GetInfo response
   Dim cbMax As Long             'Length of output buffer

cbMax = 255                   'Initialize length of output buffer
```

```
rgbInfoValue = String$(255, 0)    'Allocate string & clear to bin zero
rc% = SQLGetInfo(hdbc, SQL_ODBC_VER, ByVal rgbInfoValue, cbMax, cbOutL)
```

> **Note:** SQLGetInfo is one of the few ODBC functions that actually passes a data type of PTR, or pointer. Because, as mentioned earlier, Visual Basic does not handle pointer data types, special attention is needed for this function. In particular, be certain that the function declaration in the include file ODBEXT_M.BI does not have the ByVal qualifier in front of the rgbInfoValue parameter. In addition, in the actual function call itself include the ByVal qualifier, as shown in the preceding example, if the result is to be a character string. If the result expected is to be a 32-bit binary value, leave off the ByVal qualifier in the function call. In this way, you are fooling Visual Basic into actually passing the pointer value rather than the value.

C++ Syntax

The *SQLGetInfo* Function

The prototype for the SQLGetInfo function is

```
RETCODE SQL_API SQLGetInfo(
    HDBC        hdbc,
    UWORD       fInfoType,
    PTR         rgbInfoValue,
    SWORD       cbInfoValueMax,
    SWORD  FAR *pcbInfoValue);
```

The function is used to get general information about the data source and its driver. The function parameters are as described in the preceding Visual Basic code fragment. The note regarding pointers does not apply when you use C++ because pointers are a known data type and are handled appropriately in the C++ environment.

The SQLGetInfo function will return a pointer to the field rgbInfoValue. The value of rgbInfoValue, referred to by this pointer, can be in any of five formats, depending on the type of data requested. These formats include

- ☐ A null-terminated character string
- ☐ A 32-bit bitmask
- ☐ A 16-bit integer
- ☐ A 32-bit integer
- ☐ A 32-bit binary field

Not all information types are valid for all versions of ODBC. In the following paragraphs listing the various information types, the ODBC version follows the rgbInfoValue in parentheses. If the information type is inappropriate for the driver version or is not supported by the driver, the SQLGetInfo function will return SQL_ERROR. A subsequent call to SQLError will return the SQLSTATES of S1C00 (driver not capable) or S1096 (invalid argument value) in such cases.

The following sections provide a description of the various rgbInfoValues, including those defined in ODBC version 2.01. Each description includes the purpose of the information returned and possible values that can be returned, as well as the type of return expected. These rgbInfoValues are grouped by type of information provided.

Driver Information

The following twenty-one fInfoType values used with SQLGetInfo will return data specifically related to the ODBC driver itself. The different versions of ODBC are denoted by (1.0) or (2.0).

SQL_ACTIVE_CONNECTIONS (1.0)

This is the maximum number of active connections that the driver can support, expressed as a 16-bit integer value. In this context, a *connection* is an active connection using its own hdbc connection handle. This limitation can be imposed by either the data source or the driver. If the limit is unknown or there is no limit, a zero value is returned.

SQL_ACTIVE_STATEMENTS (1.0)

This is the maximum number of active statements that the driver can support for any active connection. Each active statement is represented by an hstmt handle, whereas each active connection is represented by an hdbc handle. This 16-bit integer value can be imposed by either the data source or the driver. If no limit is imposed, or is unknown, this value returns zero. It is important to note that a statement is still considered active as long as result set rows have not been fetched.

SQL_DATA_SOURCE_NAME (1.0)

This is the data source name used during a connection, returned as a character string. If the connection was made using the SQLConnect function, the value of szDSN is returned. If the connection was made with SQLDriverConnect or SQLBrowseConnect, the DSN attribute value is returned if the DSN keyword was used. If the DSN keyword was not used (for example, because the DRIVER keyword is used instead), this value will be an empty string.

SQL_DRIVER_HDBC (1.0)

This is the 32-bit driver's connection handle, used in hdbc.

SQL_DRIVER_HENV (1.0)

This is the 32-bit driver's environment handle. This value is implemented by the Driver Manager.

SQL_DRIVER_HLIB (2.0)

This is the 32-bit handle of the driver library. This handle is returned to the Driver Manager when it loads the driver DLL and is specific to the hdbc used in this call to SQLGetInfo.

SQL_DRIVER_HSTMT (1.0)

This is the 32-bit handle of the driver's statement. This will not be the same as the Driver Manager's statement handle seen by the application, which must be passed as input to SQLGetInfo in the rgbInfoValue parameter. The input value is the handle given to the application by the Driver Manager, the output value is the handle given to the Driver Manager by the driver.

SQL_DRIVER_NAME (1.0)

This is the filename of the driver, returned as a character string. This filename is not the same as the driver used in the connection functions. For instance, in the case of the Watcom driver used in some examples in this book, the driver parameter as defined in the ODBCINST.INI file and used in the DRIVER keyword is "WATCOM SQL". The data source name used in these examples is "WATCOM_SAMPLE". The value return from the SQLGetInfo call for SQL_DRIVER_NAME is "WSQLODBC.DLL".

SQL_DRIVER_ODBC_VER (2.0)

This is a character string in the form ##.## designating the version of ODBC that the driver supports. (Note: this is the driver, not the Driver Manager.) The first two digits of the string are the major version, defined as SQL_SPEC_MAJOR, and the last two digits are the minor version, defined as SQL_SPEC_MINOR. If the driver does not support this fInfoType, the Driver Manager will return "01.00". This value is much more meaningful in determining functionality than the similar fInfoType called SQL_ODBC_VER, which returns the ODBC version supported by the Driver Manager. If the Driver Manager is a higher level than the driver itself, you will get very few of the new features because most functionality comes from the driver itself.

SQL_DRIVER_VER (1.0)

This is a character string of the form ##.##.#### designating the version of the driver. This version number can be followed by a description of the driver. In a fashion similar to SQL_DRIVER_ODBC_VER, the first two digits are the major version, the middle two digits are the minor version, and the last four digits are the release number. This driver version number has nothing to do with, and should not be confused with, the ODBC version it supports. In other words, the DB2 ODBC driver from Fred's Software Emporium, version 2, might or might not support ODBC version 2 features. The release number for some products seems to represent a build date rather than an incremental build or release count. Typically, this build or release date is derived by doing MOD 12 division on the first two digits of the release; the result is the month, and the last two digits are the day of that month.

SQL_FETCH_DIRECTION (1.0)

This is a 32-bit bitmask enumerating all of the fetch directions supported by a SQLExtendedFetch call to this driver. The means of each fetch direction are given in the SQLExtendedFetch description on Day 17, "Using ODBC Cursors." The following values have defined bitmasks:

```
SQL_FD_FETCH_NEXT
SQL_FD_FETCH_FIRST
SQL_FD_FETCH_LAST
SQL_FD_FETCH_PRIOR
SQL_FD_FETCH_ABSOLUTE
SQL_FD_FETCH_RELATIVE
SQL_FD_FETCH_RESUME
SQL_FD_FETCH_BOOKMARK
```

The value for SQL_FD_FETCH_RESUME became obsolete for ODBC Version 2.0. The value for SQL_FD_FETCH_BOOKMARK was first introduced with ODBC Version 2.0. If SQL_FD_FETCH_RESUME is used with a version 2.0 driver or SQL_FD_FETCH_BOOKMARK is used with a version 1.0 driver, an error will result.

SQL_FILE_USAGE (2.0)

This is a 16-bit integer value indicating how files are to be viewed in a data source. This information type was added to clarify the usage of filenames in single-tier drivers. Often in such drivers, the data is not stored in a relational database model, but rather as indexed sequential access (ISAM) files. The ODBC single-tier driver then reads this file and presents its data to the application as if it were stored in a relational database. In such a model, the data is contained in individual tables, which in turn are contained in databases. In the standard naming convention, the database can be given as a qualifier to the table name because the table is "within" a database. This information type specifies whether individual files are to be treated as individual tables or as databases or systems, which are qualifiers of the individual tables contained within. The following are the defined values:

- SQL_FILE_NOT_SUPPORTED. The driver does not support the use of files as a single-tier driver. For example, a SQL Server driver is not a single-tier driver.

- SQL_FILE_TABLE. The driver treats each file as an individual table. Typically, an application using such a driver would present a standard File Open dialog box to select data, such as is the case with a dBASE driver.

- SQL_FILE_QUALIFIER. The driver treats files as if they contained multiple tables; the filename is a qualifier of the internal table names. An application using files in this manner, as Access does, would have to present a custom Select Table dialog box for data selection.

SQL_GETDATA_EXTENSIONS (2.0)

This is a 32-bit bitmask enumerating allowable extensions to or variations from the SQLGetData rules. Without these extensions, SQLGetData can retrieve data only from rowsets containing just one row, and the data must come from columns, in column order, to the right of the last bound column. These restrictions obviously limit functionality, particularly where the use of cursors returning multirow result sets is involved. For maximum interoperability, these extensions should be avoided, but when available they can make the developer's life easier. The following are the defined extensions:

- SQL_GD_ANY_ORDER. SQLGetData can be called to get data from columns to the right of the last bound column in any order rather than in left to right order. To get column data in any order and from any column, including those prior to the last bound column, this value and SQL_GD_ANY_COLUMN must both be returned.

- SQL_GD_ANY_COLUMN. SQLGetData can be called for any unbound column, including those before the last bound column. Column data must still be retrieved in left to right order unless SQL_GD_ANY_ORDER is also returned.

- SQL_GD_BLOCK. SQLGetData can be called for an unbound column in a cursor or a block of more than one row in the result set. Before returning data for the specified column, the row must be specified by calling SQLSetPos.

- SQL_GD_BOUND. SQLGetData can be called for both bound and unbound columns. Any driver supporting this feature will return this value and SQL_GD_ANY_COLUMN.

SQL_LOCK_TYPES (2.0)

This is a 32-bit bitmask value enumerating which lock types are supported by the driver and data source when the code uses the SQLSetPos function. The meaning and function of the lock types are explained on Day 17. The lock type values currently defined are

```
SQL_LCK_NO_CHANGE
SQL_LCK_EXLUSIVE
SQL_LCK_UNLOCK
```

SQL_ODBC_API_CONFORMANCE (1.0)

This is a 16-bit integer value specifying what level of ODBC conformance is provided by the driver. In order to claim conformance to either Level 1 or 2, the driver must support all of the functionality described for that level. These levels and the functionality they provide was described on Day 2. The defined values are

- ☐ SQL_OAC_NONE—Neither level is fully supported.
- ☐ SQL_OAC_LEVEL1—Level 1 functions are fully supported.
- ☐ SQL_OAC_LEVEL2—Level 2 functions are fully supported.

SQL_ODBC_SAG_CLI_CONFORMANCE (1.0)

This is a 16-bit integer value indicating whether the driver complies with the functions of the SAG specifications. If the driver is not compliant, it does not support one or more of the core functions. It is very unusual to find a driver in commercial use that does not provide the core functionality. The only values defined are

```
SQL_OSCC_NOT_COMPLIANT
SQL_OSCC_COMPLIANT
```

SQL_ODBC_VER (1.0)

This is a character string of the form ##.## designating the version of ODBC to which the Driver Manager conforms. The first two digits are the major version number, and the last two digits are the minor version number. Remember that a version 1 Driver Manager cannot pass new function calls through to a version 2 driver, but more importantly, a version 2 Driver Manager cannot provide version 2 functionality for a version 1 driver.

SQL_POS_OPERATIONS (2.0)

This is a 32-bit bitmask enumerating which of the possible positioned operations in an `SQLSetPos` function are supported by the driver and data source. The specifics of each operation's meaning is detailed in the `SQLSetPos` function, covered on Day 17. The defined values for this information type are

```
SQL_POS_POSITION
SQL_POS_REFRESH
SQL_POS_UPDATE
SQL_POS_DELETE
SQL_POS_ADD
```

SQL_ROW_UPDATES (1.0)

This is a character string designating whether a keyset driver or mixed cursor can detect changes to the row. If this `fInfoType` returns `"Y"`, it means changes since the last fetch can be detected by means of row versions or values maintained by the cursor. If detecting changes is not possible the value returned is `"N"`.

SQL_SEARCH_PATTERN_ESCAPE (1.0)

This is a character string indicating what character the driver supports as an escape character, enabling the programmer to use the standard percent (`"%"`) and underscore (`"_"`) metacharacters and as both literal characters and as operators in search patterns. The underscore metacharacter (_) is used in a search pattern to represent any single character in that position. Because the underscore is commonly also used as an actual character in table and column names, without the search pattern escape character there is an opportunity for error. If a search pattern of `"SALES_TAB"` were specified in a catalog function, the underscore would be interpreted as a metacharacter, properly returning `"SALES1TAB"`, `"SALES_TAB"`, and `"SALES-TAB"`. If you wanted only the `"SALES_TAB"` entry, you could get it by adding the escape character to give `"SALES~_TAB"` assuming you used a tilde (~) as the escape character.

SQL_SERVER_NAME (1.0)

This is a character string with the actual server name, which is data source-specific. This parameter seems to be implemented irratically; a Q+E Excel driver returns an empty string, a Microsoft Desktop Access driver returns the string `"ACCESS"`, and a Watcom driver returns the same string as the data source name.

DBMS Product Information

The three fInfoTypes explained in the following sections return either specific information about the underlying DBMS product, or, in single-tier drivers, information about the source of the data.

SQL_DATABASE_NAME (1.0)

This is a character string containing the name of the database in use if an object called database has been defined by this data source. This information type was introduced in ODBC version 1.0, and has been replaced in version 2.0 by the fInfoType SQL_CURRENT_QUALIFIER. Applications written to the ODBC 2.0 standard should use this information type only when they access ODBC version 1.0 drivers.

SQL_DBMS_NAME (1.0)

This is a character string with the name of the DBMS product accessed by the current driver. In the case of single-tier drivers accessing an ISAM file, SQL_DBMS_NAME will usually return the name of the product that created the file.

SQL_DBMS_VER (1.0)

This is a character string indicating the product version of the DBMS product accessed by the current driver. This version number is supposed to be of the form ##.##.####, but this standard is not well followed. For example, the Microsoft Desktop driver for Access returns the string "1.1".

Data Source Information

The following fInfoType values provide information about the specific capabilities and features of the data source being used.

SQL_ACCESSIBLE_PROCEDURES (1.0)

This is a character string indicating whether or not the user can execute all of the procedures enumerated by an SQLProcedures call. Returns a value of "Y" if the user can execute all procedures, "N" if the user cannot.

SQL_ACCESSIBLE_TABLE (1.0)

SQL_ACCESSIBLE_TABLE is a character string that indicates whether or not the user has rights to read all of the tables returned by SQLTables. It returns a value of "Y" if the user can SELECT from all tables, "N" if the user cannot.

SQL_BOOKMARK_PERSISTENCE (2.0)

This is a 32-bit bitmask enumerating the conditions under which a bookmark will persist. The following are the defined values:

☐ SQL_BP_CLOSE. Bookmarks are valid after the statement has been freed with a call to SQLFreeStmt using the SQL_CLOSE option.

☐ SQL_BP_DROP. Bookmarks are valid after the statement has been freed with a call to SQLFreeStmt using the SQL_DROP option.

☐ SQL_BP_DELETE. The bookmark for a particular row remains valid after that row has been deleted.

☐ SP_BP_SCROLL. This value is misnamed or misdesigned. It is said to indicate whether bookmarks are valid after any scrolling call to SQLExtendedFetch. However, by definition, all bookmarks must remain valid after scrolling calls to SQLExtendedFetch. For that reason, this value can be used to determine if the data source supports bookmarks.

☐ SQL_BP_TRANSACTION. Bookmarks are valid after a transaction is ended with a commit or rollback operation.

☐ SQL_BP_UPDATE. The bookmark for a row remains valid after update operations have been performed on any column in that row, including key and bookmark columns.

☐ SQL_BP_OTHER_HSTMT. A bookmark associated with one statement through its handle, hstmt, can be used with other statements.

SQL_CONCAT_NULL_BEHAVIOR (1.0)

This is a 16-bit integer value indicating how the data source handles the concatenation of NULL valued character columns with other character typed columns containing non-NULL values. In this and all contexts when referring to character data types, NULL values are not the same as empty character strings. The following are the two defined values for this information type:

☐ SQL_CB_NULL. The result is NULL.

☐ SQL_CB_NON_NULL. The result is a concatenation of a non-NULL valued column or columns. In this case, the value is the same as if the NULL valued column was not mentioned in the concatenation statement.

SQL_CURSOR_COMMIT_BEHAVIOR and *SQL_CURSOR_ROLLBACK_BEHAVIOR* (1.0)

A 16-bit integer value indicating how the data source handles a cursor and/or its associated prepared statement following a COMMIT or ROLLBACK operation. The behavior of a data source on both COMMIT and ROLLBACK operations can cause many problems if the cursor is not preserved. For instance, if an application is trying to perform positioned updates against a single row at a time of a multirow cursor, having the cursor go away after the first update negates much of the value of having the cursor in the first place.

The following are the defined values, which apply for both info types:

☐ SQL_CB_DELETE. Close cursors and delete any prepared statements. To use this cursor again, the application must reprepare and re-execute the statement on this hstmt handle.

☐ SQL_CB_CLOSE. Close cursors, but do not delete the associated prepared statement. An application can call SQLExecute again on the same hstmt without needing to call SQLPrepare another time.

☐ SQL_CB_PRESERVE. Preserve the cursors in the same position and state as before the COMMIT or ROLLBACK operation was performed. This is the preferred cursor state; it enables the application to continue processing data within the cursor without interruption, or the cursor can be closed and the statement re-executed without repreparation.

SQL_DATA_SOURCE_READ_ONLY (1.0)

A character string. The value "Y" indicates that the data source itself, not just the driver, is set to READ ONLY mode. Otherwise, a value of "N" is returned.

SQL_DEFAULT_TXN_ISOLATION (1.0)

This is a 32-bit integer value indicating the driver or data source's default transaction isolation level. If the data source does not support transactions, a value of zero is returned. To determine the highest level of isolation possible, use the fInfoType of SQL_TXN_ISOLATION_OPTION. A common set of terms is used to define conditions encountered requiring transaction isolation. These terms are the following:

☐ DIRTY READ. Transaction A changes the data in a row. Transaction B reads the changed row before Transaction A commits the change. If the transaction is rolled back in A, then Transaction B will have data that in effect never existed.

☐ PHANTOM. Transaction A reads a set of rows according to a search criteria. Transaction B then inserts a row that matches the search criteria used in

Transaction A. If Transaction A re-executes its read statement, it will receive a different set of rows.

- [ ] NONREPEATABLE READ. Transaction A reads a row. Transaction B then changes or deletes that row. If Transaction A attempts to reread the row, it will receive a row that has a value that has changed, or the row will not exist.

All three of the preceding conditions are considered to have a negative effect on data integrity. The different levels of transaction isolation will prevent some or all of these conditions from occurring. The bitmap values returned indicate which conditions are possible.

- [ ] SQL_TXN_READ_UNCOMMITTED. Dirty reads, nonrepeatable reads, and phantoms are possible.
- [ ] SQL_TXN_READ_COMMITTED. Dirty reads are not possible. Nonrepeatable reads and phantoms are possible.
- [ ] SQL_TXN_REPEATABLE_READ. Dirty reads and nonrepeatable reads are not possible. Phantoms are possible.
- [ ] SQL_TXN_SERIALIZABLE. Transactions can be serialized. Dirty reads, nonrepeatable reads, and phantoms are not possible. Serialized transactions are usually implemented using locking protocols that reduce concurrency.
- [ ] SQL_TXN_VERSIONING. Transactions can be serialized, but higher concurrency is possible than with SQL_TXN_SERIALIZABLE. This is implemented using a non-locking protocol such as record versioning as seen with Oracle's Read Consistency.

SQL_MULT_RESULT_SETS (1.0)

This is a character string that has a value of "Y" if the data supports multiple result sets. Otherwise, the value will be "N". Generally, SQL_MULT_RESULT_SETS refers to having multiple result sets for one hstmt.

SQL_MULTIPLE_ACTIVE_TXN (1.0)

This is a character string that has a value of "Y" if the data source can have more than one connection with an active transaction at the same time. The value is "N" if only one connection can be active at a time. Contrast this fInfoType with SQL_ACTIVE_STATEMENTS and SQL_ACTIVE_CONNECTIONS.

SQL_NEED_LONG_DATA_LEN (2.0)

This is a character string that has a value of "Y" if the data source needs to receive the length of a long data value before the value is actually sent to the data source. The value "N" denotes that the length is not needed (or long data types are not supported). The SQL_LEN_DATA_AT_EXEC macro can be used to pass the length information.

SQL_NULL_COLLATION (2.0)

This is a 16-bit integer value specifying where fields containing a NULL value are sorted in a list. The following are the defined values:

- ☐ SQL_NC_START. NULLs are sorted at the beginning of the list, regardless of the sort order of the data source.
- ☐ SQL_NC_END. NULLs are sorted at the end of the list, regardless of the sort order of the data source.
- ☐ SQL_NC_LOW. NULLs are sorted at the low end of the list.
- ☐ SQL_NC_HIGH. NULLs are sorted at the high end of the list.

SQL_OWNER_TERM (1.0)

This is a character string with the data source vendor's name that corresponds to the ODBC concept of table owner. For example, SQL Server returns "owner", and Watcom returns "Creator".

SQL_PROCEDURE_TERM (1.0)

This is a character string with the data source vendor's name that corresponds to the ODBC concept of procedure.

SQL_QUALIFIER_TERM (1.0)

A character string with the data source vendor's name that corresponds to the ODBC concept of qualifier. In typical ODBC usage, tables are named with a three-part name. The three parts are the qualifier, owner, and table. This fInfoType helps to map between the vendor's terminology and the ODBC terminology.

SQL_SCROLL_CONCURRENCY (1.0)

A 32-bit bitmask enumerating the options possible to enable concurrent operations in this driver's scrollable cursor. The following list of values indicates which options are supported:

- ☐ SQL_SCCO_READ_ONLY. The cursor is read-only. Because updates or deletes are not allowed with this cursor, concurrent change operations need not be serialized.

- ☐ SQL_SCCO_LOCK. The cursor uses pessimistic concurrency control by using locking of the row to ensure it can be updated. Generally, the lowest possible level of locking will be used.

- ☐ SQL_SCCO_OPT_ROWVER. The cursor uses optimistic concurrency control utilizing a row version value to determine if the row has changed between the time the cursor was created and an update is attempted. A row version is typically a value of a specific data type such as TIMESTAMP that, by definition, guarantees uniqueness.

- ☐ SQL_SCCO_OPT_VALUES. The cursor uses optimistic concurrency control. The cursor is not locked, but when an update is requested the values in the cursor are checked against the same row in the table. If the values do not agree, the row has been changed, and the current update fails.

SQL_SCROLL_OPTIONS (1.0)

This is a 32-bit bitmask enumerating the scroll options supported by this driver. The defined values and their release version are

- ☐ SQL_SO_STATIC (2.0). The data in the result set is static, meaning changes in the underlying tables will not be seen. This is implemented by either taking a *snapshot* of the data, which means the data in the table can change but the changes are not reflected in the cursor, or the table is locked so that no changes can occur.

- ☐ SQL_SO_DYNAMIC (1.0). The cursor presents the data as dynamic, or always current to the underlying table. Rows that are updated, deleted, or inserted by all users and the cursor are detected by the cursor when data is next fetched.

- ☐ SQL_SO_KEYSET_DRIVEN (1.0). Representing a middle ground between static and dynamic cursors, the keyset-driven cursor gets an ordered list of all keys in a result set when the cursor is opened. When the cursor scrolls to any row in the data, the values are updated from the table. If the row has been deleted, a blank or hole is shown because the key value is retained the entire time the cursor is open. If a row is inserted it is not seen until the cursor is closed and reopened.

☐ SQL_SO_MIXED (1.0). A combination of dynamic and keyset-driven cursors, used for large tables where it is not practical to maintain a list of all key values. Values are shown as a keyset cursor within the boundaries of the keyset, but act as a dynamic cursor when scrolling outside the keyset.

☐ SQL_SO_FORWARD_ONLY (1.0). The cursor only scrolls forward.

SQL_STATIC_SENSITIVITY (2.0)

This is a 32-bit bitmask enumerating whether certain changes made by an application can be detected by that same application. The cursor type determines whether or not changes made by other applications can be detected. To be detected by the changing application, the changes must be made to a static or keyset-driven cursor either through SQLSetPos or by positioned update or delete statements. The following are the defined values:

☐ SQL_SS_ADDITIONS. Rows added by this cursor can be seen and scrolled to by this cursor. The location of the added rows in the cursor is driver-dependent.

☐ SQL_SS_DELETIONS. Deleted rows do not appear in the cursor and do not leave a hole where the row used to reside. Once a cursor scrolls away from a deleted row, it cannot return to the deleted row.

☐ SQL_SS_UPDATES. Updated data is visible to the cursor after the cursor scrolls away from the row and returns.

SQL_TABLE_TERM (1.0)

This is a character string containing the DBMS vendor's name for a table in the ODBC three-part naming convention.

SQL_TXN_CAPABLE (1.0)

This is a 16-bit integer value describing the transaction support provided by the driver and data source.

☐ SQL_TC_NONE (1.0). Transactions are not supported.

☐ SQL_TC_DML (1.0). Transactions are supported, but only for SQL Data Manipulation Language (DML) statements such as SELECT, INSERT, DELETE, and UPDATE. Any Data Definition Language (DDL) statements encountered will cause an error.

- [ ] `SQL_TC_DDL_COMMIT` (2.0). Transactions are supported for DML statements. If a transaction contains DDL statements (`CREATE TABLE`, `CREATE INDEX`, and so on), the transaction will be committed.
- [ ] `SQL_TC_DDL_IGNORE` (2.0). Transactions are supported for DML statements. If DDL statements are encountered in a transaction, they are ignored.
- [ ] `SQL_TC_ALL` (1.0). Transactions can contain intermixed DDL and DML statements.

SQL_TXN_ISOLATION_OPTION (1.0)

This is a 32-bit bitmask enumerating all of the transaction isolation levels supported by the driver or data source. These values are the same as those available and defined in the definition specified in `SQL_DEFAULT_TXN_ISOLATION`.

SQL_USER_NAME (1.0)

This is a character string containing the user name used in a particular database. This name can be blank or different from the login name.

Supported SQL

The following arguments return data used to determine if and how various parts of SQL are supported.

SQL_ALTER_TABLE (2.0)

This is a 32-bit bitmask used to find which clauses in the `ALTER TABLE` statement are supported by the data source. The following bitmasks are defined to specify the supported clauses:

- [ ] `SQL_AT_ADD_COLUMN`
- [ ] `SQL_AT_DROP_COLUMN`

SQL_COLUMN_ALIAS (2.0)

This is a character string containing `"Y"` if the data source supports column aliases, `"N"` if not.

SQL_CORRELATION_NAME (1.0)

This is a 16-bit integer indicating whether table correlation names are supported. Table correlation names are often used as table aliases within an SQL statement to shorten the reference and clarify the statement. The following are the values defined to indicate if correlation names are supported:

- ☐ SQL_CN_NONE. Correlation names are not supported.
- ☐ SQL_CN_DIFFERENT. Correlation names are supported, but the correlation name must be different from the table name it represents.
- ☐ SQL_CN_ANY. Correlation names are fully supported.

SQL_EXPRESSIONS_IN_ORDERBY (1.0)

This is a character string containing "Y" if the data source supports the use of expressions in an ORDER BY list, "N" if not supported. An example of such a statement would be

```
select cust_name from custfile order by (tot_billing - amt_paid)
```

SQL_GROUP_BY (2.0)

This is a 16-bit integer value specifying how the data source will accept columns that are specified in the GROUP BY clause and that should or should not be specified in the non-aggregated columns select list. The following are the defined values:

- ☐ SQL_GB_NOT_SUPPORTED. GROUP BY clauses are not supported by this data source.
- ☐ SQL_GB_GROUP_BY_EQUALS_SELECT. The GROUP BY clause must contain all non-aggregate columns that are in the select list, but cannot contain any other columns. An example would be

  ```
  select avg(length),title from song group by title
  ```

- ☐ SQL_GB_GROUP_BY_CONTAINS_SELECT. The GROUP BY clause must contain all non-aggregate columns that are in the select list, and it can contain other columns not being selected. For example,

  ```
  select avg(length),title from song group by title,composer
  ```

- ☐ SQL_GB_NO_RELATION. The columns specified in the select list and the GROUP BY clause have no relation to each other. The data source determines the meaning of non-aggregate, non-grouped columns in the select list. For example,

  ```
  select length,title from song group by composer,type
  ```

SQL_IDENTIFIER_CASE (1.0)

This is a 16-bit integer value specifying how identifiers such as column and table names are stored and matched. The following are the defined values:

- ☐ SQL_IC_UPPER. Identifiers in SQL are case-insensitive and are stored in the system catalog in uppercase.
- ☐ SQL_IC_LOWER. Identifiers in SQL are case-insensitive and are stored in the system catalog in lowercase.
- ☐ SQL_IC_SENSITIVE. Identifiers in SQL are case-sensitive and are stored in the system catalog in mixed case.
- ☐ SQL_IC_MIXED. Identifiers in SQL are case-insensitive and are stored in the system catalog in mixed case.

SQL_IDENTIFIER_QUOTE_CHARACTER (1.0)

This is a character string containing the starting and ending delimiter of a quoted (delimited) identifier in an SQL statement. If the data source does not support quoted identifiers, a blank is returned. This feature is typically needed to protect an embedded space or special within a name. Examples of such quoted identifiers might be 'first name', 'A.COL', or 'ABC*DEF' (assuming here that the quote character is the single quote).

SQL_KEYWORDS (2.0)

This is a character string containing a comma-separated list of all data-source specific SQL keywords. This list does not contain ODBC-specific keywords or keywords shared by the data source and ODBC, but rather keywords specific to the data source. For example, Microsoft's SQL Server lists many words, including BULK, BROWSE, and COMPUTE.

SQL_LIKE_ESCAPE_CLAUSE (2.0)

This is a character string containing "Y" if the data source supports an escape character for the percent character (%) and underscore character (_) in a LIKE predicate and the driver supports the ODBC syntax for defining a LIKE predicate escape character. If the data source does not meet this criteria, an "N" is returned. See the fInfoType SQL_SEARCH_PATTERN_ESCAPE for an explanation of how escape characters are used in a LIKE predicate for searching.

SQL_NON_NULLABLE_COLUMNS (1.0)

This is a 16-bit integer specifying whether the data source supports non-nullable columns. Specifying a column to be not nullable is a useful data integrity constraint, ensuring that data is entered. In some drivers, such as the ShowCase driver for the AS/400, setting columns to non-nullable will enhance performance. The defined values for this fInfoType are

- [ ] SQL_NNC_NULL. All columns must be nullable.
- [ ] SQL_NNC_NON_NULL. Columns can be non-nullable. In this, case the data source will enable and support the NOT NULL column constraint in a CREATE TABLE statement.

SQL_ODBC_SQL_CONFORMANCE (1.0)

This is a 16-bit integer that has a value that indicates the level of SQL grammar supported by the driver. The defined values are

- [ ] SQL_OSC_MINIMUM. The minimum grammar supported.
- [ ] SQL_OSC_CORE. The core grammar supported.
- [ ] SQL_OSC_EXTENDED. The extended grammar supported. (This generally means some extended grammar is supported, but rarely is all extended grammar supported.)

SQL_ODBC_SQL_OPT_IEF (1.0)

This is a character string containing "Y" if the data source supports the optional Integrity Enhancement Facility (IEF). This string will be "N" if IEF is not supported.

SQL_ORDER_BY_COLUMNS_IN_SELECT (2.0)

This is a character string containing "Y" if the columns used in an ORDER BY clause must also be in the select list. If not, this value will be "N". For example, if the value is "N", the following statement should be supported:

```
select SongID,Title from Song order by Composer_1
```

In this case, the field Composer_1 is used for ordering the result set but is not returned to the application in the result set.

SQL_OUTER_JOINS

This is a character string containing a single character that indicates whether and how a data source supports outer joins. Defined values and their version of introduction are

- [ ] "N" (1.0). No. The data source does not support any outer joins.

- [ ] "Y" (1.0). Yes. The data source supports outer joins between two tables, and the ODBC driver supports the standard ODBC outer join SQL syntax except for nested outer joins, which are not supported. However, the syntax is limited in that the columns on the left-hand side of the comparison operator in the ON clause must come from the table specified first in the join (the "left" table), and the columns on the right side of the comparison operator must come from the right-hand table.

- [ ] "P" (2.0). Partial. Data source support of outer joins is similar to the "Y" case in the preceding entry, and nested outer joins are also supported. As above, columns on the left side of the comparison operator in the ON clause must come from the left-hand table and columns on the right of the comparison operator must come from the right-hand table. Additionally, the right-hand table of an outer join cannot be included in an inner join.

- [ ] "F" (2.0). Full. The data source fully supports nested outer joins and the driver fully supports ODBC outer join syntax.

SQL_OWNER_USAGE (2.0)

This is a 32-bit bitmask enumerating the statements in which owners can be used. Generally, owners are used in these statements as further table qualification, and if not specified the current or default owner is used. For clarification on how the owner term is defined, see the SQL_OWNER_ITEM entry. Defined values include:

- [ ] SQL_OU_DML_STATEMENTS. Owners are supported in all Data Manipulation Language statements: SELECT, INSERT, UPDATE, DELETE, and, if supported, SELECT FOR UPDATE and positioned DELETE and UPDATE statements.

- [ ] SQL_OU_TABLE_DEFINITION. Owner terms are supported in all table definition statements, such as CREATE TABLE, CREATE VIEW, ALTER TABLE, DROP TABLE, and DROP VIEW.

- [ ] SQL_OU_PRIVILEGE_DEFINITION. Owners are supported as qualification in all privilege definition statements, such as GRANT and REVOKE.

- [ ] SQL_OU_PROCEDURE_INVOCATION. Owner terms are supported in an ODBC procedure invocation statement.

SQL_POSITIONED_STATEMENTS (2.0)

This is a 32-bit bitmask enumerating the positioned SQL statements that are supported by the data source. The fInfoType SQL_POS_OPERATIONS, detailed earlier, described how to determine the positioned statement capability of the driver. This info type specifies which SQL statements are supported when using that functionality. The defined bitmask values are

```
SQL_PS_POSITIONED_UPDATE
SQL_PS_POSITIONED_DELETE
SQL_PS_SELECT_FOR_UPDATE
```

SQL_PROCEDURES (1.0)

This is a character string containing `"Y"` if the data source supports procedures and the driver supports the ODBC procedure invocation syntax. If not supported, an `"N"` is returned. A procedure is a generic term defining an executable object. The `SQLProcedures` function can be called to determine which procedures are defined to and supported by a driver.

SQL_QUALIFIER_LOCATION (2.0)

This is a 16-bit integer value indicating whether a qualifier in a qualified table name is before or after the table name. For example, a dBASE driver would return `SQL_QL_START` because the table name includes the directory, as in D:\TYODBC\CDS.DBF. On the other hand, Oracle drivers would return the qualifier at the end of the table name because a similar qualified table name would be MUSIC.SONGS@TYODBC. The defined values are

```
SQL_QL_START
SQL_QL_END
```

SQL_QUALIFIER_NAME_SEPARATOR (1.0)

This is a character string containing the character or characters that are defined by the data source to be used between the qualifier name and the qualified name.

SQL_QUALIFIER_USAGE (2.0)

This is a 32-bit bitmask enumerating the statements in which qualifiers can be used. The definitions for these bitmasks is earlier in `SQL_OWNER_USAGE`. The defined bitmasks for this `fInfoType` are

```
SQL_QU_DML_STATEMENTS
SQL_QU_TABLE_DEFINITION
```

```
SQL_QU_INDEX_DEFINTION

SQL_QU_PROCEDURE_INVOCATION
```

SQL_QUOTED_IDENTIFIER_CASE (2.0)

This is a 16-bit integer value that specifies how case is treated with quoted identifiers. It is not uncommon to see unquoted qualifiers that are case-insensitive and quoted identifiers that become case-sensitive. The defined values are the same as those used with fInfoType SQL_IDENTIFIER_CASE, with the exception that they refer to the quoted identifier. The defined values are

```
SQL_IC_UPPER

SQL_IC_LOWER

SQL_IC_SENSITIVE

SQL_IC_MIXED
```

SQL_SPECIAL_CHARACTERS (2.0)

This is a character string containing all special characters that can be used in the name of any object in the database, such as a table name, column name, or index name. Special characters include all characters other than the lower- and uppercase alphabets and numerals 0 through 9. Some data sources such as the AS/400 enable different special characters in object names between the American and foreign language versions of the DBMS.

SQL_SUBQUERIES (2.0)

This is a 32-bit bitmask enumerating the predicates that support the specification of subqueries. The bitmasks defined include

```
SQL_SQ_COMPARISON

SQL_SQ_EXISTS

SQL_SQ_IN

SQL_SQ_QUANTIFIED

SQL_SQ_CORRELATED_SUBQUERIES
```

The SQL_SQ_CORRELATED_SUBQUERIES bitmask indicates that all predicates that support subqueries also support correlated subqueries.

SQL_UNION (2.0)

This is a 32-bit bitmask enumerating whether the data source supports the ALL keyword in the UNION clause. The defined values are

☐ SQL_U_UNION. The data source supports the UNION clause.

☐ SQL_U_UNION_ALL. The data source supports the use of the ALL keyword in the UNION clause.

SQL Limits

The following 19 fInfoTypes are used to learn about maximums applied as limits to clauses and identifiers within SQL statements. These limits can be imposed by either the driver or the data source. Note that for brevity, the fInfoType and its meaning are listed in this section similarly to the way individual defined values were specified earlier. As earlier, the ODBC version in which the fInfoType was introduced is listed in parentheses before its definition. Generally, if there is no specified limit or the limit is unknown, the value returned will be zero.

SQL_MAX_BINARY_LITERAL_LEN (2.0). A 32-bit integer value specifying the maximum number of hexadecimal characters of a binary literal in an SQL statement. For example, the binary literal value 0xF12AA4 has a length of 6.

SQL_MAX_CHAR_LITERAL_LEN (2.0). A 32-bit integer value specifying the maximum number of characters allowed in a character literal in an SQL statement.

SQL_MAX_COLUMN_NAME_LEN (1.0). A 16-bit integer value specifying the maximum length of a column name in the data source.

SQL_MAX_COLUMNS_IN_GROUP_BY (2.0). A 16-bit integer specifying the maximum number of columns that can be included in a GROUP BY clause.

SQL_MAX_COLUMNS_IN_INDEX (2.0). A 16-bit integer specifying the maximum number of columns that can be included in a composite index.

SQL_MAX_COLUMNS_IN_ORDER_BY (2.0). A 16-bit integer specifying the maximum number of columns allowed in an ORDER BY clause.

SQL_MAX_COLUMNS_IN_SELECT (2.0). A 16-bit integer value specifying the maximum number of columns that can be specified in a select list.

SQL_MAX_COLUMNS_IN_TABLE (2.0). A 16-bit integer value specifying the maximum number of columns that can be defined in a table.

SQL_MAX_CURSOR_NAME_LEN (1.0). A 16-bit integer value specifying the maximum length of a cursor name in a data source.

SQL_MAX_INDEX_SIZE (2.0). A 32-bit integer value specifying the maximum number of bytes allowed in the combined fields of a composite index.

SQL_MAX_OWNER_NAME_LEN (1.0). A 16-bit integer value specifying the maximum length of an owner name as used in the data source.

SQL_MAX_PROCEDURE_NAME_LEN (1.0). A 16-bit integer value specifying the maximum length of a procedure name in the data source.

SQL_MAX_QUALIFIER_NAME_LEN (1.0). A 16-bit integer value specifying the maximum length of a qualifier name as used in the data source.

SQL_MAX_ROW_SIZE (2.0). A 32-bit integer value specifying the maximum length of a single row in a table. This is not necessarily the maximum result set row size.

SQL_MAX_ROW_SIZE_INCLUDES_LONG (2.0). A character containing "Y" if the maximum row size returned for the fInfoType SQL_MAX_ROW_SIZE includes the length of all variable-length data type columns in the row. If not, the value "N" is returned.

SQL_MAX_STATEMENT_LEN (2.0). A 32-bit integer value specifying the maximum number of characters, including white space, allowed in a single SQL statement.

SQL_MAX_TABLE_NAME_LEN (1.0). A 16-bit integer value specifying the maximum length of a table name as used in the data source.

SQL_MAX_TABLES_IN_SELECT (2.0). A 16-bit integer value specifying the maximum number of tables that can be used in the FROM clause of a SELECT statement.

SQL_MAX_USER_NAME_LEN (2.0). A 16-bit integer value specifying the maximum length of a user name as used in the data source.

Scalar Function and Conversion Information

The SQLGetInfo function can also be used to obtain details about which scalar functions and conversion functions are available. Details concerning these fInfoTypes and the functions they refer to are provided on Day 16, "Using ODBC Functions."

Querying for Specific Index Information

Almost all DBMS systems support the use of indexes as a way to access a particular row or set of rows in a table without examining each row or scanning the table to determine which rows meet the selection criteria. Building cursors in some instances depends on whether indexes are present, so if there are no indexes, no cursor can be used, depending on the DBMS and driver being used. Even if cursors are not being used, using indexes can significantly improve performance.

Because indexes play such an important role in accessing data, it is important to be able to determine what indexes exist, and what their properties are. The ODBC functions `SQLStatistics` and `SQLSpecialColumns` are designed to meet this need.

Syntax

The *SQLStatistics* Function

The general syntax for the `SQLStatistics` function is

```
RETCODE SQLStatistics(hstmt,
                      szTableQualifier,
                      cbTableQualifier,
                      szTableOwner,
                      cbTableOwner,
                      szTableName,
                      cbTableName,
                      fUnique,
                      fAccuracy)
```

The `SQLStatistics` function is used to retrieve a list of statistics about a single table and the indexes associated with the table. The information is returned in the form of a result set.

The program in Listing 9.1 illustrates how this function can be used. It was written in C++ using MSVC 1.5 and was compiled as a QuickWin application.

Type

Listing 9.1. A sample C++ program using `SQLStatistics`.

```
1: // Test Program for SQLStatistics
2: // Compiled using MSVC++ 1.5 as a QuickWin Program
3: #include <afxdb.h>
4: #include <iostream.h>
5: #define STR_LEN 128+1
6: #define REM_LEN 254+1
7:
8: main()
9: {
```

```
10:
11: HENV    henv;
12: HDBC    hdbc;
13: HSTMT   hstmt;
14: RETCODE retcode;
15: UCHAR   szQualifier[STR_LEN], szOwner[STR_LEN];
16: UCHAR   szTableName[STR_LEN];
17: UCHAR   szIndexQualifier[STR_LEN], szIndexName[STR_LEN];
18: UCHAR   szColumnName[STR_LEN], szFilterCondition[STR_LEN];
19: UCHAR   szCollation[3];
20: SWORD   Cardinality, Pages;
21: SWORD   Type, SeqInIndex, NonUnique;
22: /* Assuming you set up your database with the alias music and the */
23: /* Table name Album */
24: UCHAR   szConnect[20] = "MUSIC";
25: UCHAR   szTable[20] = "Album";
26: /* Declare storage locations for bytes available to return */
27: SDWORD cbQualifier, cbOwner, cbTableName;
28: SDWORD cbIndexQualifier;
29: SDWORD cbColumnName, cbSeqInIndex, cbType,cbNonUnique,cbIndexName;
30: SDWORD cbCollation, cbCardinality, cbPages, cbFilterCondition;
31:
32: retcode = SQLAllocEnv(&henv);                    /* Environment handle */
33: if (retcode == SQL_SUCCESS) {
34:  retcode = SQLAllocConnect(henv, &hdbc); /* Connection handle */
35:  if (retcode == SQL_SUCCESS) {
36:
37:   /* Set login timeout to 5 seconds. */
38:
39:   SQLSetConnectOption(hdbc, SQL_LOGIN_TIMEOUT, 5);
40:
41:   /* Connect to data source */
42:
43:          retcode = SQLConnect(hdbc, szConnect,
            ➥SQL_NTS, NULL, SQL_NTS, NULL, SQL_NTS);
44:
45:          if (retcode == SQL_SUCCESS ¦¦ retcode == SQL_SUCCESS_WITH_INFO){
46:
47:              /* Process data after successful connection */
48:
49:              retcode = SQLAllocStmt(hdbc, &hstmt); /* Statement handle */
50:              if (retcode == SQL_SUCCESS) {
51:
52:
53:
54:              retcode = SQLStatistics(hstmt,
55:                      NULL, 0,            /* All qualifiers */
56:                      NULL, 0,            /* All owners     */
57:                      szTable, SQL_NTS,   /* Album table */
58:                      SQL_INDEX_ALL,      /* Return all Indices */
59:                      /* SQL_INDEX_UNIQUE would return only*/
60:                              /* unique indices */
61:                      SQL_ENSURE); /* Return the Indices Unconditionally*/
62:                              /* SQL_Quick would get the indices only */
63:                      /* if they were "readily" available from the server*/
```

continues

Listing 9.1. continued

```
64:
65:
66:                   if (retcode == SQL_SUCCESS) {
67:
68:      /* Bind columns in result set to storage locations */
69:
70:                   SQLBindCol(hstmt, 1, SQL_C_CHAR, szQualifier,
71:                   STR_LEN,&cbQualifier);
72:                   SQLBindCol(hstmt, 2, SQL_C_CHAR, szOwner, STR_LEN,
                      ➥&cbOwner);
73:                   SQLBindCol(hstmt, 3, SQL_C_CHAR, szTableName,
                      ➥STR_LEN,&cbTableName);
74:                   SQLBindCol(hstmt, 4, SQL_C_SSHORT, &NonUnique, 0,
                      ➥ &cbNonUnique);
75:                   SQLBindCol(hstmt, 5, SQL_C_CHAR, szIndexQualifier,
                      ➥STR_LEN, &cbIndexQualifier);
76:                   SQLBindCol(hstmt, 6, SQL_C_CHAR, szIndexName, STR_LEN,
                      ➥&cbIndexName);
77:                   SQLBindCol(hstmt, 7, SQL_C_SSHORT, &Type, 0, &cbType);
78:                   SQLBindCol(hstmt, 8, SQL_C_SSHORT, &SeqInIndex, 0,
                      ➥&cbSeqInIndex);
79:                   SQLBindCol(hstmt, 9, SQL_C_CHAR, szColumnName, STR_LEN,
                      ➥&cbColumnName);
80:
81:                   SQLBindCol(hstmt, 10, SQL_C_CHAR, szCollation, 1,
                      ➥&cbCollation);
82:                   SQLBindCol(hstmt, 11, SQL_C_SSHORT, &Cardinality, 0,
                      ➥&cbCardinality);
83:                   SQLBindCol(hstmt, 12, SQL_C_SSHORT, &Pages, 0,
                      ➥&cbPages);
84:                   SQLBindCol(hstmt, 13, SQL_C_CHAR, szFilterCondition,
                      ➥STR_LEN, &cbFilterCondition);
85:
86:                  while(TRUE) {
87:                    retcode = SQLFetch(hstmt);
88:                    if (retcode == SQL_SUCCESS
                          || retcode == SQL_SUCCESS_WITH_INFO){
89:                      cout << "szTableName = " << szTableName ;
90:                      cout << " NonUnique = " << NonUnique ;
91:                      cout << " szColumnName =" << szColumnName;
92:                      cout << " szCollation =" << szCollation << "\n";
93:                        switch(Type)
94:                        {
95:                          case SQL_TABLE_STAT:
96:                            cout << " Type = SQL_TABLE_STAT" ;
97:                            break;
98:                          case SQL_INDEX_CLUSTERED:
99:                            cout << " Type = SQL_INDEX_CLUSTERED";
100:                            break;
101:                          case SQL_INDEX_HASHED:
102:                            cout << " Type = SQL_INDEX_HASHED";
103:                            break;
```

```
104:                              case SQL_INDEX_OTHER:
105:                                  cout << " Type = SQL_INDEX_OTHER";
106:                                  break;
107:                          }
108:                          cout << " szIndexName =" << szIndexName;
109:                          cout << " szIndexQualifier ="
                                    << szIndexQualifier
                                    << "\n" << "\n";
110:                      } else {
111:                          break;
112:                      }
113:                  }
114:              }
115:
116:              SQLFreeStmt(hstmt, SQL_DROP);
117:          }
118:          SQLDisconnect(hdbc);
119:      }
120:      SQLFreeConnect(hdbc);
121:  }
122:  SQLFreeEnv(henv);
123: }
124:
125:
126: return 0;
127:}
```

As you can see, this program sets up the required handles and then calls the function
SQLStatistics.

```
54:              retcode = SQLStatistics(hstmt,
55:                  NULL, 0,            /* All qualifiers */
56:                  NULL, 0,            /* All owners    */
57:                  szTable, SQL_NTS,   /* Album table */
58:                  SQL_INDEX_ALL,          /* Return all Indices */
59:                              /* SQL_INDEX_UNIQUE would return only*/
60:                              /* unique indices */
61:                  SQL_ENSURE); /* Return the Indices Unconditionally*/
62:                      /* SQL_Quick would get the indices only */
63:              /* if they were "readily" available from the server*/
```

 This particular example uses the first four arguments to request all qualifiers and all
owners, but you can be more discriminating if you want. The fifth and sixth
arguments are the table and its size. The seventh argument can take either
SQL_INDEX_ALL or SQL_INDEX_UNIQUE. The former returns information on all the indices
and the latter only on those that are a unique field; that is, index fields that do not allow
duplicates. The last argument can be either SQL_ENSURE or SQL_QUICK. SQL_ENSURE will
retrieve the information no matter how busy your database is. If you don't want to tie
up your LAN with this request, SQL_QUICK will return the information only if it is readily
available from the server. The program looks like what is shown in Figure 9.1 and
produces the results shown in Table 9.1.

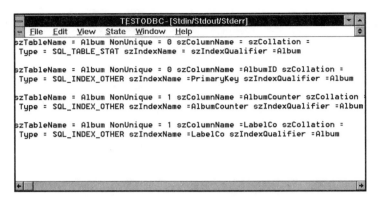

Figure 9.1. *Results of the* SQLStatistics *program.*

As you can see, after invoking the SQLStatistics function, the program binds the columns using SQLBindCol. It then loops as long as SQLFetch has data to return, showing a sampling of the returned data as shown in Figure 9.1. You can easily modify this program to look at specific values in the result set. You could also use the debugger to look at the returned values as you step through the program. Table 9.1 shows the result set returned by SQLStatistics.

Table 9.1. Result set returned by SQLStatistics.

Column name	Definition
TABLE_QUALIFIER	Of type Varchar(128). The size, 128, represents the maximum size and not the actual size of the data in the field. This value is the identifier of the table to which the statistic or index applies. This field cannot have a NULL value but will be an empty string ("") if the ODBC driver you are using does not support qualifiers.
TABLE_OWNER	Of type Varchar(128). This is just what it says; the table owner identifier of the table identified in the SQLStatistics (specified in the fifth and sixth arguments). If the table does not have an owner, then this field will return an empty string (""). It will not return a NULL.
TABLE_NAME	Of type Varchar(128). The name of the table.
NON_UNIQUE	Of type Smallint. If the value of NON_UNIQUE is TRUE (1) then the index values do not have to be unique. If it is FALSE (0) then the index values must be unique. The value is NULL if TYPE is SQL_TABLE_STAT.

Column name	Definition
INDEX_QUALIFIER	Of type Varchar(128). The name of the index that should be used in a DROP INDEX statement. If this value is NULL it means either the driver does not support an index qualifier or that TYPE is SQL_TABLE_STAT. If this value is NULL the TABLE owner should be used in the DROP INDEX statement.
INDEX_NAME	Of type Varchar(128). This is just what it says; the name of the index. If it is NULL then TYPE is SQL_TABLE_STAT.
TYPE	Of type Smallintnot. Specifies the type of information being returned and can be one of four values. If the value of TYPE is SQL_TABLE_STAT the current row contains statistics for the table specified in the SQLStatistics call. The values SQL_INDEX_CLUSTERED, SQL_INDEX_HASHED, and SQL_INDEX_OTHER indicates the type of index represented in the current row of data.
SEQ_IN_INDEX	Of type Smallint. Indicates the column number of the index. The first column is column 1. This value will be NULL if TYPE is SQL_TABLE_STAT.
COLUMN_NAME	Of type Varchar(128) . This is the column identifier. If the column is based on a relationship between other columns, such as HITS/ATBATS, then the expression is returned. An empty string ("") is returned if the driver cannot determine what expression was used. If the column is described in terms of a filter index, then each column in the filter condition will be returned. More than one condition will result in the return of more than one row. If NULL is returned then TYPE is SQL_TABLE_STAT.
COLLATION	Of type Char(1). If the column is sorted in ascending order then COLLATION will have a value of "A". A "D" value indicates descending order. If the value is NULL then one of two things have happened. Either the column sort sequence is not supported by the data source or TYPE is SQL_TABLE_STAT.
CARDINALITY	Of type Integer. This can be one of three things. It is the number of rows in the table if TYPE is SQL_TABLE_STAT. If TYPE is not SQL_TABLE_STAT, it is the number of unique values in the index. If the driver cannot find a value from the data source the value will be NULL.

continues

Table 9.1. continued

Column name	Definition
PAGES	Of type Integer. If the data source uses the concept of pages as a measure of data storage then this value is the number of pages used to store the index, unless TYPE is SQL_TABLE_STAT; then it is the number of pages used to store the table. If the value is NULL either the data is not available or not supported by the data source.
FILTER_CONDITION	Of type Varchar(128). Given a filtered index, this is the filter condition. For example, if the condition were "HEIGHT > 6" then that is what is returned. If the driver cannot determine the filter index then it will return an empty string. If TYPE is SQL_TABLE_STAT then the value will be NULL. This function is new in ODBC 2.0. A 1.0 driver could return a different column with the same column number.

Syntax

The *SQLSpecialColumns* Function

The general syntax for the SQLSpecialColumns function is

```
RETCODE SQLSpecialColumns(hstmt,
                          fColType,
                          szTableQualifier,
                          cbTableQualifier,
                          szTableOwner,
                          cbTableOwner,
                          szTableName,
                          cbTableName,
                          fScope,
                          fNullable)
```

If you need to find out more about the indices in a table, SQLSpecialColumns is the function for you. SQLSpecialColumns can tell you two things.

☐ The optimal set of columns that uniquely identifies a row in the table.

☐ Which columns are automatically updated when any value in the row is updated by a transaction.

Listing 9.2 is similar to Listing 9.1. It illustrates how SQLSpecialColumns can be used.

Listing 9.2. Test program for SQLSpecialColumns.

```
1: // Test Program for SQLSpecialColumns
2: // Compiled using MSVC++ 1.5 as a QuickWin Program
3: #include <afxdb.h>
4: #include <iostream.h>
5: #define STR_LEN 128+1
6: #define REM_LEN 254+1
7:
8: main()
9: {
10:
11: HENV     henv;
12: HDBC     hdbc;
13: HSTMT    hstmt;
14: RETCODE retcode;
15: UCHAR   szTypeName[STR_LEN], szOwner[STR_LEN];
16: UCHAR   szTableName[STR_LEN];
17: UCHAR   szIndexQualifier[STR_LEN], szIndexName[STR_LEN];
18: UCHAR   szColumnName[STR_LEN], szFilterCondition[STR_LEN];
19: UCHAR   szCollation[3];
20: SWORD   Scope, DataType, Precision, Length, Scale;
21: SWORD   Type, SeqInIndex, NonUnique;
22: /* Assuming you set up your database with the alias music and the */
23: /* Table name Album */
24: UCHAR   szConnect[20] = "MUSIC";
25: UCHAR   szTable[20] = "Album";
26: /* Declare storage locations for bytes available to return */
27: SDWORD cbQualifier, cbOwner, cbTableName;
28: SDWORD cbIndexQualifier;
29: SDWORD cbColumnName, cbSeqInIndex, cbTypeName, cbNonUnique, cbIndexName;
30: SDWORD cbDataType, cbScope, cbPrecision, cbLength, cbScale;
31:
32: retcode = SQLAllocEnv(&henv);                  /* Environment handle */
33: if (retcode == SQL_SUCCESS) {
34:  retcode = SQLAllocConnect(henv, &hdbc); /* Connection handle */
35:  if (retcode == SQL_SUCCESS) {
36:
37:   /* Set login timeout to 5 seconds. */
38:
39:   SQLSetConnectOption(hdbc, SQL_LOGIN_TIMEOUT, 5);
40:
41:   /* Connect to data source */
42:
43:   retcode = SQLConnect(hdbc, szConnect, SQL_NTS, NULL, SQL_NTS,
        ➥NULL, SQL_NTS);
44:
45:   if (retcode == SQL_SUCCESS || retcode == SQL_SUCCESS_WITH_INFO){
46:
47:           /* Process data after successful connection */
48:
49:           retcode = SQLAllocStmt(hdbc, &hstmt); /* Statement handle */
50:           if (retcode == SQL_SUCCESS) {
```

continues

Listing 9.2. continued

```
51:
52:
53:                    retcode = SQLSpecialColumns(hstmt, /* Statement handle */
54:                        SQL_BEST_ROWID , /* SQL_BEST_ROWID or SQL_ROWVER */
55:                        NULL, 0,                /* All qualifiers */
56:                        NULL, 0,                /* All owners      */
57:                        szTable, SQL_NTS,   /* Album table */
58:                        SQL_SCOPE_SESSION,
      /* SQL_SCOPE_TRANSACTION, SQL_SCOPE_CURROW, or SQL_SCOPE_SESSION*/
59:                        SQL_NULLABLE); /* SQL_NO_NULLS or SQL_NULLABLE */
60:
61:                    if (retcode == SQL_SUCCESS) {
62:
63:        /* Bind columns in result set to storage locations */
64:
65:                        SQLBindCol(hstmt, 1, SQL_C_SSHORT, &Scope, 0,
                            ➥&cbScope);
66:                        SQLBindCol(hstmt, 2, SQL_C_CHAR, szColumnName,
                            ➥STR_LEN, &cbColumnName);
67:                        SQLBindCol(hstmt, 3, SQL_C_SSHORT, &DataType, 0,
                            ➥&cbDataType);
68:                        SQLBindCol(hstmt, 4, SQL_C_CHAR, szTypeName, STR_LEN,
                            ➥&cbTypeName);
69:                        SQLBindCol(hstmt, 5, SQL_C_SSHORT, &Precision, 0,
                            ➥&cbPrecision);
70:                        SQLBindCol(hstmt, 6, SQL_C_SSHORT, &Length, 0,
                            ➥&cbLength);
71:                        SQLBindCol(hstmt, 6, SQL_C_SSHORT, &Scale, 0,
                            ➥&cbScale);
72:
73:
74:                    while(TRUE) {
75:                        retcode = SQLFetch(hstmt);
76:                        if (retcode == SQL_SUCCESS
                                ¦¦ retcode == SQL_SUCCESS_WITH_INFO){
77:                            switch(Scope)
78:                            {
79:                                case SQL_SCOPE_TRANSACTION:
80:                                    cout << " Type = SQL_SCOPE_TRANSACTION"
                                        << "\n";
81:                                    break;
82:                                case SQL_SCOPE_CURROW:
83:                                    cout << " Type = SQL_SCOPE_CURROW"
                                        << "\n";
84:                                    break;
85:                                case SQL_SCOPE_SESSION:
86:                                    cout << " Type = SQL_SCOPE_SESSION"
                                        << "\n";
87:                                    break;
88:                                default:
89:                                    cout << " Type = NULL"<< "\n";
90:                                    break;
91:                            }
```

```
92:                                cout << " szColumnName =" << szColumnName<< "\n";
93:                                cout << " DataType = " << DataType << "\n";
94:                                cout << " szTypeName = " << szTypeName << "\n";
95:                                cout << " Precision = " << Precision << "\n";
96:                                cout << " Length = " << Length << "\n";
97:                                cout << " Scale =" << Scale << "\n"<< "\n";
98:
99:                        } else {
100:                            break;
101:                        }
102:                    }
103:                }
104:
105:                SQLFreeStmt(hstmt, SQL_DROP);
106:            }
107:            SQLDisconnect(hdbc);
108:        }
109:        SQLFreeConnect(hdbc);
110:    }
111:    SQLFreeEnv(henv);
112: }
113:
114:
115: return 0;
116: )
```

Analysis The first argument of `SQLSpecialColumns` (starting on line 53 of Listing 9.2) is the familiar input statement handle that you have seen on several of the functions covered so far. The next argument, `fColType`, tells the function which of the two things it can tell us that we are interested in. If you use `SQL_BEST_ROWID`, the function will return the column or columns that you can use to uniquely identify a row. The column or columns can be either a pseudocolumn (some databases use a pseudocolumn as a unique identifier; check your database documentation for details) or the column or columns that describe a unique index. When `AlbumCounter` is the primary key, the following is the output:

```
Type = SQL_SCOPE_TRANSACTION
szColumnName =AlbumCounter
DataType = 5
szTypeName = SHORT
Precision = 5
Length = 0
Scale =2
```

In this case, the primary key is `AlbumCounter`. Therefore, the function, invoked with `SQL_BEST_ROWID`, returned information about the `AlbumCounter` column. When both `AlbumCounter` and `AlbumID` are the primary key, the following code is the output:

```
Type = SQL_SCOPE_TRANSACTION
szColumnName =AlbumCounter
```

```
DataType = 5
szTypeName = SHORT
Precision = 5
Length = 0
Scale =2

Type = SQL_SCOPE_TRANSACTION
szColumnName =AlbumID
DataType = 12
szTypeName = TEXT
Precision = 255
Length = 0
Scale =30
```

In this example the function did the expected thing and returned both parts of the primary key. If ROWVER is used, then the function will return any columns in the table that are automatically updated as a result of a transaction. Some databases use a field like `TimeStamp` that is updated when there is a transaction. SQLSpecialColumns, using SQL_ROWVER, will return information on these columns if they exist.

Of the remaining arguments only the second to last argument, fScope, is one you haven't seen already. The fScope function can be one of three values: SQL_SCOPE_CURROW, SQL_SCOPE_TRANSACTION, or SQL_SCOPE_SESSION. SQL_SCOPE_CURROW is the most restrictive. By using this value you are telling SQLSpecialColumns that your minimum requirement is for columns that will uniquely describe the currently selected row. If that row is changed by another transaction the columns you received will not be valid. SQL_SCOPE_TRANSACTION needs the columns you receive to be valid for the duration of the current transaction (until a COMMIT or ROLLBACK). SQL_SCOPE_TRANSACTION needs the returned columns to be valid for the entire database session.

The last argument, fNullable, has two settings. SQL_NO_NULLS will cause the function to not return any columns that are capable of having NULL values. The other setting, SQL_NULLABLE, enables columns that have NULLable fields to be returned.

The data set returned by SQLSpecialColumns is straightforward and is shown in Table 9.2.

Table 9.2. The data set returned by SQLSpecialColumns.

Column name	Definition
SCOPE	Of type Smallint. Returns the actual scope of the row ID. See the previous discussion on the Scope argument in the SQLSpecialColumns function. Can be SQL_SCOPE_CURROW, SQL_SCOPE_TRANSACTION, or SQL_SCOPE_SESSION. If the value is NULL the fColType is SQL_ROWVER.
COLUMN_NAME	Type of Varchar(128). This is the column identifier.

Column name	Definition
DATA_TYPE	Type of Smallint. This is the SQL data type. DATA_TYPE can be either an ODBC SQL data type or a driver-specific SQL data type.
TYPE_NAME	Type of Varchar(128). This is the string name of the DATA_TYPE.
PRECISION	Type of Integer. The value of PRECISION will depend on the data type. For a numerical data type, PRECISION refers to the number of digits used by the data type. For example, for SQL_FLOAT this value is 15. For a character data type this value refers to either the maximum or defined length of the column. The value will be NULL where precision is not applicable.
LENGTH	Type of Integer. The maximum number of bytes transferred when the field is put to its default data type. For example, The same SQL_FLOAT that has a PRECISION of 15 has a LENGTH of 8.
SCALE	Type of Smallint. The number of digits to the right of the decimal point in a numeric data type or NULL for data types where SCALE does not apply.
PSEUDO_COLUMN (ODBC 2.0)	Type of Smallint. Indicates whether the column is a pseudocolumn. Some databases use pseudocolumns to define keys. ODBC 1.0 drivers might have a driver-specific column in this position.

Summary

This chapter presented some of the functions that can be used to query the data source about its capabilities and about details of the data itself. You saw when it is important to know about specific capabilities and how they impact your development. You learned about the following topics:

- ODBC conformance levels
- Querying for a specific driver or server function
- Querying for index information

With the functions covered in this section—SQLGetInfo, SQLStatistics, and SQLSpecialColumns—you can make your program "smart" enough to adapt to its environment.

Q&A

Q **If my table has an index, but SQLStatistics does not return it, is that index still usable?**

A Yes it is. Depending on the driver and the database, SQLStatistics might not return all applicable indices. This does not preclude you from using any valid index.

Workshop

The Workshop provides quiz questions to help you solidify your understanding of the material covered and to give you experience in using what you've learned. Try to understand the quiz and exercise answers before continuing on to the next day's lesson. Answers are provided in Appendix A, "Answers."

Quiz

1. Which function can tell you the optimal set of columns that uniquely identifies a row in the table and/or which columns are automatically updated when any value in the row is updated by a transaction?

2. Which function will return information about the driver and data source?

Exercise

1. How would you modify the code, starting on line 53, to return only columns that uniquely describe the currently selected row?

SQL Syntax
for ODBC

This chapter presents the SQL syntax that is defined for ODBC. The specific syntax and grammar used for SELECT, INSERT, and UPDATE statements is covered in detail, as well as the other elements of the SQL language supported by ODBC. You also will learn the additions to supported grammar at each level of conformance. Finally, you will learn about back-end specific SQL. Today, you learn about the following:

☐ The SELECT statement and its various clauses

☐ The INSERT statement

☐ The UPDATE statement

☐ Miscellaneous SQL statements

☐ Back-end specific SQL

The goal of today's lesson is not to make you able to write the most complex or clever SQL SELECT statements. Rather, the goal is to present the standard ODBC "version" of the SQL language, and to point out where it might differ from other implementations. Likewise, this chapter assumes that you have or plan to acquire a familiarity with the finer points of SQL usage. Enough information is presented in this chapter to get you going with your ODBC application.

The *SELECT* Statement and Its Various Clauses

Because virtually every application utilizing SQL to access a database must at some time select data, the SQL SELECT statement is covered first, and probably most thoroughly. In almost all instances, the SELECT statement can be the most complex SQL element, and at times the most convoluted.

In an ODBC application, the SELECT statement is used to precisely specify which data is to be returned from the data source to the application. The SELECT statement does not actually cause the data to be moved back into the application. Instead, the SELECT statement is sent to the database engine, and that engine gathers or "selects" the corresponding data in preparation for its return to the application.

There are six possible clauses that can be used in a SELECT statement along with various predicates. The following are the available clauses and the level of SQL conformance:

Table 10.1. Parts of a SELECT statement.

Clause	Level of Conformance
FROM	Minimum
WHERE	Minimum
GROUP BY	Core
HAVING	Core
UNION	Extended
ORDER BY	Minimum

The *FROM* Clause

The basic SQL query must contain a minimum of four elements: the verb SELECT, the select list specifying which columns to select, the FROM clause, and the table reference list. The following is the simplest example of an SQL query:

```
SELECT lastname FROM artist
```

In this case, the column `lastname` from the table `artist` will be selected, with all rows going into the result set. The FROM clause refers to the table reference list, which will list all tables from which data is to be selected. The SELECT list specifies which elements from the specified tables are to be returned in the result set.

The elements in the select list can be column names (specified alone or with an alias), literals, expressions, an ODBC scalar function, or a set function, depending upon data-source conformance levels. The most common value is * (as in SELECT * FROM Table1;), which returns all the columns in a table.

The table reference list can contain either table names alone, table names with correlation names (user-created aliases to be used as a more meaningful qualifier to column names elsewhere in the query or in a subquery), or an OUTER JOIN specification, which specifies the tables and condition for an outer join.

Outer Joins

The OUTER JOIN specification is included in ODBC SQL grammar because it is used often. However, many data sources do not provide full outer-join support. To determine what level of outer-join support is provided, query SQLGetData with the value SQL_OUTER_JOINS as explained on Day 9, "Determining Driver and DBMS Capabilities."

A left outer join will return all rows from the table mentioned first (the "left" table), and will return matching information from the right table when the join condition is met. When there is no matching row in the right-hand table, null values are returned. An example of an outer join is shown in the following code. If an artist row exists, but there are no corresponding albums by that artist, null values will be returned.

```
select artist.lastname, album.albumtitle
   from {oj artist left outer join album
       on artist.artistid = album.artistid}
```

The *WHERE* Clause

The WHERE clause is used to tell the data source how to search a table for specific data. Search conditions are predicates that further refine how to choose the information to be contained in the result set. There are six types of predicates that can be used in a WHERE clause. These six are

- ☐ Relational
- ☐ BETWEEN
- ☐ LIKE
- ☐ IN
- ☐ NULL
- ☐ EXISTS

Relational Predicates

The relational predicates are expressions of the common comparison relationships between two values. The following are the ODBC comparison operators:

- ☐ < (Less than)
- ☐ > (Greater than)
- ☐ <= (Less than or equal to)
- ☐ >= (Greater than or equal to)
- ☐ = (Equal to)
- ☐ <> (Not equal to)

Note that although many DBMS systems enable the use of the NOT keyword or NOT operator (!) in relational comparison operators, this is not allowed in ODBC SQL grammar.

The relational predicates are used to include or exclude rows from the result set. Usually, these are used to specify a condition in which the value of a column equals (or doesn't equal, and so on) a specified literal value. For example:

```
SELECT LastName FROM artist WHERE ArtistID > 5
```

It is up to the application to ensure that the data type of the comparison column and the literal or other value being checked are compatible. If necessary, scalar functions can be embedded in the SELECT statement to make this occur. More often you just need to remember to enclose the literal value in quotation marks if the column being compared is a char or similar data type. For example:

```
SELECT * FROM artist WHERE LastName = 'Licad'
```

The *BETWEEN* Predicate

The BETWEEN predicate is used to specify those rows containing the value within the range specified in the clause. The following is an example of how BETWEEN is used:

```
SELECT * FROM artist WHERE artistid BETWEEN 10 AND 12
```

In this case, if the rows are numbered consecutively, the query will return rows with ArtistIDs of 10, 11, and 12. If the NOT negation operator is applied, the opposite would be true:

```
SELECT * FROM artist WHERE artistid NOT BETWEEN 10 AND 12
```

This would return all rows in the table except rows 10, 11, and 12.

The *LIKE* Predicate

The LIKE predicate enables you to perform wildcard string searches to look for a specific string, partial string, or pattern. The % character denotes a wildcard search in SQL grammar, while the underscore character (_) denotes a single wildcard character. For example, to find all ArtistIDs that might have a last name of Whiting, use the following code:

```
SELECT * FROM artist WHERE LastName LIKE 'Whi%'
```

Note that this use of the LIKE clause needs the characters 'Whi' to begin the column. If the LIKE predicate specified '%Whi%', it would find all rows with that string anywhere in the column. The % wildcard character acts the same way as the asterisk (*) character does in DOS, and the underscore acts just like the single-character wildcard ? in DOS. You must be careful about case sensitivity. If the DBMS is configured to sort in a case-sensitive manner, then generally the literal used in a LIKE clause must match the case of the searched column.

> **Note:** Although a LIKE text search for data in a database can be an appealingly easy way to identify needed rows, you should use it with caution. In most DBMS systems, the use of a LIKE clause is the slowest type of operation that can be performed, and it can be extremely resource-intensive to perform. For this reason, LIKE searches should be utilized only when there is no other way to locate the needed data.

The *IN* Predicate

There are two common forms for using the IN predicate, one simple and the other quite complex. If the comparison value can only be (or not be) one of a finite list of values, the IN clause can check that condition. For example, to see if a customer is in the local region, you would use the following syntax:

```
SELECT custID FROM customer WHERE state IN ('MN','IA','WI','SD','ND')
```

In the second case, a subquery is used to first define the set of values, with the outer or main query then comparing a column value to see if it is in the set of values returned from the subquery. An example would be a query in a sales lead tracking system. The following query will return all leads that do not have an entry in the corresponding notes table:

```
SELECT LeadID FROM leads WHERE notekey NOT IN (SELECT noteid FROM notes)
```

The *NULL* Predicate

The NULL predicate enables checking for a lack of value in a column. Note that NULL and zero or blank are not the same. NULL is a value which means that nothing has been placed in the column. Zero or an empty string, on the other hand, are actual values that have been placed into the column to indicate a specific value (or lack of value or information). Before checking for NULL values, make sure that the NULL value is allowed for that column. For example, to see which artists have been given a firstname value, you could use the following syntax:

```
SELECT artistID FROM artist WHERE FirstName IS NULL
```

The *EXISTS* Predicate

The EXISTS predicate is used to test if a particular row exists in a table. The EXISTS clause must immediately precede a SUBSELECT statement. The EXISTS predicate returns a True or False value, so it is generally ANDed with another condition to determine final row selection.

The *GROUP BY* Clause

The GROUP BY clause is used to organize the result set rows by the values contained in the column(s) specified in this clause. This is most often used to specify what column to break on for control breaks when using an aggregate function such as SUM(). The following is an example that queries sales by department:

```
SELECT deptname,SUM(salesamt)
➥from deptmast DM,saleshist SH where DM.deptID = SH.deptID
➥GROUP BY deptname
```

In this query, the result set should contain one row for each department that has rows in the sales history file. Each result set row would contain the department name and the total sales for that department. A common error in this type of query is to add another nonaggregate column, such as employee ID, invoice date, or any other. Because the grouping is performed by combining all of the nonaggregate columns together into a single concatenated key and breaking whenever that key value changes, extraneous columns can cause unexpected breaks.

Some data sources require that all nonaggregate columns be specified in the GROUP BY clause, whereas others do not. To learn the specific behavior of a data source, use SQLGetData, querying on the fDataType of SQL_GROUP_BY, as detailed on Day 9.

The *HAVING* Clause

The HAVING clause is used to apply further selection criteria on aggregated, grouped columns specified in the GROUP BY clause. The HAVING clause uses the same syntax as the WHERE clause, except that it specifies GROUPed data rather than raw data as specified in the WHERE clause.

The HAVING clause is commonly used to enable a query to show only data that is above or below a certain criteria. Using the sample that shows total sales by department, a HAVING clause could be added to show only the total sales of those departments that have overall sales that exceed one million dollars. The following is an example of such a query:

```
SELECT deptname,SUM(salesamt)
➥from deptmast DM,saleshist SH where DM.deptID = SH.deptID
➥GROUP BY deptname HAVING SUM(salesamt) > 1000000
```

The *UNION* Clause

The UNION clause is used to combine two separate result sets into a single result. To better understand this, think of it in the context of a spreadsheet. A JOIN clause will add columns

to your spreadsheet, whereas a UNION clause will add rows. Again using the spreadsheet analogy, the two result sets must have the same number of columns and the data in those columns must have exactly the same data types for them to be combined with a UNION clause.

The UNION clause might be used where historical data is kept in multiple tables that differ only by the date range of the data they contain. An example would be a situation in which employee numbers are assigned sequentially and each year a new employee table is created, holding all employees who were active during that year. To see all active employees, each table would have to be queried, with the results being the union of the two sets, as shown in the following code example. Normally, the UNION function will eliminate duplicate rows unless the ALL keyword is added to specify UNION ALL, in which case all rows of the two result sets are returned.

```
select empid,ssno from employee94 where empid < '00021'
UNION ALL
select empid,ssno from employee95 where empid >= '00020'
order by empid
```

The *ORDER BY* Clause

The ORDER BY clause is used to specify the ordering of the result set before it is returned. Multiple columns can be specified, separated by columns. When more than one column is specified for the ORDER BY clause, the primary sort is on the first column specified, with duplicate values from that sort, and then sorted by the next column specified, and so on. You can specify the keyword ASC following the column name to specify ascending sort order, and DESC specifies descending sort order. You can give an integer specifying the column number instead of a column name. In this case, the first or furthest left column in the result set is column 1, the next is column 2, and so on. This is necessary if a column in the result set is a summary column or result column that cannot be specified by name.

The *INSERT* Statement

The SQL INSERT verb is used to insert or add new rows of data to an existing table. The INSERT statement is simpler than a SELECT statement because it does not have as many optional clauses. Basically, in an INSERT statement you specify the table name and the values to be inserted. If values are to be placed in fewer than all columns of the table, the column names must also be explicitly stated.

The following code is the simplest INSERT statement you can use to add a new song to the song table:

```
INSERT INTO song VALUES (23,4,,,'Heart On The Line')
```

The third and fourth columns in this table are nullable, and for this row they have no values; therefore, NULL or the default value will be inserted into these columns.

If the value for any column is to be inserted at runtime, you can specify it in the INSERT statement (or any statement for that matter) as a dynamic parameter by placing a question mark in place of the literal value. This would be typical for a prepared statement that is then executed many times with different values. The following is an example of the same INSERT statement as the preceding example, but with dynamic parameters:

```
INSERT INTO song VALUES (?,?,?,?,?)
```

In its final form, the INSERT statement can contain a SELECT statement instead of the VALUES clause. This creates a type of "cut and paste" action, where values are selected from one table and inserted into another table in the same action.

The *UPDATE* Statement

The UPDATE statement is also a simple statement with only one variation other than the number of columns involved. In the ODBC minimum and core (as of ODBC version 2.0) grammar, the UPDATE statement must use a searched WHERE clause. The ODBC extended SQL grammar also defines a positioned UPDATE statement. Using positioned statements is conditional on using cursors, which is explained on Day 17, "Using ODBC Cursors."

An UPDATE statement can change the value of one, many, or all of the columns in a row. Some data sources, however, will not enable you to change only the primary key value. In these instances, you must delete and reinsert the row. The following example updates the artist table to add a note:

```
UPDATE artist SET note = 'Grammy Award - 1994' WHERE artistID = 4
```

Miscellaneous SQL Statements

In addition to the Data Manipulation Language (DML) SQL statements outlined previously, the ODBC SQL grammar also defines many Data Description Language (DDL) statements. It is beyond the scope of this book to detail all of the syntax for these statements. The complete syntax for these and all ODBC SQL grammar can be found in Appendix C of the Microsoft Press book *ODBC 2.0 Programmer's Reference and SDK Guide.*

The following statements are defined and supported in one of the ODBC SQL conformance levels. For more information about these statements, see Appendix A, "Glossary of Common SQL Statements," of *Teach Yourself SQL in 14 Days*, by Sams Publishing.

- [ ] ALTER TABLE
- [ ] CREATE INDEX
- [ ] CREATE TABLE
- [ ] CREATE VIEW
- [ ] DELETE
- [ ] DROP INDEX
- [ ] DROP TABLE
- [ ] DROP VIEW
- [ ] GRANT
- [ ] CALL
- [ ] REVOKE

Although some of these statements are almost self-explanatory, such as the DELETE statement, others such as CREATE TABLE can be much more complex, which is why they are not discussed in detail here. Specifically, the CREATE TABLE statement does not use the standard ODBC data types, but rather requires specification of data source-specific data types. You can obtain these by calling SQLGetTypeInfo, or using the appropriate classes in odbc/ClassLib.

Back-End Specific SQL

When the X/Open and SQL Access Group SQL CAE specification was written, the writers recognized that there would need to be exceptions and additions to the standard syntax. They provided for this in the specification by defining the escape clause as the method to send SQL extensions through to the DBMS.

The ODBC specification defined several extensions to SQL using this escape clause, although there are also shorthand ways to express the same statements. The ODBC extensions were added primarily because they enhanced functionality and were already supported natively by most DBMSs. These extensions by ODBC include:

- [ ] Scalar functions such as string, numeric, and data type conversion functions (covered on Day 16, "Using ODBC Functions")

- [ ] Date, time, and timestamp data types
- [ ] Outer joins
- [ ] Procedure calls
- [ ] LIKE predicate escape characters

If you use these standard ODBC extensions to the SQL grammar with the escape clause notation, they should be supported by all ODBC drivers. If there are other DBMS extensions to the syntax, you can use them also, but at the cost of application portability. Any application that includes database-specific SQL becomes specific to that system and loses all portability, one of the features of ODBC.

The SQL pass-through functionality found on some ODBC-compliant front-end applications and development tools is used to enable DBMS-specific SQL to be passed without parsing to the back end for processing. In some ODBC-compliant front-end applications, this is generally necessary because the application contains a parser that checks SQL syntax and grammar. This is not needed for applications you build against the ODBC API because your applications will not have syntax checkers. You can also use the SQL pass-through function to disable transformation of the SQL statement, but that also is an application-specific problem that does not apply when you are developing to the ODBC API.

Summary

Today's lesson presented the SQL statements supported by ODBC and their grammar and syntax. You learned the following topics:

- [ ] The SELECT statement is used to query data to be returned to the application or prepared for changes. The SELECT statement has many clauses, some of which are options that detail what data to place into the result set.
- [ ] The INSERT statement is used to add new data to the database in the form of new rows to an existing table.
- [ ] The UPDATE statement changes the value of data that already exists in the database. You can change a single value, or one UPDATE statement can change an entire row or many rows and many columns at once. The specification of which rows to change can be made either with a WHERE clause or, if cursors and positioned updates are to be made, the WHERE CURRENT OF clause.
- [ ] Many more SQL statements are defined in the ODBC SQL specification. These enable, among other things, changing data (DELETE), changing the database (CREATE TABLE), and changing permissions (GRANT).

☐ Extensions to the X/Open SAG SQL specification were included in the ODBC specification to enhance functionality. In addition, you can use DBMS-specific SQL, but doing so will render the application nonportable.

Q&A

Q Can I write Oracle SQL syntax in my application and let the ODBC driver translate it into ODBC syntax?

A No. This is backward, if you will. You must submit ODBC syntax, and the ODBC driver will translate it into SQL syntax specific to the data source you are using. You can call SQLNativeSql to see how the driver translated the statement.

Q Okay, but if I want to use an Oracle feature in my application for better performance, can I?

A Yes, as long as you understand that if you do so, the application will be limited to working only with Oracle data sources.

Q Because outer joins are defined in the ODBC SQL specification, does that mean ODBC adds that functionality if my DBMS doesn't support outer joins now?

A Probably not. In some cases, this is added by the driver. To determine what is supported by the driver and data source, you should call SQLGetInfo with an infotype of SQL_OUTER_JOINS. This will report the level of outer-join support provided by that driver/data-source combination.

Q Can I create databases and database devices from ODBC?

A No. This functionality is not included in the ODBC specification.

Workshop

The Workshop provides quiz questions to help you solidify your understanding of the material covered and exercises to give you experience in using what you've learned. Try to understand the quiz and exercise answers before continuing on to the next day's lesson. Answers are provided in Appendix A, "Answers."

Quiz

Identify any problems that might exist with the SQL syntax and grammar in the following statements:

1. `SELECT ALL lastname FROM artist`

2. `SELECT * FROM artist WHERE LastName = Samuels`

3. `INSERT INTO song VALUES (23,4,,,'Heart On The Line')`
   `WHERE songID = 2`

4. `SELECT deptname,SUM(salesamt) from deptmast DM,saleshist GROUP BY`
   `deptname HAVING SUM(salesamt) > 1000000`

Exercise

1. Create SQL statements joining the album and artist tables, another joining the artist and song tables, and a third from the Album_Song table that returns the name of the album and the name of the composer.

10

Running SQL
SELECT
Statements

The most common database activities in most applications are selecting data from a data source and fetching that data back into the application. This chapter explains how to perform the simplest execution of a SELECT statement. Tomorrow's lesson looks at some of the techniques available to fetch the data, but today's lesson just looks at the data selection. For the first time, you'll explore using the Microsoft Foundation Classes (MFC) for database use and the Visual C++ AppWizard, as well as perform the same activities using the South Wind Design odbc/ClassLib. Today, you learn about the following topics:

☐ Allocating a statement handle

☐ Executing a SELECT statement using SQLExecDirect

☐ Building a select query using the Application Wizard and Microsoft Foundation Classes

☐ Running a query using odbc/ClassLib

☐ Setting statement options

In today's lesson, you will quickly see that theory and practice are not always closely related when it comes to developing ODBC application programs. As far as executing SELECT statements, some environments, such as Visual Basic, require you to know all of the API calls necessary and their proper order of execution. On the other hand, when you use the AppWizard and ClassWizards contained within the Visual C++ environment, you tend to not see or know what API calls are being made.

First, you look at the additional function calls necessary to perform a SELECT statement. Then you look at similar sample programs using Visual Basic and the two different class libraries, MFC and odbc/ClassLib. The purpose behind these samples is to show the backbone needed to perform the SELECT, with the expectation that you will provide the additional "bells and whistles" as appropriate to your applications.

Allocating a Statement Handle

As discussed on Day 8, "Connecting to the Data Source," to work with data, an application needs to have at least three handles: the environment handle, connection handle, and statement handle. There can be only one environment handle per application. Depending on data source and driver capabilities, there can be one or more connection handles (connections) per environment, and one or more statement handles (statements) per connection. It is not uncommon to allocate more than one statement handle per connection, with the application ensuring that only one is active at a time, if that is the driver constraint.

VB

The *SQLAllocStmt* Function

The general syntax for the SQLAllocStmt function in Visual Basic is

```
RETCODE SQLAllocStmt(hDBC, hStmt)
```

The function allocates memory for the statement information and associates the statement with the connection specified by hDBC. It accepts the connection handle hDBC as input, and returns a pointer in the form of an integer to the new statement handle just created.

Example:

```
Global hDBC As Long        'Connection handle
Global hStmt As Long       'Pointer to handle for statement
Global rc% As Integer      'Return code

rc% = SQLAllocStmt(hDBC, hStmt)
```

The variable hStmt now contains the address pointing to the handle for the new statement. Errors from this function, which can be obtained by calling SQLError, are usually caused by not having an open connection at the time the statement allocation request is made. The connection must already have been opened successfully before this call can be used. Another common cause for error is if the Driver Manager or the driver are not able to allocate memory for the connection.

C++

The *SQLAllocStmt* Function

The prototype for the SQLAllocStmt function is

```
RETCODE SQL_API SQLAllocStmt(HDBC hdbc, HSTMT  FAR *phstmt);
```

The function allocates memory for the statement information and associates the statement with the connection specified by hDBC. It accepts the connection handle hDBC as input and returns a pointer in the form of an integer to the new statement handle just created.

Example:

```
HDBC   hdbc;
HSTMT  hstmt;

RC = SQLAllocStmt(hdbc, &hstmt);
```

In the following sections you will use Visual Basic to show how the SQLAllocStmt function is called directly from an application. In the Visual C++ samples, this function is called from within the classes rather than being coded by the application developer.

11

Executing a *SELECT* Statement

As you learned on Day 3, "Application Design Considerations," SELECT statements (and all other SQL statements) can be executed in one of two ways using ODBC. They can be either executed directly, using SQLExecDirect, or they can be first prepared using SQLPrepare and then executed multiple times using SQLExecute. The direct execution of a statement combines the preparation and execution of the statement, providing less complexity in the application, but generally worse performance with multiple executions of the same statement. Today you learn about direct execution.

VB4 **Syntax**

The *SQLExecDirect* Function

The general syntax for the SQLExecDirect function in Visual Basic is

```
RETCODE SQLExecDirect(hStmt, szSqlStr, cbSqlStr)
```

The function will execute a preparable statement contained in szSqlStr, using the current values of the parameter marker variables if any parameters exist in the statement. The parameter hStmt is the handle to the current statement. The parameter cbSqlStr contains the length in bytes of the SQL string being submitted. Many return codes are possible; the most common is SQL_SUCCESS and SQL_ERROR. If SQL_ERROR is returned, the function SQLError should be called to determine the SQLSTATE. Nearly three dozen different SQLSTATE values could be returned, depending on the specific type of SQL statement submitted and the error encountered.

Example:

```
Global hStmt As Long            'Handle for statement
Global rc% As Integer           'Function return code

Dim SqlString As String * 60    'SQL string to execute

SqlString = "select count(*) from artists"

rc% = SQLExecDirect(hStmt, SqlString, Len(SqlString))
```

The function returns SQL_SUCCESS if execution of the SQL statement was successful.

C++ **Syntax**

The *SQLExecDirect* Function

The prototype for the SQLExecDirect function is

```
RETCODE SQL_API SQLExecDirect(
    HSTMT        hstmt,
    UCHAR  FAR *szSqlStr,
    SDWORD       cbSqlStr);
```

The function will execute a preparable statement contained in szSqlStr, using the current values of the parameter marker variables, discussed in detail on Day 14, "Using Prepared Statements and Parameter Markers," if any parameters exist in the statement.

Example:

```
char  szSQL[cbMAXSQL]
//load the parameters
lstrcpy(szSQL, "select count(*) from artists");
//execute that statement
  SQLExecDirect(hstmt, lpInst->szSQL,
      lstrlen(lpInst->szSQL)
);
```

Remember that when the SQL statement is executed using this function, the data is selected from the database and ready to return to the application, but it needs another step to bring it back into the application. For the purposes of illustration, this example fetches this data using the SQLFetch and SQLGetData functions. Other options are covered in tomorrow's lesson.

Today you'll look at three specific examples that illustrate some of the basics of executing an SQL statement. The first example uses Visual Basic calls directly to the ODBC functions in the ODBC Driver Manager. Using the ODBC API in this way provides the greatest flexibility and very good performance, but requires you to write the most program code. The developer must know SQL and the ODBC API using this technique.

The second sample program, called CPEXEC, was written using the Microsoft Visual C++ Application Wizard and the MFC foundation classes. This application represents the opposite end of the spectrum, providing the least flexibility but requiring the least knowledge. This particular example was created without writing any code or SQL statements.

The third example today, named SWEX2, was designed to present a middle ground between flexibility and ease of creation. This program was created using the Microsoft AppWizard and MFC classes, but the ODBC database support uses the odbc/ClassLib classes rather than the database classes built into MFC. In this case, flexibility was retained without having to write large amounts of code. All three examples attempt to display the same data in a similar fashion. The goal is to display album title and artist name from the ARTIST and ALBUM tables of the sample database. All error checking and other normal program elements have been left out for clarity. The Visual Basic program, VBEXEC, is shown first in Listing 11.1.

 Listing 11.1. Source code for the main form of VBEXEC.

```
Sub Form_Load ()

    Dim ConnOut As String * 255    'Global connection string
    Dim ConnIn As String * 255     'Temporary for first connection
    Dim cbOut As Integer           'Receives length of actual string returned
    Dim SQLStr As String * 255     'SQL statement string
    Dim Timeout As Long            'To prevent timeout on slow system

    ConnIn = "DSN=;DATABASE=TY_ODBC;"
    ConnOut = Space$(255)

    rc = SQLAllocEnv(hEnv)
    rc = SQLAllocConnect(hEnv, hDBC)
    Timeout = 240
    rc = SQLSetConnectOption(hDBC, SQL_LOGIN_TIMEOUT, Timeout)
    rc = SQLDriverConnect(hDBC, GetParent(GetFocus()), ConnIn, _
                        255, ConnOut, 255, cbOut%, 1)

    SQLStr = "select Alb.AlbumTitle,Art.FirstName, _
            Art.LastName from TY_ODBC..Album Alb, TY_ODBC..Artist Art where
            [ic:ccc]Alb.ArtistID = Art.ArtistID"
    rc = SQLAllocStmt(hDBC, hStmt)
    rc = SQLExecDirect(hStmt, SQLStr, Len(SQLStr))
    NextRec
End Sub
```

 The few lines of code in Listing 11.1 perform the bulk of the work in this tiny application. The first four function calls establish a connection to the data source. The `SQLSetConnectOption` call was added to overcome time-out problems to an SQL Server data source running on a slow system. Normally, this should not be necessary, but it can be a lifesaver when troubles arise.

The SQL SELECT statement to be executed is defined as a constant placed in the variable `SQLStr`. Immediately following the assignment of that string, a statement handle is allocated and the statement is executed, using the `SQLExecDirect` function. Note that no return-code checking is done in this example, but it should never be left out in a production application. After the SELECT statement is executed, the data must be retrieved from the data source and displayed. This is performed in the `NextRec` function, which is shown in Listing 11.2.

The SQL statement used in Listing 11.1 includes a two-table join condition to explicitly highlight the capabilities of the three alternative development environments shown. Specifically, when you use Visual Basic and the odbc/ClassLib libraries with Visual C++, you can use joins. When you use the built-in database support in MFC, however, joins

are not easy to implement. Although there are many ways this limitation can be dealt with in the application design, it can be a significant consideration, and should be kept in mind.

 Listing 11.2. Source code for the NextRec display function.

```
Sub NextRec ()
  Dim rc  As Integer
  Dim RetLen As Long

  rc = SQLFetch(hStmt)

  TitleWork = Space$(76)
  lpStrAddress = lstrcpy(ByVal TitleWork, ByVal TitleWork)
  rc = SQLGetData(hStmt, 1, SQL_C_CHAR, lpStrAddress, 76, RetLen)
  FirstWork = Space$(51)
  lpStrAddress = lstrcpy(ByVal FirstWork, ByVal FirstWork)
  rc = SQLGetData(hStmt, 2, SQL_C_CHAR, lpStrAddress, 51, RetLen)
  LastWork = Space$(51)
  lpStrAddress = lstrcpy(ByVal LastWork, ByVal LastWork)
  rc = SQLGetData(hStmt, 3, SQL_C_CHAR, lpStrAddress, 51, RetLen)
  Chap11.TitleBox = TitleWork
  Chap11.NameBox = Trim(FirstWork)
  Chap11.NameBox = Chap11.NameBox + " " + Trim(LastWork)
End Sub
```

Analysis
Listing 11.2 shows the few lines necessary to return data from the result set on the data source to the client system (using SQLFetch) and the calls to SQLGetData to bring the data into the application program. These functions are discussed in detail on Day 12, "Returning Data to the Program." Note that the SQLGetData function does not return the data, but instead a pointer to the data. Therefore, in Visual Basic, the lstrcpy string copy function must be used to copy the actual data from the ODBC buffer to the Visual Basic variable. The final lines in this subroutine concatenate the first and last names of the artist before moving that name and the album name into the text boxes shown in Figure 11.1.

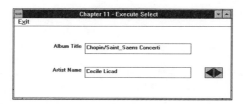

Figure 11.1. *Output from VBEXEC program, showing data displayed.*

The VBEXEC program might seem easy to do, and it is, but accomplishing the same result can be nearly as simple using Visual C++ and the Microsoft MFC libraries. The next example, CPEXEC, shows such a program. Follow the creation of this program using the Application Wizard to show how the basic building blocks contained in the MFC libraries can be utilized.

When you create a new application in Visual C++ using the AppWizard, one of the first choices to make is the type of database support you want. Figure 11.2 shows the AppWizard dialog box with check boxes for various levels of database support, including support for a database view without file support. If multiple database queries are to be utilized, with each presenting different views, the MFC file support might be useful. The MFC presents a serialized paradigm such as you would have when creating, opening, and saving files. When you choose to include a database view in your application, you must select a data source by pressing the Data Source button. Obviously, this implies that if you are developing an application that will be distributed to other workstations, the same data source must be available to both the development and production systems and will be installed using the data source name referenced in your application.

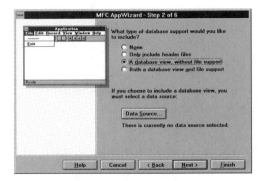

Figure 11.2. *Selecting database support when creating a new application.*

After you press the Data Source button during step 2 of the AppWizard application setup, you will be prompted to select and optionally log in to a data source. Many times in this login process you must also specify a default database. Figure 11.3 shows the list that is presented showing all tables found in the default or specified database.

As implied in the dialog box header, you can select one table for use in this application. Later, you will learn additional techniques for accessing other tables, but at this point you should select the primary table to be used. After you select the table to be used, you will be guided through the remaining steps of the AppWizard. For this example, the defaults were taken, resulting in the options shown in Figure 11.4.

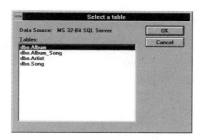

Figure 11.3. *Selecting a table to use with the AppWizard.*

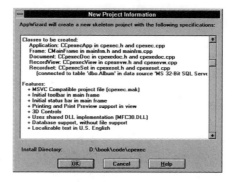

Figure 11.4. *Project specifications generated by AppWizard.*

Part of what the AppWizard in MFC does for you in creating your application is to query the data source for a list of columns in the table you selected. Members in the class derived from the CRecordset class are automatically created to correspond with each column in the table. You can look at these member variables by starting the Class Wizard, selecting the Member Variables tab, and then selecting the (YourClassNameHere)Set class name. Figure 11.5 shows this display for the CPEXEC application.

Although each column is enumerated with its data type and corresponding member variable name, these might not all be needed if the data from certain columns will not be used or displayed in the application. In this case, you should delete the member variables in this dialog box. Because this class determines what will be contained in the record set (which is the result set), removing unnecessary columns from the set will reduce the query overhead to the data source and reduce the amount of data being returned to the application.

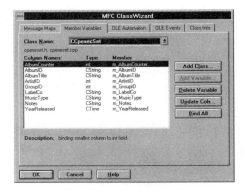

Figure 11.5. *Variables, automatically created and bound by the Class Wizard.*

The next step in building this particular application is to create the user interface. You can do this easily by double-clicking the resource file shown in the project window. In this case, that file is named CPEXEC.RC. Create the interface as you would in any application, adding the static text labels and edit boxes in this case to hold the artist ID and album title data.

A nice feature of the Class Wizard is that if the tab order of the static labels and edit text boxes is sequential (check by temporarily turning on Tab Order in the Layout menu), and the static label name is the same (or similar) to the column name, the member variable name will be automatically filled in when the variable is created for the view. You can easily create this member when you edit the dialog box by holding down the Ctrl key and double-clicking the edit text box. This will bring up the Add Member Variable dialog box, as shown in Figure 11.6.

Figure 11.6. *Creating an application interface with the Class Wizard.*

After member variables have been added in this fashion for each data item to be displayed, you are finished with the application development. You have just created an application

that will perform useful work—displaying data from a table—without writing a single line of code.

Unquestionably, building an application as just described is very easy to do, but the limitations are also somewhat obvious. When you compare the output of CPEXEC in Figure 11.7 to VBEXEC in Figure 11.1, the presentation of an artist ID rather than the artist's name can be a major drawback. Imagine a sales application in which the customer number was presented but the customer name was not because that field was in another table. You can overcome this limitation, but at the expense of the simplicity of application-building seen here. When you zoom through this example of running SQL SELECT statements, you could easily overlook the fact that nowhere was any SQL written or even seen! Again, the AppWizard and MFC hide this from the developer. The SQL is so well hidden that a search on the string "SELECT" in all of the files associated with this project will fail to find the SELECT statement.

Figure 11.7. *The completed application CPEXEC display when running.*

To determine what SQL statement is being sent to the data source, you must use another method other than searching the source code. The easiest way to determine this posthumously is to use a tool such as ODBC Spy, one of the Dr. DeeBee Tools from Syware. ODBC Spy is detailed on Day 21, "Using ODBC Test and Trace Tools." So that you can better understand this sample application, the output from an ODBC Spy trace log is presented as a portion of the session seen when running the CPEXEC application.

This log, shown in Figure 11.8, shows the SQL SELECT statement sent in an SQLPrepare call rather than an SQLExecDirect call. Although this is probably less efficient if the statement is to be executed only once, there appears to be no developer control over the choice of function calls.

Figure 11.8. *The ODBC Spy log listing from CPEXEC execution.*

The third approach to application development using ODBC is using Visual C++ with its MFC libraries for all support except database support. For the database support, the example uses the odbc/ClassLib, a set of commercially available class libraries available from South Wind Design, Inc. These class libraries seem to be the most capable third-party ODBC-specific tools available.

Again for the sake of simplicity, the SWEX2 application was created to display artist name and album title information from the sample database. In this case, instead of using the MFC MDI multiple document interface, we will use a dialog-based application. The specifications for this project are shown in Figure 11.9, and the code is presented in Listing 11.3.

Figure 11.9. *The AppWizard specifications for building the SWEX2 application.*

 Listing 11.3. Source from SWEx2.CPP main module.

```
//////////////////////////////////////////////////////////////////////////////
// CSWEx2App initialization

BOOL CSWEx2App::InitInstance()
```

```
{
    // Standard initialization
    Enable3dControls();

    CSWEx2Dlg dlg;
    m_pMainWnd = &dlg;

    int nResponse = dlg.DoModal();

    // we've exited, clean up before leaving
    if ( cursor )
    {
        delete cursor;
        cursor = NULL;
    }
    if ( pConnect )
    {
        pConnect->Disconnect();
        delete pConnect;
        pConnect = NULL;
    }
    if ( pEnv )
    {
        delete pEnv;
        pEnv = NULL;
    }
    // Since the dialog has been closed, return FALSE so that we exit the
    //   application, rather than start the application's message pump.
    return FALSE;
}
```

In the code presented in Listing 11.3, we have only added those few lines needed to clean up upon exiting from the dialog box before ending the program. These few lines are simple and straightforward; they check for the existence of the ODBC objects. If the objects exist, they are deleted. Listing 11.4 shows the code used to connect to the data source.

Listing 11.4. Source code for connection to data source.

```
void CSWEx2Dlg::OnConnect()
{
    static char szConnStrOut[ 1024 ];

    // perform odbc initialization and connection
    pEnv = new odbcENV;
    if ( pEnv )
    {
        pConnect = new odbcCONNECT( pEnv );
        if ( pConnect )
            pConnect->bTrimAllTrailingBlanks = TRUE;

        pEnv->SetWnd( m_hWnd );
```

Listing 11.4. continued

```
        pEnv->AutoRetrieve( odbcREPERRS );
        pEnv->AutoReport( odbcREPERRS );
        // use the cursor library for this example
        pEnv->nCursorLibUsage = SQL_CUR_USE_ODBC;

        // connect with user selected data source
        if ( pConnect )
        {
          pConnect->DriverConnectPrompt(
                      m_hWnd,
                      szConnStrOut,
                      sizeof(szConnStrOut));
          cursor = new odbcCURSOR( pConnect );

          if (cursor->sqlsuccess())
          {
            //execute the select statement
            cursor->ExecDirect(
                      (LPUCSTR)
                      "select Alb.AlbumTitle,Art.FirstName,Art.LastName from "
                      "TY_ODBC..Album Alb, TY_ODBC..Artist Art "
                      "where Alb.ArtistID = Art.ArtistID ");
          }
        }
      }
    }
```

Analysis

The code in Listing 11.4, which is executed when the Connect button is pressed, performs both the connection to a data source and the execution of the SQL SELECT statement. After the odbcENV and odbcCONNECT classes are constructed, some housekeeping is done, including the setting of error-reporting options with the AutoRetrieve and AutoReport member functions of the pEnv class. Next, the DriverConnectPrompt function of the pConnect class is executed. This function executes the SQLDriverConnect function (as explained on Day 8), prompting for needed additional connection attributes. Once the connection is successful, a cursor class is created. The ExecDirect function of the cursor class is executed to execute the SQL SELECT statement, which is contained as a string in the ExecDirect call.

Note in this application that we have again used a JOIN statement as in the VBEXEC Visual Basic application. Because the odbc/ClassLib functions enable the entry of any SQL statement, this JOIN can be done without any problem. Listing 11.5 shows how you can retrieve the data set from the query.

Listing 11.5. Source code for the `OnNext` function to fetch data.

```
void CSWEx2Dlg::OnNext()
{
    SDWORD pcbValue = 0;     // actual length of returned data is placed here
    char *scratch = "";

    // fetch and show a row
    cursor->Fetch();
    if ( cursor->sqlsuccess() )
    {
        cursor->GetData(
                    1,
                    SQL_C_CHAR,
                    scratch,
                    35,
                    &pcbValue);
        CWnd* pCtlTitle = GetDlgItem(IDC_ALBUMTITLE);
        pCtlTitle->SetWindowText(scratch);

        cursor->GetData(
                    2,
                    SQL_C_CHAR,
                    scratch,
                    35,
                    &pcbValue);
        CWnd* pCtlFirst = GetDlgItem(IDC_FIRSTNAME);
        pCtlFirst->SetWindowText(scratch);

        cursor->GetData(
                    3,
                    SQL_C_CHAR,
                    scratch,
                    35,
                    &pcbValue);
        CWnd* pCtlLast = GetDlgItem(IDC_LASTNAME);
        pCtlLast->SetWindowText(scratch);
    }
}
```

In this sample application, the connection is made and the SQL SELECT statement is executed as soon as the Connect button is pressed. This leaves the result set at the data source, ready for you to retrieve back into the application. Because no WHERE clause was specified in the SELECT statement, all rows meeting the join criteria will be returned. To view any data, the Next Record button must be pressed to fetch the next record and display it in the output dialog box. The source code shown in Listing 11.5 is executed when this Next Record button is pressed.

This function shows a good example of using the odbc/ClassLib and MFC libraries in harmony. The odbc/ClassLib `GetData` function is used to bring the data back to the application, and the MFC `SetWindowText` function is used to display that data in the dialog box. Again, one `Fetch` function is performed each time the Next Record button is pressed, followed by one execution of `GetData` for each column to be displayed.

As described in the documentation for both Visual C++ and the odbc/ClassLib, the library files referenced from within an application must be explicitly or implicitly located for the linker. With MFC applications, this is taken care of by default. With odbc/ClassLib applications, the proper library must be more explicitly specified or "unresolved external" errors will occur.

Odbc/ClassLib features two versions of its ODBCM232.LIB library, one for static linking and one for use with ODBCM232.DLL. Because these can be rebuilt locally, it is often easier to use and refer to the ODBCM232.LIB file from its default installation location. The easiest way to do this in Visual C++ is to include ODBCM232.LIB in the project. Figure 11.10 shows a new group of files being added to the project from the Project menu. Then, by using a right mouse button click on the project and selecting the Files command menu item, you can select this library file as shown in Figure 11.11.

Figure 11.10. *Adding a new group for Libraries from the Project menu.*

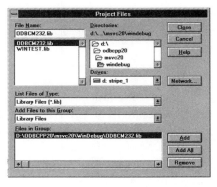

Figure 11.11. *Adding the DLL version of the ODBCM232.LIB file to a project.*

As shown in Figure 11.12, the output from this SWEX2 application is similar to that shown in Figure 11.1 from the Visual Basic VBEXEC application. Other than the obvious cosmetic differences in button appearance, the most significant change is that the artist name is shown in two distinct fields. These two fields simplify the program because, although concatenating two strings is very easy in Visual Basic, it is a little more complex in C++.

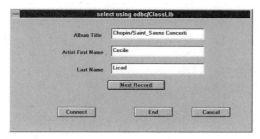

Figure 11.12. *The output dialog box from the SWEX2 application.*

Although the Visual Basic application and the MFC application used in this chapter featured buttons indicating that the data could be navigated in both a forward and backward direction, this was not actually the case, and the backward buttons did nothing. Adding this functionality is discussed on Day 16, "Using ODBC Functions."

Setting Statement Options

Controlling the execution behavior of a particular SQL statement as performed on a particular data source and driver is often helpful or even necessary. You can control this behavior at the statement level using the SQLSetStmtOption function, and the current behavior can be determined using SQLGetStmtOption. Similarly, behavior at the connection level is controlled with SQLSetConnectOption and SQLGetConnectOption. If cursors are being used, you can control their options by calling SQLSetScrollOption or SQLGetScrollOption.

Figure 11.8, earlier in the chapter, showed a common way to use this functionality where the MFC application automatically tries to set the asynchronous execution option to on. This is done without any control by the developer in this case. Next, take a look at how to call this function under your control.

The *SQLSetStmtOption* Function

The general syntax for the SQLSetStmtOption function in Visual Basic is

```
RETCODE SQLSetStmtOption(hStmt, fOption, vParam)
```

This function sets options related only to the specific statement handle specified by hStmt. The parameter fOption refers to the option to be changed, and vParam is the new value to set for that option. If this function returns SQL_ERROR or SQL_SUCCESS_WITH_INFO, a subsequent call to SQLError will return the SQLSTATE value indicating the nature of the error. If SQLSTATE 01S02 is returned with a message of Option value changed, it means that the driver does not support the specific option value specified in vParam, but a similar value was substituted and will be used. If SQLSetStmtOption returned SQLSTATE S1C00 with a message of Driver not capable, it means that an option value specified in fOption is valid for the current version of ODBC, but is not supported by the driver being used.

The available statement options and their possible values are listed next. This list will be expanded in future versions of ODBC, and each driver vendor can specify their own driver-specific options. Often, these driver-specific options are not made public, but can be seen in use when you trace with tools like Dr. DeeBee's Peek.

Example:

```
Global hStmt As Long            'Pointer to handle for statement
Global rc as Integer            'Return code

rc = SQLSetStmtOption(hStmt, SQL_ASYNC_ENABLE,SQL_ASYNC_ENABLE_ON)
```

The constants used in this example are defined as usual in the INCLUDE files that ship with the ODBC Software Development Kit (SDK). In the case of Visual Basic, they are in the VBDEMO sample directory under SAMPLES in the SDK.

The *SQLSetStmtOption* Function

The prototype for the SQLSetStmtOption function is

```
RETCODE SQL_API SQLSetStmtOption(
    HSTMT       hstmt,
    UWORD       fOption,
    UDWORD      vParam);
```

This function sets options related to the statements used with the statement handle hstmt. The parameter fOption specifies the option to be changed, and the parameter vParam specifies the new value to which that option is to be set. The following is an example (from MFC source):

```
RETCODE nRetCode;

if (m_dwQueryTimeout != -1)
{
    // Attempt to set query timeout.  Ignore failure
    AFX_SQL_SYNC(::SQLSetStmtOption(hstmt, SQL_QUERY_TIMEOUT,
        m_dwQueryTimeout));
    if (!Check(nRetCode))
        // don't attempt it again
        m_dwQueryTimeout = (DWORD)-1;
}
```

Available Statement Options

The following options can be specified in the fOption parameter of SQLSetStmtOption to set a new value or SQLGetStmtOption to retrieve the current value of the option. The version of ODBC in which the option was released is indicated in parentheses after the option name.

SQL_ASYNC_ENABLE (1.0)

A 32-bit integer value specifying whether the function called using the specified hstmt is executed asynchronously. The defined values and their constants are

```
SQL_ASYNC_ENABLE_ON = On
SQL_ASYNC_ENABLE_OFF = Off (default value)
```

Asynchronous processing is used when it will take significant processing time for the data source to complete the function and there is other work the application can perform while this is processing. If asynchronous processing is disabled, the application will wait without performing any other processing until the function returns from the data source. Once asynchronous processing is enabled and a function is called with this hstmt, no other functions can be called using this same hstmt or hdbc until the same function is called again and returns any return code besides SQL_STILL_EXECUTING. All of the following functions can be executed asynchronously:

SQLColAttributes	SQLNumParams
SQLColumnPrivileges	SQLNumResultCols
SQLColumns	SQLParamData
SQLDescribeCol	SQLPrepare
SQLDescribeParam	SQLPrimaryKeys
SQLExecDirect	SQLProcedureColumns
SQLExecute	SQLProcedures
SQLExtendedFetch	SQLPutData

SQLFetch	SQLSetPos
SQLForeignKeys	SQLSpecialColumns
SQLGetData	SQLStatistics
SQLGetTypeInfo	SQLTablePrivileges
SQLMoreResults	SQLTables

SQL_BIND_TYPE (1.0)

A 32-bit integer value setting the binding orientation to be used by SQLExtendedFetch when it is called on this hstmt. If the constant value SQL_BIND_BY_COLUMN is specified for vParam, the binding is performed in a column-wise fashion. This is the default behavior. To achieve row-wise binding, the vParam value must be set equal to the amount of space required to hold one entire row, including all padding and spaces. Using the sizeof operator in Visual C++ will ensure that this value is correct.

SQL_CONCURRENCY (2.0)

A 32-bit integer value specifying how the cursor is to maintain concurrency. These values are also defined on Day 9. The currently defined values include the following:

- ☐ SQL_CONCUR_READ_ONLY. Cursor is read-only. Updates are not allowed. This is the default value.
- ☐ SQL_CONCUR_LOCK. Cursor uses the lowest level of locking sufficient to ensure that the row can be updated.
- ☐ SQL_CONCUR_ROWVER. Cursor uses optimistic concurrency control based on a row version. This row version is usually a TIMESTAMP or ROWID type of data item.
- ☐ SQL_CONCUR_VALUES. Cursor uses optimistic concurrency control by comparing data values.

SQL_CURSOR_TYPE (2.0)

A 32-bit integer value specifying the cursor type to be used. The following are the values:

- ☐ SQL_CURSOR_FORWARD_ONLY. The cursor scrolls only forward. This is the default value.
- ☐ SQL_CURSOR_STATIC. The data in the result set is static.

- [ ] SQL_CURSOR_KEYSET_DRIVEN. The driver saves the keys for the number of rows specified in the SQL_KEYSET_SIZE option, and uses these keys for record ordering.

- [ ] SQL_CURSOR_DYNAMIC. The driver only saves and uses the keys for the rows in the rowset.

SQL_KEYSET_SIZE (2.0)

A 32-bit integer value specifying the number of rows contained in a keyset driven cursor. The default value is zero, meaning the cursor is fully keyset driven. If the keyset size is greater than zero, the cursor is mixed.

SQL_MAX_LENGTH (1.0)

A 32-bit integer value specifying the maximum amount of data that the driver will return from a character or binary column. If the vParam value set is less than the length of the available data, the data will be truncated and SQL_SUCCESS will be returned. If the value is zero, the driver will attempt to return all available data.

SQL_MAX_ROWS (1.0)

A 32-bit integer value specifying the maximum number of rows to return to the application from a result set. The default value of zero indicates that all rows are to be returned. This option was intended to reduce network traffic, not processing overhead on the data source.

SQL_NOSCAN (1.0)

A 32-bit integer value specifying whether the driver scans the SQL string looking for escape clauses. The following are the defined values:

- [ ] SQL_NOSCAN_OFF. The driver scans SQL strings for escape clauses. This is the default value.

- [ ] SQL_NOSCAN_ON. The driver does not scan the SQL string for escape clauses. Instead, the driver passes the string to the data source unchanged.

SQL_QUERY_TIMEOUT (1.0)

A 32-bit integer value specifying the number of seconds to wait for an SQL statement to complete before returning to the application with a time-out error. The default value is zero, indicating that there is no time out.

SQL_RETRIEVE_DATA (2.0)

A 32-bit integer value specifying whether SQLExtendedFetch is to retrieve data after positioning the cursor. This can be done to verify the existence of a row or retrieve a bookmark without actually having to retrieve data. The values are

- ☐ SQL_RD_ON. SQLExtendedFetch retrieves data after it positions the cursor to the specified location. This is the default action.
- ☐ SQL_RD_OFF. SQLExtendedFetch does not retrieve data after it positions the cursor.

SQL_ROWSET_SIZE (2.0)

A 32-bit integer value specifying the number of rows that will be returned in each call to SQLExtendedFetch. This is the rowset size. The default value is one row.

SQL_SIMULATE_CURSOR (2.0)

A 32-bit integer value specifying whether or not the driver guarantees that positioned update and delete statements that are simulated will affect only a single row. The defined values include the following:

- ☐ SQL_SC_NON_UNIQUE. The driver cannot guarantee that simulated positioned update or delete statements will affect only a single row. The application must take steps to ensure this happens.
- ☐ SQL_SC_TRY_UNIQUE. The driver will attempt to guarantee that a simulated positioned update or delete will affect only one row. The driver will always execute such statements even if they will affect more than one row.
- ☐ SQL_SC_UNIQUE. The driver guarantees that simulated positioned update or delete statements affect only one row.

SQL_USE_BOOKMARKS (2.0)

A 32-bit integer value specifying whether an application will use bookmarks with a cursor. The value SQL_UB_ON must be specified before opening the cursor if bookmarks are to be used. The values are

- ☐ SQL_UB_OFF. Off, the default.
- ☐ SQL_UB_ON. On.

Summary

Today's lesson presented the important steps necessary to execute an SQL SELECT statement. You learned about the following topics:

☐ A statement handle must be allocated against a connection before the statement can be executed.

☐ SQL SELECT statements can be executed by either calling SQLPrepare and SQLExecute, or by just calling SQLExecDirect. SQLExecDirect was shown today as the easiest and fastest method to execute a statement one time only.

☐ When you use Visual C++ with the Application Wizard and the MFC database classes, you can build a very simple data-display application without entering any C code. Although this technique is quick and easy, very little flexibility is provided.

☐ The odbc/ClassLib third-party database classes enable more flexibility in accessing the ODBC data source. These classes can be used in conjunction with the MFC windows classes for display functionality.

☐ Statement options can be set or changed, affecting the way a statement executes or returns its data.

Q&A

Q When would I use SQLExecDirect instead of SQLPrepare coupled with SQLExecute?

A If you are only going to use a query once, SQLExecDirect is the way to go. However, if a query is repeated more than once, then SQLPrepare, followed by SQLExecute, would give you a notable performance improvement.

Q When would I use asynchronous processing?

A You would use asynchronous processing when it will take significant processing time for the data source to complete the function and there is other work the application can perform while this is processing. If asynchronous processing is disabled, the application will wait, seemingly forever, without performing any other processing, until the function returns from the data source.

Workshop

The Workshop provides quiz questions to help you solidify your understanding of the material covered and to give you experience in using what you've learned. Try to understand the quiz and exercise answers before continuing on to the next day's lesson. Answers are provided in Appendix A, "Answers."

Quiz

1. Use `SQLSetStmtOption` to change the cursor type to where the driver only saves and uses the keys for the rows in the rowset.

2. Use `SQLSetStmtOption` to change the maximum number of rows returned from a query to 10.

Exercise

1. Rewrite the program in Listing 11.1 to return all columns and the first 20 rows from the Album table.

Returning Data to the Program

Yesterday you learned how to execute an SQL query, which generates a result set at the data source. Today, you learn the details of how to return that result set to your application. The lesson covers how to learn about the result set and the different techniques to retrieve the data. Today you learn about the following topics:

☐ Advantages of bound versus unbound columns

☐ Determining result set characteristics

☐ Binding columns

☐ Returning a row of data to the application buffer

☐ Getting unbound data from the buffer to the application

The Advantages of Bound Versus Unbound Columns

When you perform a query using ODBC to return data to an application, you must follow at least two basic steps (disregarding the allocation of environment and other setup matters). These two steps are to execute the SQL statement to determine what data is to be returned, and to actually return that data to the application.

To execute the SQL SELECT statement, yesterday you learned about SQLExecDirect. You can also learn about using SQLPrepare with SQLExecute on Day 14, "Using Prepared Statements and Parameter Markers."

To bring the data from the data source to the application, you must use the SQLFetch statement (or SQLExtendedFetch, as discussed on Day 17, "Using ODBC Cursors") and either SQLBindCol or SQLGetData. So far, most of the examples presented in this book have used SQLGetData when possible for the sake of simplicity. The differences between getting data using bound columns or unbound columns are generally subtle, although in many cases you can see better performance by using bound columns. Because this performance difference comes from the way in which the ODBC driver manipulates data internally, it is impossible to predict which function will be faster and is best determined by testing.

On the other hand, using SQLGetData does provide advantages when you are returning long data. With SQLBindCol, the receiving buffer space must be allocated before the fetch, and it must be large enough to hold all data returned in the bound columns. If not, SQLBindCol will fail. On the other hand, if SQLGetData encounters more data than will fit in the buffer, it will fill the buffer and return SQL_SUCCESS_WITH_INFO. SQLGetData can then be called as many times as necessary to get all of the data. A pointer is used to keep track of the starting point of the column, and when a "partial" return of data such as this happens, the pointer is moved so the next SQLGetData call will get the next portion of data.

Note: Predicting the amount of buffer space required at runtime without knowing the structure of the data is very complicated. A good programming rule of thumb is to use `SQLBindCol` in applications in which the buffer space can be quantified at design time and use `SQLGetData` in more dynamic situations.

The `SQLFetch` call also moves a pointer that will always point to the beginning of a result set row. Following the execution of the `SELECT` statement, the pointer is at the top of the result set. Each time `SQLFetch` is called, this pointer is moved down one row. If columns have been bound prior to the fetch by calling `SQLBindCol`, the `SQLFetch` call will also move the data into the bound locations within the application automatically. If no columns are bound, the only action caused by an `SQLFetch` call is that the row pointer moves down one row. Therefore, if your application is only concerned with the fifteenth row of data in a result set, `SQLFetch` could be called 15 times, then `SQLGetData` could be called to move data from that fifteenth row into the application.

Binding data becomes especially useful when you are retrieving multirow cursors. In this case, the columns can be bound to array variables within the application, and an extended fetch will bring back many rows of data into this cursor with a single call. Again, this is covered on Day 17.

At times, the binding behavior cannot be controlled. When you use the MFC database classes, for instance, all result columns are automatically bound. When you use the Microsoft Access Jet Engine with ODBC drivers, one of the performance problems is that it only does `SQLGetData` calls. It is important for an ODBC application developer to understand when each function is appropriate to use, and when it doesn't make much difference.

Determining Result Set Characteristics

Before result set data is returned to the application, the characteristics of that result set must be known. These characteristics include the number of columns in the result set, what data type the data is to returned in, and the size of the data. Knowing how many rows are available is not necessary to bring them back, and many times this information is not available for a `SELECT` statement.

12

If the database is a known environment, the data can be returned immediately because its characteristics are already known. For instance, consider the following query:

```
SELECT empid,empname FROM employee
```

You know that this will return two columns—the first will be numeric of a known precision and type and the second will be a character field of known length. On the other hand, some queries are less well known, such as

```
SELECT * FROM employee
```

The result set from this query will return an unknown result set. The number of columns, their order, their description, and their data type will not be known. Before this result set can be fetched, this information must be determined. The ODBC specification has APIs that are designed to be called in this situation to obtain just this needed information.

VB4 **Syntax**

The *SQLNumResultCols* Function

The general syntax for the SQLNumResultCols function in Visual Basic is

```
RETCODE SQLNumResultCols(hStmt, pcCol)
```

The function returns the number of columns contained in a result set. The parameter hStmt is the statement handle that owns the result set. This statement must have been prepared, executed, or positioned for the SQLNumResultCols function to be called successfully. The parameter pcCol points to an integer that will receive the number of columns.

Example:

```
Global hStmt As Long
Global pcCol As Integer
Global rc% As Integer

rc% = SQLExecute(hStmt)
rc% = SQLNumResultCols(hStmt, pcCol)
```

C++ **Syntax**

The *SQLNumResultCols* Function

The prototype for the SQLNumResultCols function is

```
RETCODE SQL_API SQLNumResultCols(
    HSTMT       hstmt,
    SWORD  FAR *pccol);
```

The function returns the number of columns contained in the current result set owned by hstmt. This function will succeed only if the hstmt is in a state of having just been prepared, executed, or positioned. The parameter pccol is a pointer to the word that is to receive the number of columns in the result set.

Syntax

The *SQLDescribeCol* Function

The general syntax for the SQLDescribeCol function in Visual Basic is

```
RETCODE SQLDescribeCol(hStmt,
                       icol,
                       szColName,
                       cbColNameMax,
                       pcbColName,
                       pfSqlType,
                       pcbColDef,
                       pibScale,
                       pfNullable)
```

The function returns the description for one column in the result set. It cannot return information about the bookmark column (column 0). The first parameter, hStmt, is the statement handle that owns the result set. The parameter icol is the column number in the result set, numbered sequentially from the left starting with column 1. The column name is returned to a storage location pointed to by szColName. The length of this name buffer must be input in cbColNameMax. The actual length of the column name, not counting the null termination byte, is returned in pcbColName. If the name will not fit in the buffer, it will be truncated. The data type of the column is returned in the area pointed to by pfSqlType. The SQL data type constants should describe this value unless it is a driver-specific data type. The precision or number of digits that the column can contain are returned in the storage location pointed to by pcbColDef. Similarly, the scale or number of digits to the right of the decimal is returned to the location pointed to by pibScale. The final parameter, pfNullable, indicates whether the column can contain NULL values. This field can contain SQL_NO_NULLS, SQL_NULLABLE, or if the value is not known, SQL_NULLABLE_UNKNOWN.

An example program, VBDESC (Listing 12.1), is shown following the Visual C++ syntax section.

C++

Syntax

The *SQLDescribeCol* Function

The prototype for the SQLDescribeCol function is

```
RETCODE SQL_API SQLDescribeCol(
    HSTMT        hstmt,
    UWORD        icol,
    UCHAR  FAR *szColName,
    SWORD        cbColNameMax,
    SWORD  FAR *pcbColName,
    SWORD  FAR *pfSqlType,
    UDWORD FAR *pcbColDef,
    SWORD  FAR *pibScale,
    SWORD  FAR *pfNullable);
```

12

The function returns the description for one column in the result set. The individual parameters are exactly the same as the Visual Basic syntax you saw at the beginning of this section.

Now look at a sample program using the SQLDescribeCol function. Later functions will build on this example.

Listing 12.1. The source code for the NextRec subroutine using SQLDescribeCol.

```
Sub NextRec ()
  Dim Nullable As Integer          'Nullable
  Dim lpNameAddr As Long           'Address for column name
  Dim NameLen As Integer           'Length of name
  Dim DataType As Integer          'Data type
  Dim Precision As Long            'Precision
  Dim ColScale As Integer          'Scale
  Dim NameWork As String           'Work area for column name
  Dim rc   As Integer

  NameWork = Space$(128)
  lpNameAddr = lstrcpy(ByVal NameWork, ByVal NameWork)
  rc = SQLDescribeCol(hStmt, CurCol, ByVal NameWork, Len(NameWork), NameLen, _
                DataType, Precision, ColScale, Nullable)
  ColNoBox = Str$(CurCol)
  If Nullable = SQL_NO_NULLS Then
    NullableBox = "No Nulls"
  ElseIf Nullable = SQL_NULLABLE Then
    NullableBox = "Nulls Allowed"
  Else
    NullableBox = "Nullability unknown"
  End If
  ColNameBox.Text = NameWork
  Select Case DataType
    Case SQL_BIGINT
      DatatypeBox = "SQL_BIGINT"
    Case SQL_BINARY
      DatatypeBox = "SQL_BINARY"
    Case SQL_BIT
      DatatypeBox = "SQL_BIT"
    Case SQL_CHAR
      DatatypeBox = "SQL_CHAR"
    Case SQL_DATE
      DatatypeBox = "SQL_DATE"
    Case SQL_DECIMAL
      DatatypeBox = "SQL_DECIMAL"
    Case SQL_DOUBLE
      DatatypeBox = "SQL_DOUBLE"
```

```
   Case SQL_FLOAT
     DatatypeBox = "SQL_FLOAT"
   Case SQL_INTEGER
     DatatypeBox = "SQL_INTEGER"
   Case SQL_LONGVARBINARY
     DatatypeBox = "SQL_LONGVARBINARY"
   Case SQL_LONGVARCHAR
     DatatypeBox = "SQL_LONGVARCHAR"
   Case SQL_NUMERIC
     DatatypeBox = "SQL_NUMERIC"
   Case SQL_REAL
     DatatypeBox = "SQL_REAL"
   Case SQL_SMALLINT
     DatatypeBox = "SQL_SMALLINT"
   Case SQL_TIME
     DatatypeBox = "SQL_TIME"
   Case SQL_TIMESTAMP
     DatatypeBox = "SQL_TIMESTAMP"
   Case SQL_TINYINT
     DatatypeBox = "SQL_TINYINT"
   Case SQL_VARBINARY
     DatatypeBox = "SQL_VARBINARY"
   Case SQL_VARCHAR
     DatatypeBox = "SQL_VARCHAR"
   Case Else    ' Must be something else.
     DatatypeBox = "Type unknown"
   End Select

 PrecisionBox.Text = Str$(Precision)
 ScaleBox.Text = Str$(ColScale)
End Sub
```

Analysis Listing 12.1 presents the code needed to execute the function `SQLDescribeCol` and then, in this case, display the results. Normally, the results would be used to bind the output rather than for display purposes. Notice that the function is performed after an `SQLPrepare` call. The program never executes the SQL or returns data. All the `SQLDescribeCol` function returns is metadata.

The dialog box shown in Figure 12.1 shows the VBDESC program running.

NEW☞ TERM *Metadata* refers not to the data itself, but to data about the data. This is a description of the data. All of the information returned from the `SQLDescribeCol` function is *metadata* rather than the actual data.

12

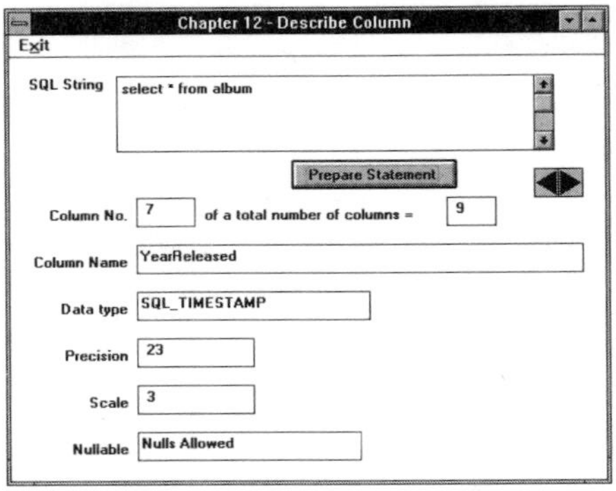

Figure 12.1. *VBDESC dialog box showing a column description.*

VB

Syntax

The *SQLColumnAttributes* Function

The general syntax for the `SQLColumnAttributes` function in Visual Basic is

```
RETCODE SQLColumnAttributes(hStmt,
                            icol,
                            fDescType,
                            rgbDesc,
                            cbDescMax,
                            pcbDesc,
                            pfDesc)
```

This function returns descriptor information about a specific column in the result set. It cannot be used to return information about the bookmark column 0. The returned descriptor information can be returned as a character string, a 32-bit descriptor-dependent value, or an integer.

The parameter `hStmt` is the statement handle that owns the result set for which metadata is being queried. The parameter `icol` is the column number being referred to, as numbered from the left in the result set, with the first column being column 1. The parameter `fDescType` must be a descriptor value from Table 12.1. `rgbDesc` is the output parameter that will be a pointer to the descriptor information, with a maximum length input in `cbDescMax`. The actual number of bytes available to return is placed in `pcbDesc`. Some descriptor types will return an integer value, which is returned in `pfDesc`.

C++

Syntax

The *SQLColAttributes* Function

The prototype for the `SQLColAttributes` function is

```
RETCODE SQL_API SQLColAttributes(
    HSTMT       hstmt,
    UWORD       icol,
```

```
UWORD        fDescType,
PTR          rgbDesc,
SWORD        cbDescMax,
SWORD  FAR *pcbDesc,
SDWORD FAR *pfDesc);
```

This function returns descriptor information about a specific column in the result set. It cannot be used to return information about the bookmark column 0. The returned descriptor information can be returned as a character string, a 32-bit descriptor-dependent value, or an integer.

Table 12.1 lists the currently defined descriptor values and what they mean. The sample program following Table 12.1 shows the function being used in an artificial environment.

Table 12.1. Descriptor types for the `SQLColAttributes` function.

Descriptor Type	Results in	Description
SQL_COLUMN_AUTO_INCREMENT (1.0)	pfDesc	A column is autoincrement if it is numeric and is incremented automatically. An application can insert values into an autoincrement field but not update them. The returned values could be TRUE—the column is autoincrement. FALSE—the column is not autoincrement or not numeric.
SQL_COLUMN_CASE_SENSITIVE (1.0)	pfDesc	TRUE if the column is considered case-sensitive for ordering and comparisons. FALSE if the column is noncharacter or not case-sensitive for ordering and comparisons.
SQL_COLUMN_COUNT (1.0)	pfDesc	The number of columns in the result set. The parameter icol is ignored for this descriptor.

continues

Table 12.1. continued

Descriptor Type	Results in	Description
SQL_COLUMN_DISPLAY_SIZE (1.0)	pfDesc	Maximum number of characters required to display the data contained in this column. For numerics this will include space for all digits as well as decimal point and sign.
SQL_COLUMN_LABEL (2.0)	rgbDesc	The column label or title, if defined, or the column name if a label is not defined or allowed.
SQL_COLUMN_LENGTH (1.0)	pfDesc	The number of bytes transferred when the column is fetched using the default data type. This is also commonly referred to as the storage length of the data.
SQL_COLUMN_MONEY (1.0)	pfDesc	TRUE if the column is a money data type, FALSE if not.
SQL_COLUMN_NAME (1.0)	rgbDesc	The column name or an empty string if the column is un-named.
SQL_COLUMN_NULLABLE (1.0)	pfDesc	SQL_NULLABLE if the column will accept NULL values. SQL_NO_NULLS if NULL is not accepted. SQL_NULLABLE_UNKNOWN if it is not known.
SQL_COLUMN_OWNER_NAME (2.0)	rgbDesc	The owner of the table if that can be determined. The value returned is implementation-defined if the column is part of a view or is an expression.
SQL_COLUMN_PRECISION (1.0)	pfDesc	The precision of the column, which is the total number of digits contained in the value.

Descriptor Type	Results in	Description
SQL_COLUMN_QUALIFIER_NAME (2.0)	rgbDesc	The qualifier of the table if that can be determined. The value returned is implementation-defined if the column is part of a view or is an expression.
SQL_COLUMN_SCALE (1.0)	pfDesc	The scale of the column on the data source, which is the number of digits to the right of the decimal.
SQL_COLUMN_SEARCHABLE (1.0)	pfDesc	SQL_SEARCHABLE if the column can be used in a WHERE clause with any comparison operator. SQL_UNSEARCHABLE if the column cannot be used in a WHERE clause under any circumstances. SQL_ALL_EXCEPT_LIKE if the column can be used in all WHERE clauses except those containing a LIKE predicate. SQL_LIKE_ONLY if the column can only be used with the LIKE predicate in a WHERE clause.
SQL_COLUMN_TABLE_NAME (2.0)	rgbDesc	The table name of the table containing the column. If the result set column does not have a table, such as when the column is from an expression or a view, the value is implementation-defined.
SQL_COLUMN_TYPE (1.0)	pfDesc	SQL data type. Any ODBC SQL data type or a driver-specific data type.

continues

12

Table 12.1. continued

Descriptor Type	Results in	Description
SQL_COLUMN_TYPE_NAME (1.0)	rgbDesc	The name of the data type corresponding to the numeric data type specification.
SQL_COLUMN_UNSIGNED (1.0)	pfDesc	TRUE if the column is not numeric or unsigned. FALSE if the column contains a sign.
SQL_COLUMN_UPDATABLE (1.0)	pfDesc	Whether the column can be updated. Values: SQL_ATTR_READONLY, SQL_ATTR_WRITE, or SQL_ATTR_READWRITE_UNKNOWN.

In the sample program VBATTR12.EXE (Listing 12.2), the SQLColAttributes function is run after the user selects the descriptor and a column number. SQLColAttributes then returns the metadata.

Listing 12.2. Source from VBATTR12 program executing SQLColAttributes.

```
Sub NextRec ()
    Dim lpDescAddr As Long          'Address for column name
    Dim DescLen As Integer          'Length of name
    Dim DescWork As String          'Work area for column name
    Dim rc  As Integer
    Dim pfDesc As Long
    Dim iCol As Integer

    DescWork = Space$(128)
    lpDescAddr = lstrcpy(ByVal DescWork, ByVal DescWork)
    iCol = ColNoBox
    rc = SQLColAttributes(hStmt, iCol, DescList.ItemData(DescList.ListIndex), _
                     ByVal DescWork, Len(DescWork), DescLen, pfDesc)
    rgbDescBox.Text = DescWork
    pfDescBox.Text = Str$(pfDesc)

End Sub
```

Analysis In Visual Basic, you can make the display of column attributes much easier by not converting the value of pfDesc, returned in SQLColAttributes, into its corresponding constant name. This more accurately reflects actual usage because passing of the parameter from one function to another would not require a reconversion. The program described in Listing 12.2 is shown running in Figure 12.2.

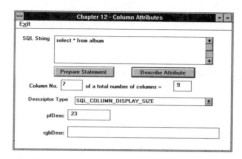

Figure 12.2. *The VBATTR12 dialog box showing the returned attribute.*

Binding Columns

Yesterday you constructed a sample application that executed an SQL query and then used the SQLFetch and SQLGetData calls to return data to the application. In a moment, you will look at the syntax for these function calls, but first you will learn an alternative.

If many fetches are to be performed against a result set, especially if many columns are being fetched, using SQLBindCol can provide performance enhancements. Consider a table of 100 columns and 1,000 rows. If all data is to be returned using the first method, SQLFetch must be called 1,000 times, once for each row. However, between each fetch, SQLGetData must be called 100 times to get each column into the application. This means a total of 101,000 function calls must be made to get all data back into the application.

With SQLBindCol, on the other hand, there will be 100 bind calls followed by 1,000 uninterrupted fetch calls, for a total of 1,100 function calls. The same amount of data is moved, but the overhead to perform those decreases by two orders of magnitude.

VB4

Syntax

The *SQLBindCol* Function

The general syntax for the `SQLBindCol` function in Visual Basic is

```
RETCODE SQLBindCol(hStmt, iCol, fCType, rgbValue, cbValueMax, pcbValue)
```

The function assigns the storage and data type for a column in the result set before the data is retrieved. When `SQLFetch` or `SQLExtendedFetch` is called, the driver will place into the assigned locations the data for all bound columns.

An application can bind all columns in the result set, bind no columns and retrieve data entirely by using `SQLGetData`, or use a combination of both techniques. However, in most cases, `SQLGetData` can be used only to retrieve data from columns to the right of the last bound column.

You make the `SQLBindCol` call after a receiving buffer has been allocated in the proper length to hold the largest possible amount of data from the column. `SQLBindCol` is used to pass the pointer to a storage buffer for a column to the driver and also to specify how the driver should convert the data type while retrieving the data.

An application can call `SQLBindCol` at any time to bind a column to a new storage location, regardless of whether data has already been fetched from that column. This new binding overrides the old binding, but the previously fetched data is not affected.

The parameter `hStmt` is the handle for the statement that owns the result set. The binding is made to the column specified by `iCol`, which is the column number in the result set, beginning with column one on the left. Any data type conversion to be performed is specified with `fCType`, which is the C data type of the result data. The driver is responsible for converting from the storage SQL data type to this C data type. If `SQL_C_DEFAULT` is specified here, the driver is to convert to its default C data type. The parameter `rgbValue` is a pointer to the storage location for the data. If this is a `NULL` pointer, the call will unbind the column. `cbValueMax` is the length of the `rgbValue` buffer. For character data, this must include room for the `NULL`-termination byte. In other words, if a field is defined in the data source as `CHAR(30)`, the `rgbValue` buffer must have a length of 31. The final parameter, `pcbValue`, contains either `SQL_NULL_DATA` or the number of bytes available to return in `rgbValue` before calling the fetch function.

As always, the best way to understand how a function such as `SQLBindCol` works is to see it in use. Listing 12.3 uses the same code demonstrated on Day 11 to connect to the data source and enable the user to enter an SQL statement.

What is different in this example is that the `SQLDescribeCol` function is used to determine the column titles used in the result set, and these columns are then bound to edit boxes in the output dialog box.

Listing 12.3. Module CHAP12.FRM showing the `ExecSQL` subroutine.

```
Sub ExecSQL_Click ()
  Dim Nullable As Integer          'Nullable
  Dim lpNameAddr As Long           'Address for column name
  Dim NameLen As Integer           'Length of name
  Dim DataType As Integer          'Data type
  Dim Precision As Long            'Precision
  Dim ColScale As Integer          'Scale
  Dim NameWork As String           'Work area for column name
  Dim cbValueMax As Long           'Size of buffer
  Dim pcbValue As Long             'Number of bytes to return
  Dim rc  As Integer
  Dim ColNo As Integer
  Dim ColIdx As Integer

  rc = SQLFreeStmt(hstmt, SQL_CLOSE)   'clear pending results, if any
  rc = SQLExecDirect(hstmt, SQLBox.Text, Len(SQLBox.Text))
  If rc <> SQL_SUCCESS Then
    DescribeError hdbc, hstmt
  End If
  rc = SQLNumResultCols(hstmt, pccol)
  If rc <> SQL_SUCCESS Then
    DescribeError hdbc, hstmt
  End If
  If pccol = 0 Then
    MsgBox "No results"
    Exit Sub
  ElseIf pccol > 9 Then
    pccol = 9                'maximum displayable columns
  End If
  pcbValue = 254
  cbValueMax = 254
  For ColIdx = 0 To 8
    Label1(ColIdx).Caption = ""  'Clear captions
    Text1(ColIdx).Text = ""      'Clear data display
  Next

  For ColIdx = 0 To pccol - 1
    NameWork = Space$(128)
    lpNameAddr = lstrcpy(ByVal NameWork, ByVal NameWork)
    ColNo = ColIdx + 1
    rc = SQLDescribeCol(hstmt, ColNo, ByVal NameWork, Len(NameWork), _
                  NameLen, DataType, Precision, ColScale, Nullable)
    Label1(ColIdx).Caption = NameWork
    Strings(ColIdx) = String$(255, 0)
    rc = SQLBindCol(hstmt, ColNo, SQL_C_CHAR, _
                  ByVal Strings(ColIdx), cbValueMax, pcbValue)
  Next
  Spin1_SpinUp
End Sub
```

12

Listing 12.4. Subroutine `Spin1_SpinUp`, which performs the fetch.

```
Sub Spin1_SpinUp ()
  rc = SQLFetch(hstmt)
  If rc <> SQL_SUCCESS Then
    DescribeError hdbc, hstmt
  End If
  For ColIdx = 0 To pccol - 1
    Text1(ColIdx).Text = Strings(ColIdx)
  Next
End Sub
```

This example points out one of the shortcomings of Visual Basic—its inability to handle pointers well. Because `SQLBindCol` uses a pointer for the parameter `rgbValue`, the declaration and calling of this function must match, as shown in this example. The other problem this presents in the example is that a pointer cannot be obtained for the control array named `Text1`, which receives and displays the returned data. Therefore, the temporary work areas called `Strings` were created to receive the data, and the pointers to `Strings` are passed in `SQLBindCol`. Then, in the last lines of `Spin1_SpinUp`, the data is copied from these temporary work areas into the controls for actual display.

The benefit of using bound columns can be seen in the log shown in Listing 12.5. In the last portion of this trace log (which was created by the Driver Manager), you can see several consecutive `SQLFetch` calls. If `SQLGetData` was used to retrieve the data, there would be one call for each column to get data between each fetch call. The example program is shown running in Figure 12.3.

Figure 12.3. *The output dialog box from VBBIND12 showing input SQL string and output column labels and data.*

Listing 12.5. SQL.LOG from the execution of VBBIND12.

```
SQLAllocEnv(phenv43CF0000);
SQLAllocConnect(henv43CF0000, phdbc438F0000);
SQLSetConnectOption(hdbc438F0000, 103, 000000F0);
SQLDriverConnect(hdbc438F0000, hwnd0000,
        "DSN=MS 16-bit SQL Server;UID=www;PWD=****;DATABASE=TY_ODBC;
", 255, szConnStrOut, 255, pcbConnStrOut, 1);
SQLAllocStmt(hdbc438F0000, phstmt447F0000);
SQLFreeStmt(hstmt447F0000, 0);
SQLExecDirect(hstmt447F0000, "select * from artist", 20);
SQLNumResultCols(hstmt447F0000, pccol);
SQLDescribeCol(hstmt447F0000, 1, szColName, 128,
                pcbColName, pfSqlType, pcbColDef, pibScale, pfNullable);
SQLBindCol(hstmt447F0000, 1, 1, rgbValue, 254, pcbValue);
SQLDescribeCol(hstmt447F0000, 2, szColName, 128,
                pcbColName, pfSqlType, pcbColDef, pibScale, pfNullable);
SQLBindCol(hstmt447F0000, 2, 1, rgbValue, 254, pcbValue);
SQLDescribeCol(hstmt447F0000, 3, szColName, 128,
                pcbColName, pfSqlType, pcbColDef, pibScale, pfNullable);
SQLBindCol(hstmt447F0000, 3, 1, rgbValue, 254, pcbValue);
SQLDescribeCol(hstmt447F0000, 4, szColName, 128,
                pcbColName, pfSqlType, pcbColDef, pibScale, pfNullable);
SQLBindCol(hstmt447F0000, 4, 1, rgbValue, 254, pcbValue);
SQLFetch(hstmt447F0000);
SQLFetch(hstmt447F0000);
SQLFetch(hstmt447F0000);
SQLFetch(hstmt447F0000);
SQLFetch(hstmt447F0000);
SQLFetch(hstmt447F0000);
SQLDisconnect(hdbc438F0000);
SQLFreeConnect(hdbc438F0000);
SQLFreeEnv(henv43CF0000);
```

12

C++

Syntax

The *SQLBindCol* Function

The prototype for the function SQLBindCol is

```
RETCODE SQL_API SQLBindCol(
    HSTMT        hstmt,
    UWORD        icol,
    SWORD        fCType,
    PTR          rgbValue,
    SDWORD       cbValueMax,
    SDWORD FAR  *pcbValue
```

The function assigns the storage and data type for a column in the result set before the data is retrieved. When SQLFetch or SQLExtendedFetch is called, the driver will place into the assigned locations the data for all bound columns.

The use of the specific SQLBindCol function from Visual C++ becomes more obscure than when using Visual Basic because much of the data retrieval and binding functionality is

hidden in the MFC code. However, it is easy to see by examining logs that this function is being used. In fact, the developer has little choice in this matter. Listing 12.6 shows another SQL.LOG trace file from the CPEXEC program, which was introduced yesterday. This log shows the `SQLBindCol` calls, one for each column, with the `SQLFetch` calls coming together at the end of the log.

Listing 12.6. The SQL.LOG trace log from the execution of CPEXEC.EXE.

```
SQLAllocEnv(phenv43CF0000);
SQLAllocConnect(henv43CF0000, phdbc438F0000);
SQLSetConnectOption(hdbc438F0000, 103, 000000F0);
SQLDriverConnect(hdbc438F0000, hwnd0000,
"DSN=MS 16-bit SQL Server;UID=www;PWD=****;DATABASE=TY_ODBC;
", 255, szConnStrOut, 255, pcbConnStrOut, 1);
SQLAllocStmt(hdbc438F0000, phstmt447F0000);
SQLFreeStmt(hstmt447F0000, 0);
SQLExecDirect(hstmt447F0000, "select * from artist", 20);
SQLNumResultCols(hstmt447F0000, pccol);
SQLDescribeCol(hstmt447F0000, 1, szColName, 128,
               pcbColName, pfSqlType, pcbColDef, pibScale, pfNullable);
SQLBindCol(hstmt447F0000, 1, 1, rgbValue, 254, pcbValue);
SQLDescribeCol(hstmt447F0000, 2, szColName, 128,
               pcbColName, pfSqlType, pcbColDef, pibScale, pfNullable);
SQLBindCol(hstmt447F0000, 2, 1, rgbValue, 254, pcbValue);
SQLDescribeCol(hstmt447F0000, 3, szColName, 128,
               pcbColName, pfSqlType, pcbColDef, pibScale, pfNullable);
SQLBindCol(hstmt447F0000, 3, 1, rgbValue, 254, pcbValue);
SQLDescribeCol(hstmt447F0000, 4, szColName, 128,
               pcbColName, pfSqlType, pcbColDef, pibScale, pfNullable);
SQLBindCol(hstmt447F0000, 4, 1, rgbValue, 254, pcbValue);
SQLFetch(hstmt447F0000);
SQLFetch(hstmt447F0000);
SQLFetch(hstmt447F0000);
SQLFetch(hstmt447F0000);
SQLFetch(hstmt447F0000);
SQLFetch(hstmt447F0000);
SQLDisconnect(hdbc438F0000);
SQLFreeConnect(hdbc438F0000);
SQLFreeEnv(henv43CF0000);
SQLAllocEnv(phenv00144A38);
SQLAllocConnect(henv00144A38, phdbc001451A8);
SQLSetConnectOption(hdbc001451A8, 103, 0000000F);
SQLSetConnectOption(hdbc001451A8, 110, 00000001);
SQLDriverConnect(hdbc001451A8, hwnd00020342,
    "DSN=MS 32-Bit SQL Server; ", -3, szConnStrOut, 512, pcbConnStrOut, 1);
SQLError(henv00144A38, hdbc001451A8, hstmt00000000,
         szSqlState, pfNativeError, szErrorMsg, 512, pcbErrorMsg);
SQLError(henv00144A38, hdbc001451A8, hstmt00000000,
         szSqlState, pfNativeError, szErrorMsg, 512, pcbErrorMsg);
SQLError(henv00144A38, hdbc001451A8, hstmt00000000,
         szSqlState, pfNativeError, szErrorMsg, 512, pcbErrorMsg);
SQLError(henv00144A38, hdbc001451A8, hstmt00000000,
         szSqlState, pfNativeError, szErrorMsg, 512, pcbErrorMsg);
```

```
SQLGetInfo(hdbc001451A8, 9, rgbInfoValue, 2, pcbInfoValue);
SQLGetInfo(hdbc001451A8, 15, rgbInfoValue, 2, pcbInfoValue);
SQLGetInfo(hdbc001451A8, 23, rgbInfoValue, 2, pcbInfoValue);
SQLGetInfo(hdbc001451A8, 24, rgbInfoValue, 2, pcbInfoValue);
SQLGetInfo(hdbc001451A8, 81, rgbInfoValue, 4, pcbInfoValue);
SQLGetInfo(hdbc001451A8, 25, rgbInfoValue, 10, pcbInfoValue);
SQLGetInfo(hdbc001451A8, 29, rgbInfoValue, 2, pcbInfoValue);
SQLGetInfo(hdbc001451A8, 17, rgbInfoValue, 64, pcbInfoValue);
SQLGetInfo(hdbc001451A8, 18, rgbInfoValue, 64, pcbInfoValue);
SQLAllocStmt(hdbc001451A8, phstmt00145688);
SQLSetStmtOption(hstmt00145688, 0, 0000000F);
SQLSetStmtOption(hstmt00145688, 4, 00000001);
SQLGetFunctions(hdbc001451A8, 59, pfExists);
SQLPrepare(hstmt00145688,
    "SELECT AlbumCounter,ArtistID,AlbumTitle  FROM dbo.Album", -3);
SQLExecute(hstmt00145688);
SQLExecute(hstmt00145688);
SQLNumResultCols(hstmt00145688, pccol);
SQLDescribeCol(hstmt00145688, 1, szColName, 0,
               pcbColName, pfSqlType, pcbColDef, pibScale, pfNullable);
SQLBindCol(hstmt00145688, 1, 4, rgbValue, 4, pcbValue);
SQLNumResultCols(hstmt00145688, pccol);
SQLDescribeCol(hstmt00145688, 2, szColName, 0,
               pcbColName, pfSqlType, pcbColDef, pibScale, pfNullable);
SQLBindCol(hstmt00145688, 2, 4, rgbValue, 4, pcbValue);
SQLNumResultCols(hstmt00145688, pccol);
SQLDescribeCol(hstmt00145688, 3, szColName, 0,
               pcbColName, pfSqlType, pcbColDef, pibScale, pfNullable);
SQLBindCol(hstmt00145688, 3, 1, rgbValue, 76, pcbValue);
SQLFetch(hstmt00145688);
SQLFetch(hstmt00145688);
SQLFetch(hstmt00145688);
SQLFetch(hstmt00145688);
SQLFetch(hstmt00145688);
SQLFreeStmt(hstmt00145688, 1);
SQLDisconnect(hdbc001451A8);
SQLFreeConnect(hdbc001451A8);
SQLFreeEnv(henv00144A38);
```

If you compare the logs presented in Listing 12.5 and 12.6, you will see very few differences despite the fact that one came from a Visual Basic application and the other from a Visual C++ application. This log comparison is also food for thought when you compare performance levels between development platforms.

The final, and perhaps best, alternative in the choices to retrieve data to the application is to use the odbc/ClassLib member functions in the CURSOR class. The first of these is the AutoBind function, which will set up fully automatic column binding for a result set. The first step in this automatic binding is to allocate memory for a data structure to contain one row in the result set according to sizes determined from the SQLDescribeCol calls also done within the member function. Once the structure is allocated, each column is bound to the appropriate storage location. In the case of cursor operations using `SQLExtendedFetch` with multirow result set cursors, `AutoBind` will allocate arrays for the result set.

In addition to the `AutoBind` and `BindCol` class member functions, the odbc/ClassLib `CURSOR` class also includes many functions that make display and dialog box manipulation much simpler. This is accomplished through the provision of functions such as `FillComboBox`, `FillBrowserListBox`, `FillListBox`, and others.

Returning a Row of Data to the Application Buffer

You have learned how to create a result set on the data source, and how to declare bound columns so that when the data is retrieved it will be moved into the application's variables. Now look at the function that performs this retrieval. This is something of an anticlimax because the function is so very simple and you've been using it in almost all the examples already.

The *SQLFetch* Function

The general syntax for the `SQLFetch` function in Visual Basic is

```
RETCODE SQLFetch(hStmt)
```

The function fetches a row of data from the result set. If any columns have been bound at the time this function is called, the driver will return data to the application for all columns that were bound to storage locations. After each call to `SQLFetch`, the cursor is positioned to the next row in the result set. After the last row of data in the result set is fetched, this function will return `SQL_NO_DATA_FOUND` and the cursor is positioned after the end of the result set.

The *SQLFetch* Function

The prototype for the function `SQLFetch` is

```
RETCODE SQL_API SQLFetch(
    HSTMT        hstmt);
```

The function fetches a row of data from the result set. If any columns have been bound at the time this function is called, the driver will return data to the application for all columns that were bound to storage locations. After each call to `SQLFetch`, the cursor is positioned at the next row in the result set. After the last row of data in the result set is fetched, this function will return `SQL_NO_DATA_FOUND`, and the cursor is positioned after the end of the result set.

Getting Unbound Data from the Buffer to the Application

The final function used for basic data retrieval is SQLGetData. You have heard about and used this function many times already. SQLBindCol and SQLGetData can and should be used in harmony as the situation dictates. In situations in which long data types are used, using SQLGetData is almost mandatory. In other situations in which performance is at a premium, SQLBindCol would probably be better.

Using both function is not uncommon; those columns that are returned with each fetch are bound, and other columns that are needed only on demand are retrieved with a SQLGetData call. Care must be taken in this situation because normally the SQLGetData can only be used on those columns to the right of the last bound column. Some drivers allow more flexibility, but it is safest to check by performing SQLGetInfo with the fInfoType of SQL_GETDATA_EXTENSIONS to determine what is allowed.

VB4

Syntax

The *SQLGetData* Function

The general syntax for the SQLGetData function in Visual Basic is

```
RETCODE SQLGetData(hStmt, icol. fCType, rgbValue, cbValueMax, pcbValue)
```

This function returns data from a single unbound column in the current row of the result set. The function SQLFetch or SQLExtendedFetch must have been performed before calling this function. The input parameters hStmt and icol refer to the owned result set and the column within that result set from which the data is to be retrieved. The fCType parameter specifies the data type the driver is to return from this column. This means the driver must make the conversion between the stored data type and the returned data type specified by this parameter. rgbValue is a parameter that contains an address pointer, which points to the storage location where the data is to be returned. The maximum length of the buffer receiving data is specified in cbValueMax. If the data is longer than the receiving buffer, pcbValue specifies how many bytes are available to return in rgbValue before the current call to SQLGetData.

C++

Syntax

The *SQLGetData* Function

The prototype for the SQLGetData function is

```
RETCODE SQL_API SQLGetData(
    HSTMT       hstmt,
    UWORD       icol,
    SWORD       fCType,
    PTR         rgbValue,
```

```
SDWORD      cbValueMax,
SDWORD FAR *pcbValue);
```

This function returns result set data for a single column from the current row. The application must have called SQLFetch or SQLExtendedFetch before calling SQLGetData. All of the parameters for this function and their usage are explained in the Visual Basic syntax of the preceding section.

No specific sample applications are included for the functions SQLFetch or SQLGetData because these functions were shown in samples presented on Days 10 and 11.

Summary

Today's lesson presented the techniques for returning result set data from the data source into your application. You learned about the following topics:

☐ There are two methods of returning data, either with bound or unbound columns. Bound columns offer less flexibility but usually better performance. Unbound columns do not have to be returned. In addition, unbound columns must be used to return very long data types.

☐ It is important to know what the result set looks like before dealing with the returning data. This includes the number of columns and their data types and sizes. If this number of columns is variable, there are three functions you can use to query this information: SQLNumResultCols, SQLDescribeCol, and SQLColAttributes.

☐ Using SQLBindCol once for each column will cause the data in the result set for that column to be automatically returned to the specified memory location in the application when the row is fetched.

☐ The SQLFetch and SQLExtendedFetch functions are used to return one or more rows of data from the result set. If there are no bound columns, no data is actually moved; the row counter is simply incremented. If columns are bound, the bound data is returned to the application.

☐ If a column has not been bound, its data can still be brought into the application by calling SQLGetData after SQLFetch has been called.

Q&A

Q When I perform `SQLExecDirect` with my `SELECT` statement it always returns `SQL_SUCCESS`, but when I perform `SQLGetData` it returns `SQL_NO_DATA_FOUND`. What is wrong?

A No rows in the data source match the query specifications in your SQL statement. Running `SQLNumResultCols` will return zero in the same situation. Change your SQL query statement and try again.

Q I try specifying the name of my edit box in the `SQLBindCol` call, but Visual Basic says I can't pass this variable by value. The data type of an edit box is `String`, and I'm trying to pass a pointer anyway. How can I do this?

A Because Visual Basic doesn't use or know about pointers, this becomes difficult. Generating an address pointer to a dialog control is not allowed in Visual Basic. Define a working variable that will receive the bound data, and then move it into the dialog control after the fetch statement.

Q I'm getting a return of `SQL_ERROR` from my fetch with an additional message of `Numeric value out of range`. I thought the driver had to convert data types?

A The driver will attempt to convert data types as specified in the `SQLBindCol` or `SQLGetData` function calls. However, if the conversion is from a larger to smaller data type and the actual value of the data being converted does not fit into the new data type, this error will result.

Workshop

The Workshop provides quiz questions to help you solidify your understanding of the material covered and to give you experience in using what you've learned. Try to understand the quiz and exercise answers before continuing on to the next day's lesson. Answers are provided in Appendix A, "Answers."

Quiz

1. When in a program can the function `SQLBindCol` be used?
2. What function can you use to determine where it is safe to mix the `SQLGetData` and `SQLBindCol` functions?

Exercise

1. Compare the number of function calls using the SQLFetch/SQLGetData method versus the SQLBindCol/SQLFetch method for a 50 column by 3,000 row data base.

Determining the
Return Status of
a Call

Whenever an application calls a function from another source, there must be a way to signal to the calling program the success or failure of that function. When a program calls ODBC functions, this return code does little more than signal success or failure and indicate conditions of no data. To aid the user or developer in determining the underlying cause of failures, ODBC includes a defined set of additional error and state codes and a mechanism for retrieving this information. Today you learn about the following:

☐ ODBC return codes

☐ The meaning of SQLStates and when they change

☐ Recovering from errors

ODBC Return Codes

Unlike some functions, which can return many values and many data types, the ODBC functions are defined to return only one of a very small set of defined return codes. As you examine the defined return codes shown in Table 13.1, you can easily see that they are broken into three types of returns:

☐ Success

☐ Success with warning

☐ Error

Table 13.1. Possible ODBC function return codes.

Return code	Description
SQL_SUCCESS	Function completed successfully; no additional return information is available.
SQL_NO_DATA_FOUND	No rows remain unfetched in the result set. The cursor is positioned after the last row of data.
SQL_SUCCESS_WITH_INFO	The function completed successfully, but there is additional information. This could be informational, warning, or nonfatal error information that can be retrieved by calling SQLError.
SQL_STILL_EXECUTING	A statement that was started asynchronously is still processing. The call that started this statement processing must be repeated (after waiting) until the return changes to SQL_SUCCESS or an error return code.

Return code	Description
SQL_NEED_DATA	The statement contains parameterized variables that have not yet received a data value.
SQL_INVALID_HANDLE	The called function failed because one of the three needed handles was invalid. Calling SQLError at this point will not provide additional information. Good programming technique and return code checking of previous allocation calls should prevent the reception of this return code.
SQL_ERROR	The function failed. Call SQLError to retrieve detailed information about this failure.

When an ODBC function returns SQL_ERROR or SQL_SUCCESS_WITH_INFO, the application usually needs to obtain more details about this problem and behave appropriately. You can obtain this additional information by calling the function SQLError. Errors can be associated with the henv, the hdbc, or the hstmt handles, or more than one of these handles. The Driver Manager can maintain up to 64 errors at one time; therefore, multiple calls to SQLError are often required to obtain all of the error information.

Any ODBC function can post zero or more errors each time it is called, regardless of the function return code; therefore, calling SQLError after each and every function call would not be improper. You must be careful not to abort program execution just because an ODBC function did not return SQL_SUCCESS.

VB4

Syntax

The *SQLError* Function

The general syntax for the SQLError function in Visual Basic is

```
RETCODE SQLError(henv,
                 hDBC,
                 hStmt,
                 szSqlState,
                 pfNativeError,
                 szErrorMsg,
                 cbErrorMsgMax,
                 pcbErrorMsg)
```

13

This function returns error or status information. If a valid handle is passed in the parameter henv, the connection and statement handles are ignored and errors most recently called with the same henv are returned. In this case, hdbc should contain SQL_NULL_HDBC and hstmt should contain SQL_NULL_HSTMT. To retrieve errors associated with a connection, the application passes the appropriate connection handle in hdbc and

SQL_NULL_HSTMT in hstmt. In this case, the driver will ignore the henv parameter and will return the error status of the function most recently called using the passed hdbc. If a statement handle is passed in the parameter hstmt, the driver will return an error status for that statement and ignore the values passed in the parameters henv and hdbc.

The parameter szSqlState will return a null-terminated string specifying the SQL state of the last function call. If this is "00000", the function call was successful. The possible values for SQLState are defined by the X/Open and SQL Access Group (SAG) specifications of 1992. These valid SQLStates and the functions that can return them are listed in the Microsoft Press publication *ODBC 2.0 Programmer's Reference and SDK Guide*. Although these state values can be useful, it is generally much more informative to inspect the error message text that should be returned in the same SQLError call. The error code returned in pfNativeError is code-specific to the data source. This field would contain AS/400 error codes if the data source is an AS/400, or Oracle error codes if the data source was an Oracle database.

The error message text is returned to the storage buffer pointed to by szErrorMsg. The length of this buffer is passed to the driver in cbErrorMsgMax. Following execution of SQLError, the actual number of bytes returned in szErrorMsg is returned in pcbErrorMsg.

Example:

```
Dim sState As String * 16
Dim sBuffer As String * 256
Dim iOutLen As Integer
Dim lNative As Long
Dim iRC As Integer

sState = String$(16, 0)
sBuffer = String$(256, 0)

Do
  iRC = SQLError(SQL_NULL_HENV, hdbc, hstmt, _
                 sState, lNative, sBuffer, 256, iOutLen)
  If iRC = SQL_SUCCESS Or iRC = SQL_SUCCESS_WITH_INFO Then
    If iOutLen = 0 Then
      MsgBox "Error — No error info available"
    Else
      MsgBox Left$(sBuffer, iOutLen)
    End If
  End If
Loop Until iRC <> SQL_SUCCESS
```

In Visual Basic programming with ODBC API calls, all of the error handling must be provided by the application developer. This can usually be done with two simple routines to handle fatal errors and display the error for less serious problems. Although these routines, as shown in Listings 13.1 and 13.2, will adequately display the error message text, the program flow after an error is left to the developer.

You can see an example of this type of logic flow by examining the ODBC trace logs from a Microsoft Access application that attaches to a remote data-source table. In the Dr. DeeBee Spy log shown in Listing 13.1, a query is executed looking for security data in the table msysconf. The log shows that the SQLExecDirect function returns SQL_ERROR, so Access next calls SQLError. The error text shows that this object does not exist. Under normal conditions, an application would probably display this message to the user with instructions to call the help desk immediately. Access does not do this because this message is expected if the user has not implemented security, so the application (Access in this case) continues normally.

Listing 13.1. Dr. DeeBee Spy log from Microsoft Access table attach attempt.

```
SQLExecDirect
    0x01010001
    [35]SELECT Config, nValue FROM MSysConf
    SQL_NTS
    SQL_ERROR
SQLError
    NULL
    NULL
    0x01010001
    [5]S0002
    208
    [79][Microsoft][ODBC SQL Server Driver]
        [SQL Server] Invalid object name 'MSysConf'.
    512
    79
    SQL_SUCCESS
```

Listing 13.2 is a subroutine you can use over and over in your own ODBC applications to show errors.

13

Listing 13.2. The ShowError subroutine, which will display errors.

```
Sub ShowError (ByVal hdbc As Long, ByVal hstmt As Long)
  Dim sState As String * 16
  Dim sBuffer As String * 256
  Dim iOutLen As Integer
  Dim lNative As Long
  Dim iRC As Integer

  sState = String$(16, 0)
  sBuffer = String$(256, 0)
```

continues

Listing 13.2. continued

```
Do
  iRC = SQLError(SQL_NULL_HENV, hdbc, hstmt, sState, _
                lNative, sBuffer, 256, iOutLen)
  If iRC = SQL_SUCCESS Or iRC = SQL_SUCCESS_WITH_INFO Then
    If iOutLen = 0 Then
      MsgBox "Error — No error info available"
    Else
      MsgBox Left$(sBuffer, iOutLen)
    End If
  End If
Loop Until iRC <> SQL_SUCCESS
End Sub
```

Listing 13.3 is another routine to add to your error detection arsenal.

Listing 13.3. The Attempt subroutine, which will display fatal errors.

```
Sub Attempt (ResultCode As Integer, ErrorMessage As String)

  If (ResultCode <> SQL_SUCCESS) Then    'Exit if no errors
    screen.MousePointer = Normal
    MsgBox ErrorMessage, StopIcon, "Unexpected ODBC Function failure"
    Stop
  End If

End Sub
```

Now that you have the error display functions, make some errors. First, try to connect to a nonexistent data source, as shown in Listing 13.4.

Listing 13.4. The BadConnBtn subroutine.

```
Sub BadConnBtn_Click ()
  Dim ConnIn As String * 255        'Temporary for first connection
  Dim ConnOut As String * 255
  Dim cbOut As Integer              'Receives length of actual connection string

  Attempt SQLAllocConnect(henv, hdbc), "Cannot allocate connection"
  ConnIn = "DSN=Goofy;UID=nobody;PWD=spies"
  ConnOut = Space$(255)
  rc% = SQLDriverConnect(hdbc, 0, ConnIn, 255, ConnOut, 255, cbOut%, 1)
  If rc% <> SQL_SUCCESS Then
    ShowError hdbc, SQL_NULL_HSTMT
  End If
End Sub
```

The `GoofyBtn` subroutine in Listing 13.5 submits an invalid SQL statement.

 Listing 13.5. The `GoofyBtn` subroutine.

```
Sub GoofyBtn_Click ()
  Dim ConnIn As String * 255        'Temporary for first connection
  Dim ConnOut As String * 255
  Dim cbOut As Integer              'Receives length of actual connection string
  Dim hstmt As Long

  Attempt SQLAllocConnect(henv, hdbc), "Cannot allocate connection"
  ConnIn = "DSN=MS 16-bit SQL Server;UID=www;PWD=bill;DATABASE=TY_ODBC"
  ConnOut = Space$(255)
  rc = SQLDriverConnect(hdbc, GetFocus(), ConnIn, 255, ConnOut, 255, cbOut%, 1)
  If rc = SQL_ERROR Or rc = SQL_INVALID_HANDLE Then
    ShowError hdbc, SQL_NULL_HSTMT
  End If
  Attempt SQLAllocStmt(hdbc, hstmt), "Cannot allocate statement"
  ConnIn = "select phonycolumn from dumbtable"
  rc = SQLExecDirect(hstmt, ConnIn, Len(ConnIn))
  If rc <> SQL_SUCCESS Then
    ShowError hdbc, hstmt
  End If
End Sub
```

 These examples demonstrate a number of subtle points about error trapping and reporting that can be useful in determining the source of a problem. The first of these is to determine what module generated the error.

When you examine the error message boxes shown in Figures 13.1 through 13.4, notice that the information displayed includes more than just a textual description of the error. Specifically, the vendor, ODBC component, and data source are identified in portions of the text contained within brackets ([]). In Figure 13.1, the vendor is Microsoft and the component is ODBC.DLL, the Driver Manager. Similarly, the text in brackets indicates that the error passed through the ODBC SQL Server driver, but came from SQL Server itself, which in this case makes sense because only the DBMS would know what objects it contains. Figures 13.1 and 13.2 show the consequences of the errors.

Figure 13.1. *The error message that appears when you try to connect to a data source that does not exist.*

Figure 13.2. *The error message generated by SQL Server returned by* SQLError.

In Figure 13.3, a different message format is displayed. In this case, a fatal error was encountered that would not provide data from a call to SQLError. In this case, the message text format is different from the previous messages, and the message box caption is different, which can be an important clue when you are trying to determine what caused an error.

Figure 13.3. *The fatal error message generated by the* Attempt *subroutine.*

The final example from Visual Basic, shown in Figure 13.4, is an error message box that was not generated by any user-written code. This error, as hinted at by the box caption, was generated from the driver when a connection failure was simulated by shutting down SQL Server and performing the "goofy query" example. There are two distinct errors generated in this example. The first comes from the DBNMP3.DLL net library, the second from the ODBC SQL Server driver itself. Both of these messages refer to the same failure and point out the need to retrieve all errors to get a full picture of what's wrong. In this case, error trapping within the program could be affected by the fact that the SQLDriverConnect call generated no errors. Instead, because the window handle was provided in the call, the driver presented the error messages as shown, and then displayed a login screen for a retry. Unless a connection is made, the only way out of this loop is to press the Cancel button in the login dialog box. This will cause the SQLDriverConnect function to return SQL_NO_DATA_FOUND.

Figure 13.4. *Multiple error messages generated by the ODBC driver.*

The *SQLError* Function

The prototype for the SQLError function is

```
RETCODE SQL_API SQLError(
    HENV        henv,
    HDBC        hdbc,
    HSTMT       hstmt,
    UCHAR   FAR *szSqlState,
    SDWORD  FAR *pfNativeError,
    UCHAR   FAR *szErrorMsg,
    SWORD       cbErrorMsgMax,
    SWORD   FAR *pcbErrorMsg);
```

This function returns error or status information. If a valid handle is passed in the parameter henv, the connection and statement handles are ignored and errors most recently called with the same henv are returned. In this case, hdbc should contain SQL_NULL_HDBC and hstmt should contain SQL_NULL_HSTMT. To retrieve errors associated with a connection, the application passes the appropriate connection handle in hdbc and SQL_NULL_HSTMT in hstmt. In this case, the driver will ignore the henv parameter and will return the error status of the function most recently called using the passed hdbc. If a statement handle is passed in the parameter hstmt, the driver will return the error status for that statement and ignore the values passed in the parameters henv and hdbc.

Error Handling Using MFC

It would be the exception rather than the rule that the SQLError function would be called by the application developer in a Visual C++ program because the C++ exception-handling routines are much easier to use. In MFC before version 3.0, the TRY and CATCH macros were used to "try" a function, and then "catch" any errors bubbling up from that try. Beginning with MFC version 3.0, Microsoft is recommending that the C++ exception keywords try and catch be used instead of the macros because of problems with the macros. Listing 13.6 shows how error handling is implemented using MFC.

Listing 13.6. The `OnInitialUpdate` function showing try/catch error handling blocks.

```
void CCperrView::OnInitialUpdate()
{
   m_pSet = &GetDocument()->m_cperrSet;
   m_pSet->m_strFilter = "garbage = 2";
   try
   {
      CRecordView::OnInitialUpdate();
   }
   catch( CDBException* e )
   {
      AfxMessageBox(e->m_strError,MB_ICONEXCLAMATION);
   }

}
```

 The short function shown in Listing 13.6 shows a try/catch block, which should catch a `CDBException` triggered in the `OnInitialUpdate` function or its lower-level functions. The `CDBException` exception handler should then load the appropriate ODBC error message text coming from the `SQLError` error message text into the class member `m_strError`, with member variables `m_strStateNativeOrigin` and `m_strRetCode`. The `RetCode` can contain any of the previously listed ODBC error codes as well as AFX-specific return codes defined for use in MFC.

Here we have specified a filter string that will cause MFC to generate a WHERE clause in the SQL statement. However, the column name "garbage" does not exist in the table referenced, which will force an error. The ODBC driver will generate an error stating that `SQLPrepare` failed because the column name "garbage" is invalid. The results of this error are show in Figure 13.5.

Figure 13.5. *The message box that should show an ODBC error. (See note following.)*

 Note: In MFC version 3.0, the proper error message does not surface when using the `CDBException` try/catch error handlers. This error appears to come from code within the module DBCORE.CPP, which creates error text twice, causing the original error message to be lost. Until this problem is fixed within MFC, an application developer would have to override the ::Open() function to correct the error trapping around the SQLPrepare and SQLExecute functions.

Using odbc/ClassLib

The odbc/ClassLib C++ class libraries from Intersolv provide both flexibility and ease of use. These routines assume that errors will normally be handled by the application rather than the library. The odbc/ClassLib libraries provide an installable error handler. Two steps must be taken to turn on the use of this error handler:

1. Install the error handler function address with a call to the member function SetErrHandler.

2. Determine the level of severity at which the error handler is to be invoked by calling the member function AutoReport() with either the constant odbcREPERRS to only report errors or odbcREPSUCCESSWITHINFO to report both errors and returns with the return code SQL_SUCCESS_WITH_INFO.

Listing 13.7 features the use of odbc/ClassLib's installable error handler returning an error similar to that forced in Listing 13.6. In this case, the SQL statement has appended to its end a WHERE clause condition that refers to a column that does not exist. Otherwise, this application is the same as that used on Day 11, "Running SQL SELECT Statements."

Listing 13.7. The OnConnect function from SWEX2 application showing forced error and error handling.

```
void CSWEx2Dlg::OnConnect()
{
    static char szConnStrOut[ 1024 ];

        // perform odbc initialization and connection
    pEnv = new odbcENV;
    if ( pEnv )
    {
        pConnect = new odbcCONNECT( pEnv );
        if ( pConnect )
            pConnect->bTrimAllTrailingBlanks = TRUE;

        // use the cursor library for this example
        pEnv->nCursorLibUsage = SQL_CUR_USE_ODBC;
```

continues

13

Listing 13.7. continued

```
// connect with user selected data source
if ( pConnect )
{
    pConnect->DriverConnectPrompt(
                m_hWnd,
                szConnStrOut,
                sizeof(szConnStrOut));
    cursor = new odbcCURSOR( pConnect );

    if (cursor->sqlsuccess())
    {
        //execute the select statement
        cursor->AutoRetrieve(odbcREPSUCCESSWITHINFO);
        cursor->AutoReport(odbcREPSUCCESSWITHINFO);
        cursor->SetErrHandler(PrintErr);
        cursor->ExecDirect(
                (LPUCSTR)
                "select Alb.AlbumTitle,Art.FirstName,Art.LastName from "
                "TY_ODBC..Album Alb, TY_ODBC..Artist Art "
                "where Alb.ArtistID = Art.ArtistID and "
                "garbage = 2");
    }
  }
 }
}
```

Listing 13.8 does in C++ what Listing 13.2 did in Visual Basic—it shows the error.

Listing 13.8. The error handler `PrintErr`, which is called when an error is detected.

```
// this error routine will be called automatically when
// an error occurs
void CALLBACK PrintErr(
    RETCODE          lastRet,
    UCHAR FAR *      szSqlState,
    SDWORD           fNativeError,
    UCHAR FAR *      szErrorMsg,
    odbcBASE FAR *   pObj
    )
    {
        AfxMessageBox( (LPSTR)szErrorMsg,
                MB_OK);
    }
```

Analysis

The simple examples in Listings 13.7 and 13.8 show all of the odbc/ClassLib error code together in one small routine. Before the `SQLExecDirect` function call, the error handling is set to automatically retrieve and report all errors and successes with

information. The error handler is identified with the SetErrHandler call on a per-object basis rather than globally. In this case, the error-handling routine PrintErr is very simple; it just prints the error text returned from the SQLError call. The complexity of this function is entirely application-dependent.

Figure 13.6 shows what this error looks like.

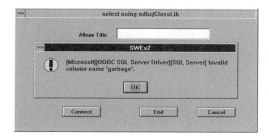

Figure 13.6. *The error message box produced from the PrintErr installable error routine.*

The Meaning of *SQLStates* and When They Change

As mentioned earlier, part of the return information from an SQLError call is the SQLState. This is expressed as a five-character string; the first two characters are the class and the last three are the subclass. Any SQLState with a class code of "01" comes from a warning, and the return code with this SQLState will always be SQL_SUCCESS_WITH_INFO. A class code of "IM" comes from warnings and errors derived from the implementation of ODBC. The assignment of all of these class and subclass values is defined by ANSI SQL-92.

Regardless of the underlying data source, all SQL functions in ODBC must transition between specific states of the environment, connection, and statement. It is the state of the environment, connection, or statement that determines when the corresponding handle can be used by an ODBC function successfully. Tables 13.2 through 13.4 show the possible states for ODBC environment, connections, and statements.

13

Table 13.2. ODBC environment states.

State	Description
E0	Unallocated henv
E1	Allocated henv, unallocated hdbc
E2	Allocated henv, allocated hdbc

Table 13.3. ODBC connection states.

State	Description
C0	Unallocated henv, unallocated hdbc
C1	Allocated henv, unallocated hdbc
C2	Allocated henv, allocated hdbc
C3	Connection function needs data
C4	Connected hdbc
C5	Connected hdbc, allocated hstmt
C6	Connected hdbc, transaction in progress

Table 13.4. ODBC statement states.

State	Description
S0	Unallocated hstmt.
S1	Allocated hstmt.
S2	Prepared statement. No result set will be created.
S3	Prepared statement. A result set will be created.
S4	Statement executed and no result set was created.
S5	Statement executed and a result set was created. The cursor is open and positioned before the first row of the result set.
S6	Cursor positioned with SQLFetch.
S7	Cursor positioned with SQLExtendedFetch.
S8	Function needs data. SQLParamData has not been called.
S9	Function needs data. SQLPutData has not been called.

State	Description
S10	Function needs data. `SQLPutData` has been called.
S11	Still executing.
S12	Asynchronous execution canceled.

For each ODBC function, there is a specific set of states the environment, connection, and statement must be in for successful execution to occur. If functions that change states are executed out of sequence, errors will prevent execution. An example that is commonly seen during application testing and exploration is the error message `Function sequence error`, `SQLState S1010`. This error would happen if you tried to execute a statement (using `SQLExecute`) that had not been prepared.

A complete matrix of the combinations of states and the results of improper sequence can be found in Appendix B of the Microsoft Press *ODBC 2.0 Programmer's Reference and SDK Guide.*

Recovering From Errors

When you are trying to develop a strategy for handling errors encountered during execution of an ODBC application, you must look carefully at both the type of error and where it happened within the program logic flow. The types of errors can generally be divided into exceptions that prevent further activity, and errors and warnings, which could be overcome within the application if they do not occur at a critical time in program logic. Remember that what are called exceptions can at times really be just warnings, whereas errors can be truly fatal to program execution.

As a general rule, if memory allocation errors are encountered during ODBC connection setup, the application should report the error and exit as gracefully as possible. Remember that in a low-memory situation, the application might not even be able to display a message box.

If the ODBC driver is a two-tier driver that interacts with a data source across a network, consideration must be given to communications problems, both during initialization and throughout the session. The developer must plan around what will happen (what errors will be presented) if the connection is lost at any time during program execution. This is particularly important if the application is adding or updating data to more than one table in a single transaction. In this case, using transactions is essential to maintain data integrity. This topic is covered in more detail on Day 18, "Using Transactions and Commitment Control."

13

Finally, a reminder is in order that if an application is written using ODBC, it might be connecting with an unfamiliar data source or driver at some time in the future. No matter how adamant the developer or designer might be today that an application will always run to only one data source, chances are that things will change in the future. During design and development, keep in mind the types of errors that could be produced if a change in data sources were made, and allow for this in error handling. Ask yourself: What will I have the application do if the return is "Driver not capable"?

Summary

Today's lesson presented the mechanism for recognizing and reporting errors. You learned about the following topics:

- ☐ There are a fixed, small set of ODBC return codes that will be returned from each ODBC function execution. These return codes indicate at a high level whether that execution was successful or not, but provide few details.

- ☐ The ODBC environment, connection, and statements must be in a fixed state at any given moment. If any of these states are not correct, function execution will fail. There are a set of predefined SQLStates that specify various state error conditions.

- ☐ There is no generalized method for recovery from ODBC errors. The recovery technique depends on the type and severity of error as well as the application context.

Q&A

Q If I duplicate the same error in a commercial application, I get different error messages than I display in my program. Why?

A There are many possible causes, but the most likely are just related to formatting. Although the SQLState, native error number, return code, and error text are available from most errors by calling SQLError, many applications will display only the error text.

Q Can't I just call SQLError once if an error return code is returned?

A No. It should be called until it returns SQL_NO_DATA_FOUND. Frequently, a single failure will create multiple error messages, and it is important to see them all to accurately diagnose the problem.

Q Can I mix and match error trapping and reporting functions between MFC and odbc/ClassLib?

A You probably could, but it would not be a very good idea from an application maintenance standpoint. It is safest to trap MFC class errors with MFC error handlers and use odbc/ClassLib error handlers for functions called from the odbc/ClassLib libraries.

Q Do I have to check every return code and call `SQLError` after every ODBC function call?

A No. Although coding this way would be the safest, it would not be the most efficient. Most developers judiciously check for errors in those locations most likely to fail.

Workshop

The Workshop provides quiz questions to help you solidify your understanding of the material covered and to give you experience in using what you've learned. Try to understand the quiz and exercise answers before continuing on to the next day's lesson. Answers are provided in Appendix A, "Answers."

Quiz

1. If the `SQLExecDirect` function returns `SQL_ERROR`, what should you call?
2. If `SQLError`'s `szSqlState` is equal to C0, what is the `szSqlState`?

Exercise

1. Fix the `BadBtn` and `GoofyBtn` subroutines in Listings 13.1 and 13.2.

13

14

Using Prepared Statements and Parameter Markers

Earlier this week, you learned how to execute a fixed SQL query that generates a result set at the data source. Today, you learn how to prepare that SQL query for better performance by using dynamic parameters. You will also study the techniques available to pass dynamic data from your application into the SQL statement. Today you will learn about the following topics:

- ☐ Advantages of preparing statements
- ☐ Filling parameter markers at execution time
- ☐ Executing prepared statements

Advantages of Using Prepared Statements Versus Direct Execution

On Day 3, "Application Design Considerations," you learned that execution of an SQL statement by a typical Database Management System (DBMS) involves two steps: preparing the access plan and executing that plan. You learned that if a statement is to be executed more than once, it is better to first prepare the statement using SQLPrepare and then execute it as often as needed using SQLExecute instead of just executing it each time with SQLExecDirect.

Preparing an SQL statement is the process the DBMS goes through to figure out how best to access the rows of data specified in the SQL statement. This frequently involves checking whether a usable index exists and weighing the performance considerations of using an existing index, building a new one, or scanning the table without indexes. This process of building an access path is different for each DBMS and is not used or supported on all data sources, particularly those for a single-tier driver.

> **Note:** It can be important to know whether your targeted DBMS supports the use of prepared statements. Because the SQLPrepare function is an ODBC core function, all drivers must support this function even if the DBMS does not. As a result, some drivers for data sources that don't support the prepare functionality simulate this behavior by fully executing the statement and inhibiting a result set by adding a WHERE clause condition of WHERE 1 = 0 to ensure no rows are returned. The net effect of this process is that nothing is gained for later executions of the statement, and the prepare will waste resources.

Preparing a statement enables the best execution speed and preserves any options that were applied to the statement. It is common practice to prepare all statements that will be used multiple times during the program initialization after the connection is open, and then just execute the appropriate statement handle as needed. A prepared statement must be unique to the statement handle so that if another SQLPrepare is performed on the same statement handle, the earlier prepare is lost.

A final benefit of preparing statements is that the parameter data can be inserted into the statement at runtime rather than fixed in the SQL. Parameters can be passed at runtime into SQLExecDirect statements, but this offers no advantage and therefore does not make sense to use.

This chapter offers a good real-world example of bound parameters passed into a prepared statement at runtime. This example features two tables, in this case the Artist and Album tables. All artists are presented in a list box. When a particular artist is selected from that list, the corresponding artist ID is passed to the second query, which then selects all albums featuring that artist. A similar functionality could be provided using a join between the two tables, but this is more difficult when using MFC because the database classes are implemented at the top level with single-table support. You can add joins by specifying the join condition in the m_strFilter member variable of your document class, but this goes beyond the limits of this chapter.

The emphasis of today is more on the application rather than on the underlying ODBC API calls because the calls are often hidden, particularly when you use MFC with Visual C++. This application, which you'll use today and tomorrow, is one that can be valuable when you are examining header and detail data, such as that found with customers and sales records, purchase orders and purchase-line items, employees and payroll events, and many similar business applications.

Using Prepared Statements in an Application

The dialog box portion of this application will display two parts: the detail data from one table and a selection list of master items from another table. These two parts of the display each have their own SQL statements to select the data from two different tables, but they share the same ODBC connection. In the example using MFC with Visual C++, there is an Album recordset and an Artist recordset, both sharing the same Cdatabase object. Using Visual Basic with direct ODBC API calls, there is only one connection, with two statements, one for each table.

Step 1: Display Album Data

Begin creating this application in Visual C++ by using the AppWizard to create a new project. Specify database support without file support, and make it a multidocument application. The names used are shown in Figure 14.1.

Figure 14.1. *New Project Information.*

In the last step of specifying the new project, you are presented with a list of the classes that will be created, along with the filenames for the interface and implementation files for each class. Because you will be having two recordsets in this project, it would be a good idea to rename the first recordset class and its files at this point to reflect the name of the table used in this recordset. In this example, the first recordset will be called CP14AlbSet because it will contain the Album records.

After the project and its initial set of files have been created, the next step is to design the dialog box with controls to display the data from the Album records. At this point, don't worry about the Artist list box except to insert a single edit box to keep track of the amount of space used by the final control and its title. The static text item at the very top is initially given the caption of Not Connected, which will change dynamically when a connection to a data source is made.

To best utilize the help of the Class Wizard, it is important during the creation of the dialog box that the static text labels and their associated controls have adjacent tab orders. If you are familiar with products such as Visual Basic version 3 and others, you will grimace at the prospect of changing tab order, but with Visual C++, it is very easy. With the dialog box displayed, select Tab Order from the Layout menu. This will superimpose the tab order number for each object on the dialog box that has a tab stop. Changing the order is as simple as clicking each item with your mouse. The first item clicked will become tab stop number one, the second item will be tab stop two, and so on. Figure 14.2

shows the completed initial dialog box for the project with tab stops displayed in the correct order.

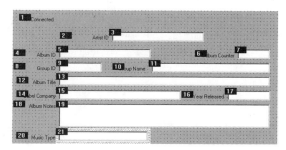

Figure 14.2. *The completed initial dialog box.*

After the dialog box is created with the tab stops in order, mapping the appropriate fields in the database table to the edit boxes in the dialog box becomes Class Wizard child's play. For each item in the dialog box, hold down the Ctrl key on your keyboard and double-click the control with your mouse. This will bring up the Class Wizard Add Member Variable dialog box, as shown in Figure 14.3. If the tab orders are correct and the static text label is anything close to the actual column name in the database table, the member variable name will be incorrect; pick the correct one from the list. Repeat this for each column in the table.

Figure 14.3. *Class Wizard's Add Member Variable dialog box showing pre-filled member name.*

Date columns are a problem, at least as of version 3.0 of the MFC classes. There is not a Record Field Exchange (RFX) function for Date data types. It might be fixed in the latest version of MFC by the time you read this.

14

By design, the MFC implementation of ODBC connections performs the connection during application initialization before the first dialog box is displayed. In addition, the default behavior is to connect to the data source specified during project creation, without user intervention or prompting. We decided to change this behavior in two ways. First, we wanted prompting so that the user could select the appropriate data source at connect time. To permit this, the OnInitialUpdate function must be overridden. The code is simple.

```
void CP14AlbView::OnInitialUpdate()
{
    m_pSet = &GetDocument()->m_p14AlbSet;
    // CRecordView::OnInitialUpdate();
    CFormView::OnInitialUpdate();
}
```

Because the ODBC connection is made in the OnInitialUpdate function in CRecordView, that call is commented out. Looking at the code in DBVIEW.CPP, it appears that the function establishes a connection, and then finishes creating the visual environment. To retain the non-connecting functionality, add back the call to OnInitialUpdate in the CFormView class that would have been made from the CRecordView implementation.

To make the connection on demand, you need to add a menu option and map a function to that option. You can do this easily using the resource editor to add the menu option, and the Class Wizard to map that menu call to a function. Because the Cdocument class "owns" the recordsets, perform the connection from within the CPPreDoc.CPP implementation file. The Class Wizard will create an OnFileConnect function shell, and we will populate that shell.

The easiest way to perform the connection within OnFileConnect is to copy the code from the MFC source. This will look like the following:

```
void CCPPrep14Doc::OnFileConnect()
{
    // CRecordset* pRecordset = OnGetRecordset();
    // recordset must be allocated already
    //ASSERT(m_p14AlbSet != NULL);

    if (!m_p14AlbSet.IsOpen())
    {
        BeginWaitCursor();
        TRY
        {
            m_p14AlbSet.m_strSort = "AlbumCounter";
            m_p14AlbSet.Open();
        }
```

```
CATCH(CDBException, e)
{
    EndWaitCursor();
    AfxMessageBox(e->m_strError, MB_ICONEXCLAMATION);
    THROW_LAST();
}
AND_CATCH_ALL(e)
{
    EndWaitCursor();
    THROW_LAST();
}
END_CATCH_ALL
EndWaitCursor();
```

This code not only includes the `m_p14AlbSet.Open()` call, which actually opens the ODBC connection, but it also is cluttered with TRY, CATCH, and THROW statements that sound as if they came from a ball game. These are MFC macros that implement database exception handling. Any database functions within the TRY block that cause errors will throw an exception (of the `CDBException` class), which will be caught by the following CATCH block, which will display a text description of the error. The implementation of these exception-handling routines throughout the MFC database classes is not perfect, and the release notes point developers toward using the C++ exception-handling routines rather than the corresponding MFC macros initially used. Let the buyer beware on this one!

You probably also noted the line immediately above the `.Open()` call, which sets the `m_strSort` member variable to the name of a column in the Album table. This variable is used to specify a sort order for the result set and is appended to the SQL SELECT string, in this case as `ORDER BY AlbumCount ASC`, which means that the result set will be sorted by the `AlbumCount` field in ascending order. Similarly, an `m_strFilter` variable is defined, which can be used before an open to specify an SQL WHERE clause. If a join condition is to be used, the join would also be specified in the `m_strFilter` variable.

> **Note:** Some editions of the MFC document are incorrect when they imply that a new `m_strFilter` or `m_strSort` value takes effect when the Requery function is invoked. This is not correct because MFC uses prepared SQL statements where the statement is prepared once, and then each time Requery is executed, an SQLExecute function is executed. Because both `m_strFilter` and `m_strSort` change the SQL string itself, the SQL must be re-prepared for these changes to take effect. SQLPrepare is run only when the recordset is opened, not when it is requeried.

14

> The use of a parameterized query, as in the example in this chapter, enables the parameter values to change without changing the SQL string. In this way, a change of the parameter value will be reflected in the next `Requery` execution.

Once the connection is made, you can gather the information to display at the top of the dialog box where it previously displayed Not Connected. To gather this information, you use two SQLGetInfo calls. This code directly follows the connect code in the OnFileConnect function.

```
SWORD   nResult;
RETCODE nRetCode;

// Get name of database and dbms
char szDatabaseName[30];
AFX_SQL_SYNC(::SQLGetInfo(m_p14AlbSet.m_pDatabase->m_hdbc,
    SQL_DATABASE_NAME, szDatabaseName,
    sizeof(szDatabaseName), &nResult));
char szDBMSName[30];
AFX_SQL_SYNC(::SQLGetInfo(m_p14AlbSet.m_pDatabase->m_hdbc,
    SQL_DBMS_NAME, szDBMSName, sizeof(szDBMSName), &nResult));

CString ConnS;
CString DBMS(szDBMSName);
CString Database(szDatabaseName);
ConnS = "Connected to: " + Database + " using: " + DBMS;
    }
}
```

The AFX_SQL_SYNC macro is used to provide protection from asynchronous requests that might still be running on the same connection. You can use this same syntax to call any and all ODBC API functions from anywhere within a Visual C++ application. At the end of this code, the Cstring object ConnS should contain "Connected to: c:\book\ty_odbc.mdb using: ACCESS" or similar phrasing depending on your driver and data source configuration. It is up to you to get the contents of that Cstring into the dialog box static text control.

Compiling and running the code at this point should provide output as shown in Figure 14.4. The Album rows are displayed as the toolbar forward and back arrows are clicked (or the Record menu commands are selected). The MFC environment has provided all the navigation and SQL generation and execution code for you. For the sake of simplicity in this example, when you add a second recordset, you bypass this code and allow the default behavior of OnInitialUpdate to open the recordsets.

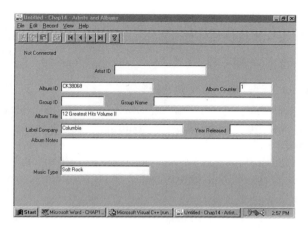

Figure 14.4. *The output from the CPPrep14 application after initial steps with one recordset.*

Step 2: Add Recordset for Artist Table

To access the data in the Artist table, you need to add a recordset class to contain that data. You can do this easily by using the Class Wizard again. Open the Class Wizard and select the Class Info tab. Then click the Add Class button. Fill in the dialog box as shown in Figure 14.5. Give the class and the files meaningful names. Then click the Create Class button. You again are prompted to select a data source name and then select a table name from that data source.

Figure 14.5. *The Add Class dialog box from Class Wizard.*

14

Next, you must add code to attach the new CArtistSet recordset to the one document in your application. While you're at it, open this recordset, populate the ArtistList combo box, and close the recordset. In the document interface file, CPPredoc.h, there already exists a member variable for the albumset class. Add another for the ArtistSet.

```
// Attributes
protected:
    CDatabase m_database;

public:
    CArtistSet  m_pArtSet;
    CP14AlbSet m_p14AlbSet;
```

The `ArtistSet` recordset is opened and the combo box filled in this case in the `OnInitialUpdate` member function of the document class. The `FirstName` and `LastName` are concatenated, and that string is added to the combo box control. Then the corresponding `ArtistID` value is added as a data item. When all the artists are added to the combo box, the recordset is closed and the first item is selected.

```
void CP14AlbView::OnInitialUpdate()
{
    int nTemp;      // Hold the index when adding combo box items
    CString S;      // For concatenating first and last names

    CCPPrep14Doc* pDoc = GetDocument();
    m_pSet = &pDoc->m_p14AlbSet;
    m_pSet->m_pDatabase = pDoc->GetDatabase();
    if (!m_pSet->m_pDatabase->IsOpen())
        return;

    // Open the artist recordset
    pDoc->m_pArtSet.m_strSort = "ArtistID";
    if (pDoc->m_pArtSet.m_pDatabase == NULL)
        pDoc->m_pArtSet.m_pDatabase = pDoc->GetDatabase();
    if (!pDoc->m_pArtSet.Open())
        return;

    // Filter, parameterize and sort the album recordset
    m_pSet->m_strFilter = "ArtistID = ?";
    m_pSet->m_intArtistIDParam = pDoc->m_pArtSet.m_ArtistID;
    m_pSet->m_strSort = "AlbumID";

    CRecordView::OnInitialUpdate();

    // Fill the ArtistList combobox
    m_ctlArtistList.ResetContent();
    if (pDoc->m_pArtSet.IsOpen())
    {
        while (pDoc->m_pArtSet.IsEOF() != TRUE)
        {
            S = pDoc->m_pArtSet.m_FirstName + " " + pDoc->m_pArtSet.m_LastName;
            nTemp = m_ctlArtistList.AddString(S);
            // Insert the ArtistID as item data at the same index
            m_ctlArtistList.SetItemData(nTemp,
                                (DWORD)pDoc->m_pArtSet.m_ArtistID);
            pDoc->m_pArtSet.MoveNext();
        }
    }
    m_ctlArtistList.SetCurSel(0);
}
```

In the third section of this code, the album recordset is parameterized and then opened. This parameterization is accomplished by initializing the m_strFilter member variable with the value "ArtistID = ?". The effect of initializing this variable is to have a WHERE clause appended to the SQL SELECT string, which will be WHERE ArtistID = ?. The question mark character is the parameter placeholder, which is replaced with an actual value when the query is executed.

When the recordset is opened, SQLPrepare is performed to prepare this statement with the parameter marker in place. Subsequently, SQLExecute is performed with a value to pass into that parameter. MFC automatically passes that ArtistID value from the selected artist in the combo box to the executing query if you add the correct code for the DDX routines. The first such addition is to the params/fields section of the albumset interface file, cpalbset.h. Note that the additional parameter is added outside of the AFX comment lines.

```
// Field/Param Data
    //{{AFX_FIELD(CP14AlbSet, CRecordset)
    CString     m_AlbumID;
    int         m_AlbumCounter;
    int         m_ArtistID;
    int         m_GroupID;
    CString     m_AlbumTitle;
    CString     m_LabelCo;
    CTime       m_YearReleased;
    CString     m_Notes;
    CString     m_MusicType;
    //}}AFX_FIELD
    int m_intArtistIDParam;
```

Similarly, in the cpalbset.cpp implementation, the number of parameters must be declared and initialized.

```
    //{{AFX_FIELD_INIT(CP14AlbSet)
    m_AlbumID = "";
    m_AlbumCounter = 0;
    m_ArtistID = 0;
    m_GroupID = 0;
    m_AlbumTitle = "";
    m_LabelCo = "";
    m_Notes = "";
    m_MusicType = "";
    m_nFields = 9;
    //}}AFX_FIELD_INIT
    m_nParams = 1;
    m_intArtistIDParam = 0;
```

The final addition to implement parameterization is to add the RFX functions to move the parameter data to the recordset. This also is done in the cpalbset implementation in the DoDataExchange function.

14

```
void CP14AlbSet::DoFieldExchange(CFieldExchange* pFX)
{
    //{{AFX_FIELD_MAP(CP14AlbSet)
    pFX->SetFieldType(CFieldExchange::outputColumn);
    RFX_Text(pFX, "AlbumID", m_AlbumID);
    RFX_Int(pFX, "AlbumCounter", m_AlbumCounter);
    RFX_Int(pFX, "ArtistID", m_ArtistID);
    RFX_Int(pFX, "GroupID", m_GroupID);
    RFX_Text(pFX, "AlbumTitle", m_AlbumTitle);
    RFX_Text(pFX, "LabelCo", m_LabelCo);
    RFX_Date(pFX, "YearReleased", m_YearReleased);
    RFX_Text(pFX, "Notes", m_Notes);
    RFX_Text(pFX, "MusicType", m_MusicType);
    //}}AFX_FIELD_MAP
    pFX->SetFieldType(CFieldExchange::param);
    RFX_Int(pFX, "ArtistIDParam", m_intArtistIDParam);
}
```

Note in the DoFieldExchange function that we have added our additional lines after AFX_FIELD_MAP, which is placed by Class Wizard. The first of these two additional lines changes the field type from outputcolumn to param fields. The final line declares the movement of int data to the param variable.

All the additions so far have enabled the selection of albums based on the artist ID from the artist list box. Although they are enabled, they don't actually do the lookup. For this, you need to tie some action with the combo box to the execution of code to display the corresponding album(s). Begin this process with the Class Wizard. Figure 14.6 shows the selections in Class Wizard, where you can add a function to process the SELENDOK action from the combo box.

Figure 14.6. *Class Wizard dialog box for adding a message map to the ArtistList combo box.*

The ON_CBN_SELENDOK message is sent when the user selects an item from the drop-down list and then presses Enter or selects the down arrow. When this happens, you want to requery the recordset with the parameter value of the artist ID taken from the ItemData value stored with the selected item from the combo box. If there are no corresponding records in the album recordset, you want the dialog box controls to be blank to reflect the lack of data. If an artist ID has more than one album record, you use the standard navigational commands of the MFC database classes to enable the user to step forward and backward through these records.

```
void CP14AlbView::OnSelendokArtistList()
{
    if (!m_pSet->IsOpen())
        return;
    m_pSet->m_intArtistIDParam =
        m_ctlArtistList.GetItemData(m_ctlArtistList.GetCurSel());

    m_pSet->Requery();
    if (m_pSet->IsEOF())
    {
        m_pSet->SetFieldNull(&(m_pSet->m_ArtistID), FALSE);
        m_pSet->m_ArtistID = m_pSet->m_intArtistIDParam;
    }
    UpdateData(FALSE);
}
```

Analysis   This code is very simple but performs many actions. First, if the recordset is open, the artist ID is retrieved from the combo box and assigned to the parameter member variable of the album recordset. The Requery function executes SQLExecute with the statement handle of the prepared SQL SELECT statement and the parameter value just placed in the parameter variable. If the recordset is at end-of-file (EOF), the ArtistID field is marked as NULL (C++ NULL and ODBC database NULL are not the same thing). The final function of UpdateData(FALSE) updates the dialog box from the recordset.

Figure 14.7 shows the application so far. Although this application is by most standards very primitive and needs additional features, many end users would love to have this much functionality for viewing their data. Don't be afraid to start small and take little steps to greatness. If you try to start with the best application in the world, your users will never see anything!

14

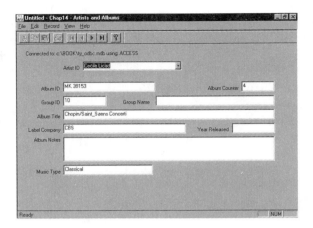

Figure 14.7. *The finished Artist/Album application.*

The Visual Basic Version of the Same Application

In today's lesson, you'll use Visual Basic to create the same application as the one you just completed using Visual C++. The most interesting aspect of this exercise might be to learn how simple it is to perform the same functions using Visual Basic. Performing this dual-application generation will also help you understand how things work in the opposite environment.

The first step of generating this application in Visual Basic is to create the form used for the visual interface to the user. In this example, use Visual Basic version 4 to demonstrate how similar its development environment is to version 3. Version 4 provides many new, powerful, and useful features such as the capability to generate OLE in-proc automation servers, but there are other books from Sams that teach you about those features. For more information about these books, see the Sams section of the Macmillan Computer Publishing World Wide Web site on the Internet at http://www.mcp.com/.

Figure 14.8 shows the fully created (and in this case, active) form for this application. Your first reaction should be how similar it is to the dialog box you created using Visual C++. The most obvious difference should be the lack of toolbars in the Visual Basic version, but creating toolbars is easy with version 4.

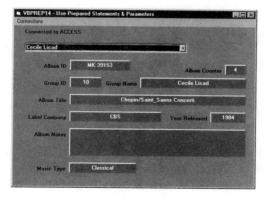

Figure 14.8. *The Artist/Album application interface in Visual Basic.*

The majority of the basic code in this example is contained in just two subroutines. The first contains the connection functionality and it loads the Artist combo box as you did in the C++ application. This subroutine is called from the Connect menu.

```
Private Sub MenuConn_Click()

    Dim Conn1In As String          'Connection string input to function
    Dim Conn1Out As String         'Connection string returned after connection
    Dim ConnLen As Integer            'Length of output connection string
    Dim FirstN As String              'First name work storage
    Dim LastN As String               'Last name work storage
    Dim ArtId As Integer              'Work storage
    Dim cbID As Long                  'For Bind Param
    Dim pvParam As Long               'Parameter for connection options
    Dim FocusOut As Long
    Dim ParentIn As Long
    Dim LenOut As Long


    Conn1Out = String$(255, 0)        'Initialize for size and value
    Screen.MousePointer = aHourGlass  'Put up hourglass to show wait mode
    Conn1In = ""                      'Prompt for all ODBC connection info
    FocusOut = GetFocus()
    ParentIn = GetParent(FocusOut)
    RetCode = SQLDriverConnect(hdbcArt, VBPREP14.hwnd, _
             Conn1In, Len(Conn1In), Conn1Out, 255, ConnLen, SQL_DRIVER_PROMPT)
    'RetCode = SQLDriverConnect(hdbcArt, 0, Conn1In, _
                  Len(Conn1In), Conn1Out, 255, ConnLen, SQL_DRIVER_NOPROMPT)
       'only show fatal errors below, filter out CHANGED CONTEXT type messages
    If (RetCode = SQL_ERROR) Or (RetCode = SQL_INVALID_HANDLE) Then
       ShowError hdbcArt, 0
       Screen.MousePointer = aNormal
    Else
         'we're connected to the first connection OK - used for ARTISTS
       ArtState = 4                   'Set Current State for artist to connected
```

14

```
'now we'll use the same connection info and connect for ALBUM without prompting

    RetCode = SQLDriverConnect(hdbcAlb, 0, Conn1Out, _
                    Len(Conn1Out), Conn1Out, 255, ConnLen, SQL_DRIVER_NOPROMPT)
      'likewise, only show fatal errors
    If (RetCode = SQL_ERROR) Or (RetCode = SQL_INVALID_HANDLE) Then
      ShowError hdbcAlb, 0
    Else
      AlbState = 4                        'Set current state for album to connected
    End If
End If
```

Through this point in the subroutine, you have created two connections to the data
source: one for the Artist table and another for the Album table. This functionality could
have been provided using two statement handles to one connection, but some data
sources don't support this, so we took the safe route.

Next, you execute a SELECT statement that returns all of the ArtistID, FirstName, and
LastName data from the Artist table. Then the rows are fetched, the three columns are
retrieved, and the combo box is loaded with these names and IDs.

```
Conn1In = String$(255, 0)                      'Initialize string for size and value
    'Get name of DBMS to display
  RetCode = SQLGetInfo(hdbcAlb, SQL_DBMS_NAME, ByVal Conn1In, 255, ConnLen)
  If RetCode <> SQL_SUCCESS Then
    ShowError hdbcAlb, 0
  End If
  ConDesc = "Connected to " & Conn1In       'Display info about driver name

  Attempt SQLAllocStmt(hdbcArt, hstmtArt), _
                     "Cannot allocate handle for Artist Statements"
  Attempt SQLAllocStmt(hdbcAlb, hstmtAlb), _
                     "Cannot allocate handle for Album statements"

    'We'll reuse the string because we don't need it any more
  Conn1In = "select ArtistID,FirstName,LastName from Artist"

    'Now execute this query once, bringing back all artists
  RetCode = SQLExecDirect(hstmtArt, Conn1In, Len(Conn1In))
  If RetCode <> SQL_SUCCESS Then
    ShowError hdbcArt, hstmtArt
  End If
  FirstN = String$(51, 0)                        'Initialize work strings
  LastN = String$(51, 0)
  RetCode = SQLFetch(hstmtArt)           'Perform initial fetch to prime the pump
  RetCode = SQLGetData(hstmtArt, 1, SQL_C_USHORT, ArtId, 5, LenOut)
  RetCode = SQLGetData(hstmtArt, 2, SQL_C_CHAR, ByVal FirstN, 51, LenOut)
  RetCode = SQLGetData(hstmtArt, 3, SQL_C_CHAR, ByVal LastN, 51, LenOut)

    'Now loop through each row of the artist table to load list box
  While (RetCode <> SQL_NO_DATA_FOUND) And (RetCode <> SQL_ERROR)
    If (InStr(FirstN, Chr$(0)) > 1) Then
        'if the first name is null, only load the last name
      f_ArtList.AddItem Mid$(FirstN, 1, _
```

```
        InStr(FirstN, Chr$(0)) - 1) & " " & _
        Mid$(LastN, 1, InStr(LastN, Chr$(0)) - 1)
    Else
       f_ArtList.AddItem Mid$(LastN, 1, InStr(LastN, Chr$(0)) - 1)
    End If
    f_ArtList.ItemData(f_ArtList.NewIndex) = ArtId
     'load the artistid to the same index
    RetCode = SQLFetch(hstmtArt)
    RetCode = SQLGetData(hstmtArt, 1, SQL_C_USHORT, ArtId, 5, LenOut)
    RetCode = SQLGetData(hstmtArt, 2, SQL_C_CHAR, ByVal FirstN, 51, LenOut)
    RetCode = SQLGetData(hstmtArt, 3, SQL_C_CHAR, ByVal LastN, 51, LenOut)
Wend

  'Now we'll prepare the album select statement
Conn1In = "select AlbumID,AlbumCounter,GroupID, _
          AlbumTitle,LabelCo,YearReleased,Notes, _
          MusicType from Album where ArtistID = ?"
   'Prepare but don't execute this select
RetCode = SQLPrepare(hstmtAlb, Conn1In, Len(Conn1In))
If RetCode <> SQL_SUCCESS Then
   ShowError hdbcAlb, hstmtAlb
End If

wAlbumId = String$(31, 0)
wAlbumCounter = String$(6, 0)
wAlbumTitle = String$(76, 0)
wLabelCo = String$(31, 0)
wNotes = String$(255, 0)
wMusicType = String$(21, 0)
wYearReleased = String$(24, 0)
   'Bind the artist id (which we get from the list box selection)
   ' to the query parameter
RetCode = SQLBindParameter(hstmtAlb, 1, SQL_PARAM_INPUT, _
                        SQL_C_USHORT, SQL_INTEGER, 10, 0, wArtID, 0, cbID)
If RetCode <> SQL_SUCCESS Then
   ShowError hdbcAlb, hstmtAlb
End If
   Screen.MousePointer = aNormal          'Turn off hourglass
End Sub
```

The final part of this routine prepares the SQL statement used to retrieve the album records. Work variables also are created and initialized to receive the data in case SQLBindCol calls were used. The final function used in this routine, SQLBindParameter, is the key to its speed.

The *SQLBindParameter* Function

The general syntax for the SQLBindParameter function in Visual Basic is

```
RETCODE SQLBindParameter(hstmt,
                         ipar,
                         fParamType,
                         fCType,
                         fSqlType,
```

```
                          cdColDef,
                          ibScale,
                          rgbValue,
                          cbVAlueMax,
                          pcbValue)
```

This function binds a buffer space to a parameter marker in an SQL statement. An application calls SQLBindParameter to bind each parameter marker contained in an SQL statement. These bindings remain in effect until SQLBindParameter is called again for the same marker or until the application calls SQLFreeStmt with either the SQL_DROP or SQL_RESET_PARAMS options.

The fParamType parameter specifies the type of parameter. Normally, this would be SQL_PARAM_INPUT. fCtype and fSqlType specify the data type of the value being passed in and the corresponding data type on the database. The precision of the column is specified with the cbColDef parameter. The buffer containing the data is pointed to by the rgbValue parameter. The length of the buffer in most cases is contained in the cbValueMax argument. The final argument, pcbValue, points to a buffer that contains the length of the actual data stored in the data buffer.

The next important section of code in the Visual Basic edition of this application is executed when an artist is selected from the combo or list box.

```
Private Sub f_ArtList_Click()
  Dim n As Integer
  Dim AnyAnds As Integer
  Dim LenOut As Long
'starting new execute, get rid of last time
  RetCode = SQLFreeStmt(hstmtAlb, SQL_CLOSE)
  wArtID = f_ArtList.ItemData(f_ArtList.ListIndex) 'set bound parameter value
  RetCode = SQLExecute(hstmtAlb)                    'execute the query
  If RetCode <> SQL_SUCCESS Then
    ShowError hdbcAlb, hstmtAlb
  End If
  RetCode = SQLFetch(hstmtAlb)                     'fetch the bound data
      'Bind the output columns to work areas
  RetCode = SQLGetData(hstmtAlb, 1, SQL_C_CHAR, ByVal wAlbumId, 31, LenOut)
  RetCode = SQLGetData(hstmtAlb, 2, SQL_C_CHAR, ByVal wAlbumCounter, 6, LenOut)
  RetCode = SQLGetData(hstmtAlb, 3, SQL_C_USHORT, wGroupID, 0, LenOut)
  RetCode = SQLGetData(hstmtAlb, 4, SQL_C_CHAR, ByVal wAlbumTitle, 76, LenOut)
  RetCode = SQLGetData(hstmtAlb, 5, SQL_C_CHAR, ByVal wLabelCo, 31, LenOut)
  RetCode = SQLGetData(hstmtAlb, 6, SQL_C_CHAR, ByVal wYearReleased, 24,LenOut)
  RetCode = SQLGetData(hstmtAlb, 7, SQL_C_CHAR, ByVal wNotes, 255, LenOut)
  RetCode = SQLGetData(hstmtAlb, 8, SQL_C_CHAR, ByVal wMusicType, 21, LenOut)
  If RetCode = SQL_ERROR Then
    ShowError hdbcAlb, hstmtAlb
  Else
    f_AlbumID = wAlbumId                           'display it
    f_AlbumTitle = wAlbumTitle
    f_AlbumCounter = wAlbumCounter
    f_GroupID = wGroupID
```

```
    If wGroupID > 0 Then
      For n = 0 To f_ArtList.ListCount - 1
        If wGroupID = f_ArtList.ItemData(n) Then
          f_GroupName = f_ArtList.TEXT
        End If
      Next
    End If
    AnyAnds = InStr(wLabelCo, "&")
    If AnyAnds Then
      wLabelCo = Mid$(wLabelCo, 1, AnyAnds) & "&" & Mid$(wLabelCo, AnyAnds + 1)
    End If
    f_LabelCo = wLabelCo
    f_AlbNotes = wNotes
    f_MusicType = wMusicType
    f_YearRel = Mid$(wYearReleased, 1, 4)
  End If
End Sub
```

This code executes the already prepared statement selecting those rows from the Album table that have the correct ArtistID value. Then the data is fetched and a series of SQLGetData calls brings that data into variables within the application.

Summary

Today's lesson demonstrated how to build a complete application utilizing the most common ODBC functions in a useful manner. Specifically, you learned about the following:

☐ Using prepared statements as a way to save steps and improve processing speeds on repetitive database accesses.

☐ Using parameter markers within prepared statements as a way to pass changing data into an otherwise unchanged SQL statement. This is especially important when you use the MFC database classes where you must close and reopen a recordset to implement changed SQL. With a parameterized and prepared statement, you can change the value of an item used in the WHERE clause of the SQL SELECT statement (or any other SQL statement) without reopening the recordset, resulting in far better performance.

☐ You can create the same application to perform a common business type of functionality using either Visual C++ or Visual Basic.

14

273

Q&A

Q Do I have to prepare a statement to use parameter markers?

A No, but it makes no sense to use parameter markers with `SQLExecDirect`. The benefit of preparing statements is to avoid the cost of continually re-preparing as is done when executing direct.

Q Won't using Visual C++ always be faster than using Visual Basic in an application like this?

A Not necessarily. Visual C++ does an excellent job of optimizing code for performance, but the Jet Engine, which is used in many of the drivers, causes inefficient use of the ODBC CLI.

Q Can I show all the artist data in a separate dialog box?

A Sure, but in Visual C++ you should create another view in that case.

Workshop

The Workshop provides quiz questions to help you solidify your understanding of the material covered and to give you experience in using what you've learned. Try to understand the quiz and exercise answers before continuing on to the next day's lesson. Answers are provided in Appendix A, "Answers."

Quiz

1. What function does ODBC provide to figure out how best to access the rows of data specified in the SQL statement?

2. What class, in MFC, encapsulates your conversation with the database?

Exercise

1. Change the `CCPPrep14Doc::OnFileConnect()` function described in the first part of the chapter to sort on AlbumID.

This week covered the nuts and bolts of your conversation with your database using ODBC. You saw how to make a connection to the database (Day 8) and once connected how to find out what capabilities the connection will support (Day 9). Then, after a day spent learning the basics of Structured Query Language (Day 10), you went right to the mechanics of how to send the SQL queries via ODBC and how to get the requested data back (Days 11 and 12). Day 13 gave you the methods and syntax to recognize and report errors, and on Day 14 you moved from working with static SQL queries to inserting parameters into your queries, making them dynamic.

During week three you will learn about some of the advanced ODBC functions and how to test, debug, and deliver your application.

Day 15, "Running UPDATE, INSERT, or DELETE Statements," gives you the syntax you need to make changes to your database. Day 16, "Using ODBC Functions," shows how you can use standard and server-specific Structured Query Language functions from within ODBC. Day 17, "Using ODBC Cursors," describes how to use cursors to improve your access. Day 18, "Using Transactions and Commitment Control," covers the important topic of data protection and data integrity. Day 19, "Ending Transactions and Connections," discusses the proper methods to end transactions within a connection and how to disconnect cleanly. Day 20, "Completing the Entire Application," gives you suggestions for code cleanup and walks you through how to prepare your code for installation. Day 21, "Using ODBC Test and Trace Tools," is your introduction to the debugging tools available in the Microsoft Software Development Kit (SDK).

Running *UPDATE*, *INSERT*, or *DELETE* Statements

WEEK

3

So far, you've learned most of the basics of creating ODBC connections, retrieving data, and managing the connection. Today you learn about the final aspect of data manipulation on the database: changing the data. Such changes can be in the form of adding data, changing existing data, or deleting data. How this is accomplished using ODBC varies greatly depending on whether you are using Visual C++ or Visual Basic. In today's lesson, you will learn about the following:

☐ ODBC syntax for data change statements

☐ Differences between Visual C++ and Visual Basic

☐ Determining the impact of the changes on the database

ODBC Syntax for Data Change Statements

Regardless of which development environment you are using, the SQL statement syntax you use will be the same. What differs is how the syntax of the SQL statement is used and the way in which the ODBC API functions are used with the SQL statement. When writing Visual Basic calls to the actual ODBC API functions, the developer must write the complete SQL statement and explicitly call each ODBC function. When using Visual C++ with MFC, on the other hand, the developer is generally not writing SQL at all, nor are the ODBC functions called directly. As you'll see shortly, MFC functions are called, and they will make the ODBC calls.

Whenever you consider changing data in the database, you must also consider how to protect the data and prevent errors. This can be handled at two levels. The first, and most important, level is the application level. If a delete is requested, the application should prompt the user for verification of the delete before actually performing that action. Similarly for updates and inserts, the users should be given the option of changing their mind partway through the operation and terminating the update or addition before it takes effect.

Some, but by no means all, database systems provide a second way to protect data by enabling the user, the application, or in some cases the DBMS to undo partially completed actions through the use of the rollback function in conjunction with a transaction journal or log file. This journal keeps track of the "before" and "after" state of all transactions, and if a rollback is requested, the DBMS will restore the data to its "before" state. The use of transaction control with journals is discussed in more detail on Day 18, "Using Transactions and Commitment Control."

ODBC *DELETE* Statement Syntax

The SQL syntax for a DELETE statement is very simple. To delete all rows from the Album table, the statement would be DELETE FROM ALBUM. This statement is simple—and dangerous. Note that no columns are specified because only entire rows can be deleted. To remove the data from a column would require an UPDATE statement, and to remove the entire column from the table requires an ALTER statement.

Note: The only way that data can be truly removed from a column is to set the column value to NULL. In this context, NULL in SQL terms has a different meaning than NULL used in the C language. In SQL, a value of NULL means the column does not contain a defined value. Unfortunately, not all database systems treat NULL alike. The ANSI/ISO SQL specifications need NULLs to be allowed by default unless the CREATE TABLE statement contains "not null" in the column specification. In non-standard systems or when a column is defined to not allow NULL values, the data cannot be deleted with an UPDATE statement. Instead, the current value can be replaced only with a neutral value such as a space in a character column or a zero in a numeric column. There is no standard other than NULL in the case of date fields.

To delete specific rows you just need to add a WHERE clause to specify a search condition for the rows to be deleted. If you want to delete only a specific row, you must be careful to delete it using the correct column specification in the WHERE clause. To delete a certain Bryan Adams album, you could say DELETE FROM ALBUM WHERE ARTISTID = 99, if Bryan Adams' artist ID were 99, but this will delete all of his albums. To delete a specific album, it is much better to write DELETE FROM ALBUM WHERE ALBUMCOUNTER = 5. Because AlbumCounter is a unique key field, specifying it as the delete key will ensure that only one row is deleted.

Maintaining Referential Integrity

When you delete rows on any table, the application must take into consideration methods to maintain the *referential integrity* of the data. This means simply that if one table refers to the data in another table, the data being referred to must exist. Most relational database systems use the terms *primary key* and *foreign key* to refer to the fields that relate one table to another. The Artist table has ArtistID as its primary key. ArtistID also exists in the Album table as a foreign key referring back to the Artist table.

A very common example of how to lose data integrity would be to delete Bryan Adams from the Artist table, but leave all rows intact in the Album table. After you delete Bryan Adams, Album rows would exist that refer to an artist ID that no longer exists, a serious referential integrity problem.

In some database systems that support referential integrity, the system will not enable the previously mentioned error to occur. Instead, the delete will fail, with an appropriate message returned to the application. In many cases, however, the database will not protect against such problems. When this happens, the symptoms of referential integrity errors are very subtle and can be just empty windows or missing data; however, program logic that is expecting data to exist can fail when integrity is broken.

Good programming practice can minimize this problem; you can take up to three steps proactively. First, the application logic should only enable you to delete artists and corresponding albums at the same time, without the ability to cancel the operation after deleting from one table and not the other. Second, where available, the DBMS should have triggers programmed to perform the cascading deletes automatically. In this case, if Bryan Adams is deleted, the trigger will automatically delete all albums with Bryan Adams as an artist. Finally, no matter what steps are taken to prevent it, your application should gracefully handle the occasion when it encounters missing rows, because it probably will happen sometime, no matter how careful you are.

ODBC *INSERT* Statement Syntax

The INSERT statement is a little different from the other common statements you will be using in that it never contains a WHERE clause. The other selection and similar statements use the WHERE clause to specify which rows to select or affect with their action. An INSERT statement, on the other hand, must contain all of the data to create a complete row. Take a look at some examples.

INSERT INTO ARTIST VALUES(22,'Pearl','Jam','Famous rock group'). In this case, we have not specified any column names, but we have provided values for all columns in left-to-right column order. If no column names are specified, you must provide values for all unless the column has a default value defined or the column allows NULL values. If the column allows NULL values, column data can be left out but the placeholder is required. INSERT INTO ARTIST VALUES(23,,'Nirvana',) is an example in which FirstName and Note values are omitted, but the commas are left in place to denote their place. This will work only if the default value for the missing columns is NULL.

15

An alternative would be INSERT INTO ARTIST(ArtistID, LastName) VALUES(23, 'Nirvana'). When you specify column names, you no longer have to specify all columns, nor do they have to be in any particular order. Another alternative would be to use parameter markers as in Day 14's lesson. In this case, the statement would look like this: INSERT INTO ARTIST VALUES(?,?,?,?). This statement could then be prepared, and with four bound parameters, executed each time a row was to be inserted.

Referential integrity problems are possible when you insert rows, just as when you delete them. For example, if you are inserting an album and artist and you have already inserted the album when the system crashes, you have an instant referential integrity problem because you have not inserted the artist. This is another case in which wrapping both inserts inside a single transaction and committing them when they're both finished is the safest course of action. If this seems like too much trouble or is not supported by the DBMS, make sure that your application will handle integrity problems.

Look at some pseudocode to examine the logic necessary to handle the previous example.

```
Call SQLGetInfo
If SQL_TXN_CAPABLE = 1 Then  // This driver is capable of handling transactions
    Begin Transaction
    Insert album
    If Successful Then
        Insert artist
        If Successful Then
            Commit Transaction  // Completed both inserts OK
        Else
            Rollback transaction, notify user
        EndIf
    Else
        Rollback transaction, notify user
    EndIf
Else      // This driver not capable of transactions
    If ablum not in database Then
        Insert album
    EndIf
    If artist not in database Then
        Insert artist
    EndIf
    If both inserts fail Then
        Notify user
    EndIf
Endif
```

If the application being written is going to use a known data source, the SQLGetInfo call can be left out based on known behavior of the DBMS. If the DBMS supports transactions, the bottom half of the above logic tree can also be omitted, sacrificing application flexibility for code size and maintainability. Note that if transactions are supported, the code will run much faster because to determine if an artist or album exists in the database a SELECT query must be run.

ODBC *UPDATE* Statement Syntax

If you want to add a note to an existing row, the SQL statement could be: UPDATE ARTIST SET NOTE = 'This is a note' WHERE ArtistID = 5. This update will change only one row, which is specified with the WHERE clause. You can also make mass updates against many or all rows by specifying appropriate WHERE clauses (or no WHERE clause at all—affecting all rows in the table).

The same rules for specifying values apply here as in other SQL statements: alpha literals must be surrounded by single quotes (including dates), and parameter markers can replace the actual value field. One, many, or all columns can be updated in a single statement. Some systems will update all columns, setting the value of unchanged columns to their original value, which is redundant and could cause integrity problems if record locking is not used.

Differences Between Visual C++ and Visual Basic

Microsoft's Visual C++ (and the Visual Basic Data Access Objects) support a navigational model that abstracts the calling of ODBC functions from the application. For this reason, it would be a waste of time to compare Visual Basic with C++ at the API level when it comes to handling updates, inserts, and deletes.

To make changes to data in Visual Basic, the application must collect the changed data, insert it into an UPDATE or INSERT SQL statement, and then execute that statement using an SQLExecDirect or SQLExecute statement. The application developer must make the changes directly to the database using ODBC API function calls and SQL statement manipulation.

On the other hand, in Visual C++, the recordset class in MFC abstracts all of the ODBC and SQL manipulation, requiring the application developer to call only one of the CRecordset manipulation functions: AddNew, Delete, Edit, or Update.

For instance, to add a new record to the database, the application must first determine whether the data source allows updates. This can be checked by calling the CanAppend function. Once this is checked, the application must perform the following steps:

1. Call AddNew. This will create a new, empty record at the "end" of the recordset.
2. Make changes to the data in this new, empty record. You can make these changes either by using a dialog and letting the DDX functions move them to

the recordset, or by directly making assignments to the member variables in the recordset.

3. Either accept the changes by calling Update, or discard the changes by performing any other action, such as moving to another record. To explicitly discard the added record, call Move with the parameter AFX_MOVE_REFRESH, which will restore you to where you were before calling AddNew.

4. Whether the record was accepted by calling Update or canceled by moving, the recordset will be repositioned to where it was positioned before AddNew was called. For example, if the recordset contains 10 rows and is currently positioned at row 5, the AddNew function will add row 11. Following the Update call, the current record will again be row 5. The new row will only be visible and editable by positioning to that new row. In addition, if your application is using snapshots rather than dynasets, the new row will exist in the database but not in the recordset. In this case, to view or edit the new row, the snapshot must be updated by calling Requery to be able to see the new row.

Making changes to a recordset is similar to making additions. Once it is determined that the recordset can be updated, you need to take the following steps to change a record:

1. Position the recordset on the record to be edited. Although AddNew will automatically position itself at the end of the recordset, the application must position to a record to be edited.

2. Call the Edit function. This will notify the recordset that the record can be changed.

3. Make changes to the data in the record. Again, you can do this through a dialog box or by assigning new values to member variables in the recordset.

4. Make the changes to the database by calling Update, or discard the changes by doing nothing (or by calling Move with the AFX_MOVE_REFRESH parameter).

5. Unlike with AddNew, a recordset will remain positioned at a changed record after the change is finalized.

6. Any changes you make to the snapshot will be reflected in that snapshot, but changes made to the underlying database will not be reflected in your snapshot.

The Delete function is different with recordsets in that you don't have a two-step procedure that allows you to discard or ignore changes before they become permanent. When you call Delete, the record is immediately and forever gone. Period.

Adding *AddNew* Functionality to a Sample Visual C++ Program

Because most of the INSERT functionality is embedded deep within the MFC database classes, the code additions necessary to implement the AddNew function are simple and straightforward.

Begin by adding a new member to the AlbView class to keep track of whether you're in Add mode.

```
// Attributes
protected:
    CDatabase m_database;
    BOOL m_bAddMode;
```

Then, you need to add code to the class constructor to initialize this member so that the class is not constructed in Add mode.

```
CP15AlbView::CP15AlbView()
    : CRecordView(CP15AlbView::IDD)
{
    //{{AFX_DATA_INIT(CP15AlbView)
    m_pSet = NULL;
    m_GroupName = _T("");
    m_YearReleased = _T("");
    //}}AFX_DATA_INIT
    m_bAddMode = FALSE;
}
```

To enable editing and setting the dialog READ_ONLY property off, you must make another member variable for one of the controls. We have chosen AlbumID. Bring up the resource editor and enter Class Wizard. Then select AlbumID and Add Variable, adding a control variable rather than a value one. Figure 15.1 shows this step.

Figure 15.1. *Using Class Wizard to add a control CEdit variable.*

You must add an Add menu item to the Record menu, and then use Class Wizard to map that menu control to a corresponding function. The code in that function should save the current artist ID because you'll be creating a new album for the same artist.

```
void CP15AlbView::OnRecordAdd()
{
    // If already in add mode, complete the previous new record
    if (m_bAddMode)
        OnMove(ID_RECORD_FIRST);

    CString strCurrentArtist = m_pSet->m_ArtistID;
    m_pSet->AddNew();
    m_pSet->SetFieldNull(&(m_pSet->m_AlbumID), FALSE);
    m_pSet->m_ArtistID = strCurrentArtist;
    m_bAddMode = TRUE;
    m_ctlAlbumID.SetReadOnly(FALSE);
    UpdateData(FALSE);
}
```

Again, use Class Wizard to add an OnMove function to the Albumview class. This function is available in the right-hand list box; just select it and click the Add Function button as shown in Figure 15.2.

Figure 15.2. *Using Class Wizard to add the OnMove function.*

The OnMove function should be populated something like the following:

```
BOOL CP15AlbView::OnMove(UINT nIDMoveCommand)
{
    if (m_bAddMode)
    {
        if (!UpdateData())
            return FALSE;
        TRY
        {
            m_pSet->Update();
        }
```

```
        CATCH(CDBException, e)
        {
            AfxMessageBox(e->m_strError);
            return FALSE;
        }
        END_CATCH

        m_pSet->Requery();
        UpdateData(FALSE);
        m_ctlAlbumID.SetReadOnly(TRUE);

        m_bAddMode = FALSE;
        return TRUE;
    }
    else
    {
        return CRecordView::OnMove(nIDMoveCommand);
    }
}
```

With the addition of this little bit of code, your application will not support the addition of Album records by merely selecting the Add menu option under the Record menu. Figure 15.3 shows the results of such an addition.

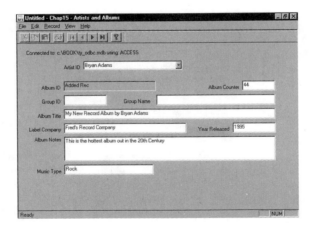

Figure 15.3. *The added record shows on view dialog and is in database.*

Because adding records in Visual Basic is a matter of creating an SQL string with an INSERT statement and then executing the statement directly, you will not see an example here, but rather do that exercise yourself. This should be very simple to accomplish.

Determining the Impact of Changes on the Database

When you make changes to a record from a Visual C++ recordset class, the only possible impact is on the one record involved, either for adding or changing (or deleting for that matter). Unless the SQL is modified, no more than one record from a recordset can be affected.

Using Visual Basic (or other tools) enables the impact to be much heavier. If the SQL WHERE clause is missing or incorrect, the wrong rows or even the entire table can be changed or deleted. In this case, it might be useful to know how many rows of the underlying database were actually affected. The SQLRowCount function can help with this by determining, after the fact, how many rows were affected by an UPDATE, INSERT, or DELETE operation.

Many people have seen this API and are disappointed that they cannot use it to determine how many rows will be returned by a SELECT statement. This is not possible in most cases from most drivers and/or DBMSs. A few systems have extended the standard so that this function will indicate the number of rows to be returned from a prepared but not yet executed SELECT statement. However, the number of rows in a result set can usually only be obtained by returning all rows to the application and determining the count of rows from that result set.

Summary

Today's lesson showed you how to manipulate data in the database. It included the following topics:

- [ ] How to create the proper SQL grammar for INSERT, UPDATE, and DELETE statements. This included where to use a WHERE clause to specify the rows to be affected and where a WHERE was not used.

- [ ] The differences between using the recordset functions AddNew, Update, Edit, and Delete with Visual C++ versus using the INSERT, UPDATE, and DELETE SQL statements with an SQLExecDirect call from Visual Basic.

- [ ] The SQLRowCount function can return the number of rows affected by an INSERT, UPDATE, or DELETE function, but it is not useful in learning how many rows will be returned by a SELECT statement.

Q&A

Q Why didn't the examples include `Edit` and `Delete` functionality?

A Implementing these functions is very easy and makes a good exercise.

Q Wouldn't it be dangerous if the ArtistList combo box were changed during an `Add`?

A Yes. For this reason, you should include a check against the `m_bAddMode` variable before allowing change to the selected item in the combo box.

Q Is adding records in the recordset manner efficient?

A No, but generally, additions are not done in large quantity. If you will be adding a lot of rows, it would be much better to implement a looping `SQLExecute` with a parameterized `INSERT` statement, just executing with different data. The performance improvement will be dramatic!

Workshop

The Workshop provides quiz questions to help you solidify your understanding of the material covered and to give you experience in using what you've learned. Try to understand the quiz answers before continuing on to the next day's lesson. Answers are provided in Appendix A, "Answers."

Quiz

1. Name the standard functions that can be called in MFC when you use Visual C++ to modify data in an existing database.

2. What are a primary key and a foreign key?

3. Specify one or more techniques to ensure referential integrity.

16

Using ODBC
Functions

Today you learn the scalar functions supported by ODBC. The lesson presents the available functions, how to use them, and how to determine which functions are supported by a particular ODBC driver. Today you learn the following topics:

- ☐ Overview of scalar functions
- ☐ String functions
- ☐ Numeric functions
- ☐ Time and date functions
- ☐ System functions
- ☐ Data type conversion functions
- ☐ Determining which scalar functions are supported by a particular ODBC driver

In addition, with each of the topics listed, a few Microsoft Foundation Class (MFC) functions that correspond with the ODBC scalar functions are discussed. Most of the ODBC scalar functions do not have an equivalent function within the CDatabase and CRecordset classes. However, other functions that perform the same operation exist in the rest of the MFC library.

Scalar Function Overview

You learned on Day 9, "Determining Driver and DBMS Capabilities," that ODBC defines three levels of SQL conformance (minimum, core, and extended), and that core compliance is based upon the X/Open SAG 1992 specification. Scalar function support is a part of ODBC's extension to the SQL grammar defined by this specification.

Most DBMSs support scalar functions in one form or another. However, at present there is no accepted syntactical standard for using scalar functions across DBMSs. ODBC bridges this gap and defines a standard SQL grammar for using scalar functions, as well as other SQL extensions such as outer joins and procedure calls.

The Pros and Cons of Scalar Functions

There are both benefits and drawbacks to using scalar functions. The most obvious benefit is the portability of code written using the ODBC scalar functions. Unfortunately, at the present time the ANSI SQL standard defines only five SQL functions that must be supported to comply with the ANSI standard.

- [ ] MAX
- [ ] MIN
- [ ] AVG
- [ ] SUM
- [ ] COUNT

These five functions also happen to be the most common functions used; however, you can be sure that the need will eventually arise to use date/time or money functions, for instance. Although it is possible to embed the function call in your SQL statement, and then bind a variable to the results returned by the SQL statement, the SQL function chosen will probably work only with the current database system. Each manufacturer provides a wide range of functions, many of which are designed to work exclusively with data types unique to that database system's SQL. The ODBC scalar functions listed in this chapter will work with any ODBC driver that supports them. This gives the developer added functionality that might or might not come with his chosen database management system.

This increased portability and functionality can come with a performance improvement, however. Using database-vendor specific function calls within an SQL statement will result in this function call being "compiled" at the time the statement is processed, optimized, and then executed. It is always desirable to do this type of processing on the database server, instead of on each local machine; the data returned to the program will be in finished form. However, if the ODBC scalar functions are used, data will be returned from the data source, and the ODBC driver will continually run this data through the ODBC scalar function before returning the result to you, the programmer. In many instances, this performance penalty might be negligible; however, it is something to be aware of, particularly when a large number of results are being returned to the user.

Because one of the important features of ODBC is its interoperability among a variety of database systems, it might not be in your long-term best interest to limit your options by using a proprietary SQL function. This, of course, is a decision each individual developer will have to make during the design of the application at hand.

The mechanism that enables you to write interoperable SQL statements across DBMSs is the escape clause. The escape clause enables the driver to easily parse the SQL extension so that it can be translated from the ODBC syntax into the native SQL syntax. The escape clause is based on the X/Open SAG 1992 specification, and its generic format looks like the following:

```
--(*vendor(vendor-name), product(product-name) extension *)--
```

Because the vendor name of ODBC is Microsoft, this format can be reduced to

```
--(*vendor(Microsoft), product(ODBC) extension *)--
```

Furthermore, ODBC has defined an abbreviated version of the escape clause notation, which simplifies the expression to

```
{extension}
```

Applying this shorthand notation to the discussion on scalar functions yields

```
{fn scalar-function}
```

All of the examples in this chapter that illustrate scalar functions are presented using the abbreviated ODBC escape clause notation.

What Is a Scalar Function?

Before you begin looking at the specific ODBC scalar functions in detail, take a look at a simple example illustrating the use of a scalar function.

Basically, *scalar functions* provide the capability to manipulate or restrict the columns of a result set. You can use them to trim leading spaces from character data, round numeric results to a specified number of decimal places, calculate the difference between dates in two columns, determine the day of the week from a column of dates, and so on. Don't confuse scalar functions with aggregate functions, such as group by, sum, count, and so forth. Aggregate functions typically return a single record that summarizes all records, or a group of records, from a particular column, whereas scalar functions typically return a record for each row in the result set.

For example, suppose that you issue the following SELECT statement to retrieve the area code and fax number columns from a sample data source:

```
SELECT areacode, faxnumber FROM customers
```

Also suppose that instead of receiving two columns back, you wanted to receive a single column in the form `areacode faxnumber` to send to your modem dialing software. ODBC defines the scalar function, CONCAT, which concatenates result data from two columns into a single column.

Incorporating this scalar function into the preceding SQL command (using the ODBC shorthand escape clause) yields the following:

```
SELECT {fn CONCAT(areacode,faxnumber} FROM employees
```

Executing this SELECT statement would return a single column of results, which would look something like 4045556794, 3125552466, 7145551839, and so on.

Using the ODBC function CONCAT to simply combine the results of two columns into a single column is by no means a demonstration of ODBC's support for extraordinary SQL grammar. Many DBMSs provide native support for this functionality. SQL Server, for example, supports the following SQL syntax to achieve the same results:

```
SELECT areacode+faxnumber FROM employees
```

The intent of using CONCAT, however, is to illustrate how to achieve common functionality across multiple DBMSs using the same SQL syntax.

This chapter shows you the specific string, numeric, system, time/date, and data type conversion scalar functions supported by ODBC. Later on, you will also look at how to determine which scalar functions are supported by a particular ODBC driver.

String Functions

You have already taken a look at the CONCAT string function. Now look at the other scalar string functions supported by ODBC. You will notice that there are four basic arguments used throughout all of the string functions. Following is a description for each of the argument types:

Argument	Description
string_exp	Valid values for this argument are
	☐ Column name
	☐ String literal (surrounded by quotes)
	☐ Result of another scalar function

> **Note:** The *string_exp* argument must be represented by one of the following data types: SQL_CHAR, SQL_VARCHAR, or SQL_LONGVARCHAR.

start	Valid values for this argument are
	☐ Numeric literal
	☐ Result of another scalar function

length	Valid values for this argument are
	☐ Numeric literal
	☐ Result of another scalar function
count	Valid values for this argument are
	☐ Numeric literal
	☐ Result of another scalar function

Note: The arguments start, length, and count must be represented by one of the following data types: SQL_TINYINT, SQL_SMALLINT, or SQL_INTEGER.

Table 16.1 lists each string function and its description. Additional examples illustrating these functions are presented after Table 16.1.

Table 16.1. String functions.

Function	Description
ASCII(*string_exp*)	Returns the furthest left character's ASCII representation.
CHAR(*code*)	Returns the ASCII code equivalent for the specified character.
CONCAT(*string_exp1*, *string_exp2*)	Returns the resulting string from concatenating *string_exp1* and *string_exp2*.
DIFFERENCE(*string_exp1*, *string_exp2*)	Returns the difference between the SOUNDEX values for *string_exp1* and *string_exp2*. The result is returned as an integer value.
INSERT(*string_exp1*, start, length, *string_exp2*)	Returns a string obtained from deleting length characters from *string_exp1* beginning at start and inserting *string_exp2* into *string_exp1* beginning at start.
LCASE(*string_exp*)	Converts *string_exp* to lowercase.
LEFT(*string_exp*, count)	Returns the furthest-left count characters from *string_exp*.

Function	Description
LENGTH(*string_exp*)	Returns the number of characters in *string_exp*, excluding trailing blanks and the string termination character.
LOCATE(*string_exp1*, *string_exp2*[, start])	Returns the position of the first occurrence of *string_exp1* within *string_exp2*. The comparison starts with the first character of *string_exp2* unless the optional start parameter is specified. The first character position starts with 1. If no match is found, then 0 is returned.
LTRIM(*string_exp*)	Removes the leading (leftmost) blanks from *string_exp*.
REPEAT(*string_exp*,count)	Returns *string_exp* repeated count times.
REPLACE(*string_exp1*, *string_exp2*, *string_exp3*)	Replaces all occurrences of *string_exp2* in *string_exp1* with *string_exp3*.
RIGHT(*string_exp*, count)	Returns the furthest right count characters from *string_exp*.
RTRIM(*string_exp*)	Returns *string_exp* with the trailing (rightmost) spaces removed.
SOUNDEX(*string_exp*)	Returns a data source–dependent character string representing the sound of the words in *string_exp*. For example, SQL Server returns a four-digit SOUNDEX code; Oracle returns a phonetic representation of each word.
SPACE(count)	Returns a string of count spaces.
SUBSTRING(*string_exp*, start, length)	Returns a string obtained from taking length characters from *string_exp* beginning at the start character.
UCASE(*string_exp*)	Converts *string_exp* to uppercase.

Examples of String Functions

Most of the following examples will work with the Access 1.1 driver using the North
Wind database.

☐ Convert a results column to uppercase:

```
SELECT {fn LCASE(Address)} FROM employees
```

☐ Return the furthest left five characters of a results column:

```
SELECT {fn Left(Address,5)} FROM employees
```

☐ Return the first name from a results column that contains both first name and
last name separated by a space character:

```
SELECT {fn SUBSTRING('Contact Name',1,
➡{fn LOCATE(' ','Contact Name',1))}} FROM customers
```

MFC String Functions

The Microsoft Foundation Classes provide an entire class (CString) designed to greatly
ease string operations. Included in this class are many useful string manipulation
functions. Some of these functions are listed in Table 16.2. These functions can be used
directly with strings read in from the database using the CRecordset class. This is because
these strings are stored into a CString object.

Table 16.2. MFC string functions.

Function	Description
GetLength	Returns the number of characters in the CString
IsEmpty	Tests whether the CString is empty
Empty	Zeroes out a CString object
GetAt	Returns the character at the given offset from the first character
Compare	Compares two strings
CompareNoCase	Compares two strings (case-insensitive compare)
Mid	Extracts middle part of the CString
Left	Extracts left part of the CString

Function	Description
Right	Extracts right part of the Cstring
MakeUpper	Converts all characters to uppercase
MakeLower	Converts all characters to lowercase
MakeReverse	Reverses the characters in the Cstring
Find	Finds a substring within the larger Cstring
GetBuffer	Returns a char pointer to the characters in the Cstring object
ReleaseBuffer	Releases buffer obtained from the GetBuffer function

Numeric Functions

Using the numeric scalar functions is really no different than using the string functions. Notice that there are three basic arguments used throughout all of the numeric functions. Here is a description of each argument.

Argument	Description
numeric_exp	Valid values for this argument are
	☐ A column name
	☐ A numeric literal
	☐ The result of another scalar function

This argument should be represented by one of the following data types: SQL_NUMERIC, SQL_DECIMAL, SQL_TINYINT, SQL_SMALLINT, SQL_INTEGER, SQL_BIGINT, SQL_FLOAT, SQL_REAL, or SQL_DOUBLE.

float_exp	Valid values for this argument are
	☐ A column name
	☐ A numeric literal
	☐ The result of another scalar function

This argument should be represented by the data type SQL_FLOAT.

integer_exp	Valid values for this argument are
	☐ A column name

☐ A numeric literal

☐ The result of another scalar function

This argument should be represented by one of the following data types: SQL_TINYINT, SQL_SMALLINT, SQL_INTEGER, or SQL_BIGINT.

Table 16.3 describes each of the numeric scalar functions. Additional examples illustrating these functions are presented after Table 16.3.

Table 16.3. Numeric functions.

Function	Description
ABS(*numeric_exp*)	Returns the absolute value of *numeric_exp*.
ACOS(*float_exp*)	Returns the arccosine of *float_exp* as an angle, expressed in radians.
ASIN(*float_exp*)	Returns the arcsine of *float_exp* as an angle, expressed in radians.
ATAN(*float_exp*)	Returns the arctangent of *float_exp* as an angle, expressed in radians.
ATAN2(*float_exp1*, *float_exp2*)	Returns the arctangent of *float_exp1* and *float_exp2* as an angle expressed in radians.
CEILING(*numeric_exp*)	Returns the smallest integer greater than or equal to *numeric_exp*.
COS(*float_exp*)	Returns the cosine of the *float_exp* angle expressed in radians.
COT(*float_exp*)	Returns the cotangent of the *float_exp* angle expressed in radians.
DEGREES(*numeric_exp*)	Returns the number of degrees in *numeric_exp* radians.
EXP(*float_exp*)	Returns the exponential value of *float_exp*.
FLOOR(*numeric_exp*)	Returns the largest integer less than or equal to *numeric_exp*.

Function	Description
LOG(*float_exp*)	Returns the natural logarithm of *float_exp*.
LOG10(*float_exp*)	Returns the base 10 logarithm of *float_exp*.
MOD(*integer_exp1*, *integer_exp2*)	Returns the remainder (modulus) of *integer_exp1* divided by *integer_exp2*.
PI()	Returns the constant value of PI (3.1415...) as a floating-point value.
POWER(*numeric_exp*, *integer_exp*)	Returns the value of *numeric_exp* to the power of *integer_exp*.
RADIANS(*numeric_exp*)	Returns the number of radians in *numeric_exp* degrees.
RAND(*integer_exp*)	Returns a random floating-point value using *integer_exp* as the optional seed value.
ROUND(*numeric_exp*, *integer_exp*)	Returns *numeric_exp* rounded to *integer_exp* places right of the decimal point. If *integer_exp* is negative, *numeric_exp* is rounded to *integer_exp* places to the left of the decimal point.
SIGN(*numeric_exp*)	Returns an indicator or the sign of *numeric_exp*. If *numeric_exp* is less than zero, -1 is returned. If *numeric_exp* equals zero, 0 is returned. If *numeric_exp* is greater than zero, 1 is returned.
SIN(*float_exp*)	Returns the sine of the *float_exp* angle expressed in radians.
SQRT(*float_exp*)	Returns the square root of *float_exp*.
TAN(*float_exp*)	Returns the tangent of the *float_exp* angle expressed in radians.
TRUNCATE(*numeric_exp*, *integer_exp*)	Returns *numeric_exp* truncated to *integer_exp* places right of the decimal point. If *integer_exp* is negative, *numeric_exp* is truncated to *integer_exp* places to the left of the decimal point.

Examples of Numeric Functions

Now take a look at a few examples illustrating the use of the numeric scalar functions.

☐ Round the discounted price calculation to two decimal places:

```
SELECT {fn ROUND('Unit Price'*(100-Discount),2)} FROM 'Order Details'
```

☐ Multiply PI times the square root of the unit price:

```
SELECT {{fn PI()} * fn SQRT('Unit Price')} FROM 'Order Details
```

Time and Date Functions

Moving on to the time and date scalar functions, you will find the following three arguments used throughout these functions.

Argument	Description
timestamp_exp	Valid values for this argument are
	☐ Column name
	☐ Result of another scalar function
	☐ Time, date, or timestamp literal

The underlying data type could be represented as SQL_CHAR, SQL_VARCHAR, SQL_TIME, SQL_DATE, or SQL_TIMESTAMP.

date_exp	Valid values for this argument are
	☐ Column name
	☐ Result of another scalar function
	☐ Date or timestamp literal

The underlying data type could be represented as SQL_CHAR, SQL_VARCHAR, SQL_DATE, or SQL_TIMESTAMP.

time_exp	Valid values for this argument are
	☐ Column name
	☐ Result of another scalar function
	☐ Time or timestamp literal

The underlying data type could be represented as SQL_CHAR, SQL_VARCHAR, SQL_TIME, or SQL_TIMESTAMP.

Earlier in this chapter, you saw that ODBC supported the X/Open SAG escape clause mechanism to denote the presence of scalar functions. Similarly, the escape clause mechanism is also used to represent time, timestamp, and date data types. Notice that in the preceding listing, these data types can be used as arguments to the time and data scalar functions. Before looking at each of these functions, this section reviews the time, timestamp, and date data types and how to represent them using the escape clause syntax.

Recall that the generic short version of the escape clause applied to scalar functions is

`{extension}`

When the escape clause is applied to scalar functions, it becomes

`{fn scalar-function}`

The escape clause notation for the time, date, and timestamp data types, as well as the format for each data type, is summarized in Table 16.4.

Table 16.4. Time, date, and timestamp data types.

Date Type	Escape Notation	Format of `'value'`
Time	(t 'value')	hh:mm:ss
Date	(d 'value')	yyyy-mm-dd
Timestamp	(ts 'value')	yyyy-mm-dd hh:mm:ss

For example, to represent the date of June 1, 1994, you would use the notation, (d '1994-06-01'). Later in the chapter, you will take a look at some examples that use these data types as literals for scalar function arguments.

Now look at Table 16.5, which describes each of the time and date functions included in the ODBC scalar function set.

Table 16.5. Time and date functions.

Function	Description
CURDATE()	Returns the current date as a date value.
CURTIME()	Returns the current local time as a time value.
DAYNAME(*date_exp*)	Returns a character string containing the data source–specific name of the day (for example, Sunday through Saturday or Sun. through Sat. for a

continues

Table 16.5. continued

Function	Description
	data source that uses English, or Sonntag through Samstag for a data source that uses German) for the day portion of *date_exp*.
DAYOFMONTH(*date_exp*)	Returns the day of the month in *date_exp* as an integer value in the range of 1–31.
DAYOFWEEK(*date_exp*)	Returns the day of the week in *date_exp* as an integer value in the range of 1–7, where 1 represents Sunday.
DAYOFYEAR(*date_exp*)	Returns the day of the year in *date_exp* as an integer value in the range of 1–366.
HOUR(*time_exp*)	Returns the hour in *time_exp* as an integer value in the range of 0–23.
MINUTE(*time_exp*)	Returns the minute in *time_exp* as an integer value in the range of 0–59.
MONTH(*date_exp*)	Returns the month in *date_exp* as an integer value in the range of 1–12.
MONTHNAME(*date_exp*)	Returns a character string containing the data source–specific month name for the month portion of *date_exp*. For example, January through December or Jan. through Dec. for a data source that uses English, or Januar through Dezember for a data source that uses German.
NOW()	Returns current date and time as a timestamp value.
QUARTER(*date_exp*)	Returns the quarter in *date_exp* as an integer value in the range of 1–4, where 1 represents January 1 through March 31.
SECOND(*time_exp*)	Returns the second in *time_exp* as an integer value in the range of 0–59.
TIMESTAMPADD(*interval*, *integer_exp*, *timestamp_exp*)	Returns the timestamp calculated by adding *integer_exp* intervals of type *interval* to *timestamp_exp*. Valid values of *interval* are the following keywords:

Function	Description
	SQL_TSI_FRAC_SECOND, SQL_TSI_SECOND, SQL_TSI_MINUTE, SQL_TSI_HOUR, SQL_TSI_DAY, SQL_TSI_WEEK, SQL_TSI_MONTH, SQL_TSI_QUARTER, SQL_TSI_YEAR, where fractional seconds are expressed in billionths of a second. For example, the following SQL statement returns the name of each employee and their one-year anniversary dates: SELECT NAME, {fn TIMESTAMPADD (SQL_TSI_YEAR, 1, HIRE_DATE)} FROM EMPLOYEES. If *timestamp_exp* is a time value and *interval* specifies days, weeks, months, quarters, or years, the date portion of *timestamp_exp* is set to the current date before calculating the resulting timestamp. If *timestamp_exp* is a date value and *interval* specifies fractional seconds, seconds, minutes, or hours, the time portion of *timestamp_exp* is set to 0 before calculating the resulting timestamp. An application determines which intervals a data source supports by calling SQLGetInfo with the SQL_TIMEDATE_ADD_INTERVALS option.
TIMESTAMPDIFF(*interval*, *timestamp_exp1*, *timestamp_exp2*)	Returns the integer number of intervals of type *interval* by which *timestamp_exp2* is greater than *timestamp_exp1*. Valid values of *interval* are the following keywords: SQL_TSI_FRAC_SECOND, SQL_TSI_SECOND, SQL_TSI_MINUTE, SQL_TSI_HOUR, SQL_TSI_DAY, SQL_TSI_WEEK, SQL_TSI_MONTH, SQL_TSI_QUARTER, and SQL_TSI_YEAR, where fractional seconds are expressed in billionths of a second. For example, the following SQL statement returns the name of each employee and the number of years they have been employed: SELECT NAME, {fn TIMESTAMPDIFF ('SQL_TSI_YEAR', {fn CURDATE()},HIRE_DATE)}

16

continues

Table 16.5. continued

Function	Description
	FROM EMPLOYEES. If either timestamp expression is a time value and *interval* specifies days, weeks, months, quarters, or years, the date portion of that timestamp is set to the current date before calculating the difference between the timestamps. If either timestamp expression is a date value and *interval* specifies fractional seconds, seconds, minutes, or hours, the time portion of that timestamp is set to 0 before calculating the difference between the timestamps. An application determines which intervals a data source supports by calling SQLGetInfo with the SQL_TIMEDATE_DIFF_INTERVALS option.
WEEK(*date_exp*)	Returns the week of the year in *date_exp* as an integer value in the range of 1–53.
YEAR(*date_exp*)	Returns the year in *date_exp* as an integer value. The range is data source–dependent.

Examples of Time and Date Functions

Here are some examples that illustrate the use of the time and date scalar functions.

☐ Select those orders that are less than a year old:

```
SELECT 'Order ID','Order Date' FROM orders WHERE {fn NOW( )}-'Order
Date' < 365
```

☐ Select the order dates that occurred on Friday:

```
SELECT 'Order Date' FROM Orders WHERE {fn DAYOFWEEK('Order Date')}=6
```

☐ Return the month number of the order date:

```
SELECT {fn MONTH('Order Date')} FROM Orders
```

☐ Select the order dates that occurred on the same day of the week as 1991-06-04:

```
SELECT 'Order Date' FROM Orders
➡WHERE {fn DAYOFWEEK('Order Date')}={fn DAYOFWEEK({d '1991-06-04'}}
```

Notice that the last example used the escape clause to represent a date literal for the second argument of the DAYOFWEEK function. As discussed earlier in this chapter, you should use the escape clause notation to represent the date, time, and timestamp data types to ensure that your SQL grammar will be supported across DBMSs.

MFC Time and Date Functions

As with the Cstring class, which greatly aids string operations, the Microsoft Foundation Classes also provide a class that is used to perform time and date operations. This class is the CTime class. Table 16.6 lists a number of useful member functions in this class. Also provided by MFC is the CTimeSpan class, which holds relative time and date values. Any field in the database that has a datatype of Time/Date will be cast to a CTime object within the Crecordset class.

Table 16.6. MFC time and date functions.

Function	Description
CTime::GetCurrentTime	Used to obtain current time
CTime::GetYear	Returns the year
CTime::GetMonth	Returns the month
CTime::GetDay	Returns the day
CTime::GetHour	Returns the hour
CTime::GetMinute	Returns the minute
CTime::GetSecond	Returns the second
CTime::GetDayOfWeek	Returns the day of the week
CTime::Format	Breaks down a CTime object into a formatted string
CTimeSpan::GetDays	Returns the number of days in this CTimeSpan
CTimeSpan::GetTotalHours	Returns the number of hours in this CTimeSpan

continues

Table 16.6. continued

Function	Description
CTimeSpan::GetMinutes	Returns the number of minutes in the current hour
CTimeSpan::GetTotalMinutes	Returns the number of minutes in this CTimeSpan
CTimeSpan::GetSeconds	Returns the number of seconds in the current hour
CTimeSpan::GetTotalSeconds	Returns the number of seconds in this CTimeSpan

System Functions

System functions return information about the user name, the database name attached to the given connection handle (hdbc), and how Null values are represented. At present there are only three system functions, as shown in Table 16.7, and only one of them, IFNULL, requires arguments. Here is a look at this argument:

Argument	Description
exp	Valid values for this argument are
	☐ Column name
	☐ Result of another scalar function
	☐ Literal

The underlying data type could be represented as SQL_NUMERIC, SQL_DECIMAL, SQL_TINYINT, SQL_SMALLINT, SQL_INTEGER, SQL_BIGINT, SQL_FLOAT, SQL_REAL, SQL_DOUBLE, SQL_DATE, SQL_TIME, or SQL_TIMESTAMP.

value	Valid values for this argument are
	☐ Column name
	☐ Result of another scalar function
	☐ Literal constant

The underlying data type can be represented as SQL_NUMERIC, SQL_DECIMAL, SQL_TINYINT, SQL_SMALLINT, SQL_INTEGER, SQL_BIGINT, SQL_FLOAT, SQL_REAL, SQL_DOUBLE, SQL_DATE, SQL_TIME, or SQL_TIMESTAMP.

Table 16.7. System functions.

Function	Description
DATABASE()	Returns the name of the database corresponding to the connection handle (hdbc). (The name of the database is also available by calling SQLGetConnectOption with the SQL_CURRENT_QUALIFIER connection option.)
IFNULL(*exp*,*value*)	If exp is NULL, value is returned. If exp is not NULL, exp is returned. The possible data type(s) of value must be compatible with the data type of exp.
USER()	Returns the user's DBMS name that is identical to using SqlGetInfo with the SQL_USER_NAME option.

Note: the description of the USER function is incorrect in the ODBC SDK, which states that the user's authorization, or login, name is returned.

Examples of System Functions

The following are some examples that illustrate some system scalar functions:

☐ Simply calling a scalar function can return the DBMS's user name:

```
SELECT {fn USER()}
```

☐ Scalar functions can be used to return the database name for the corresponding connection handle:

```
SELECT {fn DATABASE()}
```

Data Type Conversion Functions

Data type conversions are done through a special scalar function, CONVERT, which uses the following abbreviated escape clause notation:

```
{fn CONVERT(value_exp, data_type)}
```

The data types that can be converted are specific among DBMSs. You shouldn't assume that a particular DBMS will support a particular conversion type. Later in this chapter you will learn how to use the SQLGetInfo function to determine which of the conversion functions are supported by a particular DBMS.

The two arguments used by the CONVERT function are as follows:

Argument	Description
value_exp	Valid values for this argument are
	☐ Column name
	☐ Scalar function result
	☐ Numeric or string literal
data_type	Valid values for this argument are shown in the following list:

SQL_CONVERT_BIGINT
SQL_CONVERT_BINARY
SQL_CONVERT_BIT
SQL_CONVERT_CHAR
SQL_CONVERT_DATE
SQL_CONVERT_DECIMAL
SQL_CONVERT_DOUBLE
SQL_CONVERT_FLOAT
SQL_CONVERT_INTEGER
SQL_CONVERT_LONGVARBINARY
SQL_CONVERT_LONGVARCHAR
SQL_CONVERT_NUMERIC
SQL_CONVERT_REAL
SQL_CONVERT_SMALLINT
SQL_CONVERT_TIME
SQL_CONVERT_TIMESTAMP
SQL_CONVERT_TINYINT
SQL_CONVERT_VARBINARY
SQL_CONVERT_VARCHAR

Examples of Data Type Conversions

The following are some examples that illustrate the use of the data type conversion function:

- Use a datatype conversion function to convert a date literal to `SQL_CHAR` type:

```
SELECT {fn CONVERT({d '1991-06-04'}, SQL_CHAR)}
```

- In the following example, a datatype conversion function is used to find all employee IDs that are forty-something:

```
SELECT 'Employee ID' FROM Employees
➥WHERE {fn CONVERT('Employee ID', SQL_CHAR)} LIKE '4%'
```

Determining Your Driver's Support for Scalar Functions

As you know by now, ODBC drivers vary in their degree of support for scalar functions. All extended SQL-compliant drivers support scalar functions in general. However, this does not necessarily mean that all scalar functions are supported. Furthermore, minimum and core SQL-compliant drivers will most likely support some of the scalar function set. Now take a look at how to specifically interrogate the ODBC driver to find out which functions are supported.

You learned on Day 9, "Determining Driver and DBMS Capabilities," that the `SQLGetInfo` function is useful for determining the specific capabilities of an ODBC driver and data source. Now you will use `SQLGetInfo` to determine which ODBC scalar functions are supported. Recall the C function prototype for `SQLGetInfo`:

```
RETCODE SQL_API SQLGetInfo(
    HDBC        hdbc,
    UWORD       fInfoType,
    PTR         rgbInfoValue,
    SWORD       cbInfoValueMax,
    SWORD  FAR *pcbInfoValue);
```

Determining Availability of Numeric, String, System, and Time/Date Functions

To programatically determine which of the numeric, string, system, and time/date functions are available, call `SQLGetInfo` with one of the following define values for the `fInfoType` parameter:

- `SQL_NUMERIC_FUNCTIONS`
- `SQL_STRING_FUNCTIONS`

☐ SQL_SYSTEM_FUNCTIONS

☐ SQL_TIMEDATE_FUNCTIONS

After a successful call, the rgbInfoVal parameter will contain a 32-bit bitmask that is used to individually test each of the scalar functions belonging to the function set specified by the fInfoType parameters just listed.

Tables 16.8 through 16.11 list the define values for each of the string, numeric, time/date, and system scalar bitmasks, as well as the ODBC version supporting the function. These define values are found in the SQL.H file included in the ODBC SDK or the 1.5 or greater version of Microsoft Visual C++.

Table 16.8. String function bitmask values.

String Function Bitmask Values	ODBC Version
SQL_FN_STR_ASCII	(ODBC 1.0)
SQL_FN_STR_CHAR	(ODBC 1.0)
SQL_FN_STR_CONCAT	(ODBC 1.0)
SQL_FN_STR_DIFFERENCE	(ODBC 2.0)
SQL_FN_STR_INSERT	(ODBC 1.0)
SQL_FN_STR_LCASE	(ODBC 1.0)
SQL_FN_STR_LEFT	(ODBC 1.0)
SQL_FN_STR_LENGTH	(ODBC 1.0)
SQL_FN_STR_LOCATE	(ODBC 1.0)
SQL_FN_STR_LOCATE_2	(ODBC 2.0)
SQL_FN_STR_LTRIM	(ODBC 1.0)
SQL_FN_STR_REPEAT	(ODBC 1.0)
SQL_FN_STR_REPLACE	(ODBC 1.0)
SQL_FN_STR_RIGHT	(ODBC 1.0)
SQL_FN_STR_RTRIM	(ODBC 1.0)
SQL_FN_STR_SOUNDEX	(ODBC 2.0)
SQL_FN_STR_SPACE	(ODBC 2.0)
SQL_FN_STR_SUBSTRING	(ODBC 1.0)
SQL_FN_STR_UCASE	(ODBC 1.0)

Table 16.9. Numeric function bitmask values.

Numeric Function Bitmask Values	ODBC Version
SQL_FN_NUM_ABS	(ODBC 1.0)
SQL_FN_NUM_ACOS	(ODBC 1.0)
SQL_FN_NUM_ASIN	(ODBC 1.0)
SQL_FN_NUM_ATAN	(ODBC 1.0)
SQL_FN_NUM_ATAN2	(ODBC 1.0)
SQL_FN_NUM_CEILING	(ODBC 1.0)
SQL_FN_NUM_COS	(ODBC 1.0)
SQL_FN_NUM_COT	(ODBC 1.0)
SQL_FN_NUM_DEGREES	(ODBC 2.0)
SQL_FN_NUM_EXP	(ODBC 1.0)
SQL_FN_NUM_FLOOR	(ODBC 1.0)
SQL_FN_NUM_LOG	(ODBC 1.0)
SQL_FN_NUM_LOG10	(ODBC 2.0)
SQL_FN_NUM_MOD	(ODBC 1.0)
SQL_FN_NUM_PI	(ODBC 1.0)
SQL_FN_NUM_POWER	(ODBC 2.0)
SQL_FN_NUM_RADIANS	(ODBC 2.0)
SQL_FN_NUM_RAND	(ODBC 1.0)
SQL_FN_NUM_ROUND	(ODBC 2.0)
SQL_FN_NUM_SIGN	(ODBC 1.0)
SQL_FN_NUM_ROUND	(ODBC 2.0)
SQL_FN_NUM_SIGN	(ODBC 1.0)
SQL_FN_NUM_SIN	(ODBC 1.0)
SQL_FN_NUM_SQRT	(ODBC 1.0)
SQL_FN_NUM_TAN	(ODBC 1.0)
SQL_FN_NUM_TRUNCATE	(ODBC 2.0)

Table 16.10. Time/date function bitmask values.

Time/Date Function Bitmask Values	ODBC Version
SQL_FN_TD_CURDATE	(ODBC 1.0)
SQL_FN_TD_CURTIME	(ODBC 1.0)
SQL_FN_TD_DAYNAME	(ODBC 2.0)
SQL_FN_TD_DAYOFMONTH	(ODBC 1.0)
SQL_FN_TD_DAYOFWEEK	(ODBC 1.0)
SQL_FN_TD_DAYOFYEAR	(ODBC 1.0)
SQL_FN_TD_HOUR	(ODBC 1.0)
SQL_FN_TD_MINUTE	(ODBC 1.0)
SQL_FN_TD_MONTH	(ODBC 1.0)
SQL_FN_TD_MONTHNAME	(ODBC 2.0)
SQL_FN_TD_NOW	(ODBC 1.0)
SQL_FN_TD_QUARTER	(ODBC 1.0)
SQL_FN_TD_SECOND	(ODBC 1.0)
SQL_FN_TD_TIMESTAMPADD	(ODBC 2.0)
SQL_FN_TD_TIMESTAMPDIFF	(ODBC 2.0)
SQL_FN_TD_WEEK	(ODBC 1.0)
SQL_FN_TD_YEAR	(ODBC 1.0)
SQL_TXN_CAPABLE	(ODBC 1.0)

Table 16.11. System function bitmask values.

System Function Bitmask Values	ODBC Version
SQL_FN_SYS_DBNAME	(ODBC 1.0)
SQL_FN_SYS_IFNULL	(ODBC 1.0)
SQL_FN_SYS_USERNAME	(ODBC 1.0)

Determining if the *CONCAT()* Function Is Supported

Suppose, for example, that you wanted to determine whether or not the CONCAT string function is supported by a particular driver. Here is a code fragment, written in C, which shows you how:

```
RETCODE retcode;
PTR rgbInfoVal;

retcode = SQLGetInfo(hdbc,SQL_STRING_FUNCTION,
➥rgbInfoValue,cbInfoValueMax,pcbInfoValue)
if (rgbInfoValue && SQL_FN_STR_CONCAT){
    //function is supported
}
```

Notice that you simply "AND" the rgbInfoVal and the bitmask value for the CONCAT function. If the result is nonzero, then the function is supported. If you want to determine support for another string function, say the LTRIM function, then you would simply make another logical comparison with rgbInfoVal. You do not have to call SQLGetInfo again. The rgbInfoVal returned from the initial SQLGetInfo call can be used to test all of the string scalar functions. The following code snippet determines if the function is supported (or not).

Determining if the *LTRIM* Function Is Supported

```
if (rgbInfoValue && SQL_FN_STR_LTRIM){
    //function is supported
}
```

If you want to test the availability of a numeric function, say ROUND, then you would need to make another call to SQLGetInfo, this time using SQL_NUMERIC_FUNCTIONS as the fInfoType, and SQL_FN_NUM_ROUND as the rgbInfoVal. Determining whether system or time/date functions are supported is done similarly.

So far, you have learned how to determine whether a particular ODBC driver supports any of the numeric, string, system, and time/date functions, four of the five scalar function sets. Now you will learn how to inquire about which data conversions are supported.

16

Determining Supported Data Type Conversion Functions

To programatically determine which data type conversions are supported, call SQLGetInfo using one of the values for the fInfoType parameter. After a successful call, the rgbInfoVal parameter will contain a 32-bit bitmask that is used to individually test each of the data type conversion functions using one of the following bitmask values:

```
SQL_CVT_BIGINT
SQL_CVT_BINARY
SQL_CVT_BIT
SQL_CVT_CHAR
SQL_CVT_DATE
SQL_CVT_DECIMAL
SQL_CVT_DOUBLE
SQL_CVT_FLOAT
SQL_CVT_INTEGER
SQL_CVT_LONGVARBINARY
SQL_CVT_LONGVARCHAR
SQL_CVT_NUMERIC
SQL_CVT_REAL
SQL_CVT_SMALLINT
SQL_CVT_TIME
SQL_CVT_TIMESTAMP
SQL_CVT_TINYINT
SQL_CVT_VARBINARY
SQL_CVT_VARCHAR
```

For example, to determine whether a driver supports the conversion from integer data type to the char data type, you would call SQLGetInfo using SQL_CONVERT_INTEGER as the fInfoType. After a successful call, you would then "AND" the resulting rgbInfoVal with SQL_CVT_CHAR value from the preceding list. If the resulting value is nonzero, then the conversion is supported. The following is a code example written in C that illustrates how to determine whether the data source supports a conversion from the integer to the char and float data types.

C++ **Syntax**

Determining which Data Type Conversions are Supported

```
RETCODE retcode;
PTR rgbInfoVal;

retcode = SQLGetInfo(hdbc, SQL_CONVERT_INTEGER,
➥rgbInfoValue,cbInfoValueMax,pcbInfoValue)
if (rgbInfoValue && SQL_CVT_CHAR){
    //integer to char conversion is supported
}
if (rgbInfoValue && SQL_CVT_FLOAT){
    //integer to float conversion is supported
}
```

Summary

Today's lesson discussed the ODBC scalar function set. You looked at the different string, numeric, time/date, system, and data type conversion functions and how to use them using the escape syntax. You learned the following topics:

☐ ODBC's scalar function support is a part of ODBC's extension to the X/Open SAG 1992 specification.

☐ ODBC uses the X/Open SAG 1992 escape clause syntax to ensure a uniform scalar function grammar across DBMSs.

☐ The ODBC scalar function set is divided into string, numeric, time/date, system, and data type conversion functions.

☐ The sqlGetInfo function can be used to programmatically determine which of the scalar functions are supported by a particular ODBC driver.

☐ The Microsoft Foundation Class provides the CString class for use with strings and their corresponding operations. Many of the string scalar functions supported by the ODBC API have counterparts in this class. The functions of the CString class can be used in combination with string fields read in from the database into the CRecordset class.

☐ The Microsoft Foundation Class provides the CTime class for use with time and date fields. Many of the time and date scalar functions supported by the ODBC API have counterparts in this class. The functions of the CTime class can be used in combination with Time/Date fields read in from the database into the CRecordset class.

Q&A

Q I've noticed different results returned from the ODBC time scalar functions (for example) as compared to the Microsoft Foundation Class `CTime` class member functions. Why is this?

A This might be confusing to the beginning user, because both of these products come from Microsoft Corporation and MFC touts its database capabilities. However, the code reused from the `CTime` class, for example, is completely different code than the ODBC time scalar functions. The MFC classes return data in their own formats (which can be studied by examining the MFC documentation), whereas the results of the ODBC scalar functions conform to the ODBC standard.

Workshop

The Workshop provides quiz questions to help you solidify your understanding of the material covered and to give you experience in using what you've learned. Try to understand the quiz and exercise answers before continuing on to the next day's lesson. Answers are provided in Appendix A, "Answers."

Quiz

1. What are the five types of scalar functions?
2. Give the basic SQL syntax used to call an ODBC scalar function.

Exercises

1. Write the SQL statement used to determine the length of string NAME from the table EMPLOYEES.
2. Write the SQL statement used to return the time to your application.

Using ODBC
Cursors

Many modern relational database systems enable the use of cursors to assist in developing powerful SQL statements. A cursor enables the programmer to access a set of rows returned from a query. An SQL SELECT statement is used to return a row (or set of rows) from the database, but SQL traditionally did not support a way to scroll through these rows sequentially, one record at a time. The concept of *cursors* was introduced. Take a moment to scroll down the blinking cursor on your word processor using your keyboard's arrow keys. As you already know, this cursor can jump forward or backward one line (or record) at a time. By pressing the Page Down key, you can force the cursor to jump several lines. Conversely, the Page Up key will cause the cursor to scroll up.

A database cursor acts in this same fashion. Although some popular database systems still do not give the developer the ability to use cursors, don't be discouraged. ODBC provides a basic cursor model as well as the ability to use extended cursor models, if these are provided by your ODBC driver.

In the previous lessons, you learned how to use SQLBindCol, SQLExec, and SQLFetch to retrieve records from a pending result set. This technique uses a very simple cursor model to retrieve the records, one at a time, from the first record to the last. For simple ODBC applications, this might be all that is required; however, for many real-world ODBC applications, this basic cursor model simply is not adequate, especially when dealing with issues such as the following:

- [ ] Scrolling forward and backward through a result set
- [ ] Retrieving the result set in blocks of rows rather than a single row at a time
- [ ] Determining the sensitivity to underlying changes to a result set in a multiuser environment
- [ ] Controlling record locking and concurrency in a multiuser environment

Today's lesson explores ODBC's extended cursor models, which address these issues through sophisticated and useful ways of retrieving and controlling result set data. You will look at server-based cursors, which are implemented on the DBMS side for level 2 ODBC drivers, and at driver manager cursors, which utilize Microsoft's Cursor Library to provide cursor emulation for level 1 drivers. Today, you learn about the following topics:

- [ ] Simple cursors
- [ ] Enhanced cursors
- [ ] Server-based cursors
- [ ] Driver manager-based cursors (Microsoft's Cursor Library)
- [ ] How to determine the available cursor options

Simple Cursors

By definition, an ODBC *cursor* is simply a pointer to the current record in a result set. It is analogous to the cursor in your word processor, which indicates the current line on which you are typing. The simplest cursor model is one that you have already been using. It scrolls forward, one record at a time, with each call to SQLFetch, as illustrated in Figure 17.1.

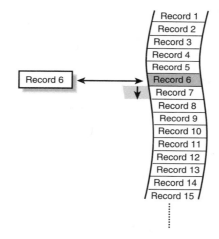

Figure 17.1. *Simple cursor operation.*

If you don't specifically set any of the extended cursor attributes using the SQLSetStmtOption function, ODBC will, by default, use this simple cursor type. If you need to give your application the functionality to scroll backward using this cursor type, however, then you would have to implement the following steps:

1. Allocate a valid statement handle, hstmt, and execute a SELECT statement.
2. Use SQLFreeStmt with the SQL_CLOSE option to close the current cursor.
3. Re-execute the SELECT statement from step 1.
4. Use SQLFetch to fetch rows from the result set until the target row is retrieved.

As you can see, this is an inefficient, brute-force technique to simulate backward scrolling for a forward-scrolling cursor. Fortunately, ODBC offers more sophisticated cursor models that, as you will soon see, provide an eloquent solution to this and other limitations imposed by the simple cursor model. Now, take a look at the extended cursor models supported by the ODBC programming interface.

Extended Cursors

The extended cursor models are defined in terms of two broad types of attributes, block and scrollable attributes, and can have components of either or both. *Block cursors* enable you to fetch data in groups of multiple rows, and *scrollable cursors* enable you to fetch data forward or backward or by a relative offset.

Extended cursor functionality is implemented either on the DBMS side for server-based cursors or through the Cursor Library for driver manager cursors. This lesson discusses these two in more detail later, but for now it concerns itself with the definition of the extended cursor attributes rather than where they are functionally implemented.

Fetching Data

In the previous lessons, SQLFetch was used to retrieve results data. However, this function is able to retrieve only one row at a time, so today let's move on to SQLExtendedFetch, which offers more versatile methods for retrieving result set data and is required for using the extended cursor types.

SQLExtendedFetch

The syntax for SQLExtendedFetch is as follows:

```
RETCODE SQLExtendedFetch(HSTMT hstmt,UWORD fFetchType,
➥SDWORD irow, UDWORD FAR* pcrow, UDWORD FAR* rgfRowStatus)
```

SQLExtendedFetch accepts the statement handle (hstmt), the fetch type (fFetchType), and number of rows to fetch as input (irow), and it returns the actual number of rows fetched (pcrow) and an array of status values as output. Table 17.1 lists the available fetch types and a description for each.

Table 17.1. Fetch types and description.

Fetch Type	Description
SQL_FETCH_NEXT	The next rowset is returned.
SQL_FETCH_FIRST	The first rowset is returned.
SQL_FETCH_LAST	The last rowset is returned.
SQL_FETCH_PRIOR	The previous rowset is returned.
SQL_FETCH_ABSOLUTE	The rowset starting at row *irow* is returned.

Fetch Type	Description
SQL_FETCH_RELATIVE	The rowset *irow* rows from the current rowset is returned.
SQL_FETCH_BOOKMARK	The rowset containing the row specified by the *irow* bookmark is returned.

Block Cursors

The block attribute specifies how many rows are returned in a single call to SQLExtendedFetch. The returned block of rows is called a *rowset*. Don't confuse a rowset with a result set. A *result set* consists of all of the rows returned from a pending query, whereas a rowset consists of a user-defined block of rows returned with each call to SQLExtendedFetch, typically less than the number of rows in the result set. Figure 17.2 illustrates the concept of a rowset.

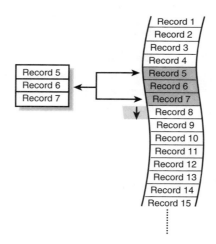

Figure 17.2. *The rowset.*

To specify the size of the rowset, call SQLSetStmtOption with the crowRowSet argument set to the number of rows you want returned. The default value is 1 as used by the simple cursor model. The following is an example of how to set the rowset size:

```
SQLSetStmtOption(hstmt,SQL_ROWSET_SIZE,5);
```

> **Note:** You can also use the `SQLSetScrollOption` to specify the rowset size. This function, however, is intended for backward compatibility with ODBC 1.0.

You can change the `crowRowSet` argument at any time. The next call to `SQLExtedendedFetch` will return the new rowset number of rows.

Forward-Only Cursor

The simplest type of extended cursor is a *forward-only* cursor. This type is a block cursor that only scrolls forward and returns the next rowset with each call to `SQLExtendedFetch`. Changes made by other users to the underlying result set are not detected. Here is how to configure a forward-only cursor:

```
SQLSetStmtOption(hstmt,SQL_CURSOR_TYPE,SQL_FORWARD_ONLY);
```

Scrollable Cursors

As mentioned earlier, SQL-based DBMSs typically support scrolling forward through a recordset but not backward. Each of the following cursor models enables multidirectional scrolling and have different sensitivities to underlying changes in a result set. You will see that static cursors offer no sensitivity to underlying changes, whereas dynamic cursors are fully aware of any modifications, updates, and deletes that occur to the underlying result set.

Static Cursors

Static cursors do not detect changes to the underlying result set if another user, or another cursor in your application, makes or tries to make such a change. This is achieved either by locking the result set so that changes can't be made or by creating a temporary snapshot of the result set so that updates from other users can occur but are not recognized while the cursor is opened. Therefore, the snapshot and the result set continually diverge as updates are made. Of course, deletions or additions made by other users also won't be detected while the cursor is open. Those of you familiar with Access or Visual Basic might recognize this type of cursor as a "snapshot." Here is how to configure a static, block cursor with a rowset of 5:

```
SQLSetStmtOption(hstmt,SQL_CURSOR_TYPE,SQL_CURSOR_STATIC);
SQLSetStmtOption(hstmt,SQL_ROWSET_SIZE,5);
```

Not all ODBC drivers natively support static cursors. If you are working with a driver that doesn't, don't worry. You will soon learn about the Cursor Library, which you can use to emulate static cursors for drivers meeting level 1 requirements.

Dynamic Cursors

Dynamic cursors are the antithesis to static cursors. All changes, updates, inserts, and deletions are detected by the cursor when data is next fetched. These changes can occur from the current cursor, from other cursors in the same application, and from other users. Dynamic cursors are very hard to implement and usually create a performance handicap due to their increased sensitivity. Compared to the other cursor models, dynamic cursors are the most sensitive to changes in the underlying result set. Here is how to configure a dynamic, block cursor with a rowset of 5:

```
SQLSetStmtOption(hstmt,SQL_CURSOR_TYPE,SQL_CURSOR_DYNAMIC);
SQLSetStmtOption(hstmt,SQL_ROWSET_SIZE,5);
```

Keyset-Driven Cursors

Keyset-driven cursors have characteristics of both static and dynamic cursors. Like static cursors, keyset-driven cursors can't change the ordering of the rows in the result set while the cursor is open. Like dynamic cursors, they are able to detect changes in the underlying result set when data is next fetched.

Keyset-driven cursors store only the primary keys of the result set. When the cursor scrolls to a particular row, the data for that row is then retrieved. This is why keyset-driven cursors, like dynamic cursors, are sensitive to modifications made by others. For those of you familiar with Access or Visual Basic, this type of cursor corresponds to the "dynaset."

For example, suppose that user A is on row 100 of the result set, and user B changes a column on row 100. User A then scrolls to row 101, then back to row 100. At this point, user A will notice the change made by user B. If user B deleted row 100, then a "hole" will appear because the corresponding key value will point to a row that no longer exists. To detect this, the driver will return a status code of SQL_ROW_DELETED, so your application should respond accordingly, such as scrolling to the next valid row. Here is how to specify a keyset-driven, block cursor with a rowset of 1:

```
SQLSetStmtOption(hstmt,SQL_KEYSET_SIZE,0;
SQLSetStmtOption(hstmt,SQL_CURSOR_TYPE,SQL_CURSOR_KEYSET_DRIVEN);
```

17

> **Note:** The first line really isn't necessary because the default value for
> `SQL_KEYSET_SIZE` is `0`. This value implies that the cursor is fully keyset-driven
> as opposed to mixed.

In case you are wondering, all of the key values are stored by the ODBC driver when the cursor is first open. This is why the membership and ordering of the results set can't be changed while the cursor is open. For small to medium result sets, buffering all the primary keys might not be a concern; however, for large result sets, this might be prohibitive. Next, we will look at the mixed cursor model and how it enables flexible setting of the keyset buffer size to get around this problem.

Mixed Cursors

Mixed cursors offer features from keyset-driven and dynamic cursors. The keyset size for mixed cursors is less than the size of the result set and greater than the size of the rowset. This cursor acts like a keyset-driven cursor scrolling within the keyset and acts like a dynamic cursor when scrolling outside the keyset. Here is how to configure a mixed cursor with a keyset size of 100 and a rowset size of 10:

```
SQLSetStmtOption(hstmt,SQL_KEYSET_SIZE,100);
SQLSetStmtOption(hstmt,SQL_ROWSET_SIZE,10);
SQLSetStmtOption(hstmt,SQL_CURSOR_TYPE,SQL_CURSOR_KEYSET_DRIVEN);
```

You might be wondering why the last line didn't specify a cursor type of `SQL_CURSOR_MIXED`. That is because there is no such type defined by ODBC. A mixed cursor is obtained by specifying a keyset-driven cursor with an `SQL_KEYSET_SIZE` greater than `0`.

For example, suppose that user A generates a result set of 200 rows using a mixed cursor with a keyset size of 50 and a row size of 10. The first 50 keys and 10 rows are initially retrieved. Suppose that user B then adds two rows corresponding to the 11 and 51 position. When user A scrolls forward to the next rowset that starts at row 11, the new record will not be picked up because it is within the current keyset. When user A scrolls to the 51 row, however, the new record will be detected because it was in the next keyset. Similarly, when user A scrolls back down to the 11 row, the new row will be picked up.

Server-Based Cursors

Cursors that are natively implemented by the DBMS are called *server-based cursors*. At the moment, there is not a proliferation of drivers that support these. This is quickly

changing, however, because Microsoft has recently released the 2.0 version of its ODBC Desktop Database Drivers, which provide keyset-driven cursors. SQL Server 95 will also have server-based cursors.

Driver Manager–Based Cursors (Microsoft's Cursor Library)

Microsoft and other ODBC driver vendors such as Informix have included extended cursor functionality in some of their ODBC drivers. In particular, Microsoft included its Cursor Library with ODBC 2.0, which provides cursor support for all level 1-compliant drivers. Not all of the extended cursor types are offered through the Cursor Library, however. At present, block and static scrollable cursors are supported.

The Cursor Library emulates `SQLExtendedFetch` calls by repeatedly calling `SQLFetch` and caching the results in disk and memory caches. If your ODBC driver natively supports extended cursors, you should probably use them rather than the Cursor Library.

Basically, the Cursor Library is a proxy DLL that emulates cursor support even when an ODBC data source does not natively provide cursor support. The driver manager calls the function in the Cursor Library instead of the driver when the Cursor Library is being used.

Because the Cursor Library offers a subset of the extended cursor features, you need to take a look at the different configurations available. Table 17.2 summarizes the different fetch types for the two types of cursors available through the Cursor Library.

Table 17.2. Cursor Library fetch type and concurrency.

Cursor Type	Fetch Type	Concurrency
Forward-only	SQL_FETCH_NEXT	SQL_CONCUR_READ_ONLY
Static	SQL_FETCH_NEXT	
SQL_FETCH_PRIOR		
SQL_FETCH_FIRST		
SQL_FETCH_LAST		
SQL_FETCH_RELATIVE		
SQL_FETCH_ABSOLUTE	SQL_CONCUR_READ_ONLY	
SQL_CONCUR_VALUES		

How to Specify Cursor Library Support

There are three options for specifying how an application can use the Cursor Library. The options are always use, use only if the driver does not support scrollable cursors, and never use. You set the desired cursor support by calling SQLSetConnectOption with fOption set to SQL_ODBC_CURSORS and vParam set to either SQL_CURS_USE_IF_NEEDED, SQL_USE_ODBC, or SQL_USE_DRIVER. Here is how to specify that the application will use the Cursor Library only if it is needed:

```
SQLSetConnectOption(hdbc, SQL_ODBC_CURSORS, SQL_CURS_USE_IF_NEEDED)
```

Limitations to the Cursor Library

For 16-bit Windows, the Cursor Library imposes a 64KB limit to the size of the rgbValue and pcbValue buffers bound using SQLBindCol to ensure that these buffers do not cross segment boundaries. If you have fields larger than this size limit, you must process them in chunks smaller than 64KB. This restriction does not apply to 32-bit ODBC applications using the 32-bit Cursor Library.

How to Determine the Available Cursor Options

The first thing to determine is whether a driver supports the SQLExtendedFetch function. Because this function is required by all extended cursor models, if it is missing you know that you will need to obtain cursor support through the Cursor Library, which has a predefined set of cursor options. Here is a code fragment written in C illustrating how to use SQLGetFunctions to determine whether SQLExtendedFetch is natively supported by the driver:

```
UWORD pfExits;
retcode = SQLGetFunctions(hdbc,SQL_API_SQLEXTENDEDFETCH,pfExits)
if (pfExists){
    //SQLExtendedFetch is supported
}
```

If SQLExtendedFetch is supported, you will need to find out which extended cursor models are available. To find out, call SQLGetInfo with the flag set to SQL_SCROLL_OPTIONS. A successful call will return a 32-bit bitmask of the supported scroll options, which then can be masked against the defined values listed in Table 17.3 to determine whether an individual scroll option is supported.

Table 17.3. Scroll options and the ODBC version introduced.

Scroll Option	ODBC Version
SQL_SO_FORWARD_ONLY	(ODBC 1.0)
SQL_SO_STATIC	(ODBC 2.0)
SQL_SO_KEYSET_DRIVEN	(ODBC 2.0)
SQL_SO_DYNAMIC	(ODBC 1.0)
SQL_SO_MIXED	(ODBC 1.0)

Determining a Driver's Cursor Support

The following C code fragment illustrates whether the keyset-driven and static cursor types are supported by a particular driver:

```
RETCODE retcode;
UDWORD rgbInfoVal;

retcode = SQLGetInfo(hdbc,SQL_SCROLL_OPTIONS,
➥(PTR)&rgbInfoValue, sizeof(rgbInfoValue),NULL)

if (rgbInfoValue && SQL_SO_KEYSET_DRIVEN){
    //keyset-driven cursor supported
}

if (rgbInfoValue && SQL_SO_STATIC){
    //static cursor supported
}
```

Now you will need to inquire about the available fetch directions using SQLGetInfo with SQL_FETCH_DIRECTION for the fInfoType parameter. After a successful call, the return value can be masked with each of the following define values for the fetch direction.

A successful call will return a 32-bit bitmask of the supported fetch directions, which then can be masked against the defined values listed in Table 17.4 to determine whether an individual fetch direction is supported. The table lists all of the possible fetch directions supported by ODBC.

Table 17.4. Fetch directions and the ODBC version introduced.

Fetch Direction	ODBC Version
SQL_FD_FETCH_NEXT	(ODBC 1.0)
SQL_FD_FETCH_FIRST	(ODBC 1.0)

continues

Table 17.4. continued

Fetch Direction	ODBC Version
SQL_FD_FETCH_LAST	(ODBC 1.0)
SQL_FD_FETCH_PRIOR	(ODBC 1.0)
SQL_FD_FETCH_ABSOLUTE	(ODBC 1.0)
SQL_FD_FETCH_RELATIVE	(ODBC 1.0)
SQL_FD_FETCH_RESUME	(ODBC 1.0)
SQL_FD_FETCH_BOOKMARK	(ODBC 2.0)

Syntax

Determining a Driver's Fetch Direction Support

```
RETCODE retcode;
UDWORD rgbInfoVal;

retcode = SQLGetInfo(hdbc,SQL_FETCH_DIRECTION,
➥(PTR)&rgbInfoValue, sizeof(rgbInfoValue),NULL)

if (rgbInfoValue && SQL_FD_FETCH_PRIOR){
    //able to scroll backward
}

if (rgbInfoValue && SQL_FD_FETCH_FIRST){
    //able to scroll to first record
}
```

The ODBC programming interface supports many flexible cursor types; however, this does not necessarily mean that all types will be implemented by a particular ODBC driver. At present, most ODBC drivers do not provide native cursor support. Microsoft's Cursor Library comes to the rescue by providing block and static scrolling cursor support for level 1-compliant ODBC drivers. This cursor support, although somewhat limited, provides bidirectional scrolling and retrieving data in blocks rather than a single row at a time.

Microsoft Foundation Class Cursor Support

The CRecordset class included within the Microsoft Foundation Class provides a degree of bidirectional cursor support. However, much of its implementation is well below the surface and out of reach of the C++ developer. (Of course, the ODBC API is available for use, but this book tries to stick to the strict MFC implementation.)

After you open a recordset with the `CRecordset::Open()` function, the first record in the corresponding table is loaded into the `CRecordset` object's member variables. Listed following is the complete source code for the `CAlbumSet` class (which is derived from the `CRecordset` class). Before you go into each `Crecordset` function used to scroll through the recordset, examine the individual parts to `CAlbumSet`, most of which was generated by Class Wizard.

```cpp
// CPAlbset.cpp : implementation of the CP15AlbSet class
//
#include "stdafx.h"
#include "CPAdd15.h"
#include "CPAlbset.h"
/////////////////////////////////////////////////////////////////////////////
// CP15AlbSet implementation
IMPLEMENT_DYNAMIC(CP15AlbSet, CRecordset)
CP15AlbSet::CP15AlbSet(CDatabase* pdb)
 : CRecordset(pdb)
{
//{{AFX_FIELD_INIT(CP15AlbSet)
m_AlbumID = "";
m_AlbumCounter = 0;
m_ArtistID = 0;
m_GroupID = 0;
m_AlbumTitle = "";
m_LabelCo = "";
m_Notes = "";
m_MusicType = "";
m_nFields = 9;
//}}AFX_FIELD_INIT
m_nParams = 1;
m_intArtistIDParam = 0;
}

CString CP15AlbSet::GetDefaultConnect()
{
return _T("ODBC;DSN=");
}

CString CP15AlbSet::GetDefaultSQL()
{
return _T("Album");
}

void CP15AlbSet::DoFieldExchange(CFieldExchange* pFX)
{
//{{AFX_FIELD_MAP(CP15AlbSet)
pFX->SetFieldType(CFieldExchange::outputColumn);
RFX_Text(pFX, "AlbumID", m_AlbumID);
RFX_Int(pFX, "AlbumCounter", m_AlbumCounter);
RFX_Int(pFX, "ArtistID", m_ArtistID);
RFX_Int(pFX, "GroupID", m_GroupID);
RFX_Text(pFX, "AlbumTitle", m_AlbumTitle);
RFX_Text(pFX, "LabelCo", m_LabelCo);
RFX_Date(pFX, "YearReleased", m_YearReleased);
```

```
RFX_Text(pFX, "Notes", m_Notes);
RFX_Text(pFX, "MusicType", m_MusicType);
//}}AFX_FIELD_MAP
pFX->SetFieldType(CFieldExchange::param);
RFX_Int(pFX, "ArtistIDParam", m_intArtistIDParam);
}
```

The CArtistSet is used to query the ARTISTS table in the database. There are nine data members: m_AlbumID, m_AlbumCounter, m_ArtistID, m_GroupID, m_AlbumTitle, m_LabelCo, m_YearReleased, m_Notes, and m_MusicType. These nine data members are "bound" to the database using the function calls in CRecordset::DoFieldExchange. The RFX_Text, RFX_Date, and RFX_Int functions essentially bind a field name to a variable name.

As the programmer scrolls forward through the recordset, these member variables are continuously updated through dynamic field exchange. Now you will learn how to actually move through the recordset.

The following is the prototype for the CRecordset::Open function:

```
virtual BOOL Open(UINT nOpenType = snapshot, LPCSTR lpszSql = NULL,
➥DWORD dwOptions = defaultOptions);
```

First, you need to concern yourself with the nOpenType argument. This basically tells MFC what type of cursor support you want. This argument can have one of three values:

☐ CRecordset::dynaset. A dynamic recordset (cursor) with bi-directional scrolling.

☐ CRecordset::snapshot. A static recordset (cursor) with bi-directional scrolling.

☐ CRecordset::forwardOnly. A read-only dynaset with only forward scrolling supported.

The framework takes the nOpenType value that you pass in and queries the ODBC driver to determine if this option is supported. If it is not supported, a CDBException will be thrown. Otherwise, the recordset will be opened using the nOpenType value.

Using the *CRecordset* Scrolling Functions

MFC also provides functionality for scrolling through the recordset once it has been opened. The following functions are used to move the cursor through the recordset and also to gain information on the cursor's location within the recordset.

```
virtual void CRecordset::Move(long lRows);
```

The CRecordset::Move function is used to jump forward (or backward) through the records in the recordset. Passing in a positive value will cause the cursor to

scroll forward that many records. Passing in a negative value will cause the cursor to scroll backward. An exception will be thrown if you try to move past the end of the recordset (see IsEOF()).

```
void CRecordset::MoveFirst();
```

The MoveFirst function makes the first record in the recordset the current record. Note that directly after calling the Open function, the first record is the current record.

```
void CRecordset::MoveLast();
```

The MoveLast function forces the cursor to jump to the last record.

```
void CRecordset::MoveNext();
```

The MoveNext function loads the recordset with the next record's data.

```
void CRecordset::MovePrev();
```

The MovePrev function loads the recordset with the previous record's data.

```
BOOL CRecordset::IsBOF();
```

The IsBOF function should always be called to determine if the recordset is currently at the beginning record. Calling MovePrev while positioned at the beginning of the file will result in an exception being thrown.

```
BOOL CRecordset::IsEOF();
```

The IsEOF function should always be called to determine if the recordset is currently at the last record. Calling MoveNext while positioned at the end of the file will result in an exception being thrown.

Summary

Today's lesson presented the simple and extended cursor models supported by ODBC. You learned the following topics:

- [ ] The simple cursor model is used by default unless SQLSetStmtOption is used to specify the particular cursor attributes. The simple cursor type retrieves one row with each call to SQLFetch in a forward direction only.

- [ ] Extended cursor models can have block and/or scrollable attributes as well as concurrency settings. The block attribute defines how many rows (the rowset) are returned with each call to SQLExtendedFetch. The scrollable attribute defines whether the cursor can move forward, backward, by a relative offset, or at the beginning or end of a result set.

☐ Server-based cursors are implemented by the DBMS engine and are part of the level 2 API requirements. Presently, the majority of ODBC drivers do not support server-based cursors. However, this trend is changing because Microsoft has recently released the 2.0 version of its ODBC Desktop Database Drivers, which utilize Microsoft's Jet Engine to provide native keyset-driven cursors.

☐ Driver manager cursors provide extended cursor functionality through caching query results to disk or to memory. Microsoft's Cursor Library is an example of this and can be used to provide simple block scrollable cursors for level 1-compliant drivers, thus providing extended cursor functionality to a great number of drivers that would otherwise do without.

Q&A

Q Can I use the extended cursors offered by my ODBC driver and the scrollable block cursors provided by the Cursor Library?

A No, you cannot use both. You specify whether to use the Cursor Library or the native driver cursors in `SQLSetConnectOption`. If you do not specify, then the Cursor Library is used only if your driver does not support scrollable cursors.

Q If I use a static cursor provided through the Cursor Library, could I run out of disk space?

A Because the Cursor Library buffers temporary result set data to your hard disk, you might run out of disk space depending on the size of the result set and the amount of available space on the drive containing the directory specified by the `TEMP` environment variable.

Workshop

The Workshop provides quiz questions to help you solidify your understanding of the material covered and to give you experience in using what you've learned. Try to understand the quiz and exercise answers before continuing on to the next day's lesson. Answers are provided in Appendix A, "Answers."

Quiz

1. What are the differences between the SQLFetch function and the SQLExtendedFetch function?

2. Explain the differences between a static ODBC cursor and a dynamic ODBC cursor. What are their advantages and disadvantages?

Exercises

1. If you have not already done so, determine the cursor capabilities of your ODBC driver of choice.

2. If you have ODBC drivers for several different databases, compare the capabilities of the different drivers.

Using Transactions and Commitment Control

Transactions and commitment control are relational database concepts that were around long before the advent of ODBC. They provide the capability to commit or recover from pending changes made to a database in order to enforce data consistency and integrity. Today's lesson discusses the concept of transactions and how to enable them; tomorrow's lesson discusses how to end them. Today, you learn the following:

- ☐ Protection provided by transactions
- ☐ Enabling transactions
- ☐ Transaction logs

Protection Provided by Transactions

A *transaction* is a recoverable series of changes you make to a database so as to ensure that your database is transformed from one consistent state to another. Typically, transactions are used to maintain the integrity of your database when records in two or more tables must be modified. You can think of a transaction as a change or series of changes to the database that is represented as a single recoverable unit of work. It either executes completely or not at all.

The ability to consider a set of operations to a database as a recoverable unit of work is like having an insurance policy for your data. For example, if you want to transfer funds from your savings account to your checking account, two things must happen. The savings account must be debited, and the checking account must be proportionally credited. Both of these operations, the debit and the credit, must complete successfully or not at all; otherwise, you or your bank will be trying to get money back. Transactions enable you to commit (save) the changes to the database, or to roll them back (undo). Figure 18.1 illustrates the typical sequence of events for using transactions.

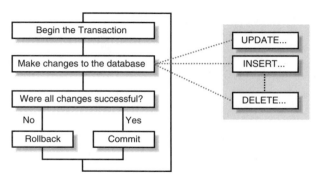

Figure 18.1. *The sequence of events for a transaction.*

SQL and Transactions

The following code listing is a typical sequence of SQL statements used to perform a transaction. ODBC duplicates this same logical flow through the use of the SQLTransact function.

The following SQL statements begin an SQL server transaction. If changes are successful, these changes are committed (or saved). If not, these changes are rolled back (or canceled).

```
begin transaction
insert table1 values (3, "Tom Thompson", $3.75)
if exists (select * from table 1
where field1 = 3 and field2 = "Tom Thompson")
begin
commit transaction
end
else
begin
rollback transaction
end
go
```

ODBC and Transactions

ODBC provides the SQLTransact command to end transactions. The syntax for this command looks like the following:

```
RETCODE SQLTransact (henv, hdbc, fType)
```

where fType can be one of two possible values: SQL_COMMIT or SQL_ROLLBACK. The command to end transactions is quite simple; however, there are many possible types of transaction support provided by the many ODBC drivers.

The ODBC programming interface supports transactions; however, not all drivers do. In order to determine whether a particular driver supports transactions, you should call SQLGetInfo using SQL_TXN_CAPABLE for the fInfoType parameter. A listing and description of possible return values are given in Table 18.1.

Table 18.1. Possible return codes indicating transaction support.

Return Code	Description
SQL_TC_NONE	Transactions are not supported.
SQL_TC_DML	Transactions can contain only data manipulation language (DML) statements such as SELECT, INSERT, and

continues

Table 18.1. continued

Return Code	Description
	UPDATE. Data definition language (DDL) statements that occur during the transaction will result in an error.
SQL_TC_DDL_COMMIT	Transactions can contain only data manipulation language statements, such as CREATE TABLE and DROP INDEX. DDL statements that occur during the transaction will cause the transaction to be committed.
SQL_TC_DDL_IGNORE	Transactions can contain only DDL statements. DML statements are ignored.
SQL_TC_ALL	Transactions can contain both DDL and DML statements.

Note: Do not rely on using SQLTransact with fType=SQL_ROLLBACK to check for transaction support. Some drivers will return SQL_SUCCESS, whereas calling SQLGetInfo with fSQLType=SQL_TXN_CAPABLE will return 0, indicating that transactions are not supported.

Determining a Driver's Transaction Support

The following listing is a code fragment illustrating how to determine the available transaction support for a given ODBC driver:

```
RETCODE retcode;
UDWORD rgbInfoVal;

retcode = SQLGetInfo(hdbc, SQL_TXN_CAPABLE,
➥(PTR)&rgbInfoValue, sizeof(rgbInfoValue),NULL)

if (rgbInfoValue && SQL_TC_NONE){
     //transactions are not supported
}

if (rgbInfoValue && SQL_TC_DML){
     //data manipulation transactions supported
}

if (rgbInfoValue && SQL_TC_DDL_COMMIT){
     //data definition transactions supported
```

```
}

if (rgbInfoValue && SQL_TC_DDL_IGNORE){
    //data definition transactions ignored
}

if (rgbInfoValue && SQL_TC_ALL){
    //all transaction types supported
}
```

Table 18.2 lists the supported transaction levels for various ODBC drivers.

Table 18.2. Transaction support for various ODBC drivers.

Driver	Transaction Support
ORACLE 7.1	SQL_TC_DML
MS SQL Server	SQL_TC_DML
MS Access 2.0	SQL_TC_ALL
MS Excel	SQL_TC_NONE

Transactions and Isolation Levels

Until now, you have considered the effect of transactions on a single user database system. These transactions are important because they provide protection against database inconsistencies by treating multiple statements as single, self-contained units of work. Each transaction occurs serially and does not have to contend with interference from other transactions.

In a multiuser database system, however, transactions can occur simultaneously and have the potential to interfere with other transactions. This potential for interference and the techniques a DBMS uses to resolve it brings us to the topic of transaction isolation levels.

The concept of *transaction isolation levels* is another relational database concept that precedes the release of ODBC. It refers to the degree of isolation among simultaneous transactions that have potential to interfere with one another.

Concurrent transactions that could interfere with one another are said to be *interleaved* or *parallel* transactions. Transactions that run isolated from each other are said to be *serializable*, which means that they produce the same effect if executed concurrently, or one right after another (serially).

Before you begin looking at the supported isolation options, look at some pertinent definitions in Table 18.3.

Table 18.3. Violations of transaction serializability.

Violation	Description
Dirty reads	Transaction T1 retrieves a row that was just modified by T2. T2 performs a rollback, thus leaving T1 with a row that no longer exists.
Nonrepeatable reads	T1 retrieves a row, and then T2 updates that row. T1 retrieves the row again, thus reading two different values for the same row.
Phantoms	T1 retrieves all rows that satisfy a search condition, and then T2 inserts rows that would have satisfied the previous search condition. T1 repeats the query and retrieves a different result.

ODBC defines five levels of transaction isolation that allow for some or none of the serializabilty of transaction violations listed in Table 18.3. You can determine which isolation levels are supported by an ODBC driver by calling SQLGetInfo using SQL_TXN_ISOLATION_OPTION for the fInfoType parameter. The return value is a 32-bit integer, which can be masked against the ODBC defined values for isolation levels listed in Table 18.4.

Table 18.4. ODBC transaction isolation levels.

Isolation level	Description
SQL_TXN_READ_UNCOMMITTED	Permits dirty reads, nonrepeatable reads, and phantoms.
SQL_TXN_READ_COMMITTED	Permits nonrepeatable reads and phantoms. Dirty reads are not permitted.
SQL_TXN_REPEATABLE_READ	Permits phantoms. Does not permit dirty reads and nonrepeatable reads.
SQL_TXN_SERIALIZABLE	Does not permit any of the serializability violations to ensure that transactions are serializable. Usually achieved with locking mechanisms that drastically reduce concurrency.

Isolation level	Description
SQL_TXN_VERSIONING	Transactions are serializable but offers higher concurrency than SQL_TXN_SERIALIZABLE because record locking is not used.

You set the driver's isolation level using SQLSetConnectOptions() with fOption=SQL_TXN_ISOLATION and one of the isolation options listed in Table 18.3 for the vParam parameter.

Note: If you do not explicitly set the isolation option, then all hdbc connections will use the default isolation level, which can be determined by SQLGetInfo using SQL_DEFAULT_TXN_ISOLATION_OPTION for the fInfoType parameter.

18

Table 18.5 lists the supported transaction isolation levels of a few ODBC drivers.

Table 18.5. Transaction isolation levels.

Driver	Isolation levels
ORACLE 7.1	SQL_TXN_REPEATABLE_READ
SQL Server	SQL_TXN_READ_COMMITTED
	SQL_TXN_SERIALIZABLE
MS Access 2.0	SQ_TXN_READ_COMMITTED, SQL_TXN_SERIALIZABLE

Now that you have gone over some transaction basics, look at how to enable transactions in the ODBC environment.

Enabling Transactions

The ODBC programming interface supports two methods of enabling transactions: auto-commit and manual commit. The *auto-commit* method begins and ends a transaction for every SQL statement submitted, therefore disabling any rollback capabilities. The *manual commit* method creates a transaction when an SQL statement is submitted while no transaction is open. Your application is responsible for submitting subsequent

SQL statements and explicitly committing or rolling back, therefore closing the transaction, at the appropriate time. If an ODBC driver supports the auto-commit method, then it will be used as the default transaction mode.

You set the desired transaction option using SQLSetConnectOptions with the fOption set to SQL_AUTOCOMMIT and vParam set to either SQL_AUTOCOMMIT_OFF or SQL_AUTOCOMMIT_ON.

Setting Your Driver's Transaction Options

The default value is SQL_AUTOCOMMIT_ON, so if your driver supports transactions, and you would like to use them, you must explicitly call SQLSetConnectOptions to disable the auto-commit. Following is a code fragment illustrating how to enable manual transactions for a given hdbc:

```
BOOL SetManualTransactions(HDBC hdbc)
{
RETCODE retcode;
retcode = SQLSetConnectOption(hdbc,SQL_AUTOCOMMIT,SQL_AUTOCOMMIT_OFF)
if retcode != SQL_SUCCESS
{
//could not turn off autocommit
return FALSE;
}
//manual transactions turned on...
....
return TRUE;
}
```

MFC Transaction Support

The Microsoft Foundation Class (MFC) provides some support for transaction management. Because the CRecordset and CDatabase classes actually encapsulate the ODBC API and use ODBC drivers to connect to a data source, the level of transaction support provided depends on which driver is being used. You learned earlier in this chapter how to use the SQLGetInfo function to determine what level of transaction support was provided by the driver.

The CRecordset class provides one function for determining whether transactions are supported by the driver associated with the current recordset. That function is the CanTransact function in the CRecordset class.

```
BOOL CRecordset::CanTransact()
```

The CanTransact function can be called to determine whether transactions are supported by the current driver. Unfortunately, this is either an on or off type of return value. Once

again, you see that flexibility was sacrificed in order to provide ease of use with MFC. To really determine the level of transaction support provided by the driver you are currently using, the API function SQLGetInfo must be called with the proper parameters.

The MFC documentation goes on to state that only one level of transaction is supported. Transactions cannot be nested and can operate only on one database. This is because the transaction is tied to the particular database handle (hdbc) that is associated with your recordset.

Using Transaction Logs

Have you wondered yet where the database management system stores the results of statements during a transaction? The results of all transactions are stored in a transaction log. The capability to log transactions is supported by many popular database management systems, including Oracle and Microsoft/Sybase SQL Server. (The SQL Server product will be the focus of our discussion on transaction logs.) These logs can be used to recover a database in the event of a system crash. In addition, they can also be "dumped" to a disk, tape, and so on, and reloaded at a later time.

Each SQL Server database has its own transaction log, which is stored in the system table *syslogs*. Each change made to the database creates an automatic entry within the transaction log. This log can then be recovered at a later date to restore the database in case of a disk failure or some other problem.

Transaction Log Storage Issues

When an SQL Server database is created, options can be passed to the create database statement to force the storage of the transaction log on a separate device. The following is the SQL syntax used by SQL Server to create a database:

```
create database database_name on database_device = size
log on database_device = size
```

This has the advantage of enabling the database administrator to be able to recover changes made to the database since the last database backup if a disk crashes. The transaction log will be sitting safely on another device. There can be a performance advantage to doing this, also. Consider the situation in which the database and transaction log reside on the same device. Disk access speed will suffer in this situation because one disk will be forced to handle all operations with the database. Putting the transaction log on a separate disk can solve this problem and can result in a performance improvement in heavy usage environments.

Placing the log on a separate device enables the database administrator to determine the default size of the transaction log. A good rule of thumb when estimating this size is to start at approximately 10 to 25 percent of the database size, depending on the level of input/output activity within the database. This implies that the transaction log has the potential of filling up—and this is very true. Dumping the transaction log periodically will reduce the size of the log itself.

SQL Server also enables the database administrator to set a "threshold" value. This threshold will call a stored procedure when it is crossed. The name of this procedure is sp_thresholdaction. By using the sp_addthreshold procedure, the administrator can designate another stored procedure to fire when the space threshold has been crossed. This procedure can be used to dump the transaction log before it becomes too full.

Although the syntax will look different for every database system, the following four commands are used to back up and restore databases and their corresponding logs. Typically, transaction logs are backed up more regularly than databases. The dump transaction command is used to dump only a transaction log. The dump database command backs up an entire database as well as that database's transaction log.

Note: The following syntax is simplified. SQL Server provides a wide variety of options for each of the following. For further information, consult the SQL Server documentation.

The *dump database* Command

The dump database command makes a backup copy of the database on the stripe device. (A *stripe device* is the physical object where the database will be backed up. This can be a physical raw device or an operating system file.)

```
dump database database_name to stripe_device
```

The *dump transaction* Command

The following version of the dump transaction command is similar to the dump database command. A backup copy of the transaction log will be made to the device. It should also be noted that the dump transaction command can be used only if the transaction log is placed on a separate device.

```
dump transaction database_name to stripe_device
```

The following `dump transaction` command does not actually make a backup copy of the transaction log. Instead, the inactive portion of the log is removed permanently from the log.

```
dump transaction database_name with truncate_only
```

The following `dump transaction` command should be used only if the transaction log has been filled to capacity. The inactive portion of the transaction log will be deleted. In addition, this action will not be recorded within the transaction log. The `with no_log` option should be used only as a last resort.

```
dump transaction database_name with no_log
```

The *load database* Command

The `load database` command restores the database from the *stripe_device* given in the command. The database should be recovered first, followed by all the transaction log dumps made since the previous database dump. Note that the `load database` command will overwrite any data existing within the database.

```
load database database_name from stripe_device
```

18

The *load transaction* Command

The `load transaction` command is a lot like the `load database` command in operation. When you are using this command, remember to first load the most recent database dump before you load the more recent transaction log backups.

```
load transaction database_name from stripe_device
```

Summary

Today's lesson presented you with the concept of transactions and how to enable them. You learned the following topics:

☐ Transactions ensure that one or more SQL statements execute completely as a group or not at all to help ensure data consistency.

☐ The ODBC programming interface defines five levels of transaction support: `SQL_TC_NONE`, `SQL_TC_DML`, `SQL_TC_DDL_COMMIT`, `SQL_TC_DDL_IGNORE`, and `SQL_TC_ALL`.

☐ In a typical single-user environment, transactions are serializable; that is, they run in isolation from each other. In a multiuser environment, however, this is not necessarily the case because concurrent transactions can exist. Transaction isolation defines the degree to which concurrent transactions can conflict. ODBC provides five levels of isolation, `SQL_TXN_READ_UNCOMMITTED`, `SQL_TXN_READ_COMMITTED`, `SQL_TXN_REPEATABLE_READ`, `SQL_TXN_SERIALIZABLE`, and `SQL_TXN_VERSIONING`.

☐ The Microsoft Foundation Classes (MFC) provide one level of transaction management support. The `CRecordset::CanTransact()` function can be called for each recordset to determine if the driver associated with that recordset supports transactions.

☐ Transaction logs are used to record transactions and changes made to a database's data. These logs can be backed up using the `dump transaction` command. Transaction logs can be restored using the `load transaction` command.

Q&A

Q My driver does not include any transaction management support, but the underlying database server does. Is there a "default" ODBC transaction management support DLL that can perform these functions, similar to the Microsoft Cursor Library?

A Unfortunately, at this time there is no support for a default library that performs rudimentary transaction management. One method that could be used is to store the transaction with its associated SQL statements inside a stored procedure. Then the procedure could be executed through ODBC. Checks could be added inside the procedure to determine whether to roll back or save the changes. In addition, some database management systems support triggers, which are stored procedures that are executed on an `INSERT`, `UPDATE`, or `DELETE` of a table's data. These objects are very useful for maintaining referential integrity.

Q What level of transaction support does the MFC function `CRecordset::CanTransact` check for? Remember, there are five levels:

```
SQL_TC_NONE
SQL_TC_DML
SQL_TC_DDL_COMMIT
SQL_TC_DDL_IGNORE
SQL_TC_DDL
```

A The `CRecordset::CanTransact` function checks for the `SQL_TC_DML` level, it appears. However, this function does not return to the programmer the actual level of support. Instead, only a Boolean (true or false) value is returned to indicate whether some form of transaction support is provided.

Q Are there performance penalties involved with using transactions in my code?

A The benefits to using transactions far outweigh any minor performance penalty from rolling back or committing a batch of statements when they are finished. Transactions enable the programmer to retain some control over the integrity of the underlying data, particularly in multiuser situations or in instances in which many records are being modified at once. Many database servers store transactions in a transaction "log." In order to fine-tune the performance of the entire server (not just your individual transactions), it is common to store the transaction log on another physical disk separate from the disk containing your database. This increases hard disk I/O performance.

Workshop

The Workshop provides quiz questions to help you solidify your understanding of the material covered and to give you experience in using what you've learned. Try to understand the quiz and exercise answers before continuing on to the next day's lesson. Answers are provided in Appendix A, "Answers."

Quiz

1. Each driver provides a default transaction isolation support type. How could you determine the default type of transaction isolation support that your driver provides?

2. The transaction isolation level of an RDBMS refers to the level of isolation one transaction's changes have from another parallel transaction's changes. Read through your database's documentation. What type of transaction isolation support does it provide?

Exercise

1. List the steps a programmer must go through in order to complete a transaction using ODBC.

Ending
Transactions and
Connections

Today's lesson shows how to end a transaction, the unit of work introduced on Day 18, "Using Transactions and Commitment Control." In addition, it covers the correct way to terminate a connection to an underlying data source.

The previous lesson covered the topic of performing a transaction. In review, a transaction is used to treat a group of statements as a unit. These statements usually perform some modification of data within a database and are intended to be performed as a single, atomic unit. If a condition arises that would cause data to be invalid, the transaction should be ended. In database terminology, this termination is called a *rollback*. To save the changes upon successful completion of all requirements, you *commit* the changes to the database.

Ending Transactions with ODBC

Naturally, the ODBC API provides support for commits and rollbacks. As you saw on Day 18, you can control the use of transactions through the use of the SQLSetConnectOptions function. By setting the fOption variable to SQL_AUTOCOMMIT and the vParam variable to SQL_AUTOCOMMIT_OFF, the programmer can enable manual commits. This means that before saving changes to the database, checks can be performed. This ensures data integrity and is an especially important feature in today's client/server, multiuser environments.

Note that if the SQL_AUTOCOMMIT capability is set to off, a new transaction is begun when an SQL command (that can be executed within a transaction) is executed against the underlying data source. This basically means that the first statement executed in an application with this option turned off begins a new transaction. To end this transaction, the SQLTransact function must be called.

The *SQLTransact* Function

The prototype for the SQLTransact function is

```
RETCODE SQLTransact( HENV henv, HDBC hdbc, UWORD fType);
```

The fType value can be either SQL_COMMIT or SQL_ROLLBACK. These values are self-explanatory: SQL_COMMIT performs an SQL commit, which ends the transaction and executes the transaction's statements; SQL_ROLLBACK also ends the transaction by canceling the transaction's statements.

SQLTransact returns the following values: SQL_SUCCESS, SQL_SUCCESS_WITH_INFO, SQL_ERROR, or SQL_INVALID_HANDLE. As explained in detail on Day 13, "Determining the Return Status of a Call," the ODBC Driver Manager maintains detailed error information, and this information can be obtained by calling SQLError. Calling the SQLError function will return an SQLSTATE value. Some of the more common SQLSTATE values returned by SQLTransact are shown in Table 19.1.

Table 19.1. SQLSTATE values returned by SQLTransact.

SQLSTATE	Error
01000	General warning
08003	Connection not open
08007	Connection failure during transaction
IM001	Driver does not support this function
S1000	General error
S1001	Memory allocation failure
S1010	Function sequence error
S1012	Invalid transaction operation code
S1C00	Driver not capable

Depending on what you pass in, SQLTransact can perform different operations. If hdbc=SQL_NULL_HDBC and henv is a valid handle, the driver manager will perform the requested operation on all database handles that are currently connected. If any one of the open hdbcs returns an SQL_ERROR error code, the driver manager returns SQL_ERROR. The programmer must then call the SQLError function to determine the exact cause of the error.

Note: If there are currently no transactions active, SQLTransact will always return SQL_SUCCESS if the driver supports transactions. If the driver does not support transaction management (SQLGetInfo fOption SQL_TXN_CAPABLE is 0 [see Day 18]), then SQL_ROLLBACK will return an SQLSTATE equal to S1C00. As expected, this means the driver is not capable of performing a rollback (see Table 19.1).

Effects of *SQLTransact* on Cursors

On Day 17, "Using ODBC Cursors," you studied the advantage of using cursors. You learned that in addition to server-side cursors, the ODBC cursor library is provided to give some rudimentary support for all data sources. The effect of transactions on open cursors can be determined by calling SQLGetInfo with the SQL_CURSOR_ROLLBACK_BEHAVIOR and SQL_CURSOR_COMMIT_BEHAVIOR options. There are three possible return values you might receive after calling SQLGetInfo with these options:

```
SQL_CB_DELETE
SQL_CB_CLOSE
SQL_CB_PRESERVE
```

By looking at the names of these three options, you can take an educated guess at what these three return values mean. If SQL_CB_DELETE is returned, a call to SQLTransact will close and delete all open cursors on all hstmts associated with the hdbc. In addition, all pending results will be discarded. If SQL_CB_CLOSE is returned, SQLTransact will close all open cursors on all hstmts associated with the hdbc. If SQL_CB_PRESERVE is returned, SQLTransact will not affect any open cursors associated with the hdbc.

MFC Transaction Support

The first part of this lesson has explained the ODBC API support for transactions. Like all of the other API functions, the SQLTransact function can be called from Visual Basic or from a C application. The Microsoft Foundation Class includes transaction support in the CDatabase class in the form of the BeginTrans member function, the CommitTrans member function, and the Rollback member function. Now that you have studied the ODBC API SQLTransact function, the meaning of these MFC functions is self-evident.

Warning: If CDatabase::BeginTrans is called, the transaction must be ended before CDatabase::BeginTrans is called again. The transaction is ended by calling either the CDatabase::CommitTrans function or the CDatabase::Rollback function.

As you have seen in earlier lessons, the MFC offers an easy-to-use, encapsulated version of the ODBC API. What the programmer loses in terms of flexibility might not be important to many developers, especially those interested in simply querying a database to retrieve static data. In the area of transaction management, once again we run into a quirk of the MFC CDatabase/CRecordset implementation.

To understand the potential for problems when calling CommitTrans or Rollback, the programmer needs to have some understanding of the CRecordset edit buffer. If the Class Wizard is used to create a CRecordset class, the fields in the selected table are linked to the member variables of the class using Record Field Exchange (RFX). These data members serve as an edit buffer that always contains the values of the current database record. During an AddNew or Edit operation, the recordset backs this edit buffer up. The current record is not backed up during a Delete operation.

The basic operation for the AddNew, Edit, and Delete functions is as follows:

- ☐ AddNew: After calling Update, the record that was current before the AddNew operation is made current again.
- ☐ Edit: After calling Update, the edited record remains in place as the current record.
- ☐ Delete: The field data members are marked NULL and the CRecordset's IsDeleted function will return a nonzero value. The programmer should scroll to another record to refill the edit buffer with another record's data.

The existence of this edit buffer eases many routine operations, but it can make performing a transaction a little more complicated. Tables 19.2 and 19.3 (paraphrased from the Microsoft Visual C++ documentation) list the results for a number of user operations.

Table 19.2. How CommitTrans affects updates.

Operation	Result at Data Source
AddNew, Update, then CommitTrans	New record added
AddNew then CommitTrans	New record is lost
Edit, Update, then CommitTrans	Edits committed
Edit then CommitTrans	Edits are lost
Delete then CommitTrans	Records deleted

Table 19.3. How Rollback affects updates.

Operation	Result at Data Source
AddNew, Update, then Rollback	Addition to data source is reversed
AddNew, then Rollback	No changes

continues

Table 19.3. continued

Operation	Result at Data Source
Edit, Update, then Rollback	Changes to data source are reversed
Edit, then Rollback	No changes
Delete, then Rollback	Deletion is reversed

> **Note:** When any of the operations are performed with an Update and then rolled back, CDatabase::Requery must be called to restore the contents of the current record back to the data members. If AddNew is called without an Update, call AddNew again to restore an empty, new buffer. If Edit is called with an Update, call Edit again to restore the unedited version of the record to the edit buffer.

Ending Statement Execution Using the ODBC API

To terminate the processing of a statement handle, the ODBC API provides two functions: SQLCancel and SQLFreeStmt. SQLCancel is used to cancel processing that is ongoing at the time the SQLCancel function is called. SQLFreeStmt is called to stop processing associated with a statement handle, close any cursors, discard results, and free resources associated with the statement handle.

SQLCancel

The SQLCancel function is used to cancel operations that are ongoing at the time the function is called. The prototype for the SQLCancel function is as follows:

```
RETCODE SQLCancel(hstmt)
```

The following types of processing can be canceled using SQLCancel:

- ☐ An asynchronous execution that was executed using the hstmt passed to SQLCancel
- ☐ A function executed using the hstmt that currently needs data
- ☐ A function running on another thread in a multithreaded application

The following process is generally followed when executing a function asynchronously: the return from the asynchronous function is called in a loop. If the function is still executing, it will return SQL_STILL_EXECUTING. Once the value SQL_STILL_EXECUTING is returned, the application can call SQLCancel at any time after that.

The second condition occurs when SQLExecute returns the value SQL_NEED_DATA. Between this time and the time when all of the data is actually sent, the application developer can cancel the statement's execution by calling SQLCancel.

Keep in mind when using SQLCancel that when SQLCancel returns SQL_SUCCESS, that only means that the SQLCancel function was executed properly. This does not necessarily mean that the original executing hstmt was canceled yet. The developer will need to check the return values for the original function until it no longer returns SQL_STILL_EXECUTING.

SQLFreeStmt

The SQLFreeStmt function is used to perform the following operations on an existing statement handle:

- [ ] End all processing associated with the hstmt
- [ ] Close all open cursors associated with the hstmt
- [ ] Discard all pending results
- [ ] Free all resources associated with a statement handle

The SQLFreeStmt has the following prototype:

```
RETCODE SQLFreeStmt(hstmt, fOption)
```

The fOption variable can accept values shown in Table 19.4.

Table 19.4. fOption values and their meanings.

Value	Meaning
SQL_CLOSE	Closes the cursor and discards pending results. After using this option, the statement handle can be reused later.
SQL_DROP	Closes the cursor, discards pending results, and frees all resources associated with the statement handle.
SQL_UNBIND	Frees all return buffers bound by SQLBindCol for the statement handle.
SQL_RESET_PARAMS	Frees all parameter buffers requested by SQLBindParameter for the statement handle.

19

It should be noted that calling SQLCancel is functionally the same as calling the SQLFreeStmt function with the SQL_CLOSE option.

Ending Statement Execution Using the Microsoft Foundation Classes

Database transactions can be canceled in essentially the same fashion as the ODBC API by using MFC. The same level of control that was given with the SQLCancel function is not allowed, however. To enable asynchronous execution, the developer must first call the CDatabase::SetSynchronousMode function as follows:

```
CDatabase::SetSynchronousMode(FALSE)
```

This is mentioned here only briefly, because the default execution processing method is in fact asynchronous. However, if the programmer wants to execute a transaction synchronously, the SetSynchronousMode function exists. Keep in mind that not all data sources support asynchronous execution, and you will need to determine this before you try it.

Once an asynchronous operation is in progress, the CRecordset::Cancel function can be called to cancel execution.

Tip: The MFC application framework provides the CRecordset::OnWaitForDataSource virtual function for the programmer to override. This function will be called by the framework each time the executed function returns SQL_STILL_EXECUTING. The OnWaitForDataSource function can be used to prompt the user if he would like to cancel the ongoing operation. By default, the CRecordset::OnWaitForDataSource function calls the CDatabase::OnWaitForDataSource function. You could also use this function to disable controls on-screen, for example, until the database operation is completed.

Terminating Connections and Environments

Recall that before any database operations can be performed using ODBC, you need to obtain a valid environment handle (henv) using SQLAllocEnv. This environment handle is used to identify a specific database environment. You were also shown how to obtain a valid connection handle (hdbc) using SQLConnect. This connection handle is used throughout an application to identify a specific connection to a database.

ODBC provides a set of functions to terminate a connection to a data source. The three functions shown in Table 19.5 terminate a connection to a data source as well as free an environment handle.

Table 19.5. Functions used to end a connection to a data source.

Function	Purpose
SQLDisconnect	Closes a connection identified by a connection handle
SQLFreeConnect	Releases the connection handle and frees all memory that was allocated for the handle
SQLFreeEnv	Releases the environment handle and frees all memory that was allocated for the handle

SQLDisconnect

The prototype for the SQLDisconnect function is as follows:

```
RETCODE SQLDisconnect(hdbc)
```

It returns the following values: SQL_SUCCESS, SQL_SUCCESS_WITH_INFO, SQL_ERROR, and SQL_INVALID_HANDLE.

The SQLDisconnect function is typically called after calling SQLFreeStmt with an SQL_DROP value. (Calling SQLFreeStmt frees all statement handles.) If values of SQL_ERROR or SQL_SUCCESS_WITH_INFO are returned, additional SQLSTATE values can be obtained by calling SQLError.

The ODBC API documentation mentions two specific state values that will be of importance to developers. SQLSTATE 25000 (invalid transaction state) is returned when a transaction associated with the connection handle has not been completed. The developer must either commit or roll back the transaction with the function SQLTransact.

The other special return value is an SQLSTATE value of S1010 (function sequence error). This value is returned if there is an existing hstmt still executing asynchronously. Calling the SQLDisconnect function will free all existing hstmts; however, it will not free those hstmts that are executing asynchronously. Be careful to check for these return values when you execute transactions or asynchronously execute statements.

SQLFreeConnect

The SQLFreeConnect function releases a connection handle and frees all memory associated with that handle. The prototype for the SQLFreeConnect function is as follows:

```
RETCODE SQLFreeConnect(hdbc)
```

It also returns SQL_SUCCESS, SQL_SUCCESS_WITH_INFO, SQL_ERROR, and SQL_INVALID_HANDLE. SQLDisconnect must be called before you call SQLFreeConnect. If SQLDisconnect is not called, the SQL_ERROR value will be returned, and the handle will remain.

SQLFreeEnv

The SQLFreeEnv function releases an environment handle and frees all memory associated with that handle. The prototype for the SQLFreeEnv function is as follows:

```
RETCODE SQLFreeEnv(henv)
```

It also returns SQL_SUCCESS, SQL_SUCCESS_WITH_INFO, SQL_ERROR, and SQL_INVALID_HANDLE. Before an environment handle can be freed by calling SQLFreeEnv, SQLFreeConnect must be called for all connection handles allocated under the environment handle, henv. (Also, remember that in order for SQLFreeConnect to be correctly executed, SQLDisconnect must have been called.)

Summary

Today's lesson discussed a range of topics that dealt with finishing off a group of ODBC transactions. You learned how to end transactions through the use of a commit or rollback, how to free a statement's handle, how to close and free a connection's handle, and finally, how to free an environment's handle.

By using the `SQLSetConnectOptions` function with the `SQL_AUTOCOMMIT_OFF` option set, the programmer essentially enables transaction support for the application at hand. A transaction must be completed with the `SQLTransact` function. One can pass either a value of `SQL_COMMIT` or `SQL_ROLLBACK` to either commit or roll back the transaction. A commit executes the previous batch of statements, whereas a rollback in effect cancels the transaction's statements.

The MFC's implementation of transactions at first glance appears to be very straightforward. However, the programmer must take care to understand what is going on "behind the scenes." If this is not done, invalid data might be left in the `CRecordset` class's member variables.

You can end statement execution using one of two methods: `SQLFreeStmt` or `SQLCancel`. `SQLCancel` is used to cancel an ongoing task such as an asynchronous execution or an execution running on another thread in a multithreaded application. If no processing is currently being done with the statement handle, calling `SQLCancel` is identical to calling `SQLFreeStmt` with the `SQL_CLOSE` option. `SQLFreeStmt` is used to free resources associated with a statement handle or to free all return buffers bound to the statement by the function `SQLBindCol`.

Finally, to completely close a connection or free an environment, three functions are provided: `SQLDisconnect`, `SQLFreeConnect`, and `SQLFreeEnv`. `SQLDisconnect` closes a connection handle, and `SQLFreeConnect` frees all resources associated with a connection handle. `SQLDisconnect` must be called before calling `SQLFreeConnect`. `SQLFreeEnv` frees all resources associated with an environment handle. `SQLFreeConnect` must be called before calling `SQLFreeEnv`.

19

Q&A

Q The database system on which my company has standardized provides full transaction support through its SQL implementation. Should I use these commands or the ODBC API?

A Powerful database management systems such as Oracle7 and SQL Server provide detailed transaction control to the SQL programmer. However, the purpose of using the ODBC API is to provide a uniform interface to the underlying database system. By using the ODBC standard's transaction control, you are assured of compatibility should your code ever need to be ported to another database system.

Workshop

The Workshop provides quiz questions to help you solidify your understanding of the material covered and to give you experience in using what you've learned. Try to understand the quiz and exercise answers before continuing on to the next day's lesson. Answers are provided in Appendix A, "Answers."

Quiz

1. (True or False) Calling SQLDisconnect will cancel all transactions and close the current connection to the database.

2. Multiple Choice. Select the proper sequence of function calls that will correctly end an ODBC session.

    a. SQLTransact -> SQLFreeEnv -> SQLFreeConnect

    b. SQLDisconnect -> SQLFreeConnect -> SQLFreeEnv

    c. SQLFreeConnect-> SQLDisconnect -> SQLFreeEnv

Exercise

1. Create a simple dialog box application that initializes an ODBC connection upon opening, and then closes the connection upon closing.

20

Completing the
Entire Application

On Day 19, "Ending Transactions and Connections," several topics were covered. You learned how to end a transaction, how to end a connection, and how to end an application.

Of these three, you will probably use the ODBC facilities for transaction control the most often. To review, transactions are essentially blocks of statements that are to be executed together. These blocks of statements can be committed or rolled back. This means that the block of statements is either executed or cancelled, a process known as transaction control. Using transactions enables developers to retain control over updates or deletions to data in a client/server database environment.

On Day 18, "Using Transactions and Commitment Control," some time was spent covering the support of transaction management by the various ODBC drivers. By using SQLGetInfo, the programmer can query the driver to determine its level of transaction support. You looked at several popular drivers and learned that the level of support varies greatly among the different manufacturer's drivers.

Finishing an ODBC Application

Once your ODBC operations are finished, there are several steps you must take to finish your application. The SQLCancel function is used to finish asynchronous processing. The SQLFreeStmt function frees a statement handle and effectively ends its use. SQLDisconnect closes a connection, followed by SQLFreeConnect, which frees the connection handle. SQLFreeEnv is used to free the environment handle when the application is finished with it.

Code Cleanup

Just when you think your job is finished and your application has been wrapped up, you have several things left to do. In this lesson you learn several of these topics. One of the first tasks the database programmer should examine once the main application has been finished is converting the most common SQL code to stored procedures. Stored procedures are discussed in some detail later in this lesson. You are probably already familiar with documentation; it is a necessary evil in the software development process and might determine your application's usability for some time to come. You will also examine the ODBC installation process. If you have installed Visual Basic, or any other product that uses ODBC, you might have noticed that its install process placed quite a few Dynamic Link Libraries (DLLs) and other files onto your hard drive. You learn the significance of those files, and what your application needs to do to install ODBC correctly.

Using Stored Procedures

Stored procedures are functional groupings of SQL statements and database operations. Typically, they are used to isolate common blocks of SQL code. The obvious advantage to using a stored procedure versus a block of SQL statements is to reduce the many statements to a single function call. This process is exactly like what programmers are used to doing with their Visual Basic or C code. For instance, all C functions start with a main() function. The entire application is not crammed into a huge main() function. Instead, it is broken up into hundreds or thousands of subfunctions. C++ or other object-oriented languages go a step further by reducing data and operations to common classes. The process of using stored procedures is identical to this process.

This book is not intended to be a reference on stored procedures or their syntax, but many new database programmers are unaware of their value. Fewer yet have used ODBC to actually execute the procedures to achieve some result. The following discussion sheds some light on their advantages.

As an example, imagine in your application that you had the group of SQL statements shown in Listing 20.1 to be executed (the following syntax is specific to SQL Server, but you can apply the logic to whatever system you are using).

Listing 20.1. SQL sample code.

```
DECLARE @NAME char(40)
SELECT @NAME = NAME FROM PRESIDENTS
WHERE AGE > 50 AND TERMS = 1
INSERT INTO ONE_TERMER VALUES (@NAME)
DELETE FROM PRESIDENTS WHERE NAME = @NAME
PRINT @NAME
```

These statements have a common thread running through them. Basically, you are doing some type of operation with the PRESIDENTS table and, when that operation is finished, you would like to print the name out. From your experience with ODBC, you know that this would require several SQLExecute() function calls. In addition, for each of the SELECT, INSERT, and DELETE statements, your database management system would need to "recompile" the syntax required to process the statement. This is usually done through some sort of a query optimizer and is repeated each time this batch of statements is finished.

A stored procedure is stored within the database as an object, just like a table or an index. The object is executed on the server machine (not the calling client machine). This reduces network traffic and aids the programmer by reducing many statements (sometimes hundreds) to the function-call level. Once again, using SQL Server, we will show

what the syntax of Listing 20.1 looks like when it is embedded within a stored procedure. Listing 20.2 actually creates a stored procedure named `PRINT_ONE_TERMERS`.

Listing 20.2. A stored procedure encapsulating Listing 20.1.

```
CREATE PROCEDURE PRINT_ONE_TERMERS
AS
DECLARE @NAME char(40)
SELECT @NAME = NAME FROM PRESIDENTS
WHERE AGE > 50 AND TERMS = 1
INSERT INTO ONE_TERMER VALUES (@NAME)
DELETE FROM PRESIDENTS WHERE NAME = @NAME
PRINT @NAME
GO
```

You can execute the stored procedure by issuing the following SQL Server command:

```
EXECUTE PRINT_ONE_TERMERS
GO
```

Note: Stored procedures are often given the suffix `dbp` or `sp` to denote to the programmer that this object is a stored procedure.

There are other advantages to using stored procedures. Perhaps the biggest advantage of all is the fact that they are compiled the first time they are used and are not recompiled every time they are used. This means that the database system will build a "map" of the procedure when it compiles it. Then it will not have to rebuild the query each time it is used. This can amount to a considerable performance improvement, particularly in situations in which a lot of data traditionally was being sent over the network.

Stored Procedures and ODBC

Stored procedures were added to the SQL syntax as part of the 1992 ANSI SQL standard (often called SQL-92). As you know by now, ODBC was designed to be a full-featured API for database applications, so it does include procedure call support. You can call a procedure in one of two ways:

1. Use the ODBC SQL syntax
2. Use server (back-end) specific syntax

You can use the server syntax by executing an `SQLPrepare` statement followed by an `SQLExecute` statement. However, that would restrict you to that specific database system,

which is not the point of using ODBC. This lesson briefly focuses on the ODBC SQL syntax before moving on to the topics of documentation and installation.

The following is the ODBC SQL syntax used to call a procedure:

```
(*vendor(Microsoft),product(ODBC)
[?=] call procedure-name[([parameter][,[parameter]]...)] *)
```

Because the vendor is Microsoft and the product is ODBC, this statement reduces to the following:

```
{[?=]call procedure-name[([parameter][,[parameter]]...)]}
```

The *procedure-name* in this function definition refers to the name of the stored procedure in the database. The *parameter* refers to an input and/or output parameter passed to the procedure. The parameter can be a literal value or a parameter marker for input or input/output parameters. For output parameters, the parameter must be in the form of a parameter marker. The [?=] parameter marker in the statement refers to the procedure's return value. This parameter marker plus all other parameter markers must be bound using the function SQLBindParameter (see Day 14, "Using Prepared Statements and Parameter Markers").

If the return value parameter is omitted, the driver will ignore the return value for the database procedure.

To determine if your data source supports the use of stored procedures, call the SQLGetInfo function with the SQL_PROCEDURES argument.

ODBC Installation Issues

One of the more trying tasks to perform with ODBC is to distribute the finished application. Because of the multitude of database drivers, networking layers, and ODBC Dynamic Link Libraries (not to mention the installation and setup of your database), the installation is a process that should not be left until the very end of your development phase. Although it might seem like a daunting task at first, there are a number of different products or tools that ease the ODBC installation process. This section examines two of these tools.

ODBC Application Components

Take the time to consider the number of things that need to be done to get your ODBC application running successfully. Assume that you are using the application in a client/server environment with the database running on a remote server.

1. The database management system must be installed and configured correctly.

2. Your database will need to be installed, along with all the appropriate stored procedures, indexes, views, and triggers. It is highly suggested that you place this database build process inside one or more SQL script files that can drop your database and rebuild it as needed. Chances are that during the start-up phase, this database will need to be rebuilt several times.

3. Decide upon a networking protocol and test the connection from all the client machines to your database server.

4. Install on each client the database's networking layer.

5. Install the actual application's executable.

6. Install any VBXs, OCXs, or DLLs required by your application.

7. Install the ODBC Driver Manager, along with associated runtime DLLs.

8. Install all appropriate ODBC drivers.

9. Install any local database files, as required.

10. Set up all required ODBC data sources.

All of these steps must be done within a professional-looking application that will not crash and will probably offer the user several different installation options. Two tools provided by Microsoft to aid in this task are the Visual Basic Setup Wizard and the ODBC Driver Setup Toolkit.

The Visual Basic Setup Wizard

The Visual Basic Setup Wizard comes packaged with the Professional Edition of Visual Basic Versions 3.0 and 4.0. It is a Wizard-type application, complete with helpful dialog boxes that automate much of the routine tasks often needed to begin an installer application. This section steps through the Setup Wizard application and builds a simple install program for the Day 14 sample program.

Step 1: Choosing a Makefile

The first dialog box you will see (see Figure 20.1) asks you to select a Visual Basic project file for the application you would like to distribute. If you like, the Setup Wizard will run Visual Basic and compile your application before continuing on to Step 2. A problem arises here for all the non-Visual Basic application developers out there. The Setup Wizard will only create an install application based on a Visual Basic .MAK file. You can

work around this by creating a dummy Visual Basic project that essentially does nothing. The Setup Wizard will examine this and continue on its way.

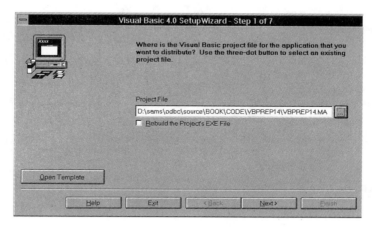

Figure 20.1. *The Setup Wizard Step 1 of 7 dialog box.*

Note that there are options on every screen to Save a Template file or Open a Template file. The Setup Wizard enables you to save the seven steps you go through for future use. In other words, once you have gone through and selected the options you would like for your install program, you don't have to go through each of these steps again.

Step 2: Select Application Features

The next dialog box (see Figure 20.2) is used to determine which DLLs you want to include with your application. As you can see, you are given the option of delivering a database engine. The screen also directs you, if your project uses ODBC, to use the ODBC install program available through the Microsoft Developer Network.

Depending on what choice you make, the appropriate DLLs will be included in your install program. This is a great idea in theory; however, there are some problems with the implementation in the Setup Wizard. If you choose Data Access, the Setup Wizard will include the Visual Basic Jet Engine DLLs. Depending on which database engine you are using, the Setup Toolkit might or might not retrieve all of the correct files. This is not really a problem, because you will be left with all of the source code for your install program. However, it should be mentioned as something to look out for.

20

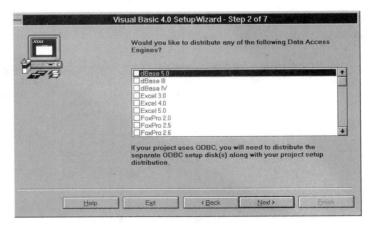

Figure 20.2. *The Setup Wizard Step 2 of 7 dialog box.*

Step 3: Select Floppy Drive and Disk Type

Step 3 enables you to select a default drive from which to install and select the size of the install disks (see Figure 20.3). The default drive will be used to alert the reader to Insert Disk #1 into Drive A:, for instance. The size of the disks is important because the Setup Wizard uses this size to "break up" your files onto separate disks after it compresses them. The most popular format at this time is the 1.44MB disk, and it will probably be the option you choose most often. You are also offered the option of installing to a subdirectory on a hard drive.

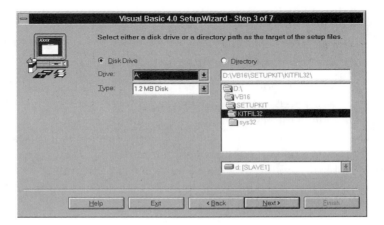

Figure 20.3. *The Setup Wizard Step 3 of 7 dialog box.*

Step 4: Add OLE Servers

New with Visual Basic 4.0 is the capability to add an OLE server to your installation. This screen enables you to select the appropriate server. (See Figure 20.4.)

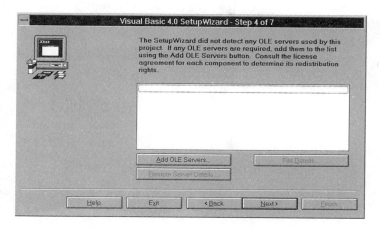

Figure 20.4. *The Setup Wizard Step 4 of 7 dialog box.*

Step 5: Additional File Dependencies

This step, shown in Figure 20.5, enables you to see what additional components Visual Basic 4.0 has determined are needed in your application. If you do not want to deliver a certain component, you uncheck it in the list box.

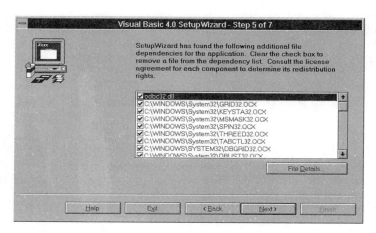

Figure 20.5. *The Setup Wizard Step 5 of 7 dialog box.*

Step 6: Determine Type of Deployment

In this dialog box (see Figure 20.6), you determine how your application will be installed. A traditional application would use the Install in application directory option. OLE components would use one or both of the other two options, Install as OLE automation shared component or Install remote OLE automation server components.

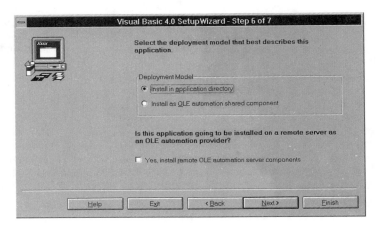

Figure 20.6. *The Setup Wizard Step 6 of 7 dialog box.*

Step 7: Adding and Deleting Files from the Installation

This dialog box (see Figure 20.7) is extremely useful for finishing up your install application. Here you are given the opportunity to add additional files such as DLLs, VBXs, help files, and any README information you want to provide. You can add files by selecting the Add Files button.

Selecting the File Details button after you select a file will give you all the pertinent file information such as Creation Date, Size, and internal comments.

Selecting the Summary Info button will give you a wrap-up of your entire install application. It gives you the number of files you are installing along with their total size. In addition, the Install program created by Setup Wizard requires several files for its operation. The total size of these files is given so that you have a good idea of the amount of space your application will take up on a user's hard drive.

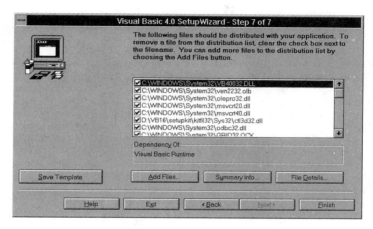

Figure 20.7. *The Setup Wizard Step 7 of 7 dialog box.*

File Compression

Finally, the Setup Wizard will compress each of your files using the COMPRESS.EXE program included with Visual Basic. Don't be overwhelmed by what happens next. The Setup Wizard will compress all of your files using the COMPRESS -d option (which compresses a file and renames it with the .XX_ option). This would compress a file named FILE1.EXE into a compressed file named FILE1.EX_. These files are stored temporarily under the Setup Wizard directory in Visual Basic.

Once these files are compressed, the Wizard automates the writing of your install application based on the information you gave it during the first five steps. Once this application is created, it is compiled into a file named SETUP1.EXE. The Wizard will then create a compressed version of this file (named SETUP1.EX_). After this file has been compressed, Setup Wizard will create your install disks for you (assuming you insert the blank, formatted disks it asks for). In a perfect world, this would be the end of your install application coding process. However, chances are you will probably want to make some modifications to the simple application that the Wizard creates for you.

Modifying Setup1.EXE

Despite its faults, at this point the Setup Wizard will have created for you a simple, straightforward application that will install the files you selected in Step 7 onto a user's hard drive. In addition, it will have left behind all of the source code to the Setup1 application. Before you examine this code more closely, take a moment to study exactly what Setup1.EXE does when it is run.

The Setup1 Install Process

The Setup1.EXE does several things behind the scenes to get itself started. If you look on disk 1 of the set of disks created for you, you will notice some files that you did not intend to be part of your project:

SETUP.EXE
SETUP.LST
SETUPKIT.DL_
VBRUN300.DL_
VER.DL_

The SETUP.EXE file is the file actually run by the user to begin the install process. This file reads the contents of the SETUP.LST file to determine which files it needs to decompress from disk 1 before running SETUP1.EXE (which is naturally included in SETUP.LST). As a minimum, your SETUP.LST file should always contain the following three entries: SETUP1.EX_, SETUPKIT.DL_, and VBRUN300.DL_. The first entry in SETUP.LST should always be SETUP1.EXE.

> **Warning:** If changes are made to the Setup1A.MAK project and then the SETUP1.EXE application is rebuilt, the SETUP1.EXE file must be compressed using the COMPRESS -d option. If this is not done, your install application will fail without any appropriate error messaging. Also, the SETUP.LST file must not be compressed using the COMPRESS tool.

Assuming that your copy of Visual Basic is located in the \VB directory, the install application source code will be located in the \VB\Setupkit\Setup1 directory. The following files are included in that directory:

Message.FRM
Path.FRM
Path.FRX
Setup1.BAS
Setup1.EXE
Setup1.FRM
Setup1.FRX
Setup1.GLB
Setup1.MAK
Setup1A.FRM

Setup1A.MAK
Status.FRM

The experienced Visual Basic programmer will notice that these are common Visual Basic project files. Note that there are two different .MAK files (the extension used by Visual Basic to denote a project). Ignore the Setup1.MAK project and concentrate only on the Setup1A.MAK project. This was the project used to create your install application. At this time, open the SETUP1A.MAK project using Visual Basic and examine the Form.Load routine of the Setup1A.FRM form. Listing 20.3 is the source code for that subroutine.

Listing 20.3. Source code for install application.

```
Private Sub Form_Load()
    Const strINI_FILES$ = "Files"       'default section to install
    Const strEXT_GRP$ = "GRP"           'extension for progman group

    #If Win16 Then
    Dim fBtrieve As Integer             'Uses Btrieve?
    #End If
    Dim strGrpPath As String            'Name for group file
    Dim strGroupName As String          'Name of Program Group
    Dim sFile As FILEINFO               'first Files= line info

    On Error GoTo MainError

    '
    'Initialize linespacing variables for message box calls
    '
    LF$ = Chr$(10)
    LS$ = LF$ & LF$

    '
    'Initialize string resources used by global vars and forms/controls
    '
    GetStrings

    '
    'Get Windows and Windows\System directories
    '
    gstrWinDir = GetWindowsDir()
    gstrWinSysDir = GetWindowsSysDir()

    '
    'If the Windows System directory is a subdirectory of the
    'Windows directory, the proper place for installation of
    'files specified in the setup.lst as $(WinSysDest) is always
    'the Windows \System directory.  If the Windows \System
    'directory is *not* a subdirectory of the Windows directory,
    'then the user is running a shared version of Windows.  In
    'this case, if the user does not have write access to the
```

continues

Listing 20.3. continued

```
'shared system directory, we change the system files
'destination to the windows directory
'
If InStr(gstrWinSysDir, gstrWinDir) = 0 Then
    If WriteAccess(gstrWinSysDir) = False Then
        gstrWinSysDir = gstrWinDir
    End If
End If


'The command-line arguments must be processed as early
'as possible, because without them it is impossible to
'call the app removal program to clean up after an aborted
'setup.
'
#If Win32 And LOGGING Then
    ProcessCommandLine Command$, gstrSrcPath,
    ⇒gstrAppRemovalLog, gstrAppRemovalEXE
#Else
    ProcessCommandLine Command$, gstrSrcPath
#End If

AddDirSep gstrSrcPath

'
'The Setup Bootstrapper (SETUP.EXE) copies SETUP1/132.EXE and SETUP.LST to
'the end user's windows directory.  Information required for setup such
'as setup flags and fileinfo is read from the copy of SETUP.LST found in
'that directory.
'
gstrSetupInfoFile = gstrWinDir & gstrFILE_SETUP

gstrAppName = ReadIniFile(gstrSetupInfoFile,
⇒gstrINI_SETUP, gstrINI_APPNAME)
If gstrAppName = gstrNULL Then
    MsgError ResolveResString(resNOSETUPLST),
    ⇒MB_OK Or MB_ICONSTOP, gstrSETMSG
    gstrTitle = ResolveResString(resSETUP, "¦1", gstrAppName)
    ExitSetup Me, gintRET_FATAL
End If

gstrTitle = ResolveResString(resSETUP, "¦1", gstrAppName)

'
'Display the background "blue-wash" setup screen
'as soon as we get the title
'
ShowMainForm

'
'If this key has a non-zero value in SETUP.LST, then set the variable to
'TRUE - otherwise set it to false
'
#If Win16 Then
```

```
            fBtrieve = IIf(Val(ReadIniFile(gstrSetupInfoFile, gstrINI_SETUP,
            ➥gstrINI_BTRIEVE)), True, False)
    #End If

        '
        'Display the welcome dialog
        '
        ShowWelcomeForm

        '
        'Get name of application's executable file.  This name will be added to the
        'program manager.  Only the EXE Name should be entered under this key in
        'the setup information file (SETUP.LST).
        '
        gstrAppExe = ReadIniFile(gstrSetupInfoFile, gstrINI_SETUP, gstrINI_APPEXE)

        'If this flag is set, then the default destination directory is used
        'without question, and the user is never given a chance to change it.
        'This is intended for installing an .EXE/.DLL as a component rather
        'than as an application in an application directory.  In this case,
        'having an application directory does not really make sense.
        If ReadIniFile(gstrSetupInfoFile, gstrINI_SETUP,
        ➥gstrINI_FORCEUSEDEFDEST) = "1" Then
            gfForceUseDefDest = True
        End If

        '
        'Read default destination directory.  If the name specified conflicts
        'with the name of a file, then prompt for a new default directory
        '
        gstrDestDir = ResolveDestDir(ReadIniFile(gstrSetupInfoFile, gstrINI_SETUP,
        ➥gstrINI_APPDIR))
        While FileExists(gstrDestDir) = True Or gstrDestDir = gstrNULL
            If MsgError(ResolveResString(resBADDEFDIR), MB_OKCANCEL
            ➥Or MB_ICONQUESTION, gstrSETMSG) = IDCANCEL Then
                ExitSetup Me, gintRET_FATAL
            End If
            ShowPathDialog gstrDIR_DEST
        Wend

        '
        'Ensure a trailing backslash on the destination directory
        '
        AddDirSep gstrDestDir

        Do
            '
            'Display install button and default directory.  The user
            'can change the destination directory from here.
            '
            ShowBeginForm

            '
            'This would be a good place to display an
            'option dialog, allowing the user
            'a chance to select installation options:
```

continues

20

Listing 20.3. continued

```
'samples, docs, help files, etc.
'Results of this dialog would be checked in the loop below
'
'ShowOptionsDialog (Function you could write
'with option check boxes, etc.)
'


'
'Initialize "table" of drives used and disk space array
'
InitDiskInfo

SetMousePtr gintMOUSE_HOURGLASS
ShowStaticMessageDialog ResolveResString(resDISKSPACE)


'
'For every section in SETUP.LST that will be installed,
' call CalcDiskSpace
'with the name of the section
'
CalcDiskSpace strINI_FILES
'CalcDiskSpace "MySection"
'CalcDiskSpace "MyOtherSection"
'
'If you created an options dialog, you need to check results here to
'determine whether disk space needs to be calculated (if the option(s)
'will be installed)
'
'If chkInstallSamples.Value = TRUE then
'    CalcDiskSpace "Samples"
'End If
'


HideStaticMessageDialog
SetMousePtr gintMOUSE_DEFAULT

'
'After all CalcDiskSpace calls are complete, call CheckDiskSpace to check
'the results and display warning form (if necessary).  If the user wants
'to try another destination directory (or cleanup and retry) then
'CheckDiskSpace will return False
'
Loop While CheckDiskSpace() = False


'
'Show copy form and set copy gauge percentage to zero
'
SetMousePtr gintMOUSE_HOURGLASS
ShowCopyDialog
UpdateStatus frmCopy.picStatus, 0, True


'
'Always start with Disk #1
'
gintCurrentDisk = 1
```

```
    '
    'Starts logging to the setup logfile (will be used for application removal)
    '
    #If Win32 And LOGGING Then
        EnableLogging gstrAppRemovalLog

        'Should go ahead and force the application directory to be created,
        'since the application removal logfile will later be copied there.
        MakePath gstrDestDir, False 'User may not ignore errors here
    #End If


    'For every section in SETUP.LST that needs to be installed,
    'call CopySection
    'with the name of the section
    '

    CopySection strINI_FILES
    'CopySection "MySection"
    'CopySection "MyOtherSection"


    'If you created an options dialog, you need to check results here to
    'determine whether to copy the files in the particular section(s).
    '
    'If chkInstallSamples.Value = TRUE then
    '    CopySection "Samples"
    'End If
    '


    UpdateStatus frmCopy.picStatus, 1, True

    HideCopyDialog

    '
    'Now, do all the 'invisible' update things that are required
    '
    SetMousePtr gintMOUSE_DEFAULT
    ShowStaticMessageDialog ResolveResString(resUPDATING)

    '
    'Add Btrieve info to win.ini if necessary
    '
    #If Win16 Then
        If fBtrieve = True Then
            DoBtrieve
        End If
    #End If

    '
    'Add file sharing (via VSHARE.386) if required
    '
#If Win16 Then
    AddShareIfNeeded
#End If
```

continues

Listing 20.3. continued

```
'
'Register all the files that have been saved
'in the registration array.  The
'CopySection API adds a registration entry
'(when required) if a file is copied.
'

RegisterFiles


'(32-bit Enterprise edition only)
'Create a separate program group and icons for the Remote Automation
'Connection Manager and the Automation Manager, if either has been
'installed.
'This program group is entirely separate from the one created for the
'application program (if any), because it will be shared by all
'VB applications which install them.
'
'NOTE: This is NOT the place to install additional icons.  This is
'NOTE: handled after the Remote Automation icons have been created.
#If Win32 Then
    ShowStaticMessageDialog ResolveResString(resPROGMAN)
    If gsDest.strAUTMGR32 <> "" Or gsDest.strRACMGR32 <> "" Then
        'At least one of these programs was installed.  Go ahead
        'and create the program group.
        Const strREMAUTGROUPPATH = "RemAutVB.GRP"
        CreateOSProgramGroup frmSetup1,
        ➥ResolveResString(resREMAUTGROUPNAME), strREMAUTGROUPPATH

        'Now create the icons for AUTMGR32.EXE and RACMGR32.EXE
        If gsDest.strRACMGR32 <> "" Then
            CreateOSLink frmSetup1, gsDest.strRACMGR32, "",
            ➥ResolveResString(resRACMGR32ICON), False
        End If
        If gsDest.strAUTMGR32 <> "" Then
            CreateOSLink frmSetup1, gsDest.strAUTMGR32, "",
            ➥ResolveResString(resAUTMGR32ICON), False
        End If
    End If
    mstrLastCreatedShellGroup = ""
    'Do not use this same group for other icons
#End If


'
'Create program groups and icons (or links, i.e. shortcuts)
'

ShowStaticMessageDialog ResolveResString(resPROGMAN)

Const fDefCreateGroupUnderWin95 = False
'If fDefCreateGroupUnderWin95 is set to False (this is the default),
'then no program group will be created under Win95
'unless it is absolutely necessary.
'
```

```
        'By default under Windows 95, no group should be created, and the
        'single program icon should be placed directly under the
        'Start>Programs menu (unless there are other, user-defined icons to create

        Dim fAdditionalIcons As Boolean
        'There are two default reasons why we will install more icons than
        'simply the program executable:
        '   1) If we are installing user-defined icons
        '   (by customizing this procedure)
        '   2) If we are creating an program removal icon
        '   (whenever we're running under NT)
        '
        'If you have modified this procedure to install
        '   more icons, make sure you set
        'this variable to True, so that a program group
        'will be created for the icons.
        fAdditionalIcons = False
        #If Win32 Then
            fAdditionalIcons = fAdditionalIcons Or (Not TreatAsWin95())
        #Else
            fAdditionalIcons = fAdditionalIcons
        #End If

        'The following variable determines whether or not we create a program
        'group for icons.  It is controlled by fNoGroupUnderWin95,
        'fAdditionalIcons, and FTreatAsWin95().
        Dim fCreateGroup As Boolean
#If Win32 Then
    If TreatAsWin95() Then
            'Win95 only:
            'We create a program group only if we have additional icons besides
            'the application executable (if any), or if fDefCreateGroupUnderWin95
            'has been set to True to override this default behavior.
#Else
    If False Then
#End If
            fCreateGroup = fDefCreateGroupUnderWin95 Or fAdditionalIcons
    Else
        #If Win32 Then
            'Win32 NT only:
            'We must always create a Program Manager group
            'because we always create an icon for the
            ' application removal program.
            fCreateGroup = True
        #Else
            'Win16 only:
            'If we are deploying this project as an application
            '(as opposed to simply
            '   a shared component), then we create a group and icon(s), or
            '   if any additional icons need to be created.
            fCreateGroup = (gstrAppExe <> "") Or fAdditionalIcons
        #End If
    End If

    If fCreateGroup Then
        strGroupName = gstrAppName
```

continues

381

Listing 20.3. continued

```
        If gstrAppExe = "" Then
            strGrpPath = Left$(gstrAppName, InStr(gstrAppName,
            ➥gstrSEP_EXT)) & strEXT_GRP
        Else
            strGrpPath = Left$(gstrAppExe, InStr(gstrAppExe,
            ➥gstrSEP_EXT)) & strEXT_GRP
        End If


        'Go ahead and create the main program group
        '
        CreateOSProgramGroup frmSetup1, strGroupName, strGrpPath
        fMainGroupWasCreated = True
    End If

    If gstrAppExe <> "" Then
        '
        'Create the main application icon or link
        '
        CreateOSLink frmSetup1, gsDest.strAppDir & gstrAppExe, "", gstrAppName
    End If


    'If you need to create more icons, insert code here,
    'and make certain that you
    'have set the variable fAdditionalIcons to True above
    '
    'If Not fAdditionalIcons Then
    '  MsgError "Internal Setup Customization Error: fAdditionalIcons = False",
        ➥vbOKOnly Or vbExclamation, gstrTitle
    '  ExitSetup Me, gintRET_FATAL
    'End If
    'CreateOSLink frmSetup1, gsDest.strAppDir & "My Exe 1.exe",
    ➥"My Exe 1 command-line arguments", "My Exe 1"
    'CreateOSLink frmSetup1, gsDest.strAppDir & "My Exe 2.exe",
    ➥"My Exe 2 command-line arguments", "My Exe 2"
    '



    'Register the per-app path for 32-bit applications
    '
    #If Win32 And LOGGING Then
        If gstrAppExe <> "" Then
            Dim strPerAppPath As String
            strPerAppPath = ReadIniFile(gstrSetupInfoFile, gstrINI_SETUP,
            ➥gstrINI_APPPATH)
            AddPerAppPath gstrAppExe, gsDest.strAppDir, strPerAppPath
        End If
    #End If

ExitSetup:
    HideStaticMessageDialog
    RestoreProgMan
```

```
        #If Win32 And LOGGING Then
            If fWithinAction() Then
                'By now, all logging actions should have been either
                'aborted or committed.
                MsgError ResolveResString(resSTILLWITHINACTION),
                ➡vbExclamation Or vbOKOnly, gstrTitle
                ExitSetup Me, gintRET_FATAL
            End If
            MoveAppRemovalFiles
        #End If
        ExitSetup Me, gintRET_FINISHEDSUCCESS

MainError:
    Select Case MsgError(Error$ & LS$ & ResolveResString(resUNEXPECTED),
    ➡MB_RETRYCANCEL Or MB_ICONEXCLAMATION, gstrTitle)
    Case IDRETRY
        Resume
    Case IDCANCEL
        ExitSetup Me, gintRET_ABORT
        Resume
    End Select
End Sub
```

As you can see, this install program actually does quite a bit of work for you at this point. The following is a list of the basic steps the program goes through when it is executing.

1. Determines Windows version.

2. Prompts user for Install disk's path name. Note that the application defaults to the drive you entered in Step 3.

3. Prompts user for destination path name.

4. Determines whether there is enough room on the disk to install your application. This amount of room is determined by comparing the amount of free space on the user's hard drive with the WINSYSNEEDED and OTHERNEEDED global variables defined in the SETUP1A.FRM general declarations section. The values of these variables were determined by the Setup Wizard based on the size of the files you included with your install application.

5. Copies files iteratively to the hard drive, decompressing them as it progresses. If your application needs more than one disk, the code will have been inserted in the install sequence to prompt for the next disk.

6. Creates Program Manager group and application icon. If you want, the code can also be modified to add help files, README files, and so on at this point.

Although the Setup Wizard is not a complete solution to every installation problem, it does produce a functioning application that gives the Visual Basic developer an excellent start on the install process. You can modify as much as you need the code for this application until the desired goal is reached.

20

ODBC Driver Setup Toolkit

Now that you have created a professional-looking install application using the Setup Toolkit (or some other tool of your choice), there is one hurdle left to be cleared. That hurdle is the correct installation of the ODBC components required by your application. The best way to install your ODBC drivers and ODBC DLLs on a user's system is by using the ODBC Setup Toolkit. This toolkit is included with the ODBC 2.0 SDK and is located in the \ODBCSDK\DRVSETUP.KIT directory. The toolkit consists of a C-language Windows application that can be customized to meet your installation needs. The base application consists of the following files:

- [ ] DRVSETUP.DEF—Module definition file
- [ ] DRVSETUP.DIB—Customizable bitmap file
- [ ] DRVSETUP.DLG—Dialog description file
- [ ] DRVSETUP.ICO—Icon control used by application's dialog boxes
- [ ] DRVSETUP.RC—Resource file
- [ ] DRVSETUP.C—C Source code for driver setup program
- [ ] DRVSETUP.H—Header file
- [ ] 3DCHECK.BMP—Bitmap file used internal to application

You can customize these files and then compile them with the Microsoft Visual C++ compiler to produce an executable named DRVSETUP.EXE. This executable performs a similar task to the SETUP1.EXE program examined in the Visual Basic Setup Wizard discussions. DRVSETUP.EXE first reads the SETUP.LST file (sound familiar?) to determine user interface settings as well as which files should be installed. The following lists the contents of the SETUP.LST file included with the 16-bit DRVSETUP.KIT example.

```
SAMPLE SETUP.LST FILE CONTENTS
[Params]
    WndTitle   = Put Your Own Title Here
    WndMess    = Put Your Own Message Here...
    TmpDirSize = 500
    TmpDirName = ~smplstp.t
    CmdLine    = _bootstp drvsetup %s %s
    DrvModName = _BOOTSTP

[Files]
    odbc.inf     = odbc.inf
    _mssetup.ex_ = _mssetup.exe
    _bootstp.exe = _bootstp.exe
    drvsetup.exe = drvsetup.exe
    odbcinst.dl_ = odbcinst.dll
    odbcinst.hl_ = odbcinst.hlp
```

Note: The odbc.inf section of the SETUP.LST file must be set to ODBC.INF.

Following the installation of the files in SETUP.LST, DRVSETUP examines the contents of the ODBC.INF file. The ODBC.INF file contains the following possible sections, according to the Microsoft ODBC SDK documentation:

☐ **Source Media Descriptions.** Describes disks used to install ODBC.

☐ **Default File Settings.** Default settings for installation properties.

☐ **ODBC Drivers.** Lists the descriptions of the ODBC drivers shipped on the disk.

☐ **ODBC Driver Manager.** Describes the files shipped for the Driver Manager.

☐ **ODBC Administration Utility.** Describes the files shipped for the ODBC Administrator program.

☐ **Files.** Describes the files shipped for the setup program.

Listing 20.4 shows the contents of the sample ODBC.INF file included with the ODBC SDK 16-bit sample application.

 Listing 20.4. Sample ODBC.INF file contents.

```
[Source Media Descriptions]
    "1", "ODBC Driver Libraries", "odbc.dl_", "."
[ODBC Drivers]
"Template Sample Driver" =

[ODBC]
"Help" = 1, odbcinst.hlp,,,, 1994-12-07,  ,,,  ,,,,,, 17412,,,,,
"Main" = 1, odbcinst.dll,,,, 1994-12-07,
➥ ,, OLDER,  ,,,,, SHARED, 92576,,,, 2.10.24.1,

[ODBC Administrator]
"Windows00" = 1, odbcadm.exe,,,, 1994-12-07,
➥ ,, OLDER,  ,,,,,, 6464,,,, 2.10.23.9,

[ODBC Driver Manager]
"Ctl3dv2" = 1, ctl3dv2.dll,,,, 1994-12-07,
➥ ,, OLDER,  ,,,,, SHARED, 26832,,,, 2.26.0.0,
"Driver" = 1, odbc.dll,,,, 1994-12-07,
➥ ,, OLDER,  ,,,,, SHARED, 56240,,,, 2.10.24.1,
"CrsrLib" = 1, odbccurs.dll,,,, 1994-12-07,
➥ ,, OLDER,   ,,,,, SHARED, 88896,,,, 2.10.23.23,
```

continues

Listing 20.4. continued

```
[Template Sample Driver]
"Driver" = 1, sample.dll,,,, 1994-12-07,
➡    ,, OLDER,  ,,,,,, 11184,,,, 2.0.20.25,
"Ctl3dv2" = 1, ctl3dv2.dll,,,, 1994-12-07,
➡    ,, OLDER,  ,,,,, SHARED, 26832,,,, 2.26.0.0,
"Setup" = 1, sample.dll,,,, 1994-12-07,  ,, OLDER,  ,,,,,, 11184,,,, 2.0.20.25,

[Win32s ODBC]
"Thunk" = 1, cpn16ut.dll,,,, 1994-12-07,  ,, OLDER,  ,,,,, SHARED, 3264,,,,,
"Main" = 1, odbccp32.dll,,,, 1994-12-07,  ,, OLDER,  ,,,,, SHARED, 5632,,,,,

[Win32s ODBC Driver Manager]
"Thunk" = 1, odbc16ut.dll,,,, 1994-12-07,  ,, OLDER,  ,,,,, SHARED, 5792,,,,,
"Driver" = 1, odbc32.dll,,,, 1994-12-07,  ,, OLDER,  ,,,,, SHARED, 12800,,,,,

[Template Sample Driver-Keys]
CreateDSN=sdk21-Sample

[sdk21-Sample]
Description=Sample Driver (null functionality)
Option1=Yes
Option2=Yes
```

We strongly recommend that you purchase a copy of the ODBC SDK by joining the Microsoft Developer Network. Included with this Software Development Kit is a 16-bit Driver Setup Sample Application that can be customized to meet users' needs.

Documenting Your Application

Next to the actual application, users will see your documentation more than anything else. For most non-trivial database tasks, some user training is required so that the user can learn his or her way through a myriad of screens and dialog boxes, some or many of which are constantly bringing the user new or updated data. This is particularly true in business environments where a formerly manual business process has been replaced by a shiny new application written by you. In situations like this, your application might be the first database application your users have ever worked with. To ease this transition, there are several things the programmer can contribute that will pay off in the months or years to come:

- ☐ Create a data dictionary for the database schema
- ☐ Document all code and database scripts thoroughly
- ☐ Create written documentation
- ☐ Convert written documentation to help files for online use

The Data Dictionary

A *data dictionary* can be thought of as a repository of all information concerning the structure and design behind your chosen database schema. The following are applicable items to be placed in the data dictionary:

- ☐ Descriptions of all databases (if multiple databases are used).
- ☐ Descriptions of all tables. This description should include a subdescription of all elements within the table (fields, field data types, field sizes) as well as some type of documentation describing the purpose of each field.
- ☐ Descriptions of all primary and foreign keys within the tables.
- ☐ Descriptions of all indexes.
- ☐ A complete listing of all rules for the database. A small amount of documentation is almost mandatory for these rules in order for future users or developers to understand the thought process behind your work.
- ☐ Listing by name of all stored procedures and triggers stored in the database. In addition to this listing, cataloging the code behind these data objects is useful for future use.

Online Documentation

Although you might be employed on a large project with an eager-to-help technical writing team on your staff, chances are that as your project develops, the need for some type of written documentation will arise. The most common form of documentation has traditionally been printed documentation, but with new forms of help systems such as Windows Help, users have grown accustomed to clicking their way through hypertext links to learn more about the topic at hand. Numerous products abound, such as Microsoft Word or Blue Sky Software's RoboHelp, which aid in the task of online help creation. The purpose of this section is not to instruct the programmer on how to use these tools but rather to stress the importance of the documentation process.

When you use ODBC or develop any type of client/server application, the possibilities or errors that are out of your control multiply. In the past, your executable running on a text-based, single-process operating system might have accessed a few data files located on the disk. About the only thing that could go wrong was either a programming error on your part or a hardware failure.

Now suppose that application has grown into a full-fledged Windows application that first of all must co-exist with many other applications at once. Add to that mix the layers of the ODBC Driver Manager talking to your ODBC driver. The ODBC driver then

20

hands off commands to some type of network protocol DLL, which might converse back and forth to a UNIX machine running SQL Server. Attached to this SQL Server are 125 other users just like yourself all running the same application. One can quickly see the need for extensive testing and excellent documentation should any problem occur. Users might encounter errors that they have never seen (or you have never seen, for that matter). Good documentation and training will help step the users through the problem-solving process and at least enable you to make an educated guess as to what is causing the difficulty.

Summary

This lesson covered a broad spectrum of topics with an emphasis on things a developer can do to create a more professional, polished application. The first of these topics was the creation and use of stored procedures. Stored procedures are database objects that encapsulate SQL code at the functional level. These procedures are popular for several reasons. In addition to reducing application complexity and lessening network load, they can also improve application performance because they are compiled and run on the database server. They can be created with a single command under most common relational database systems, and can be executed several different ways. The specific method of invocation that you studied was through the use of the SQLExecDirect function. The programmer can determine whether or not the driver being used supports procedure calls through the SQLGetInfo function.

Once much of the underlying SQL code has been converted to stored procedures, and the application itself appears to be functioning correctly, the next major step is the creation of the installation program. There are two common ways to quickly develop ODBC installation applications: through the use of the Visual Basic Setup Toolkit and the use of the ODBC Driver Setup Toolkit. These two methods produce good-looking Windows install applications that will decompress the install files from the floppy disks (or other media) into the appropriate install directory. In addition to doing this, both types of applications will install the appropriate ODBC drivers, driver manager, and data sources if requested.

The final step in producing the application is creating documentation. In this process, you learned the importance of creating a data dictionary and online help files. The data dictionary makes it much easier for other developers or administrators to go in behind your work and maintain it. Online documentation has become a standard way of providing documentation with applications, and you can create it with many common tools.

Although the bulk of your development time will go toward creating an excellent application, some time should be allotted for these tasks. They might not seem as important to the application programmer, but these steps are often the first things noticed by end users and should be treated with importance.

Q&A

Q **I've tried the Visual Basic Setup Toolkit but wasn't interested in it, for whatever reason (distributing the "overhead" DLL's, don't own Visual Basic, won't port to other platforms, and so on). I've also had a lot of problems getting the ODBC DLLs installed properly. Any suggestions?**

A Installation programs are often overlooked until the very end of many development projects; however, we often forget that the install application is the first taste of your application users get. There are many third-party toolkits (InstallShield by Stirling Technologies, Inc. is a popular one) that will enable you to produce an industrial-strength install application; however, they require a little more effort than the point-and-click approach that Visual Basic provides. Try to examine several of these options before making your final decision.

Workshop

The Workshop provides quiz questions to help you solidify your understanding of the material covered and to give you experience in using what you've learned. Try to understand the quiz and exercise answers before continuing on to the next day's lesson. Answers are provided in Appendix A, "Answers."

Quiz

1. (True or False) Each ODBC driver at a mininum enables the programmer to call stored procedures in the underlying database.
2. (True or False) The recommended method for writing ODBC install applications is the Visual Basic Setup Toolkit.

Exercise

1. Do some research on your company's (or your client's) database system(s) of choice. Several database management systems support the use of stored procedures; however, yours might not. Determine if it does, and if so, determine if your ODBC driver supports procedure calls.

Using ODBC Test
and Trace Tools

Throughout the first 20 days of this book, you have studied the ODBC Application Programming Interface (API). You learned that by using this API, you can write Visual Basic, C, or C++ code that can perform a variety of database operations. What is important about the ODBC API is that this code does not change if you decide to change your actual database underneath the code.

Today you will study the set of tools that Microsoft has included with the ODBC Software Development Kit (SDK). Specifically, the lesson covers ODBC Test, ODBC Spy, and the sample Visual Basic application included with the ODBC SDK. These tools were included with the application developer in mind, and they can be very beneficial when you are tracking down bugs within your application. In addition to this, actually tracing ODBC function calls visually can help the beginning ODBC programmer see what is going on "underneath the hood."

Tools from the Microsoft ODBC SDK

Included with the ODBC SDK are more than just a set of DLLs and ODBC drivers. This SDK comes packaged with the following tools:

- [ ] ODBC API help files
- [ ] Individual ODBC driver help files
- [ ] Visual Basic sample application (VB Demo)
- [ ] C sample application
- [ ] C++ sample application
- [ ] Cursors sample application
- [ ] ODBC Test
- [ ] ODBC Spy
- [ ] DLL Viewer Translation Spy
- [ ] ODBC drivers for popular database formats
- [ ] Information on building your own driver
- [ ] ODBC Administrator

This lesson focuses primarily on the Visual Basic sample application (called VB Demo), ODBC Test, and ODBC Spy. However, you will first learn some of the additional tools included with the SDK.

DLL Viewer Translation Spy

The DLL Viewer Translation Spy is actually a sample application provided with the ODBC SDK. It is provided to demonstrate how to write a translation DLL; however, you can also use it to examine all DLLs currently in use on your system (see Figure 21.1). Translation DLLs are DLLs used to translate data being passed to the driver or retrieved from the driver. Because they are not actually called by the ODBC application, but rather by the ODBC driver itself, they are not discussed in this book. If you are interested in this topic, study the functions SQLDataSourceToDriver and SQLDriverToDataSource in the ODBC API reference material.

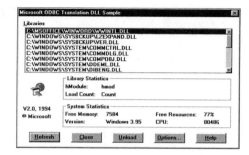

Figure 21.1. *The ODBC Test application.*

ODBC Test

ODBC Test is an application included with the ODBC SDK. This tool enables the developer to simulate ODBC function calls and examine the results as these functions are called. In addition, some common groups of functions can be executed together to save time. (An example of this would be logging into the database, where several function calls are required to accomplish one common task.) Figure 21.2 shows what the application looks like before a data source has been opened.

The following sections go through each of ODBC Test's main menus and explain what each one is for.

21

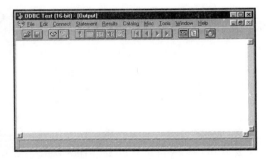

Figure 21.2. *ODBC Test before opening a data source.*

File Menu

The File menu, as in most Windows applications, is used to open and close files. If a file is opened, it will be loaded into the Input section of the main window.

Edit Menu

The Edit menu is used to perform a set of common editing commands, such as Cut, Copy, Paste, Delete, and Undo. These commands operate on text in the Input section of the main window. This section is the large area beneath the main menu that contains a blinking cursor.

Connect Menu

The Connect menu contains items for the following function calls or commands:

SQLAllocEnv
SQLAllocConnect
SQLConnect
SQLBrowseConnect
SQLDriverConnect
SQLDisconnect
SQLFreeConnect
SQLFreeEnv
SQLSetConnectOption
SQLGetConnectOption
SQLDataSources

SQLDrivers
SQLGetInfo
Full Connect
Full Disconnect
Data Sources All
Drivers All
Get Info All

With each of these menu selections, a dialog box is presented prompting you to fill in the parameters to be passed with the function call. Figure 21.3 illustrates the dialog box that corresponds to a SQLSetConnectOption menu selection.

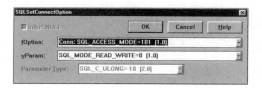

Figure 21.3. *The SQLSetConnectOption dialog box.*

Figure 21.4 shows the various options available within the fOption variable.

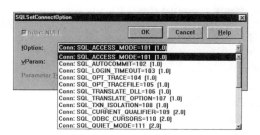

Figure 21.4. *Various options available for the fOption selection.*

Within some of the ODBC Test menus are items that you (as an experienced ODBC programmer) will recognize as not being ODBC function calls. The Connect menu has the following items: Full Connect, Full Disconnect, Data Sources All, Drivers All, and Get Info All. These menu selections perform the actions shown in Table 21.1.

Table 21.1. Connect menu actions.

Menu Selection	Purpose
Full Connect	Calls `SQLAllocEnv`, `SQLAllocConnect`, `SQLSetConnectOption`, `SQLDriverConnect`, and `SQLAllocStmt`.
Full Disconnect	Calls `SQLDisconnect` and `SQLFreeConnect`.
Data Sources All	Calls `SQLDataSources` with `fDirection` set to `SQL_FETCH_FIRST`.
	Calls `SQLDataSources` with `fDirection` set to `SQL_FETCH_NEXT` until it returns `SQL_NO_DATA_FOUND`.
Drivers All	Calls `SQLDrivers` with `fDirection` set to `SQL_FETCH_FIRST`.
	Calls `SQLDrivers` with `fDirection` set to `SQL_FETCH_NEXT` until it returns `SQL_NO_DATA_FOUND`.
Get Info All	Calls `SQLGetInfo` for each value of `fInfoType`.

Statement Menu

The Statement menu contains items for the following function calls or commands:

SQLAllocStmt
SQLSetStmtOption
SQLGetStmtOption
SQLPrepare
SQLBindParameter
SQLNumParams
SQLDescribeParam
SQLExecute
SQLExecDirect
SQLSetCursorName
SQLGetCursorName
SQLParamData
SQLPutData
SQLParamOptions
SQLFreeStmt
SQLNativeSql
Fill Param
Show Params

Like the Connect menu, the Statement menu contains two options that are combinations of ODBC API function calls: Fill Param and Show Params. These options are used in conjunction with the `SQLBindParameter` function call.

Results Menu

The Results menu contains items for the following function calls or commands:

    SQLNumResultCols
    SQLDescribeCol
    SQLColAttributes
    SQLRowCount
    SQLBindCol
    SQLFetch
    SQLExtendedFetch
    SQLSetPos
    SQLGetData
    SQLMoreResults
    SQLSetScrollOptions
    Describe Col All
    Bind Col All
    Show Bound Cols
    Fetch All
    Get Data Row
    Get Data All

Table 21.2 describes the menu options that are not standard ODBC API function calls.

Table 21.2. Results menu options.

Menu Selections	Purpose
Describe Col All	Calls `SQLNumResultCols` and `SQLDescribeCol` for each column in the result set.
Bind Col All	Calls `SQLFreeStmt` with `fOption` set to `SQL_UNBIND`. Calls `SQLNumResultCols`, `SQLDescribeCol`, and `SQLBindCol` for each column in the result set.
Show Bound Cols	Displays the bindings information for each buffer bound to a column with `SQLBindCol`.

continues

Table 21.2. continued

Menu Selections	Purpose
Fetch All	Calls `SQLGetFunctions` to determine if the driver supports `SQLMoreResults`. Calls `SQLFetch` and `SQLMoreResults` (if supported).
Get Data Row	Calls `SQLNumResultCols`, `SQLDescribeCol`, and `SQLGetData` for each column in the result set. `SQLFetch` or `SQLExtendedFetch` must be called before calling the Get Data Row function tool.
Get Data All	Calls `SQLGetFunctions` to determine if the driver supports `SQLMoreResults`. Calls `SQLNumResultCols`, `SQLDescribeCol`, `SQLFetch`, `SQLGetData`, and `SQLFetch`. If the driver supports it, calls `SQLMoreResults`.

Catalog Menu

The Catalog menu contains items for the following function calls or commands:

> SQLGetTypeInfo
> SQLTables
> SQLColumns
> SQLStatistics
> SQLPrimaryKeys
> SQLForeignKeys
> SQLTablePrivileges
> SQLColumnPrivileges
> SQLSpecialColumns
> SQLProcedures
> SQLProcedureColumns

Misc Menu

The Misc menu contains items for the following function calls or commands:

> SQLTransact
> SQLCancel
> SQLError

SQLGetFunctions
Errors All
Get Functions All

The Errors All menu option displays all pending errors. The Get Functions All option displays whether each ODBC function is supported. When executed, this menu item calls SQLGetFunctions for each ODBC function printing either a TRUE or a FALSE next to the function's name in the Test application's window.

Tools Menu

The Tools menu contains the following possible selections:

User Options
Rowset Options
Trace
Manage Test Sources
Manage Auto Tests
Manage Test Groups
Run Auto Tests

The following section discusses each of these options briefly.

User Options

The User Options menu selection prompts the user with a User Options dialog box (see Figure 21.5).

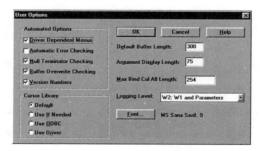

Figure 21.5. *ODBC Test User Options dialog box.*

Selecting Driver Dependent Menus will disable all menu items that are not supported by the driver you are currently using. This is much simpler than calling SQLGetInfo for each option, and it is a real time-saver. Selecting Automatic Error Checking will cause ODBC Test to call the `ErrorAll` function after each ODBC function is called.

Rowset Options

This option presents the user with a dialog box with three basic options: Status Values, Length Values, and Column names. The status of these options will be used by ODBC Test to determine how it displays data in the rowset windows.

Trace

This option turns tracing on and off. If tracing is turned off at this time, a File Save dialog box will be presented to the user asking him or her to select a filename to save trace information to. If tracing is currently turned on, selecting this menu option will turn tracing off. This is the equivalent of calling SQLSetConnectOption with the `SQL_OPT_TRACE` option.

Using Auto Tests

The Manage Test Sources, Manage Auto Tests, Manage Test Groups, and Run Auto Tests menu selections all deal with Auto Test DLLs. The ODBC Test tool also provides a capability known as an Auto Test. An Auto Test is a DLL with the following functions exported: `AutoTestName`, `AutoTestDesc`, and `AutoTestFunc`. Within these functions are standard ODBC API function calls. An Auto Test can be used to call ODBC functions with a variety of different parameters to test out the capabilities of a particular driver. For more information, consult the ODBC Test documentation.

Window Menu

The Window menu provides the standard windowing functionality such as tile, cascade, and so on.

Help Menu

This menu enables you to examine the ODBC API help files as well as the help files for the ODBC Test application.

Summary of ODBC Test

You can use the ODBC Test application to completely test out a driver before delivering that driver with your application. Each dialog box for each ODBC function call contains

a control for each possible argument of that function. This enables the user of ODBC Test (probably an ODBC programmer) to test all of the ODBC function calls with a wide variety of parameters to find out what works and what doesn't. Once you have tested this driver, your application can use it with some assurance that it will perform as expected.

VB Demo

Several useful sample applications also come packaged with the ODBC SDK. One interesting example is the sample Visual Basic application, called VB Demo (see Figure 21.6).

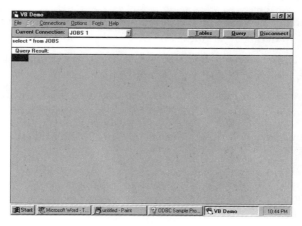

Figure 21.6. *VB Demo (Visual Basic sample ODBC application).*

The VB Demo needs you to first open a connection to a data source. Once this connection has been opened, the connection name will be added to the drop-down list box on the toolbar.

VB Demo enables you to issue standard SQL queries by typing them into the Query edit box. Once you have typed in your query, select the Query button to execute the query. The requested data will be returned into a grid in the main window of the application.

We strongly suggest that you spend some time looking at this application. It implements all of the standard ODBC API functionality, such as opening and closing connections, preparing and executing statements, and returning data from the data source. In addition, it does this in a generic manner. In other words, the application is designed to work with any data source, instead of being hard-coded for one specific data source.

Designing your database applications in this manner will lead to much greater reuse of code over a long period of time.

Tracing ODBC Calls Using ODBC Spy

The ODBC Spy application is a tool included with the ODBC SDK. It is extremely useful in debugging an ODBC application or driver. Although the ODBC Test tool can be used to test the functionality of a driver, it is not really helpful in testing your actual application. This is where ODBC Spy comes in. It enables you to test your ODBC connection in three ways.

1. Intercept and copy commands from the application to the driver. This can be used to debug an application/driver connection.
2. Mimic the actions of a driver when it receives commands from an application. This can be used to debug an application.
3. Mimic an application and send requests to a driver. This can be used to debug a driver.

The ODBC Spy application consists of the following menu items:

File
Edit
Spy
Debug
Help

The following sections describe what each of these menu items are used for.

File Menu

The File menu is used to perform operations on an ODBC Spy log file. Among the options allowed are File Save, File Clear, Log To File, and Log To Screen.

Edit Menu

The Edit menu contains only the Copy command. This will copy the contents of the log buffer to the Windows Clipboard for pasting into a text editor or whatever you choose to do with it.

Spy Menu

The Spy menu is where the "action" begins. It contains the following options:

>   Capture
>   Emulate Driver
>   Emulate App

Selecting the Capture menu item results in a dialog box that prompts you to select a data source on which to spy. Capturing this data source will result in the logging of all interaction with this data source to the log file and the screen (if you choose). After you capture a data source, and then connect to the data source using the VB Demo example, the following information (and much more) is captured by ODBC Spy (see Figure 21.7).

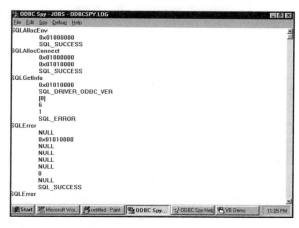

Figure 21.7. *The ODBC Spy application.*

Selecting the Emulate Driver menu selection will play back all ODBC function calls in the log file to a requesting application. This is useful to determine exactly where in an application you are having difficulties, if any. After opening a log file with the Emulate App menu selections, begin the application. As the application calls each ODBC function in the log file, this function will be highlighted on the ODBC Spy screen.

Selecting the Emulate App menu selection does the opposite of the Emulate Driver selection. It is useful in helping you debug a driver. After you open a log file with the Emulate App menu selections, simulate the running of the application by selecting the Go option from the Debug menu. You can set breakpoints within the log file using options on the Debug menu. Step through the ODBC commands in the log file to debug the application.

21

Debug Menu

The Debug menu contains many of the similar features, such as breakpoints and steps, seen in commercial debuggers. The Debug commands are to be used in conjunction with the Emulate App menu selection. The choices on this menu are

> Add Break
> Remove Break
> Remove All Breaks
> Step
> Go
> Enter Debugger

Summary

On your final day of learning to use ODBC, you learned about a variety of tools that are provided as part of the ODBC Software Development Kit. You can obtain this kit (as mentioned on earlier days) by subscribing to the Microsoft Developer's Network. With the ODBC SDK come many useful tools for testing and debugging ODBC applications and drivers. In addition, several useful application programs are provided that you can examine for tips when you begin your first ODBC application.

The ODBC Test utility is designed to fully test ODBC drivers. On its menus the user will find every ODBC API function, as well as some menu selections that combine several ODBC function calls. With each ODBC function call menu selection, a dialog box is provided with a separate control for each function parameter. This enables the users of ODBC Test to custom-tailor their function calls to whatever option they would like.

The ODBC Spy utility can be used to examine communications between an application and an ODBC driver. These communications can be stored and rerun at a later time for use in debugging the driver or the ODBC application.

Q&A

Q It's nice that the ODBC SDK comes packaged with these driver testing tools, but what I'd really like is a tool to automate my ODBC application for testing purposes. Any suggestions?

A Today there are a number of testing software packages available for Windows developers. Testing and software configuration management are areas often overlooked by many organizations, and these areas are critical to the success of any large development project. (For more on this topic, look to the volumes of books on software engineering.) Two excellent testing tools common in many shops are Microsoft Test and SQA TeamTest; however, study each product carefully and try to get an evaluation copy before spending the big bucks to outfit several users.

Workshop

The Workshop provides quiz questions to help you solidify your understanding of the material covered and to provide you with experience in using what you've learned. Try to understand the quiz and exercise answers before continuing on to the next day's lesson. Answers are provided in Appendix A, "Answers."

Quiz

1. (True or False). Both the ODBC Spy and ODBC Test tools can be purchased individually from Microsoft.

Exercise

1. Use the ODBC Test application to examine all of the capabilities of an ODBC driver you will be using. Now is a good time to catalog the information you gain from this tool. This will provide you with a handy reference that can be used with all application development with this driver.

The third week of *Teach Yourself ODBC in 21 Days* was spent covering more advanced ODBC and database management topics. By the end of the second week, you were already familiar with the concepts of opening a connection to a data source, preparing an SQL statement, executing the statement, and returning data from the data source. This constitutes the vast majority of the ODBC operations many ODBC developers will be doing.

During this final seven days, you added to your new bag of ODBC tricks by learning some other parts of ODBC's functionality. Data modification through the use of the UPDATE, INSERT, and DELETE statements was covered in Day 15. Days 17 and 18 discussed the topics of cursors and transactions. On Day 19 you learned how to end a transaction and a connection the correct way.

The final two days covered "non-ODBC API" topics. You learned the importance of a professional-looking (and acting) install application. You learned several alternatives, including the Visual Basic Install Wizard and the ODBC Setup Toolkit. On the final day, you studied the variety of tools that come packaged with the ODBC Software Development Kit. Most notable among these tools are the ODBC Test and the ODBC Spy application. These applications enable you to completely test a driver's capabilities as well as the interaction between your application and an ODBC driver.

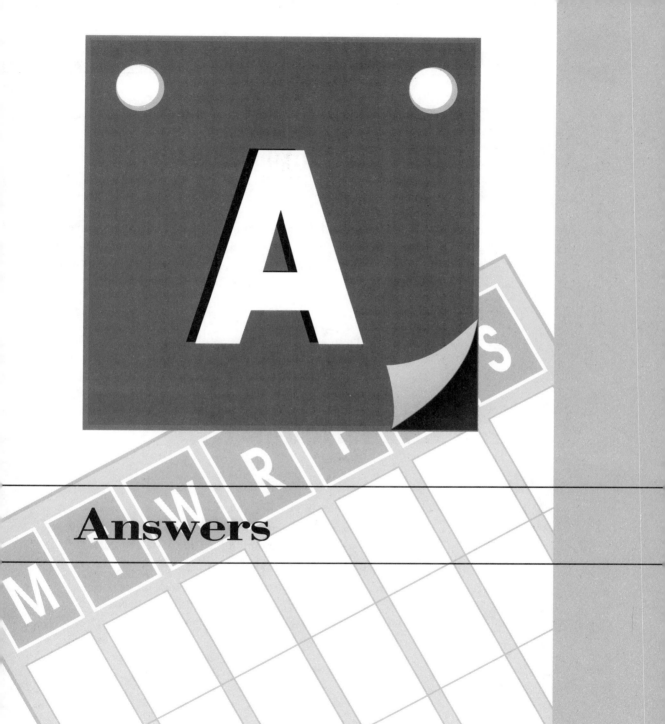

Answers

Answers for Day 2, "Overview of ODBC Concepts and Theory"

Quiz

1. What memory constraints should the programmer be aware of when using the ODBC API?

   The programmer must ensure that the pointers used to pass data back and forth are valid. Also, be aware of problems that can arise using Visual Basic strings.

2. What will be the return value of your ODBC function if it is successful? If it is not?

   You can get two return values if a function is successful: SQL_SUCCESS and SQL_SUCCESS_WITH_INFO. An unsuccessful function will return an SQL_ERROR.

Answers for Day 3, "Application Design Considerations"

Quiz

1. Does SQLRowCount return the number of rows in a result set?

   No, depending on the database; this function might not return the number of rows in the result set. Consult the documentation for your particular database.

2. What functions does the ODBC core provide for SQL execution?

   The core ODBC functionality provides two different methods for SQL execution, depending on need. These are prepared execution using SQLPrepare followed by SQLExecute, and direct execution using SQLExecDirect.

Answers for Day 4, "Installing Drivers and Configuring Data Sources"

Quiz

1. Can more than one data source be created using the same driver? Specify why or why not.

   Yes, a driver can be used to define many data sources.

2. Can the return from `SQLConfigDataSource` be checked against `SQL_SUCCESS`, and can the standard ODBC error routines be used if it fails?

   No, it returns `TRUE` or `FALSE` instead of a return code.

3. If the `SQLConfigDataSource` function needs to be used to provide a common data-source name, but the other attributes can be user configurable, how is this done?

   By using the ODBC Administrator program.

4. On a Windows NT system that uses a 32-bit SQL Server driver, can the ODBC.INI file be distributed on the network to other workstations to copy the data-source configuration rather than running the administrator or configuring programmatically at each workstation?

   No, Windows NT and Windows 95 have replaced the INI file with the registry.

Exercise

1. Modify Listing 4.4 to use the Access (32-bit) driver, create a connection named MUSIC, and connect to a database named music.mdb in the \samples subdirectory.

   The following lines were modified:

   ```
   Driver = "Access(32Bit)" & ZSTR
   Attrib = "DSN=MUSIC;Description=Music Database;
   ➥Database=\sample\music.mdb" & ZSTR & ZSTR
   ```

Answers for Day 7, "Data Types"

Quiz

1. What are the two main categories of data types used in ODBC applications?

   The SQL data type and the C data type.

2. What ODBC functions must an application use to determine whether a particular data type or a particular column of a result set is signed or unsigned?

   An application must use the ODBC functions SQLGetTypeInfo or SQLColAttributes.

Exercise

1. Using the ODBC Test tool, connect to a database, use the SQLGetTypeInfo function, and then the Get_Data_All function to return the type information.

   Using the Music database I got the following result:

```
SQLGetTypeInfo:
    In:      hstmt=#2 0x178F:0x0000, fSqlType=SQL_ALL_TYPES=0
    Return:  SQL_SUCCESS=0

    Get Data All:
    "TYPE_NAME", "DATA_TYPE", "PRECISION", "LITERAL_PREFIX",
    "LITERAL_SUFFIX", "CREATE_PARAMS", "NULLABLE", "CASE_SENSITIVE",
    "SEARCHABLE", "UNSIGNED_ATTRIBUTE", "MONEY", "AUTO_INCREMENT",
    "LOCAL_TYPE_NAME", "MINIMUM_SCALE", "MAXIMUM_SCALE"
    "BIT", -7, 1, <Null>, <Null>, <Null>, 0, 0, 2, <Null>, 0, <Null>, <Null>, 0, 0
    "BYTE", -6, 3, <Null>, <Null>, <Null>, 1, 0, 2, 1, 0, 0, <Null>, 0, 0
    "LONGBINARY", -4, 1073741824, "0x", <Null>, <Null>, 1, 0, 0, <Null>, 0,
     <Null>, <Null>, <Null>, <Null>
    "VARBINARY", -3, 255, "0x", <Null>, "MAX LENGTH", 1, 0, 0, <Null>, 0, <Null>,
     <Null>, <Null>, <Null>
    "BINARY", -2, 255, "0x", <Null>, "MAX LENGTH", 1, 0, 0, <Null>, 0, <Null>,
     <Null>, <Null>, <Null>
    "LONGTEXT", -1, 1073741824, "'", "'", <Null>, 1, 0, 0, <Null>, 0, <Null>,
     <Null>, <Null>, <Null>
    "CHAR", 1, 255, "'", "'", "MAX LENGTH", 1, 0, 3, <Null>, 0, <Null>, <Null>,
     <Null>, <Null>
    "CURRENCY", 2, 18, <Null>, <Null>, <Null>, 1, 0, 2, 0, 1, 0, <Null>, 4, 4
    "LONG", 4, 10, <Null>, <Null>, <Null>, 1, 0, 2, 0, 0, 0, <Null>, 0, 0
    "COUNTER", 4, 10, <Null>, <Null>, <Null>, 0, 0, 2, 0, 0, 1, <Null>, 0, 0
    "SHORT", 5, 5, <Null>, <Null>, <Null>, 1, 0, 2, 0, 0, 0, <Null>, 0, 0
    "SINGLE", 7, 7, <Null>, <Null>, <Null>, 1, 0, 2, 0, 0, 0, <Null>, <Null>,
     <Null>
    "DOUBLE", 8, 15, <Null>, <Null>, <Null>, 1, 0, 2, 0, 0, 0, <Null>, <Null>,
     <Null>
    "DATETIME", 11, 19, "#", "#", <Null>, 1, 0, 2, <Null>, 0, <Null>,
     <Null>, 0, 0
```

```
"TEXT", 12, 255, "'", "'", "MAX LENGTH", 1, 0, 3, <Null>, 0, <Null>, <Null>,
 <Null>, <Null>
15 rows fetched from 15 columns.
```

Answers for Day 8, "Connecting to the Data Source"

Quiz

1. Will the following connection string return any syntax errors from `SQLConnect`:

   `"DSN=mydriver;UID=Whiting;PWD=mypass;"`

   No.

2. What is the problem with the following `SQLDriverConnect` connection string?

   `"DSN=SQL Server;UID=Bill;DSN=SQL Server #2"`

   There are two `DSN` statements.

Exercises

1. Modify the `SQLDriverConnect` example to connect to each of the data sources on your desktop system. Code all of the connection attributes into your application and set `fDriverCompletion` to `SQL_DRIVER_NOPROMPT`.

2. Use the `SQLDataSources` to create your own dialog box prompts for the `SQLDriverConnect` function.

   1 and 2—Results of the exercises will vary depending on how many data sources are present on your machine.

Answers for Day 9, "Determining Driver and DBMS Capabilities"

Quiz

1. Which function can tell you the optimal set of columns that uniquely identifies a row in the table and/or which columns are automatically updated when any value in the row is updated by a transaction?

   `SQLSpecialColumns`

2. Which function will return information about the driver and data source?

   `SQLGetInfo`

Exercise

1. How would you modify the code, starting on line 53, to return only columns that uniquely describe the currently selected row?

   Change the argument in line 58 to `SQL_SCOPE_CURROW`. By using this value you are telling `SQLSpecialColumns` that your minimum requirement is for columns that will uniquely describe the currently selected row.

Answers for Day 10, "SQL Syntax for ODBC"

Quiz

Identify any problems that might exist with the SQL syntax and grammar in the following statements:

1. `SELECT ALL lastname FROM artist`

   This query runs fine. The `ALL` is not needed, because it is the default.

2. `SELECT * FROM artist WHERE LastName = Samuels`

   In the `WHERE` clause, the string `Samuels` needs to have quotations around it. The correct syntax is `SELECT * FROM artist WHERE LastName = 'Samuels'`.

3. `INSERT INTO song VALUES (23,4,,,'Heart On The Line') WHERE songID = 2`

   Here we are mistaking `INSERT INTO` for `UPDATE`. The `WHERE` clause makes no sense in the `INSERT INTO...VALUES` statement. This statement inserts a new record into the table but not at any particular position. `UPDATE`, on the other hand, uses `WHERE` to specify the row to update. The corrected query would be `INSERT INTO song VALUES (23,4,,,'Heart On The Line')`.

4. `SELECT deptname,SUM(salesamt) from deptmast DM,saleshist GROUP deptname HAVING SUM(salesamt) > 1000000`

   This query will probably run on most implementations of SQL; however, be careful what you ask for! The `FROM` clause specifies two tables but there is no `WHERE` to limit the `JOIN`. What would happen is all the columns from both

tables would be combined and then the GROUP BY would have quite a time trying to sort things out. Better syntax would be:

```
SELECT deptname,SUM(salesamt) from deptmast DM,saleshist SH where
DM.deptID = SH.deptID GROUP BY deptname HAVING SUM(salesamt) > 1000000
```

Exercise

1. Create SQL statements joining the Album and Artist tables, another joining the Artist and Song tables, and a third from the Album_Song table that returns the name of the album and the name of the composer.

```
SELECT artist.LastName, Album.AlbumTitle FROM Album, artist WHERE
(artist.ArtistID=Album.ArtistID)
```

Answers for Day 11, "Running SQL *SELECT* Statements"

Quiz

1. Use SQLSetStmtOption to change the cursor type to where the driver only saves and uses the keys for the rows in the rowset.

```
SQLSetStmtOption(hstmt, SQL_CURSOR_TYPE, SQL_CURSOR_DYNAMIC);
```

2. Use SQLSetStmtOption to change the maximum number of rows returned from a query to 10.

```
SQLSetStmtOption(hstmt, SQL_MAX_ROWS, 10);
```

Exercise

1. Rewrite the program in Listing 11.1 to return all columns and the first 20 rows from the Album table.

Simplify the query to the following:

```
SQLStr = "select * from Album" _
```

Then, after the statement

```
rc = SQLAllocStmt(hDBC, hStmt)
```

add the following line:

```
rc = SQLSetStmtOption(hStmt, SQL_MAX_ROWS, 20)
```

Answers for Day 12, "Returning Data to the Program"

Quiz

1. When in a program can the SQLBindCol function be used?

   An application can call SQLBindCol at any time to bind a column to a new storage location, regardless of whether data has already been fetched from that column. This new binding overrides the old binding, but the previously fetched data is not affected.

2. What function can you use to determine where it is safe to mix the SQLGetData and SQLBindCol functions?

   SQLGetInfo. Be careful in this situation because normally the SQLGetData can be used only on those columns to the right of the last bound column. Some drivers enable more flexibility, but it is safest to check by performing SQLGetInfo with the fInfoType of SQL_GETDATA_EXTENSIONS to determine what is allowed.

Exercise

1. Compare the number of function calls using the SQLFetch/SQLGetData method versus the SQLBindCol/SQLFetch method for a 50 column by 3,000 row database.

   Consider a table of 50 columns and 3,000 rows. If all data is to be returned using the first method, SQLFetch must be called 3,000 times, once for each row. However, between each fetch, SQLGetData must be called 50 times to get each column into the application. This means a total of 153,000 function calls must be made to get all data back into the application. With SQLBindCol, on the other hand, there will be 50 bind calls followed by 3,000 uninterrupted fetch calls, for a total of 3,050 function calls. The same amount of data is moved, but the overhead to perform those decreases by two orders of magnitude.

Answers for Day 13, "Determining the Return Status of a Call"

Quiz

1. If the SQLExecDirect function returns SQL_ERROR, what should you call?

   SQLError

2. If SQLError's szSqlState is equal to C0, what is the szSqlState?

   C0 means unallocated henv, unallocated hdbc.

Exercise

1. Fix the BadBtn and GoofyBtn subroutines in Listings 13.1 and 13.2.

   Your answer will vary according to your connections. In general, you can fix BadBtn by giving it a valid connection string to one of the databases set up on your machine. You would then fix GoofyBtn by using an SQL statement along the lines of SELECT * FROM SomeValidTableName.

Answers for Day 14, "Using Prepared Statements and Parameter Markers"

Quiz

1. What function does ODBC provide to figure out how best to access the rows of data specified in the SQL statement?

   SQLPrepare

2. What class, in MFC, encapsulates your conversation with the database?

   CRecordSet

Exercise

1. Change the `CCPPrep14Doc::OnFileConnect()` function described in the first part of the chapter to sort on `AlbumID`.

   The finished code would look like the following:

```
void CCPPrep14Doc::OnFileConnect()
{
    // CRecordset* pRecordset = OnGetRecordset();
    // recordset must be allocated already
    //ASSERT(m_p14AlbSet != NULL);

    if (!m_p14AlbSet.IsOpen())
    {
        BeginWaitCursor();
        TRY
        {
            m_p14AlbSet.m_strSort = " AlbumID ";
            m_p14AlbSet.Open();
        }
        CATCH(CDBException, e)
        {
            EndWaitCursor();
            AfxMessageBox(e->m_strError, MB_ICONEXCLAMATION);
            THROW_LAST();
        }
        AND_CATCH_ALL(e)
        {
            EndWaitCursor();
            THROW_LAST();
        }
        END_CATCH_ALL
        EndWaitCursor();
```

Answers for Day 15, "Running *UPDATE, INSERT,* or *DELETE* Statements"

Quiz

1. Name the standard functions that can be called in MFC when you use Visual C++ to modify data in an existing database.

   `AddNew`, `Edit`, `Delete`, and `Update`

2. What are a primary key and a foreign key?

A primary key is one or more columns of data in a table whose data will uniquely identify a row. A foreign key is a column in a table that references one or more columns in another table and defines the relationship between the two tables. The column or columns referred to by the foreign key will be the primary key in the other table.

3. Specify one or more techniques to ensure referential integrity.

Use database triggers to not enable deletes that will violate integrity.

Use transactions to group inserts or deletes taking place on multiple tables so that all are successful or all are rolled back.

Use application logic to perform the preceding steps when the database system does not provide trigger or transaction support.

Answers for Day 16, "Using ODBC Functions"

Quiz

1. What are the five types of scalar functions?

   The five types of scalar functions are string, numeric, system, time/date, and datatype conversions.

2. Give the basic SQL syntax used to call an ODBC scalar function.

   The basic SQL syntax used to call an ODBC scalar function looks like this:

   ```
   SELECT {fn FUNCTION(argument)} from TABLENAME
   ```

Exercises

1. Write the SQL statement used to determine the length of string NAME from the table EMPLOYEES.

   ```
   SELECT {fn LENGTH(NAME)} from EMPLOYEES
   ```

2. Write the SQL statement used to return the time to your application.

   ```
   SELECT {fn CURTIME()} from EMPLOYEES
   ```

   Note that the time returned will be in the ODBC time format hh:mm:ss.

Answers

Answers for Day 17, "Using ODBC Cursors"

Quiz

1. What are the differences between the SQLFetch function and the SQLExtendedFetch function?

   SQLFetch returns data into a simple cursor. This type of cursor can only be used for forward scrolling. SQLExtendedFetch is much more versatile. This function enables the use of more advanced cursors for forward and backward scrolling, as well as jumps to another rowset.

2. Explain the differences between a static ODBC cursor and a dynamic ODBC cursor. What are their advantages and disadvantages?

   A static ODBC cursor returns a result set that is not "sensitive" to changes by other users. (This type of cursor is referred to as a *snapshot* within Visual Basic.) A dynamic cursor has the advantage of detecting other user's changes, which can be extremely important in a client-server, multiuser environment. However, the programmer will notice a performance penalty on occasion when using a dynamic cursor.

Exercises

1. If you have not already done so, determine the cursor capabilities of your ODBC driver of choice.

   The code for this was actually given earlier in the chapter, so if you did not actually run it at that point, take the opportunity to do so now in order to learn more about your driver's capabilities. (On Day 21, you will use the ODBC Test tool to examine your driver's capabilities without writing any code.)

   Basically, the driver's cursor support can be determined by calling the SQLGetInfo function with an argument of SQL_SCROLL_OPTIONS. Once you know what type of cursors are supported, the available fetch directions can be determined by calling SQLGetInfo with an argument of SQL_FETCH_DIRECTION.

2. If you have ODBC drivers for several different databases, compare the capabilities of the different drivers.

   You will probably notice that most of the Desktop Database drivers are similar in capabilities. However, if you have access to a driver for a database server

(such as Oracle or SQL Server), compare the capabilities of these drivers to those of the Desktop Database drivers. Keep in mind that nearly all database servers now provide native cursor support through their SQL dialects. Using these proprietary cursors, however, will require some code rewrite should you ever have to "point" your code at another database.

Answers for Day 18, "Using Transactions and Commitment Control"

Quiz

1. Each driver provides a default transaction isolation support type. How could you determine the default type of transaction isolation support that your driver provides?

   A driver's default transaction isolation support can be determined by calling `SQLGetInfo` with the `SQL_DEFAULT_TXN_ISOLATION` option.

2. The transaction isolation level of an RDBMS refers to the level of isolation one transaction's changes have from another parallel transaction's changes. Read through your database's documentation. What type of transaction isolation support does it provide?

   As was mentioned earlier in this chapter, the topics of transactions and transaction isolation support were around long before the advent of ODBC. Therefore, all true database servers provide some degree of transaction management. The level of isolation support provided by your driver will then be the level provided by the database server (because transaction management is handled by the database server). However, for PC-based databases such as dBASE and Access, the driver controls the transaction management, and it is important to understand the isolation support provided by the driver. This can be determined by calling `SQLGetInfo` with the `SQL_TXN_CAPABLE` option and then calling it with the `SQL_TXN_ISOLATION` option.

Exercise

1. List the steps a programmer must go through in order to complete a transaction using ODBC.

The simplest answer to this exercise is to prepare an SQL statement, execute it, and then call SQLTransact to complete the transaction. However, in many applications, it is not quite so simple. The driver's transaction support must first be determined by calling SQLGetInfo with the SQL_TXN_CAPABLE option. Once this is known, you might also want to determine the available transaction isolation options. This can be determined by calling SQLGetInfo with the SQL_TXN_ISOLATION option. Once the driver's transaction support is fully understood, call SQLSetConnectOptions with the fOption set to SQL_AUTOCOMMIT and vParam set to either SQL_AUTOCOMMIT_OFF or SQL_AUTOCOMMIT_ON. Setting the option to SQL_AUTO_COMMIT_OFF will enable the use of the SQL_COMMIT and SQL_ROLLBACK options within SQLTransact.

Answers for Day 19, "Ending Transactions and Connections"

Quiz

1. (True or False) Calling SQLDisconnect will cancel all transactions and close the current connection to the database.

   False. Calling SQLDisconnect with open transactions will cause an error. If you call SQLError immediately afterward, an SQLSTATE 25000 (invalid transaction state) error will be raised. All transactions must be ended with SQLTransact before the connection can be closed.

2. Multiple Choice. Select the proper sequence of function calls that will correctly end an ODBC session.

   The correct answer is b, SQLDisconnect -> SQLFreeConnect -> SQLFreeEnv.

Exercise

1. Create a simple dialog box application that initializes an ODBC connection upon opening, and then closes the connection upon closing.

   To close the ODBC connection, your statements should look something like this:

```
SQLDisconnect(hdbc)
SQLFreeConnect(hdbc)
SQLFreeEnv(henv)
```

Answers for Day 20, "Completing the Entire Application"

A

Quiz

1. (True or False) Each ODBC driver at a minimum enables the programmer to call stored procedures in the underlying database.

   False. To determine whether your driver supports procedure calls, call the SQLGetInfo function with a parameter of SQL_PROCEDURES.

2. (True or False) The recommended method for writing ODBC install applications is the Visual Basic Setup Toolkit.

   This answer is left completely up to the individual developer. There are pluses and minuses associated with using the Visual Basic Toolkit. There are no runtime distribution fees (a plus); however, you must distribute the VB runtime files as well as the decompression utilities. It also requires some knowledge of Visual Basic programming (which not everyone has mastered). Other options include third-party applications such as Stirling Technologies' InstallShield, and writing your own custom install application in C/C++, VB, Delphi, or whatever you choose.

Exercise

1. Do some research on your company's (or your client's) database system(s) of choice. Several database management systems support the use of stored procedures; however, yours might not. Determine if it does, and if so, determine if your ODBC driver supports procedure calls.

   Popular database systems such as Oracle7, InterBase, and Sybase/Microsoft SQL Server provide stored procedure support. In fact, SQL Server was the first commercial database management system to provide stored procedure support. However, the capability to call these procedures using ODBC syntax depends on your driver.

Answer for Day 21, "Using ODBC Test and Trace Tools"

Quiz

1. (True or False). Both the ODBC Spy and ODBC Test tools can be purchased individually from Microsoft.

   False. The ODBC SDK (which comes with the Microsoft Development Network Level 2 Subscription) contains these useful tools. Unfortunately (or fortunately, if you work for Microsoft), at this time the API and the corresponding tools can only be obtained by joining the Developer Network. It should be mentioned, however, that this membership is well worth the money for any serious Windows developer.

Index

G

parameters

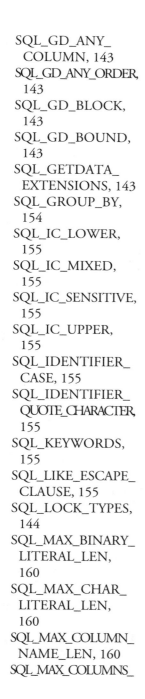

SQL_ACCESSIBLE_PROCEDURES

Add to Your Sams Library Today with the Best Books for Programming, Operating Systems, and New Technologies

The easiest way to order is to pick up the phone and call

1-800-428-5331

between 9:00 a.m. and 5:00 p.m. EST.

For faster service please have your credit card available.

ISBN	Quantity	Description of Item	Unit Cost	Total Cost
0-672-30602-6		Programming Windows 95 Unleashed (Book/CD)	$49.99	
0-672-30474-0		Windows 95 Unleashed (Book/CD)	$35.00	
0-672-30855-x		Teach Yourself SQL in 14 Days	$29.99	
0-672-30462-7		Teach Yourself MFC in 21 Days	$29.99	
0-672-30620-4		Teach Yourself Visual Basic 4 in 21 Days, 3E	$29.99	
0-672-30594-1		Programming WinSock (Book/Disk)	$35.00	
0-672-30596-8		Develop a Professional Visual Basic Application in 14 Days (Book/CD)	$35.00	
0-672-30593-3		Develop a Professional Visual C++ Application in 21 Days (Book/CD)	$35.00	
0-672-30453-8		Access 2 Developer's Guide, 2nd Ed (Book/Disk)	$44.95	
0-672-30737-5		World Wide Web Unleashed, 2E	$39.99	
0-672-30765-0		Navigating the Internet with Windows 95	$25.00	

❏ 3 ½" Disk

❏ 5 ¼" Disk

Shipping and Handling: See information below.	
TOTAL	

Shipping and Handling: $4.00 for the first book, and $1.75 for each additional book. Floppy disk: add $1.75 for shipping and handling. If you need to have it NOW, we can ship product to you in 24 hours for an additional charge of approximately $18.00, and you will receive your item overnight or in two days. Overseas shipping and handling adds $2.00 per book and $8.00 for up to three disks. Prices subject to change. Call for availability and pricing information on latest editions.

201 W. 103rd Street, Indianapolis, Indiana 46290

1-800-428-5331 — Orders   1-800-835-3202 — FAX   1-800-858-7674 — Customer Service

Book ISBN 0-672-30609-3

PLUG YOURSELF INTO...

THE MACMILLAN INFORMATION SUPERLIBRARY™

Free information and vast computer resources from the world's leading computer book publisher—online!

FIND THE BOOKS THAT ARE RIGHT FOR YOU!

A complete online catalog, plus sample chapters and tables of contents give you an in-depth look at *all* of our books, including hard-to-find titles. It's the best way to find the books you need!

● STAY INFORMED with the latest computer industry news through our online newsletter, press releases, and customized Information SuperLibrary Reports.

● GET FAST ANSWERS to your questions about MCP books and software.

● VISIT our online bookstore for the latest information and editions!

● COMMUNICATE with our expert authors through e-mail and conferences.

● DOWNLOAD SOFTWARE from the immense MCP library:
  - Source code and files from MCP books
  - The best shareware, freeware, and demos

● DISCOVER HOT SPOTS on other parts of the Internet.

● WIN BOOKS in ongoing contests and giveaways!

TO PLUG INTO MCP: ➞ WORLD WIDE WEB: **http://www.mcp.com**

GOPHER: gopher.mcp.com

FTP: ftp.mcp.com